Agricultural Development in India

A Regional Analysis

by

Surendra Singh

Department of Geography,
North-Eastern Hill University,
Shillong

Kaushal Publications

Shillong - 793 014

First Published in India
by
Kaushal Publications
Dohsgthiang, Nongshiliang,
Nongthymmai, Shillong-793014 (India)

Edition : 1994

ISBN : 81-900447-0-2

Price : Rs. 400.00 (U.S. $ 20.00)

Typeset by : Printografix, 8/4, Prem Nagar, JanakPuri, New Delhi 110058
Printed by : Deepak Offset Printers, 10/11, Subhash Gali,
Vishwas Nagar, Delhi 110032

Foreword

Agriculture has been essentially a spatial subject as it is influenced by physical, economic and institutional factors. Yet, the theme has not acquired adequate attention and hence spatial dimension unlike sectoral and temporal aspects has remained elusive both in fundamental and applied studies. In the context of agricultural development in India, the Planning Commission while accepting the fact that agro-climatic regions would be more realistic than the use of states as "regions" has adopted belatedly a scheme of agro-climatic regions and zones as the basis for the formulation of the agricultural development strategy. Various studies have attempted regional interpretation of the cropping pattern, productivity and its growth-rate over time. What is needed is the integration of studies in regional dimensions of agriculture with the formulation of regional development policy and its effective implementation by preparing regional agricultural landuse plans and formulation of area specific development programmes. Sustainability factor which ensures integration of environment with development is another challenging area of work that needs priority in the research programmes related to planning.

In this study, Dr. Surendra Singh has focussed attention on regional dimension in a *holistic* spatial perspective using district as the areal unit of analysis. There is proper blending of quantitative and cartographic techniques in the delineation of planning regions for agriculture. One may not agree with the interpretation of the observed spatial patterns of agriculture particularly the role of metropolitan centres as catalysts in modernisation of agriculture and its spatial spread to the periphery. This is where intensive regional studies would serve to reveal the myth and reality of Indian agriculture in its regional dimension. The study is an important contribution to methodology and some new findings in understanding the regional personality of Indian agriculture.

L. S. Bhat (retd.)
Professor, Regional Planning Unit
Indian Statistical Institute
Sansanwal Marg,
New Delhi

New Delhi
2nd January, 1994

Preface

Numerous studies have appeared in recent years presenting methodological and empirical issues of the agricultural growth and development of India. Undoubtedly, agriculture is the major sector of Indian economy and preparation of agricultural investment strategies and its proper implementation are the main problems which confront the planners for the last forty years of its planned economy. Various models and approaches of agricultural growth and development have been suggested by the agricultural scientists, but there are many unresolved problems and issues untouched by comprehensive planning which are equally important and needs to be resolved. These aspects would be helpful for optimising the integrated agricultural characteristics. In a vast country like India, there is a wide range of regional and sectoral variations of agricultural characteristics because of complex nature of agricultural production systems resulting in complex structural forms. They are too diversified to be interpreted as they are the parts of comprehensive and implicit facts of different agro- ecological and bio- physical conditions of agricultural systems.

The main purpose of this monograph is to present these aspects of agricultural growth and development and also to highlight regional analysis of well-validated facts of the above parameters rather than a definitive work on the subject. Nevertheless, knowledgeable readers will certainly feel that there must be more elaborations on decision - making processes in agricultural development which are parts of the preparation of regional investment strategy. Indeed, I thought of this point at the time of preparing the final draft. But this leads to other aspects of the decision which are not necessary to describe here. A good researcher may give a better analysis and pose the important issues in a scientific way and arrive at a logical solution.

For instance, I emphasized on topics of agricultural development largely associated with the regional structure of agricultural attributes in order to test the validity of facts generated by green revolution technology leading to a concentrated regional pattern of agricultural development. The primacy in the distribution of developmental attributes creates regional imbalances in the growth and productivity patterns. These problems can be detected through the analysis of the regional processes of trilateral components of agricultural development and planning. They are (i) the existing agro-ecological, bio-physical and techno- economic conditions of agricultural activities, (ii) the agricultural growth potential structure which is solely responsible for structural transformation and self-sustained growth, and (iii) the devised/predicted structure for regional balance of agricultural activities. The established relations among these components of Indian agriculture for different sets of agro-ecological phenomena are interpreted in order to delineate the agricultural planning regions which differ from the given schemes of the Planning Commission, New Delhi and the traditional classification of region-formation.

So far as coherence of the matter presented in the present volume is concerned, the performance of Indian agriculture, methdological aspects and design of the study are discussed in Chapter-1, while the regional analysis of the attributes of agricultural development, *viz.*, the growth and agricultural productivity is dealt in detail in Chapters 2 and 3. The regional processes of agricultulral growth potential, its logical reasoning and empirical specifications for the Indian agricultural conditions are arranged in coherent manner in Chapter-4. Lastly, the synthesis of regional facts of agricultural characteristics is discussed in Chapter-5 by considering the region- formations and their assimilation processes by which the priorities of cropping pattern and agricultural extension services can be fixed and the areas of optimal use of local agricultural resources can be identified. In the end, the feasible solution and its nature are also dealt with in the same Chapter. The duality of themes seems to occur in this Chapter. But agricultural regionalisation, regional characteristics and their optimisation as interpreted here are mutually interrelated and interdependent and, therefore, they are arranged in the same Chapter. Just as the table of contents reflects the coherence of the material, illustrations in the form of maps and diagrams have been designed in such a way so that the readers would be able to pick up the comprehensive and logical arguments easily.

In fact, the present piece of research would be helpful for preparing the regional investment strategy and determining the priorities of agricultural activities as well as of areas where more stress may be given in future. It would open new dimensions of the facts of Indian agriculture to agricultural economists, agronomists, regional analysts, agricultural planners and various government and non-government agencies, which are engaged in framing the agricultural policies of the country or developing new models and theories on Indian agriculture.

Shillong - 793014
January 1994.

Surendra Singh

Acknowledgements

I extend my gratitude to the people whose works I have freely utilised here. The list is far too long to enumerate everyone, though I sincerely hope sometimes, I have relied referring to the works of a few scholars, namely, Dr. G.S. Bhalla, Professor of Economics at the Centre for the Study of Regional Development and Professor Y.K. Alagh, Vice-Chancellor, Jawarlal Nehru University, New Delhi, Dr. L.S. Bhat, Professor of Regional Planning, Indian Statistical Institute, New Delhi and Professor M.N. Pal, Indian Statistical Institute, Calcutta. I am very much grateful to the Department of Statistics and Economics, Ministry of Agriculture, Government of India, New Delhi for providing published and unpublished data records.

I am especially grateful to Professor R.K. Rai, Head, Department of Geography, North-Eastern Hill Universty, Shillong for his constant encouragement and suggestions and to Dr. D.K. Nayak, Reader, Department of Geography, North-Eastern Hill Universty, Shillong for painstakingly going through the final draft of manuscript and making helpful comments. I must acknowledge the encouragement and help of our M.Sc. Students in preparing maps. I am very much thankful to Dr. B.S. Mipun, Dr. S.Sharma for cartographic assistance, Dr. N.P. Goel and Mr.P.P. Dey for computer help and Mr. P. S. Thomas for typing the manuscript. I also offer thanks to my daughter, Monika and son, Mohit Kumar, who immensely helped me in data arrangement and compilation. However, the views expressed, the conclusions drawn and the errors that may remain are attributable to the author alone.

Finally, I am indebted to University Grants Commission, New Delhi for providing partial financial assistance for data collection under Visiting Associateship Scheme.

Surendra Singh

Shillong- 793014

January, 1994.

List of Tables

Page

[illegible]

Potential Magnitude and Frequency of [illegible]

[illegible]

Figure

[illegible]

Agricultural Production [illegible]

[illegible]

4.1 Production Potential [illegible]

4.2 [illegible]

4.3 [illegible]

4.4 [illegible]

[illegible]

List of Figures

-----o0o-----

List of Appendices

Contents

Chapter - 1

Performance of Indian Agriculture

Agriculture is the main occupation in India. It shares nearly one-third of the total national income with a noticeable decrease because of fast development in the other sectors of the economy. However, economic conditions, standard of living and socio-cultural setup of rural masses are solely based on agriculture and its allied activities. The country is facing two major problems of agricultural growth and development. First is related to the increasing demand for food and the back- wash effects of agricultural growth on the socio-economic development. Second problem of Indian agriculture is associated with the assessment of optimal agricultural growth and its regional variations, so that the correct picture of required agricultural infra-structure may be depicted and the proper regional investment policies for self-sustained growth of agriculture may be prepared. These problems have been looked into and tackled for the last forty years of planned economy of the country by the agricultural scientists especially by economists, agronomists and geographers. Obviously, the problems of increasing food demand and the contribution of agriculture to the overall economic development can be better understood by giving the answer to **two** major questions related to the performance of Indian agriculture: firstly, how does agricultural sector contribute to the rate of economic growth in the country and secondly, what will be the consequences when the share of agricultural sector of Net Domestic Product (NDP) declines with a slow increase in its absolute size? Answers to these questions would be given by discussing the transformation processes of agricultural growth.

Role of Agriculture in Overall Economic Development

It is widely recognised that the share of agriculture in the structure of total output tends to decline when the economic growth of a region or country proceeds and, at advanced stage of development, the labour force employed in agriculture sector also tends to diminish absolutely (World Development Report 1982, pp. 40). Therefore, the role of agriculture in the acceleration of economic growth processes and the causes of the sectoral shift of the economic structure can be understood by describing its contribution to the national economic growth. It can be interpreted in the following manner.

(i) *The Product Contribution-* which makes the major contribution to survival of the economy, people and other related sectors like industries and services,

(ii) *The Factors' Contribution*- Agricultural sector contributes to shift the surplus capital and labour force from agricultural sector to the non-agricultural sectors of the economy because of higher degree of income elasticity of non- agricultural products (due to their higher demand), higher incremental demand for capital specially in non-agricultural sectors of the economy, and lower Incremental Capital- Output Ratio (ICOR) in agriculture than industries; it means that farmers tend to invest surplus money in the non- agricultural activities (Ghatak and Ingersent 1984, pp. 43-46),

(iii) *The Market Contribution* - under which surplus agricultural production moves from rural areas to urban centres and to other countries through market facilities. Therefore, the advanced agricultural areas of the country have more *mandi* towns which act as the collection centres of surplus agricultural products, and

(iv) *The Foreign Exchange Contribution* - The marketable agricultural surplus provides the facilities of imports, substitutes and helps to boost up the overall economy of the country in the international market.

In general, agricultural product contribution to the economic growth and development is the function of two main attributes of agriculture: share and growth rate of the net product of agriculture. Kuznets (1964) formula, which establishes the relationship between agricultural share of Net Domestic Product (NDP) growth and ratio of sectoral shares (or the ratio of sectoral growth rates), expresses inverse relationship between them. But the simplified form of the same formula as given in Appendix-I states a direct and positive relationship of non-linear nature between the agriculture's share of Gross Domestic Product (GDP) growth and the share and/or rate of agriculture's net product. This relationship follows the reciprocity law of agriculture contribution to the rate of economic growth (Appendix -I). The empirical evidences on the agriculture sector's share of the growth rate in Indian economy is in broad agreement with *a priori* expression. The evidences given in Table-1.1 confirm that

(a) Agriculture share declines over time. It decreases by 6.0 per cent (from 40.0 to 34.0 percent) in the eighties. It is inversely related to the level of NDP of the country over the same period.

(b) The agricultural contribution to the NDP growth has been fluctuating during 1980-90 (Table-1.1) because of very high temporal fluctuations in the growth rate of agriculture sector of the economy, especially in the alternative years during early eighties (1982-3,1984-5 &1986-7). Another attribute of agriculture sector, i.e., agriculture's share to NDP, has a gradual and smooth decrease over time. The product of both of these attributes was fluctuating very high in the year 1983-4 and in 1988-9. Consequently, the agricultural contribution to NDP growth (Pa.ra/NDP) has been recorded appreciably high during the same periods.

(c) There is a positive relationship between growth rate of agriculture sector, contribution of agriculture sector to NDP growth and proportional increase in NDP. It signifies the validity of the Kuznets model which generalises the related growth phenomena in the logical form.

Further, per capita income is the real indicator of economic development. It is the function of two important attributes of development: NDP and total population. The dynamics of these attributes have been interpreted by many economists for solving the problem of poverty, income and employment. The empirical evidences confirm an inverse relationship between poverty and agricultural performance (Ahluwalia 1978), population below poverty line and per capita income (Bhalla 1980) and poverty index and per capita NDP (Singhal and Gill 1991). Infact, total NDP (at factor costs) is heavily dominated by the agriculture sector of the economy, although its percentage share is declining at an average annual rate of .66 percent during 1980-1 to 1989-90. There seems, contrary to claims, that the absolute size of NDP in agriculture sector has been recorded to have increased at an annual rate of 4.03 percent in the same period, which is slower than the average annual increasing rate of the total NDP of the country (Table-1.2). On the other hand, an average annual rate of population growth of 2.32 percent has been registered in the eighties, from 685.2 million (1981) to 843.9 million (1991). As a result, the slow increase in per capita income (i.e., 3.02 percent annually in the eighties for Rs. 2097 in 1989-90) and in per capita Net National Product at factor costs (NNP) (i.e., 3.49 percent per annum from Rs. 1630 to Rs. 2142 during 1980-1 to 1989-90) have been recorded.

Table-1.1: Agriculture's Contribution to the Rate of Economic Growth in India.

Years	Total Magnitude+ (in Rs 00 crores)								
	TPa	TPn	NDP	Pa	Pn	ra	rn	Para	Pa.ra/dNDP
1980-81	441	663	1104	.3996	.6004	-	-	-	.3996
1981-82	467	704	1171	.3992	.6008	.0602	.0620	.0240	.3921
1982-83	460	743	1203	.3825	.6175	-.0155	.0560	-.0059	-.2069
1983-84	512	792	1304	.3926	.6074	.1125	.0659	.0442	.5246
1984-85	512	839	1351	.3786	.6214	-.0015	.0594	-.0006	-.0156
1985-86	512	891	1403	.3650	.6350	.0013	.0616	.0005	.0120
1986-87	503	952	1455	.3455	.6545	-.0184	.0687	-.0063	-.1647
1987-88	504	1013	1517	.3323	.6677	.0037	.0644	.0012	.0278
1988-89*	587	1097	1684	.3483	.6517	.1628	.0832	.0567	.5112
1989-90**	601	1169	1770	.3396	.6604	.0249	.0650	.0084	.1651

N.B:
* Provisional figures,
** Quick Estimates,
\+ at 1980-81 prices.

Abbreviations:

TPa = agricultural net product, TPn = non- agricultural net product, NDP = Total Net Domestic Product,

Pa = agriculture sector (agriculture, forestry & fishing) share of NDP, Pn = non-agriculture sector share of NDP,

ra = annual growth rate of agriculture sector product, rn = annual growth rate of non-agriculture sector product,

Pa.ra/dNDP = ratio of agriculture sector growth to GDP growth using Kuznets (1964) formula.

Source : Central Statistical Organisation, Ministry of Planning, Government of India, New Delhi.

Table-1.2: Average Annual Increase in the National Income according to Major Heads of Economy: 1980-81 and 1989-90 (at 1980-81 prices).

(total in Rs. crores)

Heads	1980-81 Total	1980-81 %	1989-90* Total	1989-90* %	Average annual increase (%)
1. Agriculture	44,091	39.96	60,103	33.96	4.03
2. Mining and Quarrying	1,474	1.33	2,224	1.25	5.65
3. Manufacturing	18,698	16.95	35,460	20.03	9.96
4. Electric,Gass & water supply	912	.83	2,092	1.18	14.37
5. Construction	5,771	5.23	7,639	4.32	3.60
6. Trade, Hostel & Restaurant	14,322	12.98	24,763	13.99	8.10
7. Transport, Storage & Communication	3,724	3.37	7,036	3.97	9.88
8. Financing, Insurence, Banking, Real Estates & Business Services	9,264	8.39	17,398	9.83	9.75
9. Community, Social & Personal services	12,084	10.95	20,265	11.45	7.52
10. Total Net Domestic Product at Factor costs	110,340	100.00	176,980	100.00	6.71
11. Net Factor Income from Abroad	345	-	-2,182	-	-
12. Net National Product at Factor costs	110,685	-	174,798	-	6.43
13. Per Capita NNP	**1,630**	-	**2,142**	-	**3.49**

N.B.: * Figures are quick estimates.

Source : Central Statistical Organisation, Ministry of Planning, Government of India, New Delhi.

It is interesting to note that the areas where intensive agriculture is being practiced have higher per capita State Domestic Product (SDP) with its higher growth rate and *vice-versa.* Exemplifying the case of green revolution areas of the country, per capita SDP of the states of Punjab, Haryana and Gujrat are marked very high with the high rate of its increase even before green revolution period (Table-1.3). Therefore, there seems a concentration of economic growth of the country in its regional patterns. But the fast growth of SDP in the states of Punjab and Haryana indicates higher NDP level of agriculture worker, per capita agricultural income and more opportunities of employment which can be achieved either by shifting the agricultural labour force to the non-agricultural sectors of the economy or by accelerating the agricultural output growth at faster rate. There are two main forces which operate simultaneously and produce the major transformation in the structure of economic development.

(a) The shift in the relative demand is, indeed, an important force. The pace of agricultural growth is determined by the growth of the demand of its output, which is controlled by the tendency and likings of consumers that is directly related to the income of the family. According to Engel's law, as incomes rise, they demand products, that are more and more processed than unprocessed grain food (Hagen 1975, pp. 89-100). Thus, the high income families spend less proportion of their income on food and *vice-versa.* For example, in India, with a per capita income of $240, households spend 60 to 70 percent of their income on food, while on the other hand, in a $ 10,000 per capita income countries such as Canada, they spend less then 20 percent on food and are able to enjoy varieties and qualities of processed food (World Development Report 1982, p.43).

(b) The second main force of structural transformation in agriculture is increased agricultural productivity per unit of land as well as per person of agricultural work force. In low-income countries of the world, specially the South Asian countries, where overall development is based on agricultural growth, the increase in agricultural productivity is made possible by technological innovations that came in the South Asian countries through green revolution effects specially in the early seventies. Due to increasing demand of modern agricultural inputs like chemical fertilizers, tractors and other machines, irrigation tools purchased from non-agricultural sectors of the economy, the elasticities of demand of these sectors increase faster than the agricultural products at farm-gate (Ghatak and Ingersent 1984, pp.43-59). The aggravation of rural-urban income inequalities conflicting with broader objectives of income distribution also encourages the rural people (agriculture sector) to move towards the nearby cities and urban centres (non-agricultural sectors).

Table- 1.3: State-Wise Per Capita State Domestic Product (at 1960-1 prices) and its Growth Rate.

Sl. No.	State	Per Capita State Domestic Product(in Rs)			Average Annual Growth rate(%)	
		1960-1	1970-1	1977-78	1961-71	1971-78
1.	Andhra Pradesh	275	310	322	1.27	0.55
2.	Assam *	251	270	303	.80	1.74
3.	Bihar	215	-	-	-	-
4.	Gujrat	362	439	408	2.13	-1.01
5.	Haryana	327	441	508	3.48	2.17
6.	Jammu & Kashmir	269	292	355	0.85	3.08
7.	Karnataka **	238	306	343	2.85	1.73
8.	Kerala	259	298	-	1.50	-
9.	Madhya Pradesh	260	261	-	0.03	-
10.	Maharastra	409	427	-	0.44	-
11.	Orissa	217	265	287	2.21	1.18
12.	Punjab	347	471	567	3.57	2.91
13.	Rajasthan	284	353	308	2.43	-1.82
14.	Tamilnadu	334	349	382	0.45	1.35
15.	Uttar Pradesh	252	269	284	0.67	0.79
16.	West Bengal	390	282	410	-2.77	6.48

N.B.: * at 1948-9 prices, ** at 1956-7 prices.

Source: Reserve Bank of India Bulletin, April 1978 & June 1979, data quoted from Singhal and Gill (1991).

In spite of all these forces and factors which are working behind the agricultural structure for its transformation, the increase in agriculture and food-output per capita in these low-income countries are recorded as modest at 0.3 and 0.4 percent a year in the 1960s and 1970s. To study the stagnant conditions of agriculture, the performance of Indian agriculture would be described in detail.

Performance of Indian Agriculture

Comparing main indicators of economic growth and development of five South-Asian low-income countries, it can be concluded that the socio-economic conditions of Sri Lanka is better than the other countries (Table- 1.4). In spite of high density of population (223 persons/sq. km) in Sri Lanka, the per capita GNP($240 in 1980) and its average annual growth (2.4 percent in 1960-80) have been recorded higher than that of India and the other countries. In India, agriculture and services are major sectors of the economy which contribute nearly three-fourth share of GDP, but the average annual growth rate of GDP in agriculture sector recorded lowest (only 1.9 percent in the 1970s) not only among the other sectors of Indian economy but the agriculture sector of the other countries also. The latest figures of agricultural growth indicate that there is a stagnant growth of agricultural production (i.e., 2.6 percent annual growth rate in 1991-92) because it is equal to the growth rate of GDP in the same period as Reserve Bank of India stated (The Times of India 1992). In India, the share of Gross Domestic Savings (GDS) to GDP is appreciable and highest (20.0 percent) among the South-Asian countries. It reflects the faster rate of investments for future economic development. It is pertinent to note here that saving shares in the economy of Pakistan and Bangladesh are very small for further investment although the differences between investment and saving shares of GDP in these countries are extremely high (Table- 1.4). It indicates the loan-based economy of these countries which is surviving on the external help of International Monetary Funds (IMF) and other loans.

The agricultural performance of India may be evaluated in a better way by taking into account the NDP and its distribution among different sectors of economy. The share of agriculture in NDP has declined by 18.73 percent (at an average annual rate of .62 percent) from 58.69 percent in 1950-1 to 39.96 percent in 1980-1 as the first thirty years of planned development of the country. The decline was recorded marginally higher (at an average annual rate of .66 percent) in the eighties (Table-1.2). But the share of work force dependent on agriculture (which includes two major categories of primary sector: cultivators and agricultural labourers) has not declined in the same proportion. The share of agricultural work force to total size of working population declined only 2.9 percent from 69.42 percent (1951) to 66.42 percent (1981) (Table-1.5). On account of rapid decrease in the agriculture share of NDP and the stagnant conditions of agricultural workforce, the quantity of NDP per agricultural worker will decrease proportionately. It declined by Rs. 110 during 1970s from Rs 1305 (1971) to Rs 1195 (1981). Dandekar and Rath (1971) and Dantwala (1971) suggested an appreciable shift in the occupational structure from primary sector to the other sectors of the economy for eliminating the situation of a 'pause' in agricultural growth which has been observed especially during seventh five year plan period in spite of constantly inter-shifting agricultural technology. The problems of disguised unemployment and stagnant conditions of agriculture sector may be tackled by following the same criteria of occupational shift.

Table-1.4 : Socio-Economic Development in South Low-Income Countries.

Development Indicators	Bangladesh	Nepal	India	Sri Lanka	Pakistan
	C o u n t r i e s				
(A) Basic Indicators:					
1. Density of population in 1981 (persons/km^2)	614	103	208	223	102
2. Adult literacy in 1977(%)	26	19	36	85	24
3. Life Expectance at birth 1980 (in years)	46	44	52	66	50
4. Gross National Product 1980 (us$ per capita)	130	140	240	270	300
5. Average Annual Growth of GNP(1960-80)(in %)	NA	0.2	1.4	2.4	2.8
6. Average Index of Food production per capita (1967-70=100) for 1978-80 (%)	94	88	101	121	101
(B) Structure & Growth of production:					
7. Percentage share of Gross Domestic Product (1980) in:					
(a) Agriculture	54	57	37	28	31
(b) Industry	13	13	26	30	25
(c) Manufacturing	7	4	18	18	16
(d) Services	33	30	37	42	44
8. Average annual growth rate (%) in total GDP (1970-80)	3.9	2.5	3.6	4.1	4.7
9. Average annual growth rate in GDP for 1970-80 (in%) in:					
(a) Agriculture	2.2	0.5	1.9	2.8	2.3
(b) Industry	9.5	-	4.5	4.0	5.2
(c) Manufacturing	11.8	-	5.0	1.9	4.0
(d) Services	4.9	-	5.2	4.8	6.2
(C) Structure and Growth of Demand:					
10. Percentage distribution of GDP for 1980 in:					
(a) Public consumption	7	NA	10	8	11
(b) Private consumption	91	93	70	78	83
(c) Gross Domestic savings	2	7	20	14	6
(d) Gross Domestic Investment	17	14	23	36	18
11. Annual average growth rate of consumption & Investment in 1970-80 (in%)					
(a) Public consumption	NA	-	4.2	NA	4.3
(b) Private consumption	4.0	-	3.2	2.7	4.9
(c) Gross Domestic Investment	1.8	11.7	4.8	9.8	2.4

N.B. NA = Not Available.

Source: World Development Report (1982), Oxford University Press, Table 1 to 5 .

Table -1.5: Shifting Sectoral Shares and Relative Growth Rates in India.

Year	Total Population (millions)	Annual Compound Growth rate + (%)	Working Population (millions)	Annual Compound Growth rate+ (%)	Size of labour force (millions)		Average Annual Growth rate #(%)		%Distribution of labour force	
					1	2	1	2	1	2
1951	361.1	1.25	140.0	-	97.2	42.8	-	-	69.4	30.6
1961	439.2	1.96	188.7	3.02	131.1	57.6	3.48	3.45	69.5	30.5
1971	548.9	2.20	180.5	-0.50	125.8	54.7	-0.40	-0.51	69.7	30.3
1981	658.2	2.25	222.5**	2.11	148.0	74.5	1.76	3.62	66.5	33.5
1991	836.6*	2.00	285.4**	2.50	185.2	100.2	2.51	3.45	64.9	35.1

1 = Agricultural sector, 2 = non-Agricultural sector

N.B.: * Provisional figures compiled from Provisional Population Table, paper-3, Census of India, 1991 (series 1)

** Figures related to main workers only.

+ Compound growth rate, r, is computed by simplifying the following formula $p1 = po(1+r)^t$; and

Average annual growth rate as r = (p1- po)/pot,

where p1 and po are the population figures of current and base years respectively, r is annual rate, and t is the number of years.

Source: Census of India, Office of the Registrar General of India, Government of India, New Delhi.

If agricultural performance is viewed in per capita term, all these figures of NDP and the production achievements look insignificant because of the effect of demographic pressure on the economy. In spite of significant increase in food grains production of about 120 million tones from 50.82 to 170.47 million tones during the period of last forty years (1950-1 to 1989-90), the rapid increase in the population of the country which has been recorded 483.2 million persons (361.1 million in 1951 to 844.3 million in 1991) declines marginally the food availability per capita. According to the data of per capita net availability of food grains available in the Ministry of Agriculture, Government of India, New Delhi, there seems a fluctuating trend of food grains availability during the planned period of economic growth of the country. It confirms that net availability of foodgrains was slightly improved during 1950s from 394.9 gms/day in 1951 to 468.7 grm/day in 1961. While it was constant at the same level of 468.7 grm/day in the 1960s, and recorded a decline to 15.1 grm/day during 1970s from 468.8 grm/day and is still constant at this lower level. Note here that the per capita net availability of foodgrains was sufficiently higher (548.0 grm/day) in the early period of the century (1905-6) which significatly declined to 132.0 grm/day in 1945-6. This rate of decline was very slow during pre-independence period of British India because of very slow process of production increase and the decline rate continued even in the first phase of planned development of independent India (in the 1950s). However, the starvation conditions were prevailing during British regime due to bulk export of foodgrains to England and other countries and inefficient management of foodgrains distribution system. But the stabilisation of the net availability of foodgrains after independence specially during the sixth and seventh five-year plan periods was recorded due to demographic expansion and widening gaps between geometric growth of population and arithmatic increase in foodgrains production (Fig.-1.1). Note that, comparatively, the net foodgrains availability was slightly improved in cereals from 334.2 grm/day in 1951 to 416.2 grm/day in 1981, but a rapid decline of 23.2 grm/day has been observed in the pulses (excluding gram). It was 60.7 grm/day in early 1950s and came down to 37.5 grm/day in early 1980s. These trends of foodgrains availability denote the impact of green revolution only on cereals (and especially on wheat production) not on the pulses. Therefore, per capita net availability of pulses are far lower (38.1 grm/day) than the balanced diet recommended for adults for vegetarian society (65.0 grm/day) by Indian Council of Medical Research, Hyderabad. There is still deficiency of pulses of about 28.0 grm/day per person in the production structure of foodgrains.

In another fifteen years, by the end of this century (year 2001), the population of India would touch the 1,000 million mark. It means it is expected to add nearly 160 million persons in the population of 1991. For fulfilling the food requirements of ever increasing population and the deficiency of pulses which already exists, the additional foodgrains production of about 100 million tones is required for upto the end of this century. During the next ten years of time (1991-2001), the agricultural production processes must be accelerated in such a manner so that they may produce at least six percent of annual rate of increase instead of three - and - half percent which has been observed during seventh five-year plan period. To achieve the target growth of agriculture, its regional dimensions should also be elaborated.

Regional Dimensions of Indian Agriculture

Most of the agricultural scientists interpreted the agricultural growth processes and its regional structure for solving the problems of optimisation of agricultural phenomena applying factorial-ecologic approach in the regional frame of agricultural growth characteristics. With the help of statistical techniques of correlation coefficient for the regional analysis of agricultural growth and development in the fifteen years period of planned development (specially first three-five years plan periods), it is concluded by Nath (1969) that there is a weak regional structure of agricultural growth components because of their insignificant relations with the infra-structural variables of agricultural development. It is observed further that there are no effects of moisture index (which is the most significant agro-climatic attribute) and irrigation (agro-technological attribute of modern agricultural practices) on the output growth and productivity increase especially in the fifties. It may be because of regional variations in the agro-ecological conditions and lack of policy implementation for agricultural development. No doubt, the diversified patterns are emerging in the regional frame of agricultural phenomena while, framing regional agricultural policies, the states have been considered as regions for evaluating the agricultural performance and preparing regional investment strategy. Indeed, state formations in India are on 'language-based' rather than 'based on economic parameters'. State boundaries do not have the agro-ecological identity. Therefore, the results of Nath's study might not be giving the true picture of agricultural growth phenomena. A very good deal of agricultural growth was done by

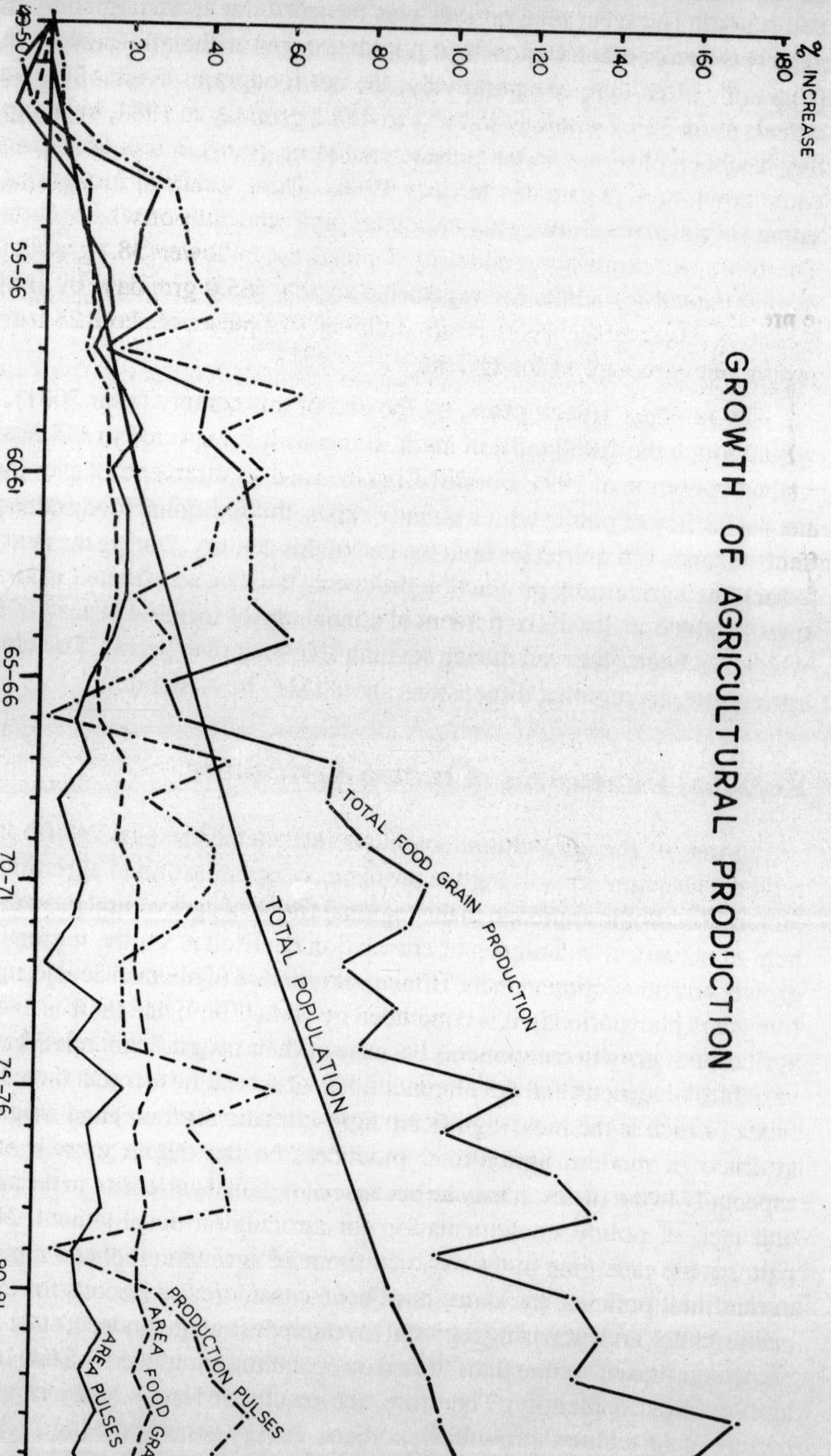
GROWTH OF AGRICULTURAL PRODUCTION
% INCREASE
20
40
60
80
100
120
140
160
180
49-50
55-56
60-61
65-66
70-71
75-76
80-81
85-86
YEARS
TOTAL FOOD GRAIN PRODUCTION
TOTAL POPULATION
PRODUCTION PULSES
AREA FOOD GRAINS
AREA PULSES

Fig 1.1

Bhat and Learmonth (1968) by following the physiographic base of agricultural patterns by collecting district-wise data of agricultural output growth (1951-4 to 1958-61) and the land productivity for 1950-4 for establishing their areal relationships on the basis of physiographic regions of India. They concluded that the areas of high productivity have low growth rates particularly in the fertile great plains of India. It seems, contrary to claims, that the areas of Western Madhya Pradesh and parts of the black- soil plateau of Maharashtra characterise low agricultural productivity level with its high growth rate (Bhat and Learmonth 1968) while cotton, a commercial crop, is grown in these areas.

Many empirical studies on the changing regional patterns of agricultural growth between the pre-and post-green revolution periods conclude the interesting findings that the impact of green revolution had been confined in certain pockets of upper parts of the northern great plains of India, while major parts of the country marked a net decline in the per capita agricultural output with an increasing intra-regional inequalities (Mahapatra 1982, pp.217-18). Increasing intra-regional inequalities indicate the diversified patterns of agriculture because the main effect of green revolution technology is marked on the area and yield of wheat crop, while its pattern was emerging in a specific area (Mahapatra 1982, pp.241-3; Bhalla and Alagh 1979). Therefore, the effects of green revolution have failed to boost agricultural production and to accelerate the production processes in its optimal manner. It is being realised now that decision making processes and fund allocations for self-sustained growth of agriculture should have followed the criterion of 'optimal level of production' instead of 'production maximisation' that is adopted for the last three five- year plans (for fifth to seventh plan periods). No doubt, overall foodgrain production has increased rapidly to meet out the demand of the increasing population of the country. But there seems a fundamental fallacy in the decision-making process which creates regional duality and imbalances in the agricultural development patterns specially after the introduction of green revolution technology. Obviously, it is a well known fact that the country has plenty of agricultural resources and their potentials to use them in the future, however, crop-yields are recorded very low in India compared to other developing countries of the world. The Indian farmers rarely achieve the record crop-yields which have been assessed on the basis of local agro-ecological conditions and 'on-farm experiments' by the agricultural scientists of Indian Council of Agricultural Research (ICAR), New Delhi (Prasad and others 1987). There are varied type of constraints and barriers which determine the farming efficiency and limit to the crop-yield increase. They are:

(a) The lack of knowledge of modern agricultural technology among the farming community and its proper implementation without understanding the local agro-ecological conditions is the major constraint at national level, while the Department of Agriculture Extension Services, Ministry of Agriculture is trying its best to introduce the agricultural technology programmes of the government to the village-level farmers. In this connection, it can be said that self-sustained agricultural growth processes must follow 'optima-limit concept' propounded by McCarty and Lindburg (1967) rather than 'equilibrium theory of profit maximisation'. The former concept of agricultural growth follows the agro-ecological criterion of agricultural production efficiency, while the latter optimises the agricultural growth processes on the basis of income elasticity of production demand. To eliminate the effects of these constraints, the regional study of agricultural growth processes must be done on the basis of delimiting homogeneous agro-ecological regions of the country rather than considering states as the agro-ecological homogeneous regions which cannot give the real picture of agricultural growth.

(b) The most significant growth constraints are related to the demand of the most rational distribution and location of infra-structural facilities and agricultural productive forces from the point of view of national agro-economic efficiency. These constraints can be envisaged by understanding the regional patterns of agricultural growth potential and 'yield-gaps' of various crops in the different agro-ecological conditions of the country.

(c) Socio-economic barriers always play the significant role and destabilise the crop-yields at micro-economic processes of agriculture growth. Land tenancy, size of operational land-holdings, price mechanism (agricultural production prices and input costs) and the social changes (which influence the food habits, domestic food requirements, and consumption patterns, etc) are the constraints which never allow the peasants to alter their cropping patterns, crop-intensity and to take the firm decisions on farm-operations and its proper management. Thus, growth processes of Indian agriculture seem slow and regionally unbalanced.

In fact, factorial ecological integrated approach of agriculture which may relax the conditions and constraints of crop-yield as discussed above should provide the sound base through identifying suitable areas of the fast growth rate of agricultural output for the purpose of proper expansion and intensification of green revolution technology. Thus, the 'region-specific approach' of agricultural growth is better than 'sectoral-priority criterion'.

The Objectives

Therefore, the attention is focused here on the detailed examination of region forming processes of agricultural growth and development by considering districts as the Operational Taxonomic Units (OTUs). District is considered as the homogeneous areal unit for interpreting the results of agricultural characteristics at micro, meso and macro-areal levels. Accordingly, the main objectives of the present study are :

(a) to estimate the growth of agricultural output, levels of agricultural productivity and its changing patterns over time specially the post-green revolution period (1970-1 to 1989-90), so that the effects of modern technology can be visualised in its regional perspective,

(b) to assess the agricultural growth potential at district level so that its rate of absorption can be calculated for analysing its role in agriculture growth and development, and

(c) to generate the relevant variables for agricultural regionalisation and to analyse the regional characteristics of agriculture in view of proper utilisation of agricultural growth potential for preparing regional investment strategy.

It may be noted here that we have been able to give the general picture of agricultural performance in its descriptive account rather than analytical evidences because the main emphasis is given on the regional aspects for preparing proper investment strategy. The growth performance of area, yield and production of crops is not described separately. Only the aggregated picture is shown in its regional frame because the cropping - patterns, crop - combination regions and crop-wise yield patterns have already been described in detail by many geographers and economists (Agricultural Commission 1964, Bhat and Learmonth 1968, Bhalla and Alagh 1979, Sen Gupta 1968, Mahapatra 1982, Dayal 1984, 1985).

In the present study, the areal patterns of growth processes and the regional characteristics of agriculture are shown by taking district as an areal unit into account. The states of Arunachal Pradesh, Nagaland, Meghalaya, Mizoram and Manipur of the North-Eastern part of the country are not included in the present study because of non-availability of comparable data of all the variables taking into account for agricultural regionalisation. On account of same problems of data availability the smaller states, namely, Goa, Daman and Diu, Sikkim and the Union Territories of Chandigarh, Dadra and Nagar Haveli, Pondichheri, Lakshadweep, Andaman and Nicobar Islands have also been excluded. Out of a total 14 districts of the Jammu and Kashmir state, only 6 districts of the foot-hills of Himalayas have been considered for describing the regional characterists. The districts which have urban characteristics (as follow urban population more than 90.0 percent to total population of the district) or those which have very low agricultural activities have also been excluded for the functional analysis. The name of these districts are Greater Bombay(Maharastra), Madras (Tamilnadu), Calcatta(West Bengal), Hydrabad(Andhra Pradesh), Delhi State, The Dangs(Gujrat), Lahaul & Spiti(Himachal Pradesh) and Nilgiris (Tamil Nadu). They are excluded primarily because they may have fluctuating effects on the results of areal variations of agricultural phenomena. Thus, total OTUs that are 348 in number of the seventeen states of India, have been considered for regional analysis of performance of Indian agriculture. Due to boundary changes over the period of study, the district boundaries at the time of 1981 have been considered as OTUs and the newly formed districts have been clubbed together according to 1981 district boundaries (Appendix- II).

Methods and Data Base

Three major issues which are closely related to the methodological aspects of agricultural growth and development are highlighted here for applying the appropriate methods in understanding the real-world situation of agricultural characteristics. They are to measure the growth of agricultural output and level of agricultural production, the role of labour and technology in the growth processes, and the demarcation of regional boundaries to understand the real regional picture of Indian agriculture.

(a) Methods Used for Measurement of Agricultural Growth

It is basically related to the analysis of changes occurred in the growth components, that are, area under cultivation, crop-yield and the cropping patterns of a particular area. Reviewing the concerned literature, it is obvious that the methods which have been used for measuring the agricultural growth of India, are based on:

(i) the additive decomposition scheme of the analysis of agricultural growth components used by Minhas and Vaidyanathan (1965),

(ii) the multiplicative decomposition scheme of growth component elements which predicts annual exponential rate of agricultural output growth, used by Bhalla and Alagh (1979 pp.40-61),

(iii)the compound rate of aggregated agricultural output used by many scientists (Mahapatra 1982, pp. 220-43) and the Department of Agriculture and Cooperation, Government of India, New Delhi for estimating the growth rates of area, production and yield of principal crops in India (Ministry of Agriculture 1991, Table- 14.2), and

(iv) the linear growth rate which is based on linear-trend equation.

According to the additive growth model of Minhas and Vaidyanathan, the observed increase in aggregate output has been decomposed into four component elements, that is the contribution of the changes in: (a) cultivated area, (b) crop-yield, (c) cropping patterns and (d) the interaction between latter two elements. Indeed, this model is based on the ' arithmetic law' of agricultural production growth rather than 'geometric law' by which production follows exponential or compound trend of production increase. Exponential and compound trends are based on semi-logarithmic distribution of agricultural production increase over time. Exponential trend follows the form:

$$p_1 = p_0(e)^{rt} \quad \dots \quad \dots \quad \dots \quad (1.1)$$

where, p_1 = production of current year, p_0 = production of base year, r = annual rate per unit and t = number of years.

Its linearised form is :

$$\log_e p_1 = \log_e p_0 + rt. \quad \dots \quad \dots \quad \dots \quad (1.2)$$

On the other hand, compound growth is based on formula:

$$p_1 = p_0(1+r)^t,$$

It follows $\log p_1 = \log p_0 + \log (1+r).t$ form of the distribution.

Note that the linear form of production increase follows as :

$$p_1 = p_0 + (p_0 r)t, \quad \dots \quad \dots \quad \dots \quad (1.3)$$

where $r = [(p_1 - p_0)/p_0 t]$, and $(p_0 r)$ = annual absolute increase in the total size of production. It has been confirmed from various empirical evidences that agricultural production follows the law of diminishing return (Miller 1966); it means production increases with decreasing rate due to various factors like land capability limitations of agricultural production, changes in the agro-ecological conditions,various levels of substitution rate of input factors operating in agricultural production processes, local food requirements and so on.

Thus, agricultural production increase follows arithmetic progression rather than geometric one; it means linear trend shows real- world situation rather than concave curve (which increases with increasing rate) of production increase. The same facts have also been tested by the Department of Agriculture and Cooperation, Ministry of Agriculture, New Delhi by fitting the straight lines in the distribution of production of various crops as well as of total foodgrains of India drawn for the last forty years of production data (Ministry of Agriculture 1991). Therefore, compound as well as exponential trends appear unsuitable to show the real picture of the growth of agriculture output. The inherent characteristics and weaknesses of these scheme of decomposition have also been shown by Bhalla and Alagh (1979, pp. 40-1 & Table-11), although they used the geometric progression method (exponential growth rate formula) for measuring district-wise growth of agricultural output. So, Minhas and Vaidyanathan's model has better expression of agricultural growth. But the average annual growth (i.e., based on linear trend equation 1.3) is used for the aggregated value-added agricultural output for each of the district of the country.

(b) Methods for Assessing Agricultural Productivity

The assessment of agricultural productivity per unit of cultivated land as well as per agricultural worker (as called land as well as labour productivities respectively, although they are not appropriate terms for agricultural productivity) is also one of the major issues of methodological consideration. The conversion of crop-production (i.e., the product of two main elements of production components: area and yield) and its aggregation to form a single index of agricultural production, are the main aspects of present discussion*. A number of techniques have been used to assess agricultural output with some of their virtues and shortcomings. Ranking coefficient which is the simplest method of showing the importance of crop-yield of various crops in different areal units was applied by Kendall(1939) for assessing the agricultural output of England and later on it was followed in the study of 20 countries of the world by Stamp (1960) and of Uttar Pradesh in India by Shafi (1960). In this method, crop-yield is merely the index without considering the areal performance of the crops which is also an important element of agricultural output. Further, the Bhatian concept of agriculture productivity (as he has used the term efficiency instead of productivity) index is slightly extended form of Ganguli's agricultural efficiency index who prepared agricultural efficiency index for Ganga valley in India by multiplying the percentage share of crop area with percentages of crop-yields in an areal unit and, later on, averaging them into one (Ganguli 1938). The yield of crops was considered merely in relation to crop-land share by Bhatia (1967) which has been termed as 'standardized yield Index by Singh and Chauhan (1977). But the relative importance of crops in a particular areal unit is the principal aspect of converting crop yield into a single unit. The crop-equivalent coefficients are calculated on the basis of crop-prices, caloric significance of crops and the relative importance of crop-production at national, state and local levels. Thirdly, the cropping intensity index is also important to evaluate productivity results on per unit of Net Sown Area instead of Gross Cropped Area. Thus, the composite index of agricultural productivity is the product of all these three indices (Singh and Chauhan 1977). It is noted here that, on account of calculating relativity of the areal patterns of agricultural productivity by 'coefficient method', the comparison of agricultural productivity is only possible among the areal units. The comparison over time is not possible because of unit mean of agricultural components. To solve the problem

---

* The detail discussion on the techniques to form the composite index of agricultural output has been published elsewhere (Singh and Chauhan 1977). The modified version of the useful part of the paper is reproduced here.

of comparability of agricultural productivity (on regional as well as on temporal bases), Dayal(1948) prepared the agricultural productivity index in value added term by converting crop production into its money value. In fact, production price is the most important factor which directly controls the cropping patterns, crop-intensity and the quantity of crop-production specially in the area of green-revolution when agriculture is also recognised as industrial occupation.

Thus, the agricultural production and productivity levels are assessed here by following the same criterion of 'value added agricultural production' rather than its physical output. Productivity maps for 1969-72, 1979-82 and 1988-90 and the maps of average annual growth of agricultural output for 1970s and 1980s are prepared by aggregating the output of sixteen principal crops in terms of money value by using constant farm harvest prices of crop production considering 1969-72 as base year. It is done because of comparability of agricultural output and productivity over time. Thus, Agricultural total output,O, is calculated as:

$$O = \sum_{i=1}^{n} A_i . Y_i . P_i, \qquad \ldots \qquad \ldots \qquad \ldots. \qquad (1.4a)$$

where i = 1,2,3,..., n as number of crops; A_i, Y_i, P_i are the area, yield and prices of a particular crop of a district; and O is total agricultural output in value term.

Agricultural productivity has been defined in relation to land as well as labour because they are the major agricultural inputs. Thus, land productivity refers to the agricultural output per unit of cultivated land as

$$Y = (O/A), \qquad \ldots \qquad \ldots \qquad \ldots. \qquad (1.4b)$$

and labour productivity ,Y_l, refers to the agricultural output per agricultural worker as

$$Y_l = (O/L). \qquad \ldots \qquad \ldots \qquad \ldots. \qquad (1.4c)$$

The physical output of agriculture is the product of three component elements: area, yield and intensity of crop, while production prices are the major determinant of value output O. If total work force engaging in agriculture is denoted by L, the labour productivity (O/L)* must be the product of two main components of agriculture: value output per unit of cultivated area (i.e., land productivity, O/A, as noted in the present context by eqn. 1.4b) and agricultural land per worker (A/L). Besides these components, the other agricultural attributes, namely, production efficiency, growth potential and its absorption rates for production increase are also taken in to account for preparing the bases of regional investment strategy. These attributes of agriculture are discussed in detail in the concerned Chapters of the present study. Now, present discussion should be proceeded towards the methods used for delineating agricultural regions of the country.

---

* It is mathematically formulated as:

$$O/L = (O/A.A/L). \qquad \ldots \qquad \ldots \qquad \ldots \qquad (1.5)$$

Note that rate of increase in labour productivity, must to a close approximate be the sum of the rates of increase in O/A and in A/L as

$$d(O/L)/dt = [d(O/A)/dt] + [d(A/L)/dt]. \qquad \ldots \qquad \ldots \qquad \ldots \qquad (1.6)$$

(c) Methods Used to Delimit Regions*

Briefly, the concept of region refers to the areal properties and their interacting nature, while region provides a framework of time and space that binds sectors and areas together and relates the effects of one point of time to the other point of time impelling us as contrary to greater cooperative environment. By strengthening the economic fabric of the country as a whole or its parts, region makes a powerful force and shown the real-world situation for self-sustained growth and integrated development of the sectors of the economy of the country because it has three particular kinds of synthesis of the forms and features of areal geographical phenomena; it shows existing reality, determines the degree of space-relations, and systematises areal hierarchy (spatial ordering) of given phenomenal properties/characteristics. Therefore, spatial interactions can be/ have been interpreted in order to consider them as a systematic description and/or areal analysis. The work of Troll (1950, pp.163-8), Berry (1961, pp.273-4 and 1964, pp.2-11), Berry and Rao (1968), Dickenson (1969, pp.179-80), Pal (1961, 1975) and so on are appreciable and noticeable on the systematic description of spatial characteristics of developmental phenomena. On the other hand, the interpretation of regional resource structure produced by Soviet geographers and regional planners through developing the planning concept of 'Territorial Production Complexes (TPCs)' is important to note on the areal analysis of spatial interactions (Kolosovsky 1958, Bandman 1978). The same concept was later on followed by Sen Gupta (1968, pp.101-16) for economic regionalisation in India.

The major issues are indicative to the regionalisation (that refers to the processes of region-formation) especially for preparing Regional Investment Strategy for which the process of segregating areal features has to be evolved. There are two fundamental processes for regionalisation: *division* and *classification*. Division follows the partitioning procedure of the whole space into its constituent parts on the basis of some norms or laws of the areal properties, while classification follows the grouping procedure of areal units into classes on the basis of homogeneity of interacted phenomenal facts (Grigg 1967, pp.461-63, Amedeo and Golledge 1975, p.168). Thus, ordering of spatial variance of the interact areal characteristics is the main tool by which homogeneous characteristics of the whole of the universe may regionally be demarcated with the help of cartographic and/or statistical techniques.

Various multivariate techniques like factor analysis, functional distance analysis, super-imposition method of cartographic techniques can be applied for finding out the hierarchical regional gradation by classifying OTUs on the basis of agricultural characteristics of the country. Having been tested the validity of these techniques, the suitable method would be chosen and applied for agricultural regionalisation. The scientific reasoning of the procedures for region-formation is discussed in detail in the concerned Chapter of the present study.

This part is the out come of the material prepared after discussing with Professor L.S. Bhat, Professor of Regional Planning, Indian Statistical Institute, New Delhi at the time of his visit at our department in the month of August-September 1991. The valuable suggestions regarding the metaphysics of regions and regional economy of the country are gratefully acknowledged.

(d) Data Collection

So far as data collection and mapping are concerned, the present research has utilised varied sources of informations at secondary levels. The district-wise crop-statistics, area, yield and production of the principal crops for early 1970s, 1980s and late 1980s have been collected from the Journals published by the Ministry of Agriculture, Government of India, New Delhi. The main sources of the data used in the present study are given in Table- 1.6.

Data-tabulation and generation of variables for agricultural regionalisation are done manually by calculators and the complex nature of data processing and formulations are successfully proceeded with the help of electronic computer. The district-wise authentic map of India is used as base-map for showing the regional patterns of agricultural attributes.

Conclusion

In the above discussion on the major issues and problems of Indian agriculture, it is concluded that the agricultural sector is facing a problem of its low growth as the GNP of agricultural sector at 1980-1 prices grew by 169 percent between 1951-2 and 1991-2, whereas for the other sectors of the economy by 610 percent. Per capita GNP, using the same base, of agricultural sector grew only by 28 percent while that of other sectors by 154 percent. Therefore, the study requires a different angle of self- sustained growth, that is 'region-specific approach' to synthesize the natural factors and to analyse the agricultural characteristics for the optimal use of agro-ecological conditions of landuse and production processes in relation to open-market economic system where agricultural production, productivity, cropping patterns, crop intensity and the other related attributes of agriculture are highly price-related. From what has been said, it follows that the regional investment strategy may only be prepared by following this approach of regional dimensions of agricultural phenomena. It would provide the sound base for productivity enhancement and optimal utilisation of agricultural resources. The areal patterns of agricultural incremental output will now be examined in the light of the regional growth characteristics of Indian agriculture separately in the next Chapter.

-----o0o-----

Table-1.6: Source of Data.

	Items	Source	Years Used
1	Normal Annual Rainfall	Indian Meteorological Deptt., Pune	1901-1950
2	Soil Fertility Rating	Some & Raychaudhary c.f. R.B.I. Bulletin, Bombay 1969.	1960
3	Landuse Statistics	D.O.E.&S., Ministry of Agriculture, N. Delhi	1950-1 to 1986-7
4	Total Cropped & Net Sown Area	Indian Statistics, Vol. II, 1978	1969-70 to 1971-2
5	Total Cropped Area and Net Sown Area	D.O.E. & S., Ministry of Agriculture, N. Delhi	1979-80 to 1981-2 1988-9 & 1989-90
6	Net & Gross Irrigated Areas	—do—	1979-80 to 1981-2 1988-9 & 1989-90
7	Production & Acreage of Crops	Agricultural Situation in India	1969-70 to 1971-2 1979-80 to 1981-2 1988-9 & 1989-90
8	Farm Harvest Prices of Crops	—do—	1970-71
9	Maximum Expected Crop Yield	Annual Reports of All India Coordinated Report on National Demonstration, ICAR, N. Delhi	1981-2 & 1985-6
10	Use of Fertiliser	Fertilizer Statistics, F.A.I., N. Delhi	1980-1 & 1988-9
11	Machine Tools	Indian Livestock Census, D.O.E.& S. Publications	1972 & 1988-9
12	Agricultural Wages	Agricultural Wages in India, D.E.O. & S. Pubtications	1970-1,1980-1 & 1988-9
13	Agricultural workers, Litercery Rate, Rural Urban Population	Census of India, P.C.A. 1971 , 1981 &1991 Provisional Population Tables	1971, 1981 & 1991

Abbreviations:

D.O.E. & S.= Directcrate of Economics & Statistics,

F.I.A. = Fertilizer Assciation of India,

R.B.I. = Reserve Bank of India,

ICAR = Indian Council of Agricultural Research, New Delhi.

Chapter - 2

Agricultural Growth and Its Regional Patterns

The general performance of Indian agriculture as described in Chapter-1 shows significant changes in agricultural attributes with a slow agricultural growth. A detailed description of growth components and their changing patterns in relation to various physical as well as techno-economic factors would be able to give clear cut reasons of slow growth. Keeping in view the physical factors (specially soils and climatic conditions) and modern agricultural technology which have direct impact on agriculture, the present chapter is devoted to three important aspects of agricultural growth,viz., (a) the anatomy of agricultural growth in order to describe its decomposed elements, (b) the general growth trends with its factors and (c) the concentration of growth in its regional frame for understanding the proper applicability of seed-fertilizer technology and optimal acceleration of regional processes of sustainable growth patterns.

So far as the required statistics of agricultural production is concerned, the growth patterns are described here by collecting district - level statistics of area and yield of sixteen principal crops* for three points of time, viz., 1969-72 (three years average) as base year, 1979-82 as middle year and 1988-90 (two years average) as current year. The total volume of agricultural output is assessed by changing physical quantity of various crop production into its money terms with the help of state -level statistics of production - prices of harvesting period. For the calculation of value added output of agricultural products for various points of time, the production prices of 1970-1 are considered as base year's prices, so that comparability among the agricultural growth patterns may be maintained and interpreted.

In fact, there are three main aspects for interpreting the growth trends and its inter-regional variations. They are directly related to three major methodological questions of the aggregation of various crop yield, decomposition of growth components and the regional variations of concentration of growth areas. The conceptual and methodological insights of these aspects have already been described in the previous Chapter, however, the workable solutions are also given side by side in the present text.

---

* The crops included in the present analysis are as: (a) cereal crops - Paddy,Wheat, Jowar, Bajra,and Maize; (b) Pulses-Gram and Tur (Arhar); (c) Oilseeds - Groundnut , Rapeseed & Mustard and other six oilseeds ; (d) Fiber Sugarcane, Cotton, Jute & Mesta; (e) Vegetables - Potato.

Anatomy of Agricultural Growth

Anatomy of an organism refers to the cross sectional study of its inter-related components and their inherent characteristics. The agricultural growth basically depends upon the volume of incremental growth output which is the result of changes occurring in the agricultural production components. Incremental agricultural output refers to the absolute size of output increase within a specific span of time, while agricultural growth rate refers to a proportionate change in the total volume of agricultural output over time. Therefore, the trends of agricultural production components would be described here before detailed study of agricultural growth processes.

(a) Trends of Agricultural Production Components

There are two important aspects to be highlighted here for the trend analysis of agricultural components: the break-up of the period for a comparative study of growth trends of production components and its measurements with its statistical significance and, secondly, the measurement of the fluctuating nature of the actual trends of agricultural components . So far as measurement of the gradient values of the tendencies of production components is concerned, the constants and coefficient values of the best-fitted straight line equations are calculated to show the rate of change (indicated by b) and the degree of fluctuation of the actual trends of production components over time (shown by the degree of determinant value R^2) (for detail, see foot notes of Table- 2.1).

In fact, green revolution of the mid sixties has altered the entire trend of agricultural structure in India with fast acceleration of agricultural growth processes. As a result, the general trend of production components can be visualised by dividing the entire span of time of planned agricultural development into two broad phases of production increase : pre-green revolution period (1950-1 to 1969-70) and post-green revolution period (1970 -1 and onwards). The comparative study undertaken to interpret the results of average annual increase in the absolute size of agricultural production as given in Table -2.1 reveals the following salient features.

(i) If the actual trends of agricultural production and its infra-structural variables are shown on the graph , it is found that linear equations represent the best fitted trend lines at their 1.0 percent significant levels for most of the agricultural variables (Fig.-2.1). It means that average annual rate of change (i.e., based on linear expression of agricultural components) is the best expression for describing the real world situation of growth phenomena rather than log-normal or semi-logarithmic expressions. This fact has already been discussed conceptually in the previous Chapter.

(ii) The value of trend-determinant, R^2, which determines the degree of temporal fluctuation of the trend, indicates that higher the value lesser is the degree of its temporal fluctuation and *vice-versa*. The evidences given in Table-2.1 confirm that the infrastructural variables of agricultural growth trends have the higher values of R^2. It means they have lesser temporal fluctuations than the agricultural production variables. Specifically, the Net Irrigated Area fluctuates significantly less during the pre- and post- green revolution periods. Comparing the degree of temporal fluctuations of agricultural growth variables for pre- and post- green revolution periods, it is evident that there is a smoothness in the trends of agricultural infra-structural variables especially during post- green revolution period. But the production variables have higher degree of temporal fluctuations during the same period of time because of many reasons like, poor responses of farmers towards adoption of modern technology, changes in the climatic and farmers' socio-economic conditions.

Table-2.1: Increasing Trends of Agricultural Production Components and Input during Pre- and Post-Green Revolution Periods.

Agricultural Components	Annual rate of Linear Increase				Annual Increase (in Thousand units)
	1950-1to1969-70 (20 Years)		1970-1to1984-5 (15 Years)		
	b	R^2(%)	b	R^2(%)	
(A) Agricultural Land					
1. Net Area Sown	9.964**	88.74	2.825*	23.89	ha.
2. Area Sown more than once	4.760**	85.09	8.333**	90.21	ha.
(B) Crop-Patterns					
3. Total Coarse cereals					
i. Area	11.374**	82.52	4.381**	38.14	ha.
ii. Production	20.010**	78.37	26.394**	68.01	tonnes
4. Total Pulses					
i. Area	1.310*	19.84	.661	11.22	ha.
ii. Production	0.812+	10.88	0.758	7.67	tonnes
5. Total Oilseeds					
i. Area	2.539**	85.15	1.595**	62.39	ha.
ii. Production	1.380**	61.44	2.448**	47.40	tonnes
(C) Agriculture Infracture					
6. Net Irrigated Area	4.447**	96.41	8.450**	98.84	ha.
7. Irrigated Area more than once	2.300**	88.74	4.247**	96.88	ha.
8. Use of Fertilizers	6.364**	77.50	29.818**	93.20	kg /ha
9. Area under H.Y.Vs.	—	—	19.011**	98.70	times

** significant at .01 level,

* significant at .05 level, and

\+ significant at .10 level.

N.B.: 1. Linear increase is calculated by fitting straight line equation in given data of time series. Its equation is as Y = a+ bt, whereY = agricultural components' value, t =time (years), b = rate of increase.

2. R^2 indicates the degree of determinant of temporal fluctuations.

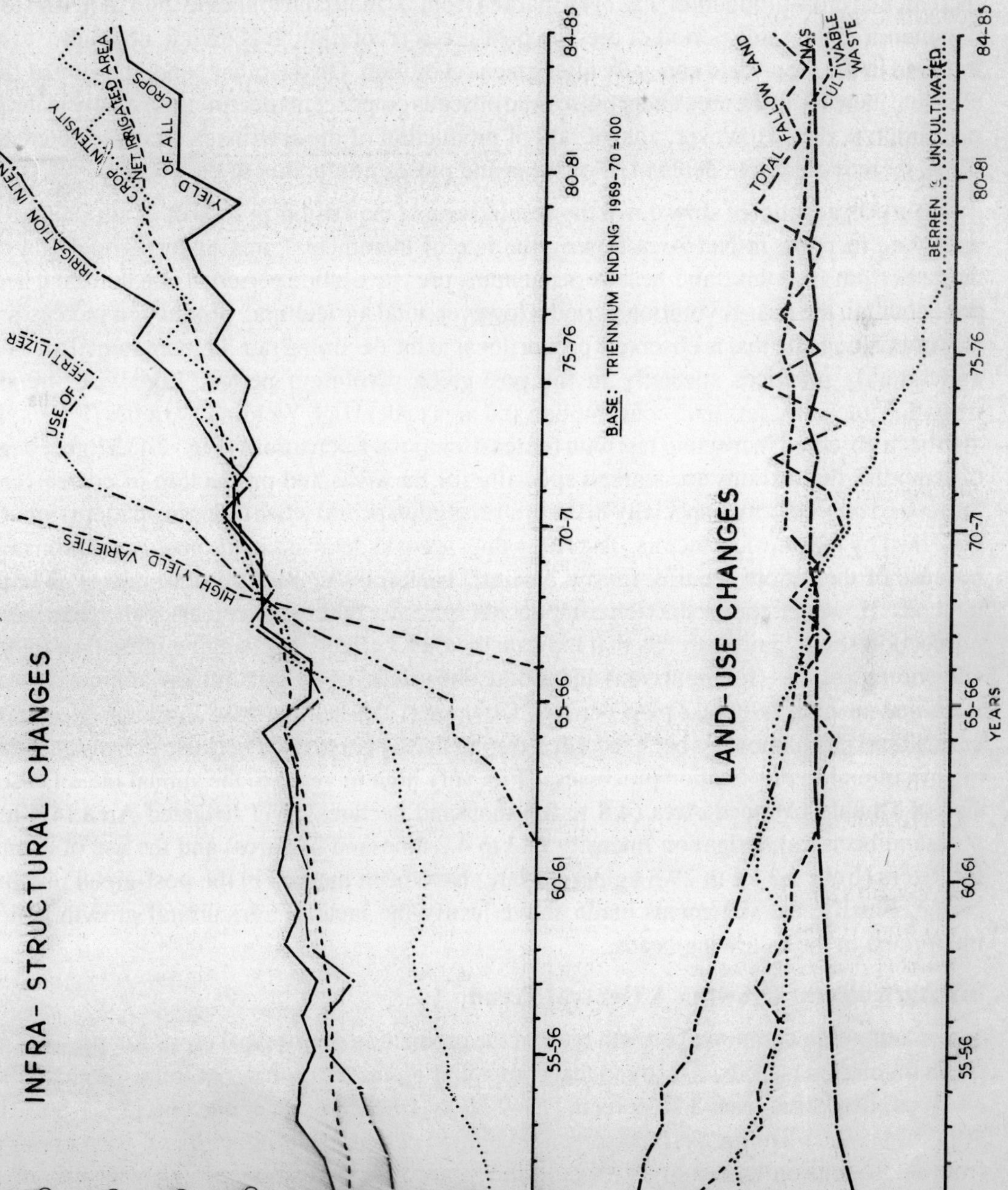
INFRA- STRUCTURAL CHANGES
IN PERCENT
160
140
120
100
80
60
40
20
1950-51
55-56
60-61
65-66
70-71
75-76
80-81
84-85
HIGH YIELD VARIETIES
USE OF FERTILIZER
IRRIGATION INTENSITY
CROP INTENSITY
NET IRRIGATED AREA
YIELD OF ALL CROPS
BASE: TRIENNIUM ENDING 1969-70 = 100
LAND-USE CHANGES
IN PERCENT
140
120
100
80
1950-51
55-56
60-61
65-66
70-71
75-76
80-81
84-85
YEARS
TOTAL FALLOW LAND
NAS
CULTIVABLE WASTE
BERREN & UNCULTIVATED

Fig 2.1

(iii) Inspite of diminishing trend of crop-area of coarse-cereals from 11.3 thousand hectare per annum (1950-1 to 1969-70) to 4.4 thousand hectare (1970-1 to 1984-5), an overall significant increase in the level and rate of the total production of its absolute size (i.e., incremental crop-production) has been marked from 20 thousand tonnes to 26.4 thousand tonnes per annum in the same period of pre-and post-green revolution. It is owing, no doubt, to rapid increase in the crop-yield specially after green revolution. On the other hand, the annual rate of absolute increase in the area under pulses and oilseeds crops seems declining specially in the post-revolution period. However, annual rate of production of these crops is recorded increasing. Thus, there is an ample demand of oilseeds and pulses production in the country.

(iv) On account of slow down the acceleration of expansion processes of agricultural land use (i.e., increase in Net Area Sown), the rate of incremental area under agricultural crops declines from 10.0 thousand hectare per annum (pre - revolution period) to 2.8 thousand hectare per annum in the post-revolution period. However, total agricultural production increases with its diminishing rate that is observed proportional to the declining rate of incremental area under agricultural practices specially in the post-green revolution period. Like-wise, trends of irrigation intensity, fertilizer consumption and area under High Yielding Varieties (HYVs) have also been observed increasing fast with the least temporal fluctuations (Fig.-2.1). Higher degrees of temporal fluctuations are marked specially for the areas and production of coarse cereals, pulses and oilseeds crops specially in the pre-revolution period when cropping patterns are solely governed by the physical factors. Their R^2 values seem to decrease in the post-revolution period, because of their more security from the natural calamities through modern means of farming methods. However, the production components specially the coarse-cereals, pulses and oilseeds production show 'pause' trends that indicate the direct effects of changing climatic conditions and pricing policies (for input costs and production prices) of the government announced during sixth and seventh five-year plan periods. Obviously, the fast increase in the absolute rate of agricultural production has been recorded during these plan periods because of fast acceleration of agricultural intensification processes. Thus, very high increase in the annual rate of absolute size of Double Cropped Area (4.8 to 8.3 thousand hectares), Net Irrigated Area (4.4 to 8.4 thousand hectares), Irrigation Intensity (2.3 to 4.2 thousand hectares) and the use of chemical fertilizers (from 6.3 kg to 29.8 kg per hectare) have been marked in the post-green revolution period. Finally, the statements made above justify the facts of agricultural growth which is interpreted in the following heads.

(b) Agricultural Growth - A General Trend

Comparing compound growth rates of the production of principal crops for pre- and post-green revolution periods, it is found that compound annual rate of agricultural production (for all crops) decreases from 3.13 percent (1949-50 to 1964-5) to 2.74 percent (1967-8 to 1989-90) (Table - 2.2). During the post -green revolution period, the production of food grains rose from 50.82 million tonnes to 89.36 million tonnes with the compound growth rate of 2.93 percent per annum ; nine major oil-seeds from 5.16 million tonnes to 8.56 million tonnes with 3.11 percent per annum; cotton from 3.04 million bales (of 170 kg each) to 6.01 million bales with 4.56 percent growth per annum ; jute and mesta from 3.31 million bales (of 180 kg each) to 7.66 million bales with an annual growth rate of 4.20 percent; and sugarcane from 57.05

million tonnes to 121.91 million tonnes with 4.26 percent annual growth . But the growth rate of each and every crop production has been recorded lower (except the production of wheat) during the post-green revolution period because of very slow growth in its areas (Table - 2.2). Although there is a significant increase in the total quantity of agricultural production, however decline its growth rate specially in the post-green revolution period is not a healthy symbol of balanced agricultural development and self sustained growth. Therefore, the growth of agricultural production must be examined in relation to the size of resource allocations in the plan periods and the agricultural technological advancements adopted specially in the post-green revolution period.

The relative performance of agricultural growth can be observed by calculating Incremental Input - Output Ratio (IIOR, which is a proportion between the rate of increase of input in agriculture and growth rate of agricultural production) for two points of time. It should give real picture of the increase of investment with respect to agricultural growth. The statistics collected and compiled by the Central statistical Organisation (CSO) and the Ministry of Agriculture show an increase in agricultural inputs (in its real terms) of 5.72 percent per annum and increase in real output (for all crops) of 3.13 percent during the 20 years of per-revolution period (1950-1 to 1969-70) . Note that the decline in the IIOR has been marked little lesser (33.0 percent per annum) during the post - revolution period (1970 -1 to 1989-90) because of slow increase in inputs (4.42 percent per annum) in this duration rather than before green -revolution period (Table- 2.3) . The worsening IIOR in the pre-revolution period was, owing to, fast increase in the consumption of chemical fertilizers in agricultural practices (146.0 percent per annum), though its total amount of consumption during that period was far less compared to that of its total amount consumed during post-green revolution period. Infact, during first three five-years plan periods, more weightage was given to multipurpose projects and industrial development of the country and, therefore, the production increase of fiber crops(jute, mesta and cotton) and cash crop (sugarcane) was recorded higher to meet out the raw material demands for agro-industries. It had to become most of the jute and mesta cultivation areas of Bengal state which had been given to the East Pakistan (now Bangladesh) after partition of the country . As a result, there was a great demand for the agricultural production of these industrial crops.

It appears that there was an overall gradual decline in IIOR during the 20 years of post-green revolution period. The value of IIOR has been recorded 1.65 for post-green revolution period as against 1.83 for pre-revolution period (Table-2.3) .It might be because of intensification of agricultural system through seed-fertilizer technology. In spite of intensive application of green revolution technology, the annual rate of production growth has been marked 2.68 percent, lesser than that of annual rate of input increase which was recorded as 4.42 percent during the post-revolution period in the country(Table-2.3). Very high rate of input investments which exceeds the rate of agricultural growth is indicative of the failure of green revolution. The causes are obvious. Inputs in agriculture are not corresponding to agro-ecological conditions of the country although green-revolution was started from the tracts of the most suitable agro-ecological conditions of the Punjab plains but it was confined in a few patches of the Great plains (the Punjab, Haryana , Western Uttar Pradesh and the major parts of west Bengal). It distorts the regional picture of agricultural growth, although the value of IIOR is seen to have diminished marginally during post green revolution period.

Table- 2.2: Compound Growth Rate of Area, Production, and Yield of Principal Crops in India for Pre- and Post-Green Revolution Periods.

(in per cent per annum)

	Crops	1949-50 to 1964-5			1967-8 to 1989-90		
		A	P	Y	A	P	Y
1.	Rice	1.33	3.49	2.13	0.57	2.74	2.92
2.	Wheat	2.68	3.99	1.27	1.91	5.14	3.15
3.	Jowar	0.99	2.50	1.50	-0.68	1.31	2.00
4.	Bajra	1.08	2.34	1.24	-0.81	0.26	1.08
5.	Maize	2.66	3.87	1.18	-0.10	1.15	1.26
6.	Ragi	0.84	3.08	2.22	0.07	1.52	1.59
7.	Small Millet	-0.30	-0.20	0.09	-2.78	-2.37	0.41
8.	Barly	-0.64	-0.28	0.36	-5.03	-3.07	2.05
	Total Cereals	**1.30**	**3.24**	**1.68**	**0.18**	**2.95**	**2.35**
9.	Gram	1.64	2.66	0.54	-0.75	-0.51	0.21
10.	Tur(Arhar)	0.57	-1.34	-1.90	1.52	2.08	0.55
11.	Other Pulses	2.07	1.28	-0.77	0.59	1.44	0.85
	Total Pulses	**1.90**	**1.39**	**-0.22**	**0.28**	**0.78**	**0.57**
	Total Foodgrains	**1.41**	**2.93**	**1.43**	**0.20**	**2.74**	**2.20**
12.	Sugar Cane	3.27	4.26	1.12	1.34	2.78	1.43
13.	Groundnut	4.01	4.33	0.31	0.29	1.45	1.16
14.	Sesamum	0.14	-0.32	-0.36	-0.35	1.53	1.89
15.	Rapeseeds & Mustard	2.97	3.36	0.37	1.63	4.27	2.60
16.	Seven Oilseeds	2.64	3.34	0.13	0.44	2.31	1.76
	Total Oilseeds	**2.69**	**3.11**	**0.20**	**0.16**	**2.15**	**1.51**
17.	Cotton	2.47	4.56	2.04	-0.34	2.18	2.54
18.	Jute & Mesta	3.86	4.20	0.73	0.05	1.89	1.57
	Total Fibers	**2.57**	**4.45**	**1.68**	**-0.31**	**2.07**	**2.28**
19.	Patato	4.37	4.27	-0.11	3.56	6.64	2.97
20.	Tobacco	1.66	2.79	0.96	-0.32	1.59	1.92
	Total Non-Foodgrains	**2.52**	**3.54**	**0.93**	**0.48**	**2.75**	**1.69**
	All crops	**1.61**	**3.13**	**1.30**	**0.26**	**2.74**	**2.02**

Abbreviations: A = Area, P= Production and Y = Yield

N.B.: 1. Seven oilseeds include Groundnut, Sesamum, Rapeseed & Mustard, Linseed, Castorseed, Niggerseed & Sunflower.

2. Total oilseeds include seven oilseeds, coconut & Cotton seed.

Source : *Agricultural Statistics At A Glance* (1991), Directorate of Economics & Statistics, Dept. of Agriculture & Cooperation, Ministry of Agriculture, New Delhi, Table-14.2, p.101.

Table- 2.3: Growth of Production Components and Incremental Input-Output Ratioin the Pre- and Post-Green Revolution Periods.

(Production in million tonnes)

Items	Pre-Revolution Period (20 Years)			Post-Revolution Period (20 years)		
	1950-1 (P_0)	1969-70 (P_1)	Ann. Growth rate+(%)	1970-1 (P_0)	1989-90 (P_1)	Ann.Growth rate+ (%)
(A) Agricultural Output						
1. Total Foodgrains	50.82	99.50	4.79	108.42	170.63	2.87
2. Total Oilseeds*	5.16	7.73	2.49	9.63	16.75	3.70
3. Groundnut	3.48	5.13	2.37	6.11	8.09	1.62
4. Sugarcane	57.05	135.02	6.83	126.37	222.63	3.81
5. Fiber crops**	6.35	12.35	4.72	10.95	19.76	4.02
Total output	—	—	**3.13**	—	—	**2.68**
(B) Agricultural Inputs						
1. Net Irrigated Area(mill. ha.)	20.85	30.20	2.24	31.10	42.00	2.33
2. Fertilizer Consumption (in ,000 tonnes)	6.56	198.24	146.10	198.24	873.74	17.03
Total input (in real terms)	—		**5.72**	—	—	**4.42**
Incremental Input-Output Ratio (IIOR) ++			**1.83**	—	—	**1.65**

N.B. : * It includes nine oilseeds crops.

** It includes cotton, jute and mesta crops, for which the production unit million bales of 170 kg each for cotton and 180 kg each for jute and mesta.

+ Annual growth rate has been calculated by simple growth rate formula as given in Eqn. - 1.3.

++ IIOR is the ratio between the rate of input increase and the rate of agricultural growth of a specific period.

(c) Conditions Created for Agricultural Growth in the Early Phases of Development

The major share of annual budgetary allocations had been given to the multi-purpose projects and industrial development for creating infra-structural facilities for agricultural development during first three-five year plan periods. The investment on heavy industries was also noticeable during the same plan periods. For fulfilling the demand of raw materials for textile industries, the production of fibers and commercial crops like cotton, jute, mesta and sugarcane had increased at a faster rate than foodgrains and, therefore, India had to import cereals and pulses during the first phase of planned development. The organisational aspects of agriculture land were strengthened for its proper management and productivity enhancement. Effective land management system was implemented through land reforms. Four major dimensions of land management which were implemented during second and third five-year plan periods were: abolition of intermediatory interests, land distribution through imposing land ceilings, abolition of absentee landlordism, and consolidation of land holdings (Bhalla 1988). These institutional factors created tempo of encouragement and free-working of the farmers on their farms, and later on, they became the causes of the increase in both production and productivity. On the other hand, studies on water and soil resources as physical factors of agricultural growth were conducted specially by Indian Council of Agricultural Research (IARI), Pusa, New Delhi in relation to moisture availability for agricultural growth which is a major attribute of the climatic conditions specially dependent on the quantity of rainfall and degree of mean temperature. In the early phases of agricultural development, the environmental conditions, particularly availability of water and soil fertility for plant growth, were the dominating factors of agriculture growth and entire agricultural activities like sowing crop seasons, crop mixing, rotation of crops, etc. were governed by the conditions and intensity of monsoons. Therefore, Indian agriculture was called 'monsoon dependent agriculture' at that time and monsoon had been the deciding factor of farmers' fate in the early period of agricultural development (specially till third five-year plan periods). The irrigation was insufficient and its effect on production growth was insignificant at that time as Nath (1969) undertook to interpret these facts, by establishing statistically the correlation between the share of irrigated area and agricultural land productivity. The relationship was observed very weak as r = .0931 during pre-green revolution period. He asserted that it might be due to regional imbalances in the distribution of irrigation facilities. However, irrigation had become the 'root- factor' and major cause of agricultural growth and development through which the other attributes of agricultural technology (HYVs seed-fertilizer technology) came into existence at the time of starting of green revolution (during late sixties).

Thus, there had been two major components of production growth operative in the pre-green revolution period: (a) the expansion of Net Area Sown (NAS) and (b) the changes in cropping patterns. The expansion of cultivation towards new lands, it means changes in the general landuse patterns, refers to the conversion of cultivable waste land into the other categories of landuse specially into the cultivated land . The geographical factors and the causes of the fast acceleration of expansion processes of agricultural landuse before introduction of green revolution have been interpreted carefully and examined logically by Singh (1971) by analysing the areal variations and the changing nature of the share of cultivable waste land specially for early period of planned development. He concluded that the percentage share of waste land is positively related to its rate of conversion specially during 1950s. In his analysis, it is clear that in most parts of Rajasthan, Madhya Pradesh and the central and northern boarder lands of Uttar Pradesh, which had a significant share of cultivable wasteland as about 16.0 percent (i.e., far higher than the national average which was recorded only 8.07 percent in 1950-51), it has been reduced to 10.0 percent in the 15 years of pre-green revolution period (1950-1 to 1965-6). It is interesting to note that the processes of agricultural expansion had been accelerated specially in the fertile tracts of these states, where irrigation and small-scale machine tool technology were available . For example, the terai areas of Uttar Pradesh extending from Saharanpur to Gorakhpur along with the hills of Sivalik ranges of the Himalayas which were full of marshy lands and bushes before independence, had been cleared and made arable by the refugees who immigrated from Punjab and Sindh provinces (now in Pakistan) at the time of partition. They used tractor as a machine tool for irrigation purpose and land cultivation. With the result, production and productivity increased fast and its level has become very high in these areas of Uttar Pradesh. But the agricultural land expansion processes in the Chambal ravine lands of Madhya Pradesh and Rajasthan were operated by small hand-operated traditional farming tools during the second five year plan period and , therefore, this land could not yield much production. Socio-economic conditions of the farmers at that time were also responsible for the areal variations in the productivity patterns.

The second major component of increasing production during pre-green revolution period had been the significant changes in cropping patterns. During first two decades of agricultural development (1950-1 to 1970-1), an increase of about 34.0 million hectare in the total cropped area of the country had been recorded owing, undoubtedly, to the rapid increase in two fundamental attributes of landuse : NAS and farming intensity . It has already been discussed that NAS was increasing at a constant rate of 10.0 thousand hectare per annum and area sown more than once (which refers to farming intensity) had increased at an annual rate of 4.8 thousand hectare in the 20 years of pre-green revolution period. The agricultural statistics reveal that the increase in farming intensity is positively related to the increase in the area under irrigation and its intensity (Table- 2.3) . Irrigation intensity rose 14.65 percent from 108.20 to 122.85 percent in the successive period of time. Another important factor of change in cropping pattern was production price mechanism. The substitution of more remunerative crops for remunerative ones was the additional factor for production increase. Inspite of rapid increase in the areas of foodgrains crops and quick requirements of their production which had to undertake imports during first three-five year plan periods, the marginal increase had been recorded in the areas under cash crops specially sugarcane and cotton (nearly half percent) because of more remunerative crops and basic raw materials of textile and sugar industries which was put in the priority list of development by the Planning Commission, New Delhi.

The details regarding the changes occurring in the cropping pattern and the influence of agricultural pricing policies on the changing agriculture structure would be discussed separately in the next chapter. But, the salient features and the trends of agricultural attributes came up after an introduction of modern input packages for agriculture is proposed to be analysed now in a systematic manner.

(d) Impact of Green Revolution Technology

Undoubtedly, the agricultural production has been enhanced fast during the 20 years of post green revolution period (1970-1 to 1989-90). The production growth of various crops vary in order to the application of modern inputs. For example, the production of total cereals rose from 96.60 million tonnes (1970-71) to 158.02 million tonnes (1989-90) at an annual compound rate of 2.97 percent . The record increase of cereal crops has been registered due to rapid increase in wheat production of 15.82 million tonnes, from 23.83 to 49.65 million tonnes at an annual rate of 5.64 percent in the two decades time of post-green revolution period. The wheat production increased by increasing its both components of production : area as well as yield. Area under wheat cultivation increased at a compound rate of 2.41 percent per annum and yield at an annual rate of 3.15 percent. But the moderate increase in the production of other foodgrains and commercial crops has also been recorded. For example, the production of oil seed has increased nearly three - fourth times from 9.63 million tonnes to 16.75 million tonnes at an annual compound rate of 1.56 per cent. The lowest rate of annual compound growth (i.e., only .65 percent) was recorded in the pulses in the successive time of post revolution period. Sugarcane production has followed very high growth rate (2.70 per cent per annum) being the constant expansion of its area at 1.58 percent annually and compound growth of yield at 1.11 percent per annum during the successive period of time. While the other commercial crops, specially fibers, increased at the moderate rates of their growth (Table-2.4). The growth structure of the post-green revolution period specifies its two important features. First feature is related to the overall growth of crop production which is influenced by the rapid increase of the production of two crops, namely, (a) wheat - a staple foodgrain which had to undertake import during pre-green revolution period at its higher prices. Maximum efforts have been made to increase the yield of wheat by inducing green-revolution technology during fifth and sixth five year plan periods. Even the area under wheat cultivation increased by 2.41 percent annually. And (b) Sugarcane - a commercial crop and the backbone of rural industralisation by which the farmers' economy is directly influenced and, therefore, area under sugarcane cultivation has been increasing at an annual rate of 1.58 percent. It is interesting to note here that increasing production prices of wheat and sugarcane during fifth five-year plan period has been the sound bases to the farmers for intensifying yield and expanding area under these crops. Thus, the farmers of wheat and sugarcane belt dispersed from Punjab to Western Uttar Pradesh (the area of Upper Ganga plains and Sivalik foot hills of *terai* and swamps) have started the use of the modern package of HYVs seed-fertilizer in the irrigated fields and farmers. Even during seventh plan period, wheat has been considered as a commercial crop instead of foodgrains and the surplus wheat was transported in the country through the markets and *mandies* for which Food Corporation of India have been playing a significant role. Note that the higher production and productivity of wheat crop are achieved by introducing modern technology at each stage of its growth and working for which medium size tractor (15HP) has become an essential and multipurpose tool for marginal and medium size land holders (2.0 to 5.0 hectares) who have mostly been using it for irrigation purposes sowing crops by seed drills, wheat threshing, leveling the fields/farms and even spraying weedicides and pesticides. Consequently, India has now sufficient stock of wheat and other foodgrains (as 13.20 million tonnes of wheat 6.94 million tonnes of rice and 1.05 million tonnes coarse grains as on July, 1,1990). Enough availability of wheat cereal at cheaper rate has altered the food consumption patterns of even rural masses. The poor people, who used to consume jowar and maize (cheaper food) specially in winter and rainy seasons since longer period of pre-revolution, have now started consuming wheat instead of these millet cereals. Expanding and intensifying cheap irrigation facilities (by regular canal system and private tubewell facilities), availability of HYVs of wheat seed and low-priced or subsidised chemical fertilizers (specially NPK) and better loan facilities for small and medium size tractors during the 20 years of post-green revolution period of agricultural modernisation have brought out fast increase in the production and productivity of agriculture specially of cereals and oil seed crops. Therefore, input costs and production prices have become the major ingredients of changing the production trends. They altered the entire ecologically oriented crop-combinations and cropping -patterns of Indian agriculture. As a result, increasing regional disparities may be observed in the areal patterns of productivity distribution. But note here that, on account of increasing input costs and stable agricultural production prices, there seems frustration among the farmers because of less profitability. Secondly, because of intensification and expansion of more remunerative crops like wheat and sugarcane of the upper Ganga plains, gram of the central Peninsular India and cotton of the Gujarat and Maharashtra states, the cropping patterns which had been evolved earlier in its diversified form, have been changing towards crop-concentration. Consequently, an over all annual growth of all crops have been recorded at 2.74 percent during post green revolution period which is far lower than the growth rate of 20 years of pre-green revolution period (Table-2.2). There seems a failure of green revolution which is hampering the self-sustained growth of agriculture. Keeping in mind the general performance of agricultural growth in order to implement of appropriate technology and the required policy measures for self-sustained growth of agriculture, Union Minister of Agriculture Mr. Singh, Buta (1985) reminded the agriculture scientists in his convocation address delivered in Indian Agriculture Research Institute, New Delhi and added that inspite of increasing the inputs in its real terms at a rate of 4.1 percent per annum in the seven years of post-green revolution period (1976-7to 1982-3) when gross irrigated area had increased at an annual rate of 5.6 per cent, irrigation pump sets (diesel and electric) at annual rate of 8.0 to 9.0 percent, the area under HYVs at 7.0 per cent annual rate and the consumption of chemical fertilizers (specially NPK) at 11.0 percent annum, the annual rate of real agriculture output had been brought out only 2.0 percent increase (i.e., about half of the input increase) during the successive period of time.

Table - 2.4 Growth of Agricultural Production in the Post- Green Revolution Period

(Production in million tonnes)

	Items	Total Production 1970-71 (P_0)	Total Production 1989-90 (P_1)	Average Growth 1970-1 to 1989-90 (TG) +	Annual Compound Growth (%) (r) ++
1.	Total Cereals	96.60	158.02	63.58	2.96
2.	Total Pulses	11.82	12.61	6.68	0.65
3.	Oil Seeds (Nine)	9.63	16.75	73.95	1.65
4.	Groundnut	6.11	8.09	32.40	0.96
5.	Sugarcane	126.37	222.63	76.17	2.70
6.	Cotton*	4.76	11.41	139.70	2.35
7.	Jute & Mesta*	6.19	8.35	34.89	2.68

N.B. : + TG (Average Total grwoth) = $\{(P_1 - P_0).100/ P_0.\}$

++ Annual compound growth figures are based on 18 years data (1967-8 to 1985-6) compiled by the Director of Economics and Statistics, Ministry of Agriculture, New Delhi.

* Cotton Production figures are in million bales of 170 kg each and Jute & Mesta figures in million bales of 180 kg each.

The emerging recent growth trends of Indian agriculture show the imbalances in the yield increase of various crops and their optimal regional patterns. For instance, the virtual stagnation in the increase of pulses and oilseeds production has been observed in spite of increasing their production prices and demands in the country. The validity of these facts of agricultural growth has also been tested by Mohapatra (1982, pp.210-18) and Bhatia (1988, p.17-18) by stating the shortcomings of green revolution growth strategy which provided seed-fertilizer technology only to wheat and sugarcane that are the dominating crops only of a specific area of the country. Bhatia (1988, pp.17-18) argued that price mechanism had been the important factor for adopting modern input technology. He exemplified that prices of crop production and fertilizer costs persuaded the growth of wheat production in the early seventies when 3.00 kg of wheat was required for 1.00 kg of nitrogen and 1.00 kilo of NPK fertilizer would add about 10.00 kg of wheat grain to the output (Bhatia 1988, p.25). Therefore, NPK fertilizer was used substantially for wheat production with introducing HYVs of Mexican wheat seeds particularly in the irrigated areas of the states of Punjab, Haryana and Uttar Pradesh in the early seventies. Note that the quantity of wheat required to buy 1.00 kg of NPK has been decreasing from 3.00 kg (1970-1) to 2.27 kg (1991-2) because of faster rate of increase in wheat price than the fertilizer costs which was available at subsidised rate of constant costs till July 1991. Therefore, the doses of NPK fertilizer may further be increased for wheat production instead of the production of other crops specially pulses and oilseeds.

The second important feature of slow growth persisting in the post-green revolution period is the imbalances and distortion brought out in the ideal cropping patterns with breaking up the norms of agro-ecological criteria of agricultural growth. These distortions are creating regional diversities in the growth patterns as Dogra (1981) concluded that the concentrated growth patterns have been emerged during green revolution period (1962-5 to 1972-5). Being diversified nature of agro-ecological conditions in the country, the regional approach of agricultural growth is essential to understand its inter-state as well as inter-district variations for self sustained growth. It should be studied in detail under the proceeding heads.

Agricultural Growth Components and their Areal Patterns

Infact, the agricultural growth patterns and their processes have three major methodological considerations, that are related to the aggregation of total agricultural output for different points of time, the absolute increase in agricultural production (incremental output) for assessing the regional variations of the volume of production increase, and the inter-district variations in the growth rate of agricultural output. The average annual growth rate of each district for the last two decades (1970-1 to 1980-1 and 1980-1 to 1988-9) is calculated separately on the basis of applying 'simple - growth rate method' which is based on linear trend of agricultural output increase.

Componental relationship of agricultural growth can be established by understanding the logical reasoning of production elements of the growth equation. The logical explanation of the aggregation of agricultural output, which has already been given in the previous Chapter (eqn.-

1.4a), produces to predict that the agricultural output is the product of three production elements : area, yield, and production-prices of the various crops as considered under the domain of calculations. Since production-prices are considered constant for calculating production growth (because it is considered as conversion factor only), cropping patterns and crop-yield have become the major elements (that may be called determinants) which have direct effects on the changes in the agricultural output over time . On definitional part, it may be referred to that the incremental output is simply the difference of total output between two points of time as considered for the study of agricultural output increase (P_1-P_0), while the growth of agricultural output refers to the proportionate change of production differentials of various crops over time because of the linear trend of crop-production increase*. Thus, the equation of agricultural growth rate, R, which is $R = (P_1 - P_0)/ P_0$, as Eqn. 1.3 given in the previous Chapter, is the result of the growth rates of various crop production. The production growth of a particular crop, r_i, is expressed as :

$$r_i = (a_{i1} \cdot y_{i1} \cdot p_{io} - a_{io} \cdot y_{io} \cdot p_{io}) / a_{io} \cdot y_{io} \cdot p_{io} \,,$$

$$= [\{(a_{i1}/a_{io}) \cdot (y_{i1}/y_{io})\} - 1.0], \quad \ldots \quad \ldots \quad \ldots \quad (2.1)$$

where a_{i1} and a_{i0} are areas under ith crop for the current and the base years, y_{i1} and y_{i0} refer to the crop-yield for the current and the base year respectively, and p_{i0} denotes prices per unit of production of ith crop. The equation of the growth of crop production (eqn. 2.1) expresses to establish an important relationship among growth components that the growth rate of crop output is the result of the product of two growth ratios the growth ratio of crop-area (a_{i1}/a_{i0}) and of the crop-yield (y_{i1}/y_{i0}) with the subtraction of unit constant to determine the actual figures of crop-growth.

Thus, the agricultural growth components, namely, the changing crop patterns as area component, the changes in crop-yield, the growth ratios of crop-area and crop-yield and the concentration of the volume of agricultural output in its areal perspective, are described in detail. For the same, state-wise statistics of area, yield, and total production of the principal crops have been compiled and used for three points of time (1969-72, 1979-82 and 1988-90) for finding the empirical evidences of the regional concentration of agricultural growth. The evidences that are in broad agreements with *a priori* expectations confirm some important facts which have been interpreted in the following heads.

(a) Changes in Cropping Patterns (An Area Component)

Obviously, Indian agriculture is foodgrains dominated because more than 80.0 per cent share of Gross Cropped Area (GCA) as 126.50 million hectare out of total 159.13 million hectare (1989-90) is under foodgrains crops(which include cereals and pulses). There seems a gradual increase specially in the areas of paddy and wheat crops (which are the staple foodgrains) during the last 20 years after green revolution (1970-1 to 1989-90) (Table-2.5). Infact, the inter-district variations and regional characteristics of the cropping patterns have been examined first by the

* Note here that decomposition of growth components is not based on interaction factors as described by Minhas and Vaidyanathan (1965) and Bhalla and Alagh (1979, pp.40-1). It follows linear growth equation in which additive rule of growth is applicable rather than multiplicative one.

Agriculture Commission, ICAR (1964) and Professor Bhat and Learmonth (1968) for the late fifties, and later on by Professor Bhalla and Alagh (1979, pp.57-139) for showing the regional patterns of the growth of foodgrains production for the late sixties. It may be generalised from these studies that the regional variations in the cropping patterns and changes therein are the results of physical factors like soils, rainfall, temperature, length of seasons, etc. rather than the application of modern technology . As a result, in the areas of humid climatic conditions (annual rainfall more than 100cm with a high range of annual temperature , 20 °C to 40 °C) with the fertile alluvial soils, namely, the middle and lower Ganga valley (mostly the areas of Bihar and West Bengal), the Brahmaputra valley (the Assam state), the coastal regions of the deltas and the costal plains (the costal parts of Orissa, Andhra Pradesh, Tamilnadu, Kerala and Maharashtra states) , monoculture is the dominating feature of the cropping patterns in which paddy enjoys as 'monopolised crop'. On the other hand, wheat cultivation is remarkable in the semi-arid conditions of the Punjab, Haryana, Western parts of Uttar Pradesh states where it is grown with the help of extensive irrigation-based modern seed-fertilizer technology. While, in the arid zones of the country which include the state of the Rajasthan, and the central parts of Peninsular India, jowar and bajra have become the major crops but with conciderable decline its area after green revolution (1970-1 to 1989-90).

Table- 2.5: Changing Crop-Patterns in India (1970-1 to 1989-90).

(Area in million hectare)

	Corps	1970-71		1980-90		Changes	
		Area	%	Area	%	Area	%
1.	Rice	37.59	22.67	42.17	26.50	4.58	3.83
2.	Wheat	18.24	11.00	23.46	14.74	5.22	3.74
3.	Jowar	17.37	10.48	14.95	9.40	-2.42	-1.08
4.	Bajra	12.91	7.79	10.89	6.84	-2.02	-0.95
5.	Maize	5.85	3.53	5.86	3.68	0.01	0.15
6.	Ragi	2.15	1.30	2.37	1.49	0.22	0.19
7.	Small millets	2.82	1.70	2.60	1.63.	-0.22	-0.07
8.	Barley	0.92	0.59	0.99	0.62	0.07	0.03
9.	Gram	7.84	4.73	6.50	4.08	-1.34	-0.65
10.	Tur	2.66	1.60	3.58	2.25	0.92	0.65
11.	Other pulses*	12.04	7.26	13.14	8.25	1.10	0.99
12.	Sugarcane	2.62	1.58	3.41	2.14	0.79	0.56
13.	Groundnut	7.33	4.42	8.71	5.47	1.38	1.05
14.	Cotton	7.61	4.59	7.33	4.51	-0.28	-0.08
15.	Jute & Mesta	1.08	0.65	0.91	0.57	-0.17	-0.08
16.	Potato	0.48	0.29	0.96	0.60	0.48	0.31
17.	Tobacco	0.45	0.27	0.45	0.27	—	—
Total Cropped Area		**165.79**	**99.99**	**159.13**	**99.99**	**—**	**—**

N.B.: * It includes Peas, Mung, Masoor, and Lobia pulses.

Source : *Agricultural Statistics At AGlance,* Ministry of Agriculture, New Delhi for 1970-71 data. The data for 1989-90 is compiled from the Directorate of Economics & Statistics, Ministry of Agriculture, New Delhi.

Table- 2.6: State-wise Changes in Crop-Patterns of 12 Principal Crops for 1970-3 to 1989-90.

(Area in thousand hectare)

Sl.	State		Paddy	Wheat	Jowar	Bajra	Maize	Gram	G. Nut	Sesamum	Rapseed	S.Cane	Cotton	Jute & Mesta
1.	A.P.	a	3016.2(31.64)	17.3(0.18)	2079.0*(21.81)	502.8(5.27)	244.3(2.56)	73.2(0.76)	1434.4(15.04)	234.3(2.45)	0.4(0.01)	121.9(1.28)	318.5(3.34)	93.3*(0.97)
		b	4190.7(36.06)	12.3(0.11)	1337.0 (11.51)	278.6(2.40)	297.3(2.56)	62.6(0.54)	2312.3(19.90)	168.4(1.45)	2.1(0.02)	162.5(1.40)	657.0(5.65)	81.9(0.71)
2.	Assam	a	2001.6(82.57)	57.6(2.37)	—	--	1[illegible].5(0.47)	2.5(0.01)	–	10.2(0.42)	133.5(5.51)	33.4(1.38)	4.8(0.20)	124.0*(5.00)
		b	2435.1(75.37)	93.1(2.88)	—	--	19.7(0.61)	3.3(0.10)	–	14.5(0.45)	323.4(10.01)	38.8(1.20)	2.3(0.07)	103.5(3.20)
3.	Bihar	a	5022.6(59.03)	1313.7(15.44)	8.4*(0.10)	13.3(0.16)	873.9(10.27)	249.1(2.93)	4.4(0.05)	26.1(0.31)	80.5(0.95)	346.0(1.72)	2.4(0.03)	29.0*(0.34)
		b	5327.6(53.81)	1967.0(19.87)	5.7 (0.06)	9.6(0.10)	702.0(7.09)	169.5(1.71)	4.9(0.05)	16.0(0.16)	82.0(0.82)	124.6(1.26)	.1(neg)	140.0(1.41)
4.	Gujarat	a	456.1(05.57)	507.7(6.19)	906.0*(11.05)	1758.6(21.46)	264.6(3.23)	47.8(0.58)	1766.0(21.55)	115.4(1.41)	37.7(0.46)	37.3(0.45)	1738.0(21.20)	–
		b	601.0(7.12)	619.1(7.34)	872.7 (10.35)	1331.6(15.79)	323.3(3.83)	109.7(1.30)	1823.4(21.62)	154.5(1.81)	241.6(2.86)	106.0(1.76)	837.0(9.92)	–
5.	Haryana	a	282.8(6.46)	1186.8(27.12)	136.0*(3.11)	886.4(20.25)	113.4(2.59)	1051.9(24.04)	8.8(0.20)	2.4(0.05)	168.3(3.84)	131.5(3.00)	231.4(5.29)	–
		b	621.0(12.72)	1859.0(38.09)	109.0 (2.20)	261.0(12.72)	38.0(0.77)	526.0(10.78)	3.0(0.06)	0.3(neg)	383.0(7.85)	126.0(2.58)	468.0(9.59)	–
6.	H.P.	a	97.6(12.68)	316.5(41.13)	—	--	252.4(32.80)	25.1(3.26)	2.0(0.03)	8.1(1.05)	4.3(0.56)	3.2(0.42)	0.5(0.05)	–
		b	88.7(10.00)	382.7(43.00)	—	--	313.6(35.23)	5.7(0.64)	0.4(0.04)	2.2(0.25)	8.3(0.93)	2.5(0.25)	0.2(0.02)	–
7.	J & K	a	221.0(29.19)	183.3(24.21)	—	19.4(2.56)	276.0(36.45)	2.5(.03)	–	7.4(1.00)	23.5(3.10)	1.8(0.23)	–	–
		b	264.0(26.94)	242.7(24.76)	—	14.5(1.48)	292.2(29.82)	1.1(0.11)	–	9.9(1.01)	52.5(5.35)	0.5(0.05)	–	–
8.	Kar.	a	1095.8(14.25)	316.6(4.12)	1625.0*(21.14)	432.5(5.62)	87.8(1.14)	147.7(1.92)	808.9(10.52)	70.5(0.92)	3.4(0.04)	102.6(1.33)	987.0(12.89)	28.3*(0.37)
		b	1183.3(11.93)	247.9(2.50)	2343.0 (23.60)	514.2(5.19)	252.8(2.55)	222.1(2.24)	1281.2(12.92)	200.1(2.02)	4.8(0.04)	319.3(2.21)	681.7(6.87)	20.0(0.20)
9.	Kerala	a	873.4(94.68)	—	—	--	--	—	15.4(1.67)	11.8(1.29)	–	7.7(0.83)	7.4(0.80)	–
		b	572.4(57.53)	—	—	---	---	—	14.9(1.50)	11.6(1.16)	–	8.1(0.81)	4.9(0.49)	–
10.	M.P.	a	4442.5(28.84)	3371.3(21.89)	2141.3*(13.90)	214.8(1.39)	590.3(3.83)	1655.8(10.75)	455.1(2.95)	329.7(2.14)	205.9(1.33)	58.4(0.38)	694.4(4.51)	–
		b	5036.1(26.66)	3202.8(16.95)	1802.1 (9.53)	166.4(0.89)	869.5(4.60)	2129.7(11.27)	337.1(1.78)	217.8(1.15)	477.5(2.53)	53.5(0.28)	574.1(3.04)	–
11.	Maha.	a	1321.7(9.17)	860.6(5.97)	6437.9*(44.67)	1447.1(10.04)	29.7(0.21)	348.0(2.41)	822.1(5.70)	136.5(0.95)	4.2(0.03)	193.3(1.34)	2573.6(17.85)	65.0*(0.45)
		b	1519.5(8.08)	841.9(4.48)	6427.8 (34.19)	1912.7(10.17)	98.3(0.50)	627.2(3.34)	917.5(4.88)	379.7(2.02)	4.8(0.02)	383.1(2.04)	2635.5(14.02)	43.0(0.22)
12.	Orissa	a	4432.0(85.61)	27.9(0.54)	35.9*(0.69)	3.5(0.06)	74.1(1.43)	19.9(0.38)	79.1(1.53)	96.2(1.86)	59.9(1.16)	30..5(0.58)	0.3(0.05)	43.4*(0.84)
		b	4391.5(54.21)	39.9(0.49)	28.2 (0.34)	7.3(0.09)	168.0(2.07)	44.7(0.55)	375.9(4.64)	307.0(3.78)	135.7(1.67)	47.5(0.59)	7.8(0.10)	64.1(0.79)
13.	Punjab	a	438.3(9.20)	2333.3(48.98)	1.2*(0.02)	157.2(3.30)	553.7(11.60)	340.7(7.15)	168.5(3.54)	14.1(0.29)	130.3(2.73)	111.9(2.35)	458.3(9.62)	–
		b	1908.0(29.08)	3251.8(49.57)	0.5 (neg)	11.0(0.16)	210.0(3.20)	54.4(0.83)	19.0(0.28)	21.0(0.32)	114.0(1.74)	103.0(1.57)	732.0(11.16)	–
14.	Raj.	a	133.6(1.10)	1464.9(12.14)	1005.7*(8.33)	5163.7(42.78)	773.7(6.43)	1505.4(12.47)	235.6(1.95)	531.6(4.40)	306.2(2.53)	32.9(0.27)	300.8(2.49)	–
		b	119.0(0.83)	1650.4(11.53)	826.8 (5.77)	4924.7(34.40)	942.5(6.58)	1143.8(7.99)	234.5(1.64)	322.3(2.25)	1527.3(10.67)	15.6(0.11)	434.2(3.03)	–
15.	T.N.	a	2665.1(45.91)	1.6(0.02)	541.6*(9.33)	476.5(8.21)	14.1(0.24)	4.3(0.07)	991.6(17.08)	129.0(2.23)	0.5(neg)	122.9(2.11)	306.8(5.28)	–
		b	2015.3(33.04)	0.1 (neg)	608.1 (9.97)	272.5(4.47)	41.3(0.68)	5.5(0.09)	1044.1(17.12)	159.4(2.61)	0.6(neg)	231.6(3.80)	267.5(4.38)	–
16.	U.P.	a	4519.2(22.69)	6014.8(30.20)	680.4*(3.41)	1052.0(5.28)	1485.7(7.45)	1980.1(9.94)	330.1(1.66)	51.2(0.31)	257.7(1.29)	1309.1(6.57)	52.9(0.26)	–
		b	5357.9(22.51)	8663.1(36.40)	573.8 (2.41)	822.0(3.45)	1107.2(4.65)	1357.7(5.70)	133.5(0.56)	373.2(1.56)	1045.0(4.40)	1755.0(7.37)	17.7(0.07)	–
17.	W.B.	a	5005.9(78.87)	383.6(6.04)	—	–	47.8(0.75)	135.4(2.13)	5.3(0.08)	11.7(0.18)	103.5(1.63)	36.8(0.58)	–	300.5*(4.73)
		b	5614.3(78.19)	326.7(4.55)	—	–	56.0(0.78)	30.9(0.43)	20.6(0.28)	69.3(0.96)	378.5(5.27)	15.1(0.21)	–	400.5(6.00)

Abbreviations : a =1970-3 & b =1989-90. * = the figures are collected from various volumes of *Agricultural Situation in India.*

N.B. : Figures in perentheses are percentage share of crop area to GCA.

Source : Three years average figures of various crops for early 1970s are compiled from Bhalla & Alagh (1979), State-wise data for 1989-90 are compiled from D.O.E.&S., Ministry of Agriculture, New Delhi

table 2.6

The changes in the share of crop-areas specially after green revolution (1970-1 till now) are, in my opinion, influenced highly by the remunerative prices of crop-production. In several states, substitution of more productive crops for less productive ones appears to be a major ingredient of agricultural output growth. For example, jowar and bajra have been replaced by groundnut and cotton in Andhra Pradesh in the last 20 years (1970-1 to 1989-90); oil seeds have marginally been substituted for paddy and stood up on second rank in Assam despite an increase in area under paddy cultivation (Table-2.6). Inspite of favourable conditions in the interior parts of Gujarat for bajra crop, its area has declined nearly by 6.0 percent and replaced by rapeseeds and mustard oilseeds because of more remunerative crops. Likewise, bajra has been replace by wheat and gram in Haryana, by gram (more remunerative pulse) in Madhya Pradesh and by sugarcane (cash crop) in Maharashtra during the same period (Table-2.6). It is also interesting to note that, inspite of unfavourable conditions for paddy cultivation in Punjab and Haryana states, the area under paddy cultivation seems to be increasing by 20.0 percent (from 9.20 in 1970-1 to 29.08 percent in 1989-90) with a negligible increase under wheat area in Punjab and by 6.3 percent (from 6.46 percent in 1970-1 to 12.72 percent in 1989-90) with the gradual increase of 11.0 percent in the wheat area in Haryana. It might be because paddy is being considered as a commercial crop rather than food grain for local consumption in these areas . With the help of modern technology, the export quality rice (for international market) is being produced by Punjabi farmers. It has occupied second place in the changing pattern of Punjab's agriculture (Table -2.6).

There seems an over all gradual shift in the cropping pattern from diversification (which are considered better for fulfilling local needs of the people) towards unification (based on commercialisation rather than local feeding) which breaks down the geographical boundaries of ideal crop-combination regions (Fig.- 2.2) with the requirements of more infra- structural facilities for properly regulating the surplus production from local level to the national and to international levels. The ideal crop- combination regions which are proposed by Husain (1979, pp.125) for the whole country, have been distorted by the effects of cost-price mechanism of agricultural production (because of intensification of seed-fertilizer technology and the production-prices which alter cropping patterns by influencing farmer's profit). Farmers always wish to achieve the maximum profit from their partials of cultivated land with maximising the marginal returns of their products through changing their crop-combinations and cropping patterns accordingly.

(b) Changes in Crop - Yields

Crop-Yield is the major component of agricultural production. Its changes have the direct impact on the changing patterns of output growth. There has been a significant increase appreciated in crop-yields specially after green revolution, although yield levels are still very low. For example, fiber crops, jute and mesta are noticeable for the record increase in their yields of 95.03 and 155.17 percents respectively, while appreciable increase in the foodgrains crop-yield ranging from 15.3 per cent in bajra to 70.86 per cent in jowar crop-yield in the last 20 years have also been recorded. But the striking features of crop-yield which have been depicted in Table-2.7 reveals a rapid decline of 32.68 percent in the yield of the pulses specially of *moong, moth, urad,* and *lobia.* Since pulses play the major role in the vegetarian food for Indian society and are the main sources of protein for sound health, there seems a deficiency of the pulses-items in the food, decrease in its production and rapid hike in its production prices specially during the last 20 years. The gram and tur *(arhar)* have crop-yield increase only to the tune of 5.0 per cent (Table - 2.7). As a result the market price of chana (i.e., famous pulses of Punjab and Haryana and delicious dish for punjabi-food) had gone upto Rs. 20.0 per kg in 1988-89. It is interesting to note that the gram cultivation requires least application of seed-fertilizer technology but the most natural conditions of clayey loam soils. Therefore, its yield recorded fast increase in Andhra Pradesh and Maharastra and marginal in the state of Madhya Pradesh.

Table- 2.7: Changes in Crop-yields in India (1962-5 to 1988-90)

(yield in kg/ha)

	Crops	1962-65	1970-73	1988-90	Changes(early 70s to 90s)	
					Absolute	%
1.	Rice	1015	1106	1637	531	48.01
2.	Wheat	811	1322	2121	799	60.44
3.	Jowar	522	453	774	321	70.86
4.	Bajra	365	472	544	72	15.29
5.	Maize	996	1085	1343	258	23.78
6.	Ragi	803	865	1080	215	24.85
7.	Barly	824	1033	1485	452	43.76
8.	Gram	569	645	678	33	5.11
9.	Tur	643	712	741	29	4.07
10.	OtherPulses*	585	661	445	-216	-32.68
11.	Groundnut	760	734	929	195	26.57
12.	Rapeseed & Mustard	418	507	826	319	63.04
13.	Sesamum	187	212	303	91	42.92
14.	Linseed	227	260	290	30	11.54
15.	Castersed	224	332	727	395	118.97
16.	Sugarcane+	456	497	621	124	24.95
17.	Cotton	119	129	203	74	57.36
18.	Jute	1237	1227	2393	1166	95.03
19.	Mesta	751	687	1753	1066	155.17
20.	Tobacco	845	852	N.A.	—	—

N.B. : N.A. = Not Available.

* It includes Moongh, Moth, Masoor, Lobia, etc. pulses. + Sugercane figures are in qu./ha.

Source: 1. Three years average figures for triennum ending1964-5 and 1972-73 have been traced out from Bhalla and Alagh (1979), Table-2, pp. 12-13.

2. Yield data for 1988-89 and 1989-90 have been compiled from the Tables provided by the Deptt. of Economics & Statistics, Ministry of Agriculture, New Delhi.

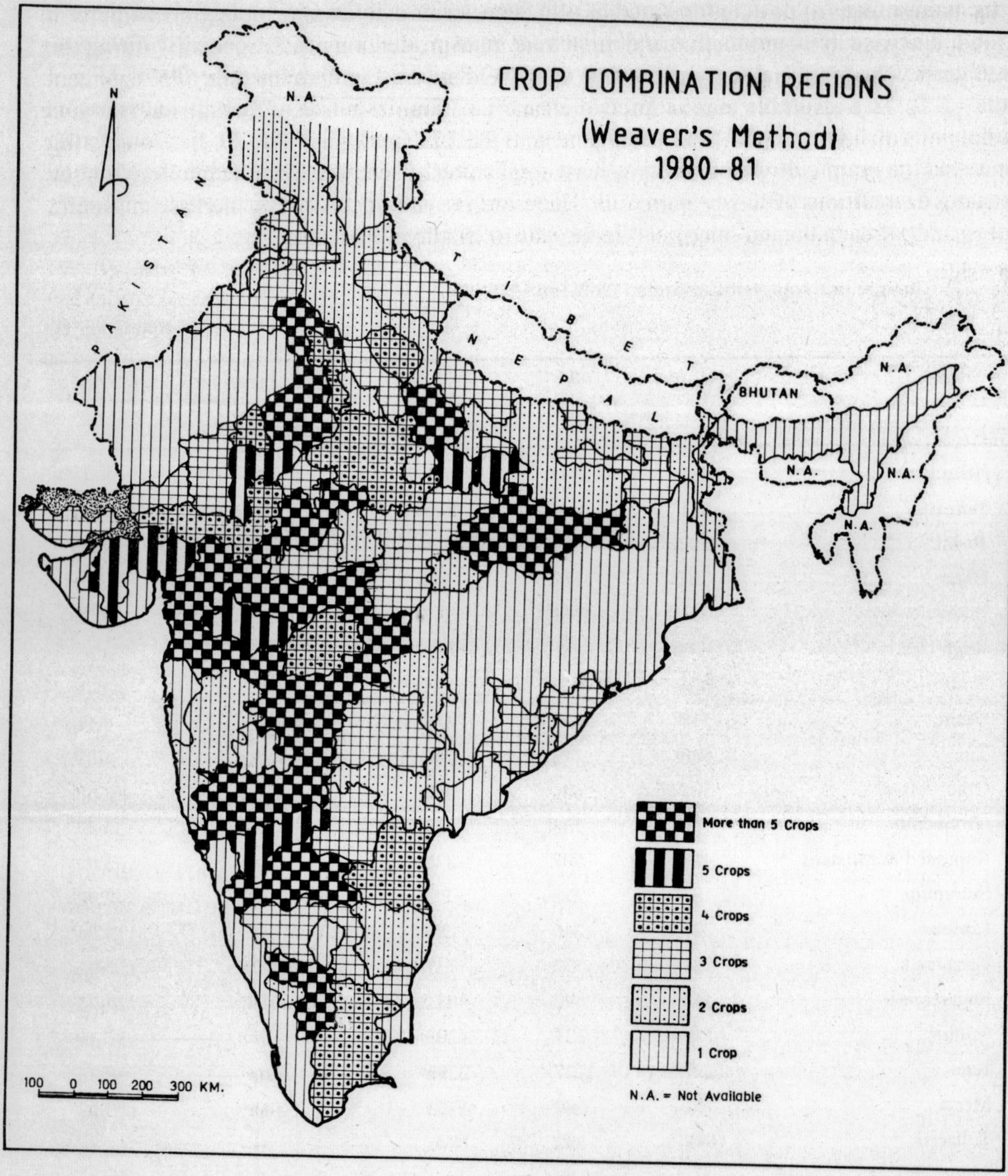
CROP COMBINATION REGIONS
(Weaver's Method)
1980-81
N
N.A.
PAKISTAN
TIBET
NEPAL
BHUTAN
N.A.
N.A.
N.A.
N.A.
More than 5 Crops
5 Crops
4 Crops
3 Crops
2 Crops
1 Crop
N.A. = Not Available
100 0 100 200 300 KM.

Fig 2.2

The state-wise patterns of crop-yield increase reveal that, in the core areas of green revolution (Punjab, Haryana and western Uttar Pradesh), the level (1988-90) and increase (1970-3 to 1988-90) in the wheat and paddy crop-yield have been recorded appreciably high. But it is pertinent to note that a remarkable increase of 615 kg/ha in wheat yield has also been recorded in Maharashtra and Tamilnadu where favourable conditions do not permit for its sustainable growth (Table-2.8). The yield of jowar, a fodder crop of Maharashtra and Uttar Pradesh, has also increased significantly although it is not significant in its areal extent in these areas. The yield of bajra seems to have decreased in most of the states except in Orissa and Maharashtra where it does not have significant place in its areal extent. Gujarat and Maharashtra covering the major industrial areas of the country, are marked record increase in the crop-yields of oilseeds (specially groundnut) and cash crop (cotton and sugarcane) because of local demands of industrial raw materials . Thus, the emerging features of crop-yield patterns may be generalised by relating them to the cropping patterns of the country which should be helpful for understanding the undergoing processes of agricultural growth of the country. They are:

(i) Inspite of remarkable changes in the cropping patterns of the country observed during the last 20 years (1970-1 to 1989-90), they are still following the physiographic basis of their changes. But the regional patterns of crop-yield are breaking the criterion of agro-ecologically based yield increase.

(ii) There must be positive relationship between the increase in crop-yield and crop-land occupancy in relation to its agro-ecological conditions for self-sustained growth of agricultural output. But the crop-yield patterns show negative relationship of these components of growth. For example, paddy is a dominating crop grown in the middle and lower parts of the Ganga and Brahamputra valleys including the costal areas of the country, but the level as well as increase in its yield have been recorded significantly high in the states of Punjab and Haryana. Likewise, gram (an important pulse) is having high land-occupancy share in the Madhya Pradesh, but its yield increase is recorded high in the Maharashtra and Andhra pradesh (Table- 2.8).

(iii) Agro- ecologically, jowar and bajra are the crops grown in the arid areas of the country and, therefore, area and yield under these crops must be increased in Rajasthan, Maharashtra, and Karnataka, but their yield have been increasing in Orissa and Tamilnadu (during 1970-1 to 1989-90) with losing the foot ground in their crop-land occupancy shares.

(iv) There seems a regional shift in the cotton belt of India from Gujarat - Maharashtra - Karnataka region to Punjab-Rajasthan-Gujarat region because Gujarat, Maharashtra and Karnataka have recorded decline in the share of its crop-land occupancy as 11.0, 3.0 and 6.0 percent respectively after the introduction of green revolution technology (see Table- 2.6).

(v) The regional trends of yield increase follow the centre-based agricultural intensification hypothesis proposed by Thuenen (cf. Dunn 1954, p.6, Hall 1966). The four biggest metropolitan centres of the country (Delhi, Calcutta, Bombay and Madras) from where the agricultural innovations (specially seed-fertilizer technology) are deffused outward in its surrounding hinterlands, have become the core areas of very high increase of crop-yield and become the main centres of concentration of agricultural output growth. The validity of these facts should be tested to study the micro-economic processes of agricultural growth under separate head.

Table - 2.8: State-wise Average Yield of the Various Crops (1969 -73 to 1988-90).

(Yield in kg/ha.)

Sl.	State		Rice	Wheat	Jowar	Bajra	Maize	Gram	Ground	Rapseed	Sugarcane*	Cotton(lints)	Jute
1.	A.P.	a	1460	331	414	428	1114	287	744	165	8582	67	—
		b	2417	734	587	667	1821	500	938	263	7109	125	—
		c	957	403	173	239	707	213	194	98	-1473	58	—
2.	Assam	a	1010	1276	—	—	549	516	—	430	3731	72	1418
		b	1148	940	—	—	635	510	—	445	4295	87	1508
		c	138	-336	—	—	86	6	—	15	564	15	90
3.	Bihar	a	857	1403	456	531	749	640	873	516	3521	648	840
		b	1206	1637	456	910	1717	779	935	820	5372	—	1460
		c	349	234	—	-21	988	139	62	304	1851	—	620
4.	Gujrat	a	912	1566	336	751	1436	779	703	453	4992	181	—
		b	1360	1780	497	995	1486	605	1577	1165	8641	356	—
		c	437	214	161	-244	50	-174	874	-712	3649	175	—
5.	Haryana	a	1700	1956	265	720	1145	629	842	552	4492	314	—
		b	2734	3181	248	696	1421	700	733	988	5357	430	—
		c	1034	1235	-17	-24	276	71	-109	436	865	116	—
6.	H.P.	a	1069	1026	—	414	1593	580	971	335	1336	256	—
		b	1065	1569	—	—	2134	—	250	253	1180	500	—
		c	-4	543	—	—	541	—	-721	-82	-156	244	—
7.	J & K	a	1674	847	544	578	1341	370	—	780	1101	438	—
		b	2195	1012	—	372	1512	—	—	520	4200	—	—
		c	521	165	—	-206	171	—	—	-260	3099	—	—
8.	Kar.	a	1764	412	715	398	3560	323	687	300	8371	81	—
		b	2009	510	693	550	2772	334	799	271	8047	221	—
		c	245	98	-22	152	-788	11	112	-29	-324	140	—
9.	Kerala	a	1524	—	490	—	—	—	1088	—	5077	190	—
		b	1832	—	—	—	—	—	1068	—	6614	212	—
		c	380	—	—	—	—	—	—	—	1537	22	—
10	M.P.	a	780	769	669	586	910	610	648	359	2660	78	—
		b	928	1208	990	763	1646	662	1095	766	3441	120	—
		c	148	439	321	177	736	52	447	407	781	42	—
11.	Maha.	a	951	466	281	284	849	261	519	197	7395	357	—
		b	1526	1078	1032	630	1129	533	1096	424	8877	1426	—
		c	575	611	751	346	280	272	577	227	1482	1069	—
12.	Orissa	a	848	1635	590	402	773	566	1194	470	6015	291	1280
		b	1431	1632	809	822	1166	644	1234	480	7000	191	1679
		c	583	—	219	420	393	78	40	10	985	-100	399
13	Punjab	a	1946	2292	579	1088	1574	821	996	610	4260	376	—
		b	3510	3593	1000	909	1900	711	1200	903	6311	570	—
		c	1564	1301	421	-179	326	-110	204	293	2051	203	—
14.	Raj.	a	932	1075	365	317	1007	639	602	627	3821	181	—
		b	1270	2060	396	371	1393	622	775	846	4585	386	—
		c	338	785	31	54	386	-17	173	219	764	205	—
15	T.N.	a	2007	385	758	649	1086	561	981	268	8476	212	—
		b	3092	1000	1072	1190	1448	610	1153	250	10123	325	—
		c	1085	615	314	541	362	49	172	-18	1647	113	—
16	U.P.	a	779	1253	582	675	891	760	706	501	4101	124	—
		b	1746	2053	1071	1062	1368	744	913	817	5534	158	—
		c	967	800	489	387	477	-16	207	316	1433	34	—
17	W.B.	a	1225	2153	—	—	871	641	—	364	5254	—	1585
		b	1948	1742	—	—	2089	579	—	894	6828	—	2111
		c	721	-411	—	—	1218	-62	—	530	1574	—	526

Abbreviations: a = 1970-3, b = 1988-90, and c = absolute change in crop-yield. * Sugarcane yield is in qu/ha.

table 2.8

(c) Patterns of Production Growth- Ratios

The changes in the crop-area and crop-yield as studied above denote the absolute picture of production increase, while its proportionate increases which are expressed by production growth-ratios (by eqn.- 2.1) are also important to find the causes of growth. The study of state-wise variations of production growth-ratios of the principal crops show a different picture of the componental distribution. Note that they are the major components of agricultural growth. According to Table-2.9, the striking features of growth of the production of various crops reveal that Orissa emerges as the most dynamic state of the country where the values of the growth-ratios* for crop-area have been recorded extremely high for all the crops except paddy and jowar. In this state, the area under cotton has increased 9.69 times, groundnut 4.75 times, Sesamum 3.19 times, gram and maize areas 2.25 and 2.27 times respectively during the last two decades of green revolution effects. The crop- ratios are also very high for Sesamum crop (5.92), groundnut (3.89) and rapeseeds and mustard crops (3.66). The high values of rapeseeds and mustard crop growth ratios are also remarkable for Rajasthan and Andhra Pradesh states of the arid areas of the country. The marginal areal expansion of wheat crop and fast expansion of paddy have been recorded in the Punjab and Haryana (the core area of green revolution). On the other hand, Maharashtra has a record growth of crop-yield of all crops except paddy (Table - 2.9). It may be because of the impact of agro-based industries on agricultural growth. The growth ratios for wheat yield have been recorded very high in Tamilnadu (2.60), Maharashtra (2.31) and Andhra Pradesh (2.22), while high ratio for paddy-yield (2.24) is marked only in Uttar Pradesh instead of west Bengal,although it has more favourable conditions for its growth. Gujarat and Maharashtra are noticeable for the proportional increase of groundnut crop-yield.

An overall performance of the regional variations of growth-ratio generalises the facts that there is a negative areal relationship between the growth ratios of crop-area and crop-yield. It means that the states of the rapid acceleration of areal expansion processes crop production increase have very low growth of crop-yield specially after green revolution period and *vice-versa.* It reflects a diverse nature of agricultural components operating the agricultural growth processes in its regional frame. Thus, there might be diversified areal patterns of agricultural output and its growth which have been interpreted in the following heads.

(d) Concentration of the Volume of Agricultural Output

Calculating total amount of agricultural output in its value term at constant (1969-72) price (with the help of out put aggregation method as discussed in the previous Chapter) for each and every district of the country for three points of time as specified earlier and arranging the districts in their descending order according to their total output strength, the number of the districts having one-fourth share of the total agricultural output of the country have been identified for each point of time (Table-2.10). The magnitude and change in the cultivated land of these districts must explain the tendency of concentration of agricultural output in its absolute degree**. There

* Note that the values above 2.00 indicate 100 percent increase (means two times) between two points of time. Only the values of growth-ratios above 2.00 have been interpreted for the proportional increase in crop-area and crop-yield.

** In the present explanation of concentration, the districts are selected according to their size of total output rather than output per unit of land or labour because district is the unit of agricultural production which may be bigger or smaller in its areal extent.

Table-2.9: State-wise Growth-Ratios of Crops-Yield and Crop-Areas of the Principal Crops (1970-73 to 1988-90).

	State		P	W	J	B	M	G	Gn	Rp	Sc	C	Ju	In
1.	A.P.	y	1.65	2.22	1.42	1.56	1.63	1.74	1.26	1.59	0.83	1.86	—	1.58
		a	1.39	0.71	0.64	0.55	1.22	0.85	1.61	5.25	1.33	2.06	0.88	1.22
2.	Ass	y	1.14	0.74	—	—	1.16	0.98	—	1.03	1.15	1.21	1.06	1.06
		a	1.22	1.62	—	—	1.71	1.32	—	2.42	1.16	0.48	8.28	1.33
3.	Bih	y	1.41	1.17	1.00	0.96	2.29	1.22	1.07	1.59	1.52	—	1.74	1.40
		a	1.06	1.50	0.68	0.72	0.80	0.68	1.11	1.02	0.85	0.04	4.83	1.16
4.	Guj	y	1.47	1.14	1.48	1.33	1.03	1.29	2.24	0.39	1.73	1.97	—	1.41
		a	1.32	1.22	0.96	0.76	1.22	2.29	1.03	3.76	2.84	0.48	—	1.03
5.	Har	y	1.61	1.63	0.93	0.97	1.24	1.11	0.87	1.79	1.19	1.37	—	1.27
		a	2.20	1.57	0.80	0.70	0.34	0.50	0.34	2.28	0.96	2.02	—	1.12
6.	H.P.	y	0.99	1.53	—	—	1.34	—	0.25	0.75	0.88	1.95	—	1.10
		a	0.91	1.21	—	—	1.24	0.23	0.20	1.93	0.78	0.40	—	1.16
7.	J&K	y	1.31	1.19	—	0.64	1.13	—	—	0.67	3.81	—	—	1.46
		a	1.19	1.32	—	0.75	1.06	0.44	—	2.23	0.28	—	—	1.29
8.	Kar	y	1.14	1.24	0.97	1.38	0.78	1.02	1.16	0.90	0.96	2.73	—	1.23
		a	1.08	0.78	1.44	1.90	2.88	1.50	1.58	1.41	2.14	0.69	0.71	1.29
9.	Ker	y	1.20	—	—	—	—	—	1.00	—	1.30	1.11	—	1.15
		a	0.66	—	—	—	—	—	0.97	—	1.05	0.66	—	1.08
10.	M.P.	y	1.19	1.57	1.48	1.30	1.81	1.08	1.69	2.13	1.29	1.54	—	1.51
		a	1.13	0.95	0.84	0.77	1.47	1.29	0.74	2.30	0.92	0.83	—	1.23
11.	Mah	y	1.60	2.31	3.67	2.82	1.33	2.04	2.11	2.15	1.20	3.99	—	2.32
		a	1.15	0.98	1.00	1.32	3.14	1.80	1.12	1.14	1.98	1.02	—	1.30
12.	Ori	y	1.68	1.00	1.37	2.04	1.51	1.13	1.03	1.02	1.16	0.66	1.31	1.26
		a	0.99	1.43	0.78	2.08	2.27	2.25	4.75	2.26	1.56	1.69	1.49	1.56
13.	Pun	y	1.80	1.57	1.72	0.84	1.21	0.86	1.20	1.48	1.48	1.55	—	1.37
		a	4.35	1.39	0.42	0.07	0.38	0.16	0.11	0.88	0.92	1.60	—	1.38
14.	Raj	y	1.36	1.62	1.08	1.17	1.38	0.97	1.27	1.35	1.20	2.13	—	1.35
		a	0.89	1.13	0.82	0.95	1.21	0.76	0.99	4.99	0.47	1.44	—	1.19
15.	T.N.	y	1.54	2.60	1.41	1.83	1.33	1.08	1.18	0.93	1.94	1.53	—	1.54
		a	0.76	0.06	1.12	0.57	2.93	1.28	1.05	1.20	1.88	0.87	—	1.05
16.	U.P.	y	2.24	1.63	1.36	1.57	1.54	0.98	1.29	1.63	1.34	1.27	—	1.49
		a	1.18	1.44	0.84	0.78	0.75	0.68	0.40	4.05	1.34	0.33	—	1.19
17.	W.B.	y	1.58	0.80	—	—	2.40	0.90	—	2.45	1.30	—	1.33	1.54
		a	1.12	0.85	—	—	1.17	0.23	3.89	3.66	0.41	—	1.44	1.13

Abbreviations: y= crop-yields, a= crop-area.

P=Paddy, W= Wheat, J= Jowar, B= Bajra, M= Maize,G= Gram, Gn=Groundnut,

Rp= Rapeseeds & Mustard, Sc= Sugarcane, C= Cotton, Ju=Jute and In= Composite Yield Index for crop-yield and Total GCA Index for crop-area.

Table -2.10 : Name of the Districts according to the Ranks of their Agricultural Output.

Rank	Triennum 1969-72			Teinnum 1979-82			Teinnum 1988-90		
	N	O	A	N	O	A	N	O	A
1.	Midnapur(WB)	195552	14081	Gaziapur(UP)	197692	3377	Midnapur(WB)	273321	14081
2.	Birbhum(WB)	164030	4544	Burdhwan(WB)	171128	7024	Murshidabad(WB)	268198	5324
3.	Murshidabad(WB)	161109	5324	Nadia(WB)	164030	3927	Faridkot(Pun)	265397	5740
4.	Sirsa(Har)	151707	4276	W.Diranjpur(WB)	154924	5358	Nadia(WB)	257627	3927
5.	W.Dinagpur(WB)	150575	5358 24	Parganas(WB)	144000	4094	Jaunpur(UP)	244803	20634
6.	24Parganas(WB)	138012	4049	Thanjavur(TN)	143951	8280	N.Arkot(TN)	243226	6077
7.	Nadia(WB)	105820	3927	Murshidabad(WB)	139025	5324	Parganas(WB)	222288	4094
8.	Purnia(Bir)	100947	3229	Azamgarh(UP)	138161	5740	Burdwan(WB)	219302	7024
9.	Ganganagar(Raj)	88970	20674	Ganganagar(Raj)	137557	20674	S.Arkot(TN)	205264	10895
10.	Bakura(WB)	87925	6882	Sangrur(Pun)	129219	5107	Thanjavur(TN)	204333	8280
11.	Kurnool(AP)	87472	17658	Bhatinda(Pun)	123706	5551	Sangrur(Pun)	200639	5104
12.	Bhatinda(Pun)	87188	5551	Hisar(Har)	118650	6279	Bhatinda(Pun)	194549	5551
13.	Cooch Bihar(WB)	86590	3387	Firozpur(Pun)	118230	5874	Hissar(Har)	193290	6279
14.	Bhiwani(Har)	85248	5140	Guntur(AP)	114685	11391	W.Godawari(AP)	170519	7747
15.	Faridkot(Punj)	84835	5740	Cooch Bihar(WB)	109259	3387	Belgaon(Kar)	161717	13415
16.	Raipur(MP)	84323	21258	Champran(Bih)	107045	3968	Moradabad(UP)	160085	5967
17.	Jalpaiguri(WB)	83934	6227	W.Godawari(AP)	105220	7742	Purnia(Bih)	152275	3229
18.	W.Godavari(AP)	79385	7742	Midnapur(WB)	130709	14081	Guntur(AP)	148536	11391
19.	Guntur(AP)	77256	11391	Jainpur(UP)	101412	4038	Birbhum(WB)	148219	4544
20.	Ferozepur(Punj)	71952	5874	Patiala(Pun)	99063	4581	Patiala(Pun)	146967	4585
21.	Burdwan(WB)	70852	7024	Ludhiana(Pun)	98570	3857	Saharanpur(UP)	146551	3860
22.	Chittor(AP)	70716	15152	Jalpaiguri (WB)	95839	6227	W.Dinajpur(WB)	145018	5358
23.	Rothas (Bih)	69255	7213	Birbhum(WB)	85727	4544	Amritsar(Pun)	144274	5874
24.	Ludhiana (Pun)	68864	3857	Bhawnagar(Guj)	84650	11155	Meerut(UP)	137087	3911
25.	Madurai(YN)	64782	6565	W.Godabari(AP)	83532	10807	Hoogli(WB)	136152	3149
26.	Kurukshetra(Har)	64320	1217	Krishna (AP)	82814	8724	Kheri(UP)	134260	7680
27.	Rohtak(Har)	62976	4411	Junagarh(Guj)	80730	10607	Krishna(AP)	132072	8724
28.	Meerut(UP)	62472	3911	Amritsar(Pun)	80280	5087	-	-	-
29.	Rajkot(Guj)	61097	11203	Kurukshetra(Har)	79740	1217	-	--	-
30.	Raishur(Kar)	60900	14017	Hoogli(WB)	77322	3149	-	-	-
31.	Mahasana(Guj)	60171	9025	Sirsa(Har)	72770	4276	-	-	-
32.	Bilaspur(MP)	59349	19897	Mehsana(Guj)	71184	9024	-	--	-
33.	Khelda(Guj)	58968	7194	Karmal(Har)	70770	1967	-	-	-
34.	Goalpara(Ass)	58713	3838	S.Arkot(TN)	70196	10895	-	--	-
35.	Karmal(Har)	58692	1967	Tirunelvali(TN)	69530	6810	-	-	-
36.	Hardoi(UP)	58435	5986	Malda(WB)	68907	3733	-	--	-
37.	Aligarh(UP)	57916	5019	Sabarkantha(Guj)	67747	7390	-	-	-
38.	Tiruchirapalli(TN)	57015	11096	—	—	—	-	-	-
	Total	**3292023**	**300948**		**4033578**	**235320**		**5055969**	**192438**

Abbreviations: N = The name of the districts. O = Total agricultural output(in 0000Rs) A = Total Area of the district (in Sq.km.).

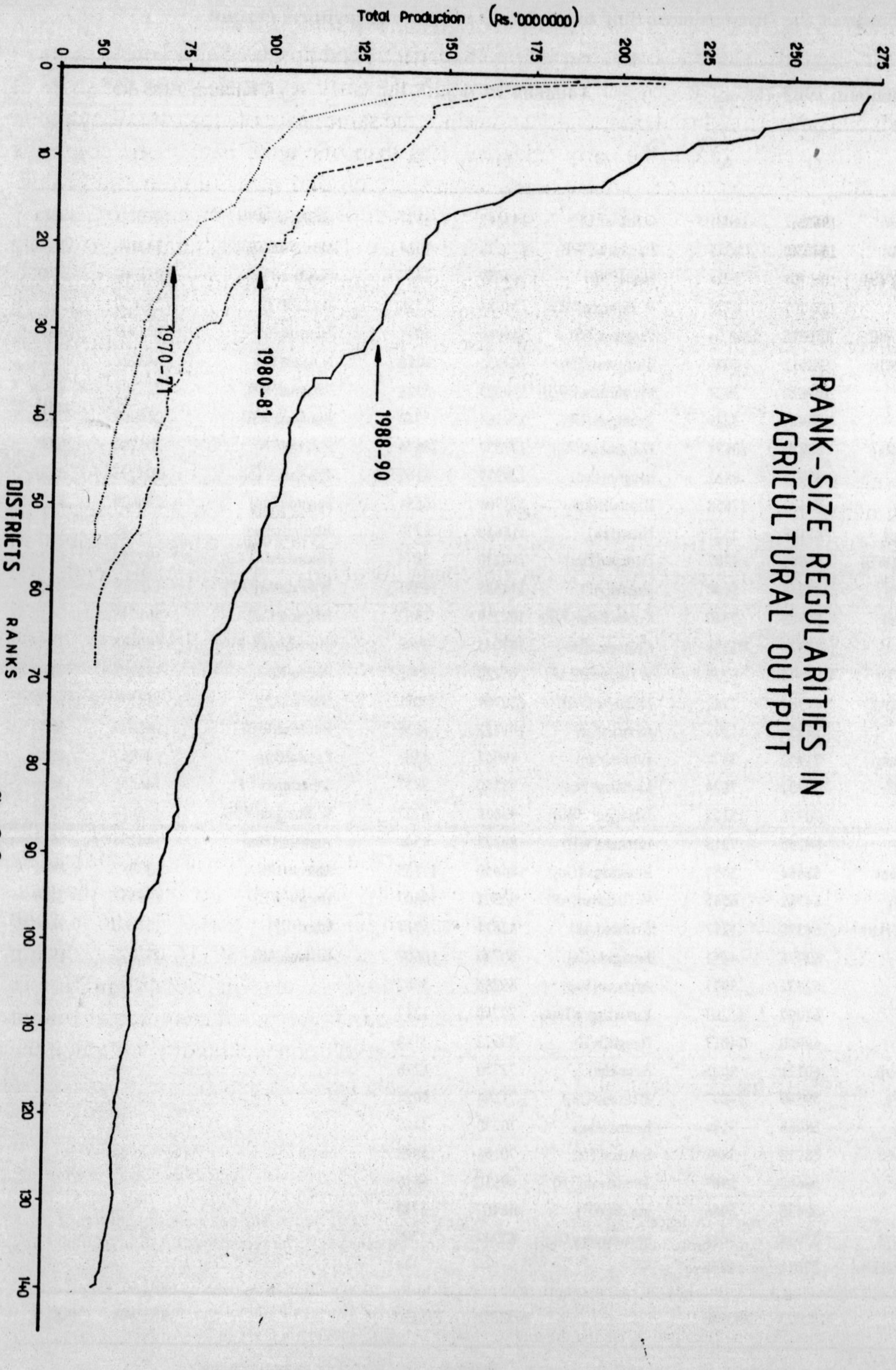
RANK-SIZE REGULARITIES IN AGRICULTURAL OUTPUT
Total Production (Rs.'0000000)
0
50
75
100
125
150
175
200
225
250
275
1970-71
1980-81
1988-90
DISTRICTS RANKS
0
10
20
30
40
50
60
70
80
90
100
110
120
130
140

fig 2.3

seems, contrary to claims of the areal expansion of green revolution effects, that 13.34 percent of the country's cultivated land (i.e., covered by 38 districts) had produced one-fourth share of the total volume of agricultural output of the country in the early seventies, while the share of cultivated land had been reduced marginally to produce the same share of agricultural output in the early 'eighties. But during the early 'nineties, less than one-tenth part of the country's cultivated land (9.77 percent) had produced the same share of total agricultural output(Table-2.11). The decline in the share of cultivated area at decadal rate of about 2.0 percent and reduction in the number of the districts from 38 to 27 to produce the same share of agricultural output during the last 20 years indicate the concentration of agricultural output in the country. It is pertinent to note that 9.77 percent cultivated land of the country has nearly 21.0 percent share of total country's irrigated land and 27.6 percent of total use of chemical fertilezers of the country. This area of very high concentration also has appreciably higher degree of crop-intensity (148.75 percent) than the national average (i.e.,126.94 percent), but irrigation intensity is recorded marginally lower (156.55) than that of the national average (165.11 percent) (Table- 2.11).

The inter-district variations of the areas of high concentration of agricultural output have been examined by preparing 'rank-size' graphs for 1969-72, 1979-82,and 1988-90. These graphs show the primacy of the spatial patterns of output distribution*. Concavity trends of distribution curve show the degree of its concentration. Greater concavity of the curve refers to higher degree of concentration in the output distributional patterns of agricultural output, and *vice-versa*. There are confirmed evidences of increasing inter-district variations in the spatial patterns of output distribution because rank-size graph for different points of time depict that there is a higher degree of concavity in the output distribution curve drawn for the early 'nineties (1988-90), while the distribution curves for early 'seventies and 'eighties show lower degree of its concavities (Fig.-2.3)**. Further, the differences among these curves generalise the trend and quantity of incremental output between two points of time. The curve-trends visualise that there is larger quantity of incremental output during the eighties (1979-82 to 1988-90) because of larger gaps between the curves of early 'eighties and 'nineties. The fact can also be confirmed by comparing the total quantity of output of the whole country over time. During, the 'seventies, the total incremental output had been recorded as Rs.30224 million (increase from Rs. 131100 in 1969 - 72 to Rs. 161324 million in 1979 - 82), which was increased to Rs. 39116 million during 'eighties (1979 - 82 to 1988 - 90) by touching a record output level of Rs. 200440 million in 1988-90 (Table - 2.11). It confirms that rapid increase in the total volume of incremental output is owing, no doubt, to the increase of the effects of green revolution technology, although the areal patterns of agricultural output have been concentrating fast.

---

* The measurement of primacy of the distribution is also one of the important aspects to show the data concentration patterns. The single - dimension data is required for the purpose. Zipf (1949) propounded 'Rank- Size Rule' for showing diversification of the spatial patterns on the basis of single - featured statistics of size of the attribute, while ranks are considered simply according to descending order of the individual size of the attribute. The concentration patterns for two-dimensional data can be presented by drawing the Lorenz Curve on cumulative frequency basis by calculating Gini Coefficient for the same purpose.

** The districts having agricultural output values more than or equal to Rs. 5000 million have been considered for preparing rank-size graphs because these districts have high degree of inter-district variations and obliterate primate patterns in the distribution. The districts having the output volume below this level are more or less uniform in size distribution.

Table- 2.11: Percentage Share of Cultivated Land, Number of Districts and the strength of other Infra-Structural Variables by 1/4th share of total Agricultural Output.

	Items	1969-72	1979-82	1988-90
1.	Total Agricultural output (in million Rs.)	131100.00	161324.00	200440.00
2.	1/4th Share of the output (in million Rs.)	32775.00	40331.00	50110.00
3.	Number of district sharing 1/4th output*	38.00	37.00	27.00
4.	NSA covered by district having 1/4th share of the putput (in million ha.)	18.715	16.454	13.305
5.	All India NSA (in million ha.)	140.271	142.122	136.185
6.	%age share of NSA coveredby districts having 1/4th share of output to total NSA	13.342	11.581	9.773
7.	Crop intensity in the areas having 1/4th share of output(in %)	—	—	148.750
8.	%age share of Net Irrigarated Area of the area having 1/4th share of output to total irrigated Area of the country	—	—	20.981
9.	Irrigation Intensity in the Areas having 1/4th share of output (in %)	--	—	156.552
10.	%age share of the Fertilizer consumtion in the area having 1/4th share of total output	—	—	27.640

N.B. : * For name of the districts having more than 1/4th share of the total agricultural output, see Table -2.10.

Patterns of Agricultural Growth

Calculating average annual growth rate of agricultural output with the help of equation(1.3) for each district of the country for the last two decades (1969-72 to 1979-82 and 1979-82 to 1988-90), the total areal units (districts) have been classified into several categories for a detailed analysis of the regional growth processes. This categorization is preferred because of very high degree of inter-district variation in the output growth, though the national average of the annual growth of output have been recorded 2.30 percent for the seventies (1969-72 to 1979-82) and 3.03 percent for eighties (1979-82 to 1988-90). Its annual rate varies from the highest rate of 116.36 percent (Pithoragarh district, U.P.) to the lowest -9.15 percent (Sehore district, M.P.) for the seventies. It has been marginally reduced in the eighties by ranging from 75.87 (North Arcot district, Tamilnadu) to -11.73 percent (Palgarh, Kerala). But the regional patterns are generalised by clubbing these categories of growth into four classes as they are the areas of :(i) high growth rate exceeding 8.0 percent of annual growth rate, (ii) medium growth rate (between 4.0 and 8.0

percent), (iii) low growth rate (0.00 to 4.0 percent, and (iv) decelerating growth (negative). The emerging features of agricultural growth patterns obliterated specially after green revolution impact are described as the following:

(1) Stating regional imbalances in agricultural growth, Dogra (1981) described its areal patterns for the duration often years of pre-green revolution period (1962-5 to 1972-5) and contended that the rapid agricultural growth was confined to one-fifth of the country's area (19.0 percent area covered by 48 districts only) recorded a growth of exceeding 4.5 percent per annum. Obviously, the acceleration rate of growth was very slow at that time and, therefore, the 4.5 percent level of growth acceleration was considered as high acceleration of agricultural growth during pre-green revolution period. But, the growth rates ranging between 4.0 to 8.0 per cents per annum are considered under the category of medium growth-rate during post-green revolution period because of upward shift of its national averages. However, the results drawn by Dogra (1981) for pre-green revolution period are comparable with the results inferred here for the post-green revolution period. Infact, the areas under the medium and high growth rate categories (above 4.0 percent) which recorded only 19.0 percent during pre-revolution period has been extended upto 36.4 percent during the seventies and increased further upto 64.4 percent during the eighties (Table - 2.12). The areal changes under these categories of high growth rate which have been shown in Table-2.12, confirm the facts of the regional expansion of agricultural growth processes. Declining percentage share of negative growth over time also confirms the validity of the same fact. For example, the marginal decline of 2.33 percent in the area of negative growth has been recorded from 27.0 percent (1962-5 to 1972-5 during pre-green revolution period) as Dogra (1981) contended, to 24.66 percent (1969-72 to 1979-82 as first phase of post-green revolution period) and again an appreciable decline of 12.05 percent has been observed during the last 20 years of post-green revolution period (Table -2.12). It is pertinent to note that agricultural growth processes are operative in the most of the agricultural tracts of country through intensifying seed-fertilizer technology and changing general landuse pattern specially decrease the waste land and increase to cultivated area of the country (Table - 2.13).

(2) The regional pattern of concentration of agricultural growth examine the validity of 'centre-based proceeded growth' specially during the post-green revolution period in the history of planned agricultural development. For example, the areas of high and vary high agricultural growth rates (exceeding 8.0 percent per annum) recorded 14.84 percent for the ten years growth average (1969-72 to 1979-82) dispersed in the peripheral areas of Delhi and Bombay metropolitan centres including coastal areas of the Andhra Pradesh state. The Punjab, Haryana and Western Uttar Pradesh areas of high growth are the peripheral areas of Delhi metropolitan centre. These concentrated patterns of agricultural growth have been expanded in the outer peripheries of these centres including Madras centre of the south-eastern coastal region where the high growth rates have been visualized during the eighties. The longitudinal belt of the terai areas of Uttar Pradesh and Bihar and dry areas of Rajasthan desert are also marked for high and very high growth rates during the eighties (See Fig.-2.5 Inset). In fact, land improvement, new farming methods and improved infra-structural facilities are all necessary requirements for agricultural growth. These centres are the diffusion centres of these agricultural innovations to the surrounding areas. As a result, growth have been recorded higher in these areas.

Table- 2.12: Agricultural Output and Area by Agricultural Growth Categories (1969-72 to 1979-82 and 1979-82 to 1988-90).

Average Annual growth rate (in %)	**Output** (1988-90)* Total (in 0000Rs)	% share	**Area** (in sq.k.m) during Growth Periods of 1969-72 to 1979-82 N	A	A(%)	1979-82 to 1988-89 N	A	A(%)	**Areal Changes** A	A(%)
> -12	5559171	27.73	41	431326	14.84	69	774975	26.67	343649	11.83
12 -10	1643558	8.20	5	26534	.91	16	94567	3.25	68033	2.34
10 - 8	2391338	11.93	22	141330	4.86	36	262954	9.05	121624	4.19
8 - 6	4090290	20.41	17	136871	4.71	48	375919	12.93	239048	8.22
6 - 4	1748278	8.72	43	458914	15.79	45	355311	12.24	-103603	-3.44
4 - 2	1799008	8.97	68	489360	16.84	40	410647	14.13	- 78713	-2.71
2 - 0	1296727	6.47	74	505444	17.39	32	265103	9.12	-240341	-8.27
-(0-2)	neg	neg	39	311316	10.72	35	194993	6.71	-116323	-4.01
-(2-4)	1515629	7.56	23	218032	7.51	13	60122	2.07	-157910	-5.44
-(>-4)	neg	neg	18	186866	6.43	16	111402	3.83	- 75464	-2.60
Total	**20044000**	**99.99**	**350**	**2905993+**	**99.9**	**350**	**2905993+**	**99.9**	-	-

N.B: * Agricultural output figures are compiled on the basis of growth categories 1979-82 to 1988-90.

\+ The figures of the total area excludes the areas of Arunachal Pradesh, Manipur, Meghalaya, Tripura, Mizoram, Nagaland, Sikkim States of the North-Eastern Region and Goa, Pandicherry, Andaman & Nicobar, Daman& Deu, Dadar & Nagar Havelli Union Territories.

Abbreviations: N = Number of districts, A = Total Areas, A(%)= Percentage share of area to total area, neg = negligible.

Table- 2.13: Percentage Change in General Landuse (1950 - 51 to 1987 - 88).

(Figures in percent)

	Landuse categories	1950-1	1960-1	1970-1	1980-1*	1987-8*
1.	Forest	14.24	18.11	21.04	22.16	21.90
2.	Not available for cultivation:					
	a. Area under non-agricultural uses	3.37	4.97	5.42	6.40	6.79
	b. Barren and uncultivable land	13.52	12.03	9.27	6.63	6.71
3.	Other cultivated land excluding Fallow land:					
	a. Permanent pastures and grazing lands	2.35	4.68	4.36	3.95	3.94
	b. Land under miscellaneous tree crops & groves	6.79	1.49	1.41	1.15	1.24
	c. Cultivable waste	8.07	6.44	5.76	5.49	5.08
4.	Fallow lands :					
	a. Fallow other than current fallow	6.13	3.74	2.88	3.22	3.62
	b. Current fallow	3.76	3.91	3.49	4.87	6.00
5.	Net Area Sown	41.77	44.63	46.34	46.12	44.72
	Total Reporting Area (million ha.)	284.32	298.46	303.76	304.17	304.85
	Total Geographical Area (million ha.)	328.73	328.73	328.73	328.73	328.73

N.B. : Percentages of landuse categories are calculated from total reporting area. * Provisional data

Source : Department of Agriculture and Cooperation, Ministryof Agriculture, Government of India, New Delhi.

(3) Two-dimensional features of growth patterns must give more detailed description of the growth process operations in India for the last 20 years of fast agricultural development. For the same, the concentration of agricultural growth patterns have been visualized by preparing the table of cross-classification of the districts by output growth rate categories (that are ten in number) for each decade (for the 1970s and 1980s). Area specific approach has been adopted for growth interpretation. Thus, the percent share of total area and number of district for each cell of growth-rate matrix containing dimensions ten (total 100 cells) have been prepared (Table-2.14). Note that for homogeneous distribution of agricultural growth, the each cell of the matrix must identically contain 1.0 percent share of the area. But there seems areal variations in the matrix. It means we will have to choose high frequency cell for generalizing our growth processes results. Those cells which have areal share of more than 2.0 percent (means more than double than that of average share) are considered for highlighting the emerging features of agricultural growth. Having identified these cells from the frequency matrix, that are 17 in number and account for nearly half of the country's total area (49.1 percent), the undergoing processes of agricultural growth are described in relation to its regional frame. Further, these identified 17 cells are classified into four broad categories on the basis of differentiations of annual growth rates occurring between the nineteen seventies and eighties. However, the values of growth rate differences indicate fast concentration of agricultural growth and *vice -versa.* These categories generalize the growth concentration patterns which have been shown by the block diagram (Fig. - 2.4). There are :

(a) The areas of marginal concentration of agricultural growth where rate-differences are less than 3.0 percent:- They have two sub-categories as (i) *Marginal concentration of growth shifting from negative (0-2%) to low growth rate (0 - 4) in the 'eighties:* It accounts for nearly one-tenth part of the total area (11.2 percent, 37 districts) which is dispersed largely in the hilly parts of Gujarat including the parts of Malwa plateau of Madhya Pradesh and the interior parts of Rayalseema areas of Andhra Pradesh (Fig.-2.5). Raipur and Bilaspur districts of Madhya Pradesh are also included in this category. Inspite of dry climatic conditions and undulating topographic features which badly affect the agriculture of these areas as a record of negative growth rate in the seventies, there has been little improvement in the agricultural growth in eighties. It may be because of extension of irrigation facilities specially in the valley parts of these areas. (ii) *The areas of second sub-category of marginal growth concentration where growth rate differences are recorded very low (1.0 percent) with the extremely high rate of agricultural growth (above 8.0 percent) during both the decades of post green revolution periods:* There is constant increase in the higher order growth rate since 1970-1. Such areas of marginal concentration by extremely high growth rates account for only 13 districts (3.9 percent of the total area) of the Upper Ganga - Jamuna *doab* including a few districts of hilly Karnataka. A constant increasing trend of agricultural growth rate, though the degree of growth concentration is very low, is observed in these areas because of high values of the growth ratios of production components. It has been discussed earlier in the present Chapter that, in Karnataka, the values of growth ratios of crop-areas specially of sugarcane, rapeseeds and mustard crops and crop-yield ratios of cotton crop have been observed very high and, in Uttar Pradesh also, the growth-ratios of crop-areas of oil seeds and yield-ratios of rice and sugarcane are marked

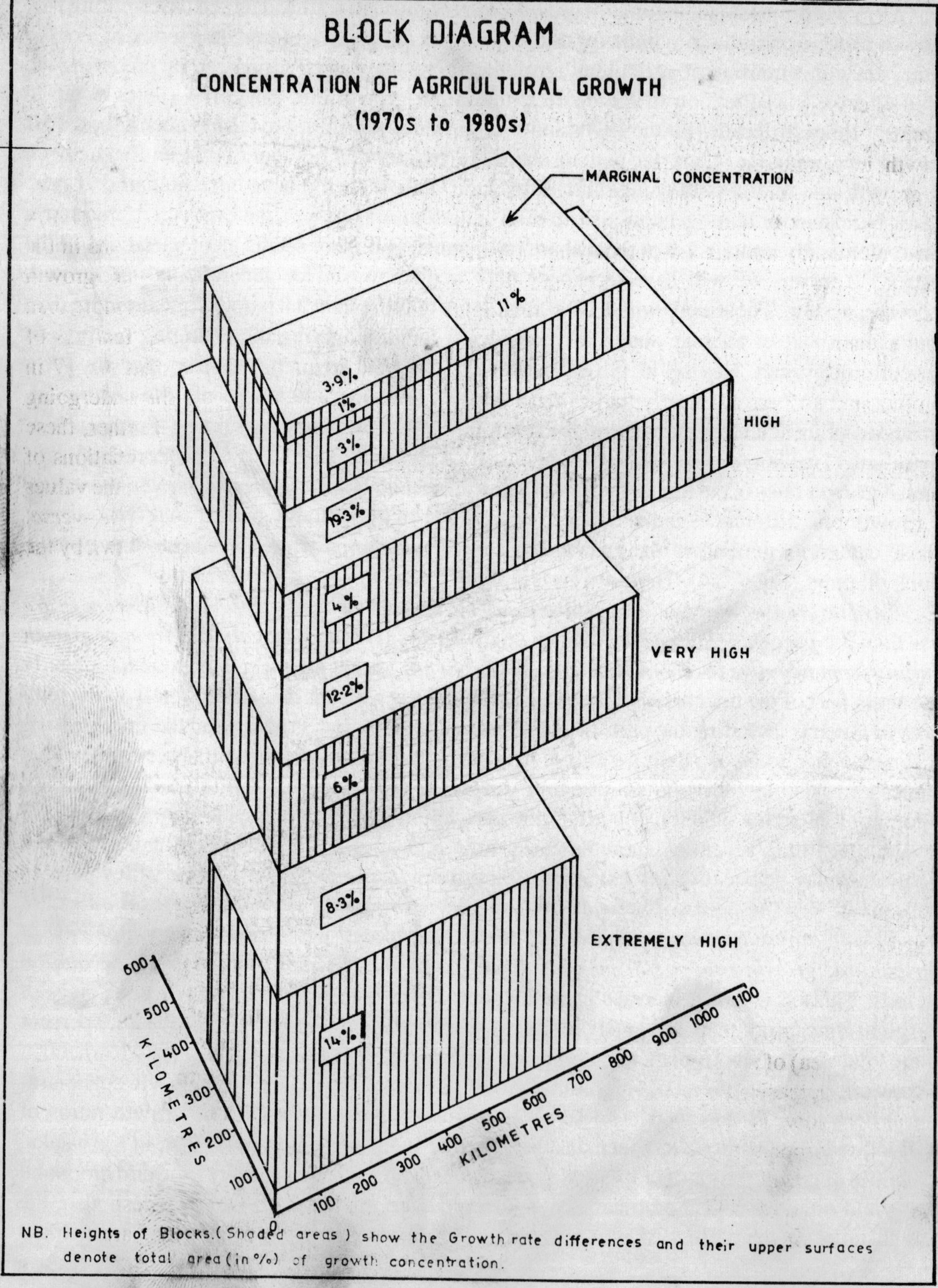
BLOCK DIAGRAM
CONCENTRATION OF AGRICULTURAL GROWTH
(1970s to 1980s)
MARGINAL CONCENTRATION
11%
3.9%
1%
3%
19.3%
HIGH
4%
12.2%
VERY HIGH
6%
8.3%
EXTREMELY HIGH
14%
KILOMETRES
KILOMETRES
0
100
200
300
400
500
600
700
800
900
1000
1100
NB. Heights of Blocks.(Shaded areas) show the Growth rate differences and their upper surfaces denote total area (in %) of growth concentration.

fig 2.4

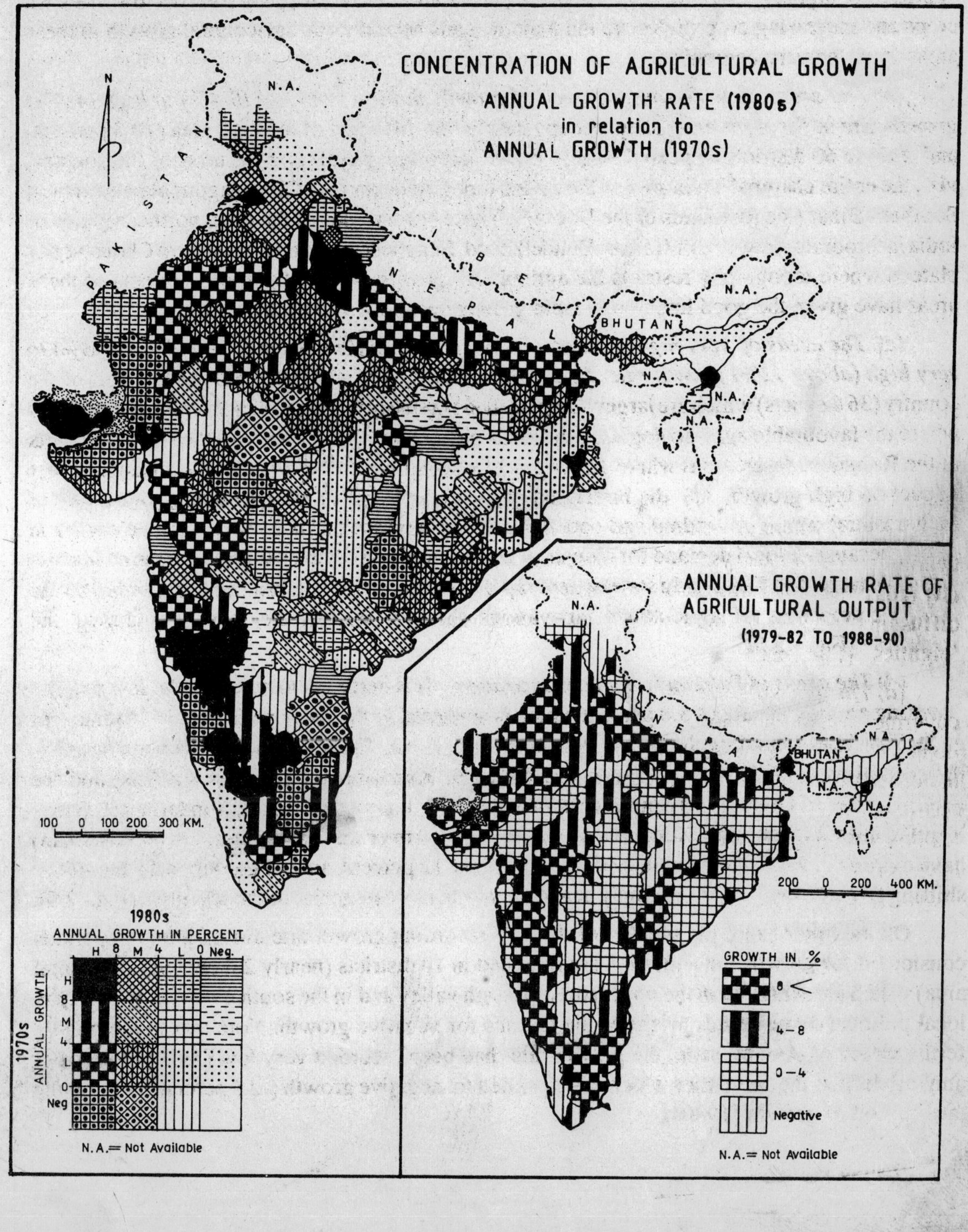
CONCENTRATION OF AGRICULTURAL GROWTH
ANNUAL GROWTH RATE (1980s)
in relation to
ANNUAL GROWTH (1970s)
N
PAKISTAN
TIBET
NEPAL
BHUTAN
N.A.
100 0 100 200 300 KM.
1980s
ANNUAL GROWTH IN PERCENT
H 8 M 4 L 0 Neg.
1970s
ANNUAL GROWTH
H
8
M
4
L
0
Neg
N.A.= Not Available
ANNUAL GROWTH RATE OF
AGRICULTURAL OUTPUT
(1979-82 TO 1988-90)
200 0 200 400 KM.
GROWTH IN %
8 <
4-8
0-4
Negative
N.A.= Not Available

Fig. -2.5

appreciably higher (see Table-2.9). Therefore, unification in the cropping patterns towards cash crops and increasing crop-yields are the main reasons behind rapid agricultural growth in these areas from the very beginning.

(b) The areas of high concentration of growth shifting from low (0-4%) to high (4-8%) growth rate in the eighties:- They occupy nearly one-fifth part of the total area (19.3 percent) and include 60 districts dispersed largely in two important physiographic units of the country, viz., the entire chambal basin area of the ravine topography and the Chotanagpur plateau area of Southern Bihar (the fore lands of the Deccan). These borderlands of the great northern plains of India incorporate Arawalies hill areas, Bundelkhand, Benghelkhand and the southern Chotanagpur plateau where topography restricts the agricultural growth but multipurpose projects of these areas have given the good impetus to rapid growth specially during the sixties.

*(c) The areas of very high concentration of growth shifting from low-medium (0-8%) to very high (above 12%) growth rate during the eighties:-*They include 18.0 percent part of the country (36 districts) which are largely dispersed in : (a) the *terai* parts of Uttar Pradesh and Bihar where the favourable agro-ecological conditions prevail for high growth, (b) the entire dry parts of the Rajasthan desert areas where Indira Gandhi canal irrigation recently started has the direct impact on high growth, (c) the hinterland areas of the Bombay metropolitan (Cotton belt of Maharashtra) where groundnut and cotton yields are increased rapidly (as described earlier in detail) because of local demand for industrial production, and (d) the peripheral areas of Madras city (coastal belt of Tamilnadu state) where rapid agricultural growth has been proceeded by the diffusion processes of agricultural innovations through Madras city specially during the 'eighties (Fig. - 2.5).

(d) The areas of Extremely high concentration:- It is pertinent to note that the few patches covering an area of about 8.0 percent which is scattered in the outer periphery of Madras city in the Tamilnadu state (the districts of North and South Arcot, Tirucherapalli and Ramanathpuram) the coastal areas of Karnataka (Uttari and Dakshine Kannada and Shimoga districts) and the boarder areas of Gujarat and South-western Rajasthan (Jamnagar, Rajkot, Sundarnagar, Banas Kantha, Gandhinagar and Mehasana of Gujarat and Barmer and Jalore districts of Rajasthan) have extremely high concentration of growth (above 12 percent annual growth rate) in eighties shifting growth range from extremely negative growth rate categories of the seventies (Fig.- 2.5).

On the other hand, the number of districts recording growth rate during both the periods considered for growth concentration are recorded in 10 districts (nearly 2.0 percent of the total area) which are scattered in the upper part of Assam valley and in the southern Bihar state where local political disturbances might be the reasons for negative growth. Note that in the middle fertile valley of Assam state, the growth rate had been recorded very low (1.05 percent per annum) during the 'seventies which has declined to negative growth (-2.5 percent) during the later period of growth (1980s).

Table- 2.14: Bivariate Frequency Matrix of the Percentage Share of Area and Number of Districts by Output Growth Rate categories during 1969-72 to 1979-82 and 1979-82 to 1988-90.

Growth rate Categories(%) 1969-72 to 1979-82	Output Annual Growth Rate (in percent) (1979-82 to 1988-90) >-12	12-10	10-8	8-6	6-4	4-2	2-0	-(0-2)	-(2-4)	-(4-<)	Total
> 12	2.83	—	1.94	0.78	1.17	4.22	1.64	1.28	—	0.97	**14.84**
	(9)	—	(4)	(3)	(5)	(6)	(6)	(6)	—	(2)	**(41)**
12-10	—	0.15	—	0.20	0.07	0.36	0.13	—	—	—	**0.91**
	—	(1)	—	(1)	(1)	(1)	(1)	—	—	—	**(5)**
10- 8	0.50	0.22	0.98	1.11	—	0.62	0.63	0.76	—	0.02	**4.86**
	(2)	(2)	(5)	(5)	—	(2)	(2)	(3)	—	(1)	**(22)**
8- 6	1.16	—	0.17	0.34	0.39	0.74	0.85	0.20	—	0.84	**4.71**
	(5)	—	(1)	(1)	(2)	(2)	(2)	(1)	—	(3)	**(17)**
6- 4	6.88	0.50	1.96	1.62	2.61	1.35	0.26	0.36	0.26	—	**15.79**
	(10)	(3)	(6)	(7)	(8)	(5)	(1)	(2)	(1)	—	**(43)**
4- 2	3.43	0.84	1.51	2.16	3.03	2.45	1.05	0.68	0.96	0.73	**16.84**
	(12)	(3)	(6)	(8)	(11)	(10)	(3)	(6)	(5)	(4)	**(68)**
2- 0	3.58	1.13	1.70	2.46	2.13	0.90	1.98	2.08	0.58	0.83	17.39
	(9)	(4)	(10)	(11)	(8)	(4)	(8)	(11)	(4)	(5)	(74)
-(0-2)	1.32	0.41	0.49	1.66	1.12	2.19	2.18	1.32	—	—	10.72
	(5)	(3)	(3)	(6)	(4)	(5)	(7)	(6)	—	—	(39)
-(2-4)	3.88	—	0.28	1.75	0.85	0.19	0.29	—	0.26	—	7.51
	(10)	—	(1)	(3)	(3)	(2)	(1)	—	(3)	—	(23)
-(4->)	3.07	—	—	0.84	0.86	1.10	0.12	—	—	0.44	6.43
	(7)	—	—	(3)	(3)	(3)	(1)	—	—	(1)	(18)
Total	**26.67**	**3.25**	**9.05**	**12.93**	**12.24**	**14.13**	**9.12**	**6.71**	**2.07**	**3.83**	**99.99**
	(69)	**(16)**	**(36)**	**(48)**	**(45)**	**(40)**	**(32)**	**(35)**	**(13)**	**(16)**	**(350)**

N.B.: Figures in parenthesses depict the number of the districts and other figures are percentage share of Area of total area of the country.

Concluding Remarks

By describing agricultural output growth trends and patterns in detail, an attempt was made to highlight the inherent characteristics of growth structure. The salient features of growth processes which have been described here bring out a few but important generalizations as given below.

It is logically proved from the empirical evidences that the linear trend of agricultural output/production growth is more significant for predicting proper growth results than the logarithmic or semi-logarithmic ones because of constant rate of production increase of various crops. A second major conclusion of this Chapter is that there seems a gradual shift in the processes and resulted forms of agricultural growth from 'demand-led growth' of pre-green revolution period to 'technology-based growth' of the post-green revolution period. In the initial stage of planned agricultural development, the diversified cropping patterns were being brought out in the frame of agro-ecological setup with accelerating expansion processes of agricultural landuse. The growth processes were operated by the local demand conditions of the areas. For example, the results of the agricultural growth study done by Bhat and Learmonth (1968) for the late fifties explain clearly that Delhi - Bombay areas as emerging industrial axel of the country were recorded very high agricultural growth because of raw material demand for the agro-based industries at that time. The growth was proceeded slowly in other areas of the country because these areas of high population concentration (specially the northern great plains and costal plains) required foodgrains for local feed, although they have intensive amount of agricultural growth potential and favourable agro-ecological conditions for self-sustained growth. Consequently, during post-revolution period (particularly after 'sixties), the agricultural growth proceeded fast as it was recorded 2.03 percent in the 'seventies and 3.03 percent in 'eighties. The big growth poles of country that are four metropolitan cities namely Delhi, Bombay, Calcutta and Madras, tend to concentrate the regional patterns of agricultural growth by diffusing agricultural new innovations to their hinterlands specially in the eighties. Therefore, high growth areas are located near by the centres and growth rate decreases towards the hinterlands of these growth poles of the nation. It confirms the fact of growth centers approach of development as proposed by Perroux (1955, 1964) and Boudavilla (1966). It is pertinent to note here that the growth has been proceeding through input shifts from labour dominated to capital (technology) enhancement. In Indian conditions of agriculture, technology may not be substitution of labour input, although it is complementary to enhance labour productivity which is marked very low in India. These productivity patterns in relation to agricultural output growth and their input-factors should be described separately in detail, so the significance of capital contribution and the choice of methods for transferring technology to agricultural development may be described for understanding the critical policy decisions.

Chapter - 3

Productivity Patterns and Agricultural Transformation in India

Agricultural output growth, its regional patterns and the growth factors which have been described in the preceding Chapter, are the result of its two major components: (a) the level of agricultural productivity and (b) the changes occurring therein over time. Therefore, an analysis of agricultural productivity at the disaggregated district level is essential for finding out the causes of self- sustained growth and regional balanced agricultural development. The changing patterns of agricultural productivity are also important to study because it should be helpful in understanding the optimal conditions of the regional processes of agricultural production. Thus, the main attention is focussed in this Chapter to study the structural changes in the regional patterns of agricultural development in order to change agricultural productivity and its input factors namely land conditions, labour as well as technological inputs, and to examine their inter-regional variations, so that the optimal pattern of productivity may be suggested in relation to its agro-ecological setting.

Since agricultural productivity is the major component of agricultural development, the study of structural transformation in the spatial patterns of agricultural development may be made in order to elaborate three main aspects of agricultural productivity. They are: (a) the changes in the regional patterns of agricultural productivity, (b)spatial features of agricultural growth in relation to agricultural productivity levels, and (c)the factors influencing the productivity patterns and their changing nature. In the present context, the productivity patterns and changes therein are interpreted by considering three points of time as early 1970s(1969-72), 1980s (1979-82) and 1990s (1988-90). But the results of structural transformation of agricultural attributes are interpreted to consider a period of 10 years, the early 1980s (1979-82) as base year and early 1990s (1988-90) as current year.

Agricultural Productivity

(A) Definition and Measurements

On the definitional parts, agricultural productivity which is a relative term, refers to agricultural output in relation to land, labour and capital inputs. Infact, capital input which reflects the application of modern technology is still being used at very low level. However, it is essential to intensify the productivity patterns and it is complementary to labour input. Only large size of landholders are benefited by the modern technology. But, in the present study, I shall consider technological application as a main factor of agricultural productivity instead of its important components. Therefore, agricultural productivity is defined here in two ways: (a) *'land productivity'* which refers to the agricultural output per unit of cultivated area (eqn. 1.4b) which is the result of physical characteristics, socio-economic set up and application of modern agricultural technological attributes of the area/region; and (b) *'labour productivity'* which refers to the agricultural output per agricultural worker (eqn. 1.4c) reflects the standard of living of agricultural workers, the effect of absolute rise of agricultural force and the degree of labour absorption capacity of agricultural sector (Bhalla and Alagh 1983,Thakur 1987). On the other hand, land productivity indicates the impact of physiographic conditions of land with human responses to increase agricultural production. It indicates how the production processes are being accelerated within the specific limits imposed by physiographic conditions of land. It is important to note that this component of agricultural productivity is very much relevant to interpret agricultural production patterns in relation to its agro-ecological setup. Labour productivity, which is equally important to study, is the main determinant of socio-economic set up of the rural population. Infact, rural migration problems, wage-rates of rural landless agricultural labourers, income earnings and purchasing capacity of rural families, which are indicators of rural development, are directly or indirectly determined by agricultural labour productivity. Of course, it is also useful for labour policy formulations because its trend may suggest labour absorbing capacity in agriculture sector (Thankur 1987).

So far as measurement of labour productivity is concerned, it is clear that the concept of labour productivity is based on the rate of marginal return of agricultural production. It means that additional agricultural production produced by the application of additional labour unit in the agricultural production processes while other inputs of agricultural production are assumed constant (Lewis 1954). Thus, the assessment of labour productivity is closely related to the mathematical theory of differentiation. But, on account of non-availability of district level data of production share produced by agricultural labour in agricultural systems in India, the correct assessment of labour productivity is not possible specially for macro-spatial analysis. The aggregated agricultural output index is infact the result of various agricultural inputs and geographical factors (e.g., physiographical conditions of land, labour and capital inputs). However, the few economic studies have made important contributions to understand the issues related to labour productivity of industrial sectors at micro-economic levels.

The second view of assessing labour productivity is to deduct the amount of capital and other inputs except labour from total agricultural output for calculating labour productivity. Since land and capital (capital includes technology and other capital factors) are also productive inputs and they are equally important in the agricultural systems, the amount of these inputs is not equal to their productivity amount. Therefore, it would not give the accurate figure for the assessment of labour productivity. But, it is a fact that these inputs have very weak share of total input strength of the system because of two reasons :(a) unlimited supply of labour in agricultural sector, and (b) very less applicabililty of modern agricultural technology due to poor socio-economic conditions and unequal distribution of land resources (size of land holdings). Thus, they are not considered for measuring labour productivity, and hence, it refers simply to agricultural output per agricultural worker (eqn. 1.4c). Thus, land productivity is one of the attributes of labour productivity. Now, it is obvious that land productivity patterns are more concerned with the physiographic conditions of land and technological factors while labour productivity is indicative to the real gains of agricultural productivity in relation to ever increasing population pressure on land. As a result, the inter-regional variations of these two indices of agricultural productivity should be evaluated under separate heads.

(B) Land Productivity- Regional Patterns and changes therein

Of course, agricultural production per hectare of land in India is low relative to the world average because of several reasons. However, the shift from traditional means of agricultural production to modern ones may be seen specially after green revolution effects. An unimpressive change in land productivity in India is due to unequal diffusion of the new agricultural technology from one area and crop to the others. The changes in the land productivity patterns have been examined here by distinguishing the total district units into seven semi-internal classes for three points of time. They show the areas of (i) Extremely High land productivity (above Rs. 1750), (ii) Very High productivity (Rs. 1750-1500), (iii) High productivity (Rs.1500-1250), (iv) Medium productivity (Rs.1250-1000), (v) Low (Rs.1000-750), (vi) Very Low (Rs.750-500), and (vii) Extremely Low productivity levels (below Rs.500). For interpretation purpose, the extreme ends of high productivity and low productivity categories have been clubbed together.

Comparing the distributional patterns of land productivity (agricultural output per hectare of cultivated land) for early 1970s, 1980s and 1990s, it is visualised that physiographic features and agro-climatic conditions had been the major determining factors for the area variations of land productivity specially during early 1970s when green revolution technology had some impact on a few pockets of agricultural growth (see Fig.- 2.5 in Ch. 2). The physiographic regions of India perfectly coincide with the boundaries with land productivity patterns. There were only 61 districts of extremely high and very high land productivity classes which incorporated only 13.1 percent (404.6 thousand sq.km.) area with nearly one-third share of total agricultural output (4374 crores of rupees) in 1969-72 (Tables- 3.1 & 3.2). These high productivity areas had emerged as the core areas of concentration of agricultural production. The areas of entire Punjab and Haryana including Meerut and Agra divisions of Western Uttar Pradesh (Punjab plains and upper parts of the Ganga-Jamuna *doab*), entire West Bengal including lower parts of Assam and North-Eastern *terai* parts of Bihar states, and the state of Kerala and Coastal Tamilnadu that are situated in the extreme southern parts of the country have been emerging as high productivity areas (Figs.- 3.1,3.2 & 3.3). It is interesting to note that these areas of very high productivity have three matropolitan cities of India, namely, Delhi, Calcutta and Madras. Thus, the development of agriculture in the early 1970s had been centre-based and because of diffusion of various innovations and modern technology of agriculture through these growth-centres, its hinterland developed to enhance land productivity. But later on during the 1980s, the hinterlands of these core productivity areas have been extended to cover the entire parts of the Ganga valley including the coastal plain areas of Eastern as well as Western coastal plains of the Peninsular India (Fig.-3.3). For example, the areas of very high and extremely high productivity have been extended from 13.0 percent (1969-72) to 33.15 percent (1988-90) with an increasing share of about 30.00 percent of the total agricultural output during the last two decades (Table- 3.2). It means that there is an areal shift with a transformation of lower productivity areas to higher productivity ones. The decadal changes in the share of total output, area and average productivity levels for various land productivity classes show the degree of areal transformation of productivity patterns. Table- 3.2 reveals that fast growth of agricultural output (14.67 percent annual) has been recorded in the extremely high productivity areas during the last two decades(1969-72 to 1988-90). It is comparatively much higher than the annual average rate of its areal expansion which is recorded only 10.08 percent during the same period of time. Very high productivity areas also have the same tendency of agricultural growth (Table- 3.3). It means that there is a tendency of the concentration of agricultural output towards the areas of higher land productivity, while the productivity patterns have been already diversified with breaking their real boundaries of agricultural growth particularly in the last two decades of green revolution period. These factors can be elaborated separately in the coming discussion by establishing relationship between agricultural growth and productivity levels in its spatial frame. But, the changing productivity patterns in relation to its level must be discussed here for explaining the reasons of productivity intensification and its inter-regional variations.

Table-3.1: Number of Districts, Output and Area in Various Land Productivity Categories.

Productivity Classes (Rs./ha)	Number of districts			Total output (in crore Rs.)			Total area (in 000 sq.km)		
	70	80	90	70	80	90	70	80	90
1750- <	42	61	106	3188.3	6180.3	11609.5	261.2	312.3	735.3
1750-1500	19	21	24	1186.4	1692.3	2269.0	143.4	142.8	228.2
1500-1250	25	37	29	1876.1	1519.7	1032.3	190.3	189.6	236.5
1250-1000	42	50	41	1314.9	1992.3	1465.2	356.8	322.9	356.8
1000- 750	53	50	49	1754.1	1621.3	1020.2	410.9	407.4	436.2
750- 500	69	85	60	1954.7	1921.4	887.9	637.3	903.3	526.8
500- >	100	46	41	1835.5	1205.1	1779.9	906.1	627.7	386.2
Total	**350**	**350**	**350**	**13110**	**16132**	**20044**	**2906**	**2906**	**2906**

Abbreviations:

70= 1969-72, 80= 1979-82, 90= 1988-90.

Table- 3.2: Productivity Levels and Percentage Share of Output and Area in Various Land Productivity Catigories.

Productivity Classes (Rs./ha)	Average Productivity (Rs./ha)			Percentage Share in: Total Output			Total Area		
	70	80	90	70	80	90	70	80	90
1750- <	1811	1848	1852	24.32	38.31	57.92	8.99	10.74	25.30
1750-1500	1611	1632	1638	9.05	10.49	11.32	4.93	4.91	7.85
1500-1250	1315	1319	1323	14.31	9.42	5.15	6.55	6.52	8.14
1250-1000	1159	1169	1171	10.03	12.35	7.31	12.28	11.11	12.28
1000- 750	829	811	802	13.38	10.05	5.09	14.14	14.03	15.01
750- 500	592	442	421	14.91	11.91	4.43	21.93	31.08	18.13
500- >	343	238	223	14.00	7.47	8.88	31.18	21.60	13.29
Total	**936**	**1135**	**1439**	**99.99**	**99.99**	**99.99**	**99.99**	**99.99**	**99.99**

Abbreviations: 70 = 1969-72, 80 = 1979-82, 90 = 1988-90.

N.B.: Average productivity for each category is calculated dividing its absolute share of total output by the total GCA for different points of time.

Table- 3.3: Annual Average Change of Land Productivity, Total Output and Area in Various Productivity Categories.

Productivity Classes (Rs./ha)	Average Annual Change in Percent in: Average Productivity			Total Output			Total Area		
	70s	80s	90s	70s	80s	70-90	70s	80s	70-90
1750- <	0.20	.03	0.12	9.38	10.98	14.67	1.95	16.94	10.08
1750-1500	0.13	.04	0.09	4.26	4.26	5.07	-0.04	7.48	3.28
1500-1250	0.03	.04	0.03	-1.90	-4.01	-2.50	-0.04	3.09	1.35
1250-1000	0.08	.02	0.06	5.15	-3.31	0.63	-0.95	1.31	0.00
1000- 750	-0.22	-.14	-0.18	-0.76	-4.63	-2.32	-0.08	0.88	0.34
750- 500	-2.53	-.59	-1.60	-0.17	-6.72	-3.03	4.17	-5.21	-0.96
500- >	-3.06	-.79	-1.94	-3.43	5.96	-0.17	-3.07	-4.81	-3.19
Total	**2.12**	**3.35**	**2.98**	**2.30**	**3.03**	**2.94**	—	—	—

Abbreviations: 70s= 1969-72 to 1979-82 (10 years averages), 80s= 1979-82 to 1988=90 (8 years averages), and 70-90 = 1969-72 to 1988-90 (18 years averages).

N.B.: Annual Average Change is calculated by applying simple growth rate formula as given by Equation- 1.3 in Ch. 1)

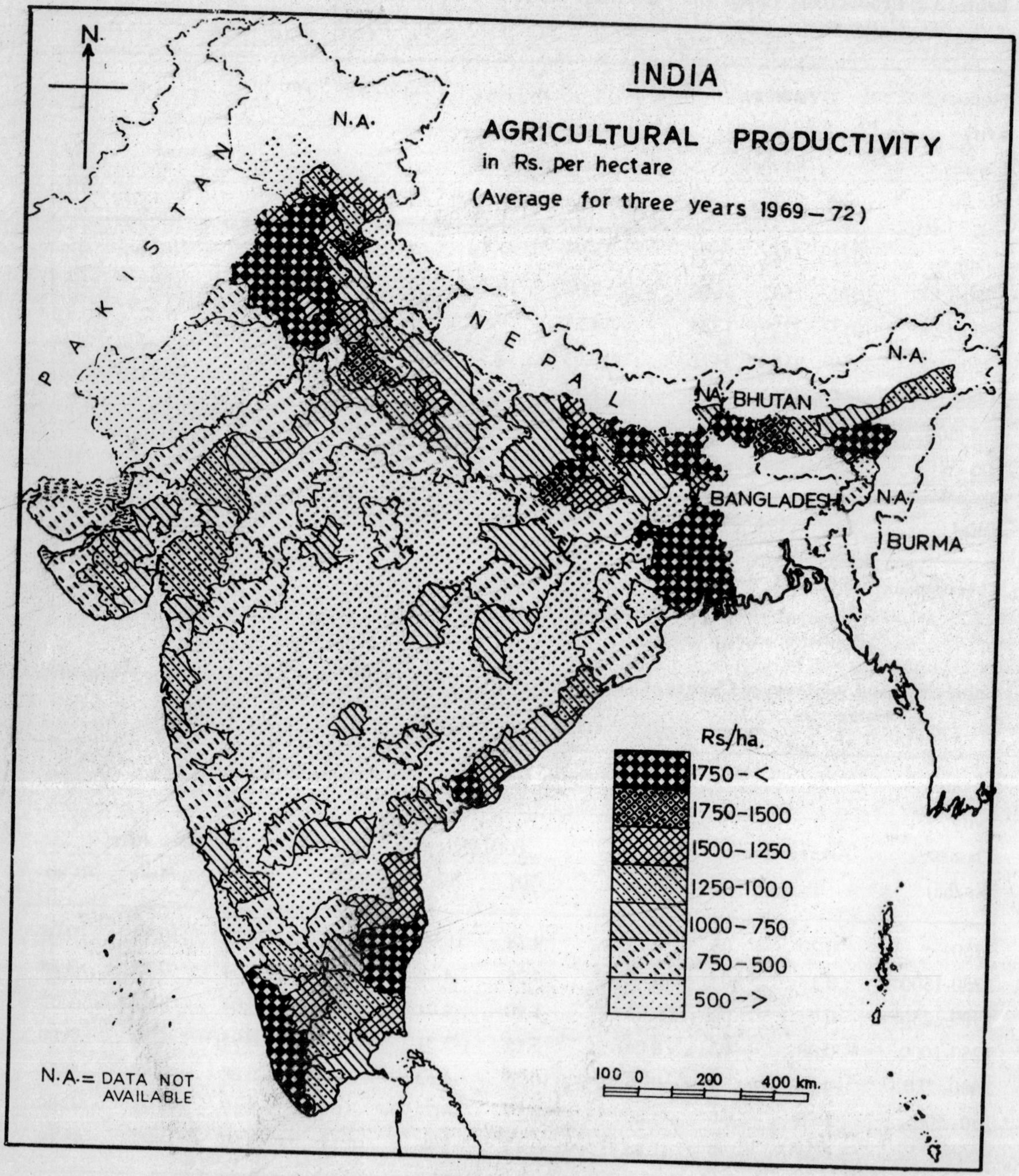
INDIA
AGRICULTURAL PRODUCTIVITY
in Rs. per hectare
(Average for three years 1969—72)
N.
N.A.
PAKISTAN
NEPAL
BHUTAN
BANGLADESH
BURMA
Rs/ha.
1750-<
1750-1500
1500-1250
1250-1000
1000-750
750-500
500->
N.A.= DATA NOT AVAILABLE
100 0 200 400 km.

Fig: - 3.1

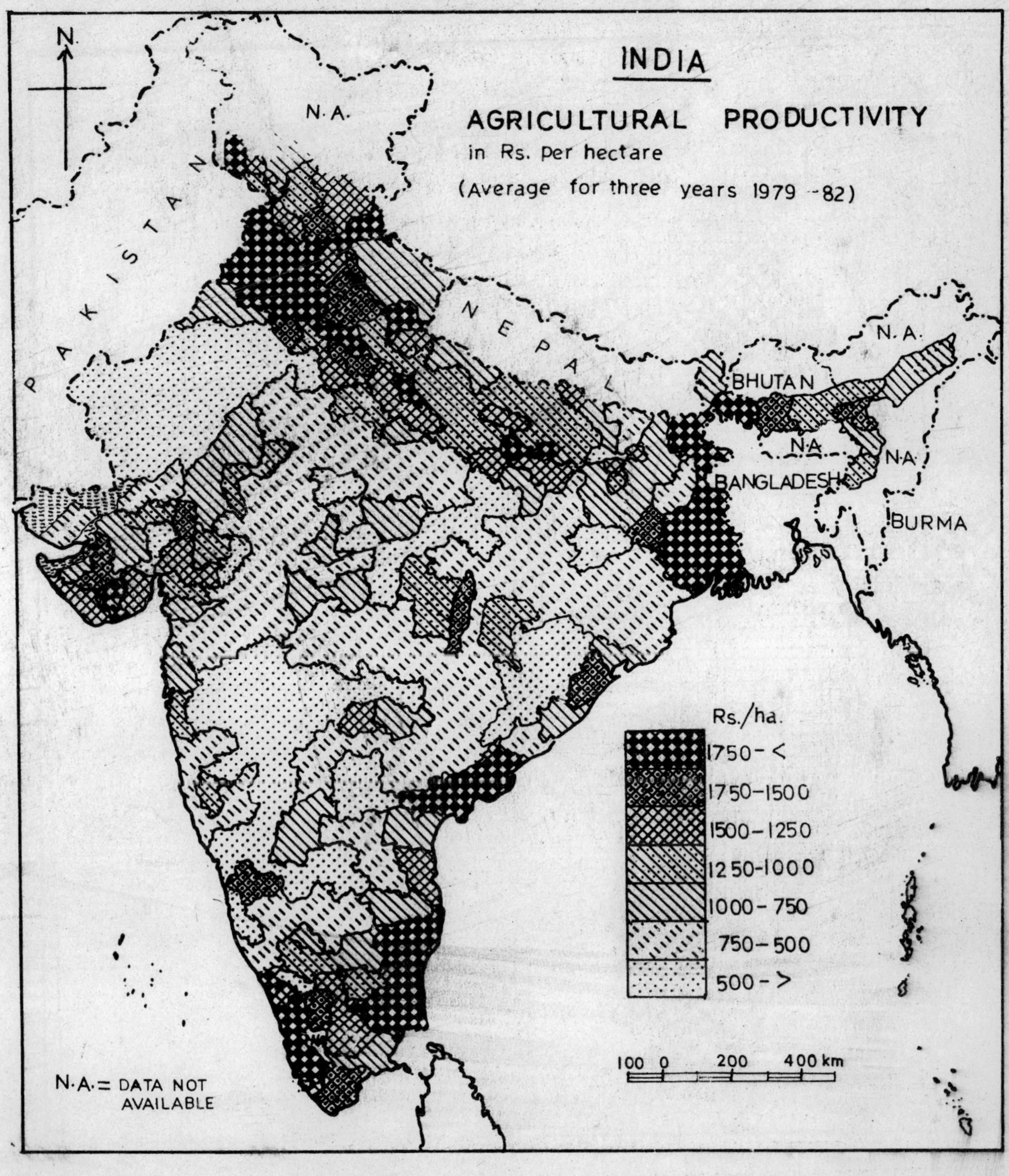
INDIA
AGRICULTURAL PRODUCTIVITY
in Rs. per hectare
(Average for three years 1979 -82)
N.
N.A.
PAKISTAN
NEPAL
N.A.
BHUTAN
N.A.
N.A.
BANGLADESH
BURMA
Rs./ha.
1750- <
1750-1500
1500-1250
1250-1000
1000-750
750-500
500- >
100 0 200 400 km
N.A.= DATA NOT AVAILABLE

Fig. - 3.2

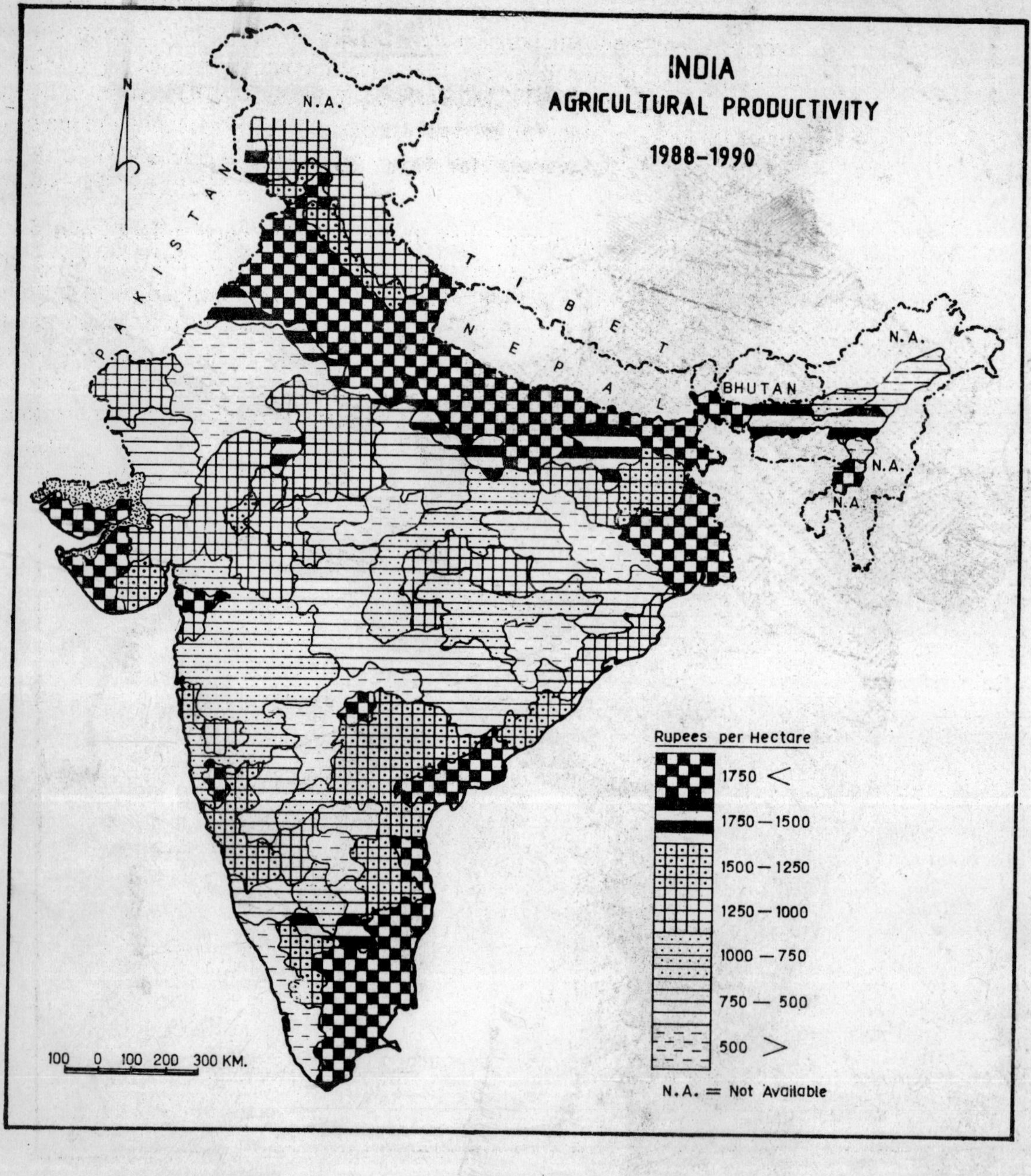
INDIA
AGRICULTURAL PRODUCTIVITY
1988-1990
N
N.A.
PAKISTAN
TIBET
NEPAL
BHUTAN
N.A.
N.A.
N.A.
Rupees per Hectare
1750 <
1750 — 1500
1500 — 1250
1250 — 1000
1000 — 750
750 — 500
500 >
N.A. = Not Available
100 0 100 200 300 KM.

Fig. - 3.3

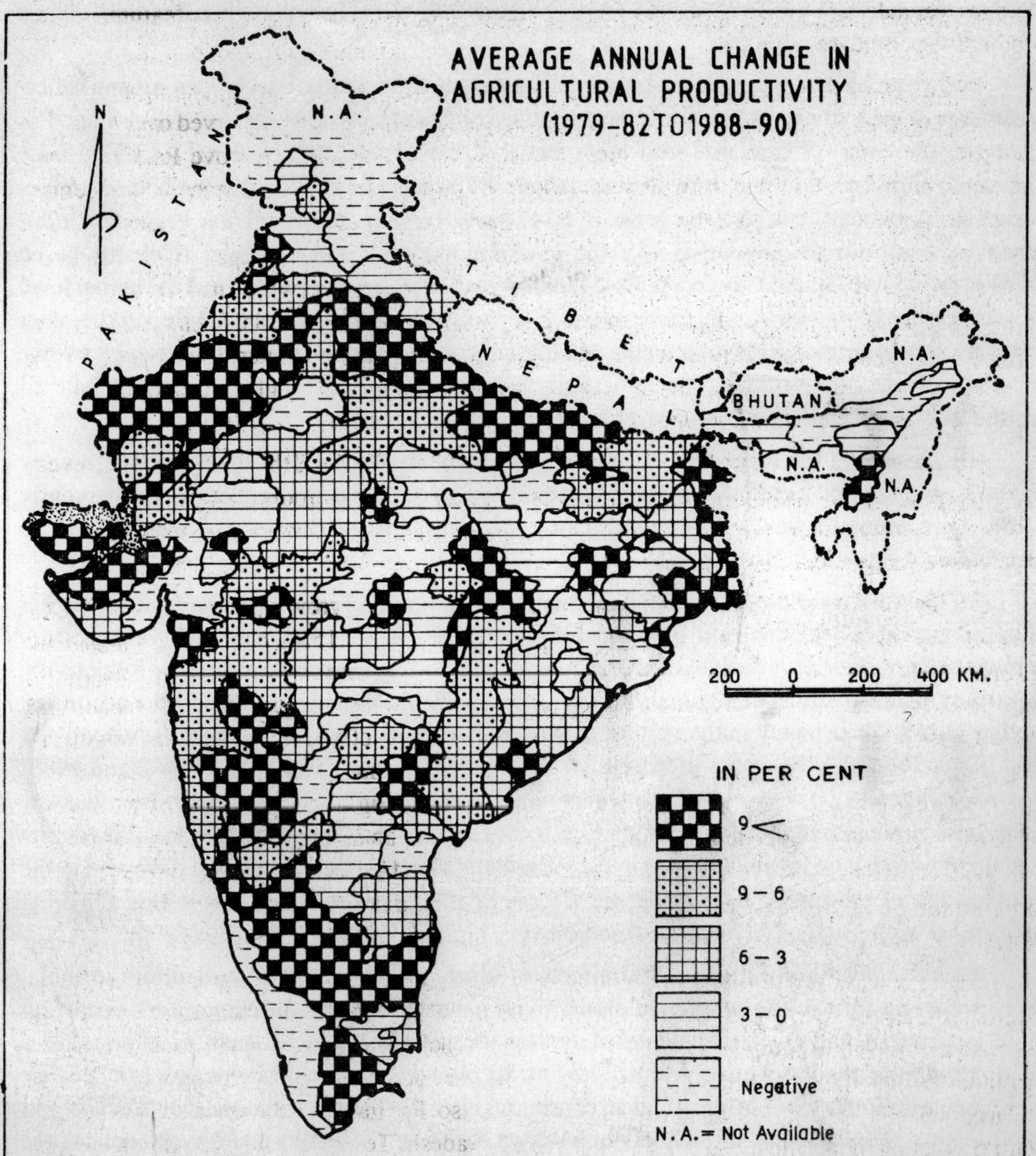
AVERAGE ANNUAL CHANGE IN
AGRICULTURAL PRODUCTIVITY
(1979-82TO1988-90)
N
PAKISTAN
N.A.
TIBET
NEPAL
BHUTAN
N.A.
N.A.
N.A.
200 0 200 400 KM.
IN PER CENT
9<
9 – 6
6 – 3
3 – 0
Negative
N. A.= Not Available

Fig. - 3.4

Comparing the distribution map of land productivity for early 1980s and the map of its change over a decade 1979-82 to 1988-90 (Fig.-3.2 & 3.4), the following salient features of land productivity increase emerge:

(a) It appears that the regional gaps in the land productivity have been widening and hence, increasing degree of diversification in land productivity patterns can be observed over time. For example, the areas of high and very high levels of land productivity (above Rs.1500) have extremely high rate of productivity increase(above 9.0 percent annually) because of their centre-based development. Note that the areas of (i) Punjab-Haryana-Western Uttar Pradesh (Delhi-based agricultural development), (ii) the southern parts of West Bengal (Calcutta-based development) and (iii) the Cauvery delta (Madras-based development) which had the higher level of land productivity, are having faster increase in their productivity levels. While, on the other hand, the entire parts of peninsular India, where productivity levels were very low in early 1980s, are still weak and backward in agriculture because they have negligible annual rate of productivity increase (even somewhere it is recorded decreased).

(b) The areas of entire Rajasthan, the arid zone of the country, and the most parts of Cauvery basin (Karnataka and Tamilnadu highlands) where the level of land productivity was low in early 1980s have emerged fast with the higher rate of increase of productivity. It may be due to expansion of irrigation facilities.

(c) The validity of the fact of the concentration of agricultural growth persisting in the higher productivity areas (where land productivity level is above Rs.1500) can also be tested by observing inter-district variations of productivity levels within these areas of higher productivity. By arranging the districts of higher productivity(above Rs.1500) in descending order according to their ranks, the primacy in the vertical distribution of productivity levels may be visualized. The Rank-Productivity curves prepared for three points of time (1969-72,1979-82 and 1988-90), reveal increasing degree of primacy in the areal patterns (Fig.- 3.5). It means more concavity in the curve indicates higher degree of inter-district variations and *vice-versa*. These curves depict that the few districts (mostly situated in the West Bengal and Punjab States) are observed at the extreme top of the ranks. As a result, the degree of inter-district variations within the areal patterns of high productivity can be observed very high in the early1990s (1988-90).

On account of multi-dimensional effects of centre-based growth of agriculture in India, there seems a poly-cyclic evolution of productivity patterns in which the changes are occurring because of varied and diversified nature of modern technological factors. In the areal patterns of productivity, the diversification is noted only on account of technological changes but because of larger variations in the agro-ecological conditions also. For instance, the areas of Western and central parts of India (most of the parts of Madhya Pradesh, Telangana and Rayalseema of the Andhra Pradesh, Widharva of Maharastra and the entire parts of Rajasthan) where arid and semi-arid agro-climatic conditions prevail, are still under very low and extremely low categories of land productivity. They are diversifying the areal patterns of land productivity through creating its regional imbalances. Of course, there will always be the higher degree of inter-regional variations in productivity patterns. Now, question is how to minimize or optimize the inter regional variations of agricultural productivity for which its main attributes and major causes will have to be found out.

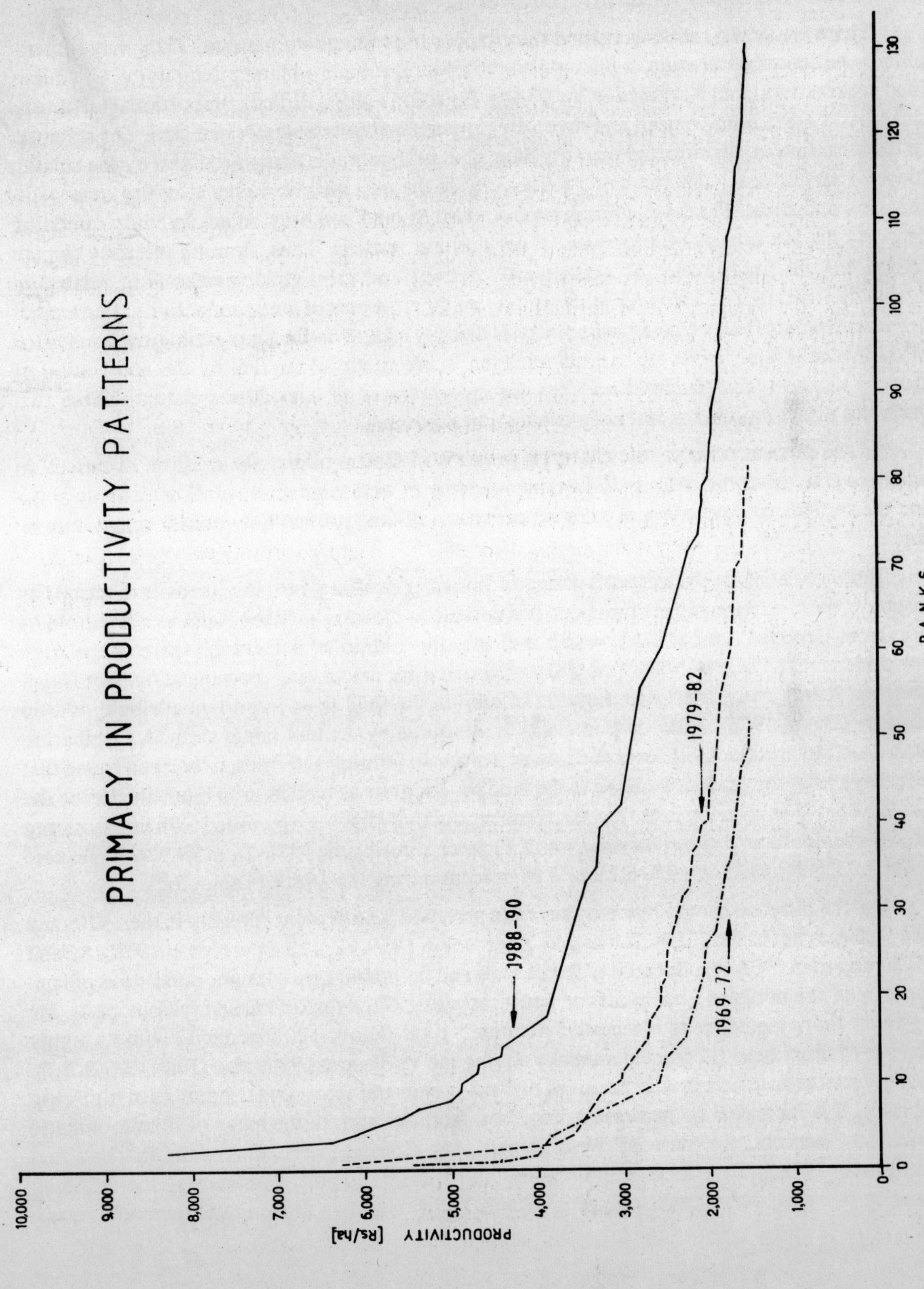
PRIMACY IN PRODUCTIVITY PATTERNS
1988-90
1979-82
1969-72
PRODUCTIVITY [Rs/ha]
10,000
9,000
8,000
7,000
6,000
5,000
4,000
3,000
2,000
1,000
0
10
20
30
40
50
60
70
80
90
100
110
120
130
RANKS

Fig.- 3.5

(C) Land Productivity Patterns- Causes of its change

There are several reasons behind the changes in productivity patterns. They may systematically be described in order to understand the major attributes of land productivity. Of course, land productivity (that is defined as Y= O/A by Equation 1.4b) is directly proportional to the total quantity of agricultural output and inversely proportional to total cultivated land. For instance, in the area/district where larger quantity of agricultural output is being produced by the smaller piece of agricultural land, the land productivity of the area will be higher than the areas of its inverse conditions. The level of high productivity of land can only be achieved by operating properly the intensification processes of agricultural landuse. Thus, farming intensity (which refers to the areal extent of agricultural output) and crop-yield increase(i.e., related to agricultural production enhancement) are two major attributes of land productivity. Remember here that first attribute of land productivity is directly related to the agro-ecological conditions of agricultural land, while the second attribute is inherently controlled by the application of modern technological factors/forces for the enhancement of agricultural output. These two attributes affect together to intensify production processes.

In the present context, the changing patterns of land productivity must be discussed in relation to the changing patterns of farming intensity as well as green revolution technology, so that the suitable interpretation of regional processes of land productivity enhancement may be made.

On account of crop dominated nature of Indian agriculture, farming intensity is termed as cropping intensity by many geographers. It is defined as the ratio between Net Sown Area (NSA) and Gross Cropped Area (GCA), which indicates the additional percentage share of the Area Sown More than Once to NSA. It is traditional index for calculating crop intensity. But Dayal modified it and considered that duration of crop in the field is an important attribute of crop intensity (Dayal 1978). Here, crop intensity is measured by the traditional method. Comparing increase in land productivity level and intensification in farming activities, it has been found that there have been the gradual increase in the land productivity as well as crop intensity during the last 20 years. The increase in the levels of land productivity has been recorded with its increasing rate. Its average annual rate of increase was 2.13 percent during the 1970s from Rs.936 per hectare in 1969-72 to Rs.1135 in 1979-82 and 2.98 percent during the 1980s (Table- 3.2).

But the increase in crop intensity has been recorded 0.56 percent annually in the 1970s and only 0.36 percent in the 1980s. It was 119.2 percent in 1969-72, 123.8 percent in 1979 - 82 and 127.0 percent in 1988-90. Because of fertile soils and favorable agro-climatic conditions of land specially of the northern great plains of India including Godavari and Cauvery delta parts, the degree of cropping intensity is recorded extremely high (above 120.0 percent) with its higher increase of more than 1.0 percent annually during the 1970s and 1980s also (Figs - 3.6 & 3.7). It is pertinent to note here that, in the areas of semi-humid and semi- arid conditions of high crop intensity, it is increased by increasing irrigation facilities and, in the areas of humid climatic conditions, namely, the state of West Bengal, the Coastal parts of Andhra Pradesh and Tamilnadu) though these areas follow mono-crop culture of paddy dominating, the cropping intensity is higher due to multi-cropping system. Paddy is grown thrice in the year. As a result, degree of farming intensity and level of land productivity have been observed high in these areas, and hence, there is significantly positive relationship between degree of crop-intensity and land productivity (r = .489).

Of course, irrigation is the integral element of intensifying modern technology through which crop- yields are increased. As a result, it intensifies farming processes, changes cropping patterns and increases land productivity. On account of changing irrigation technology in India from labour-intensive *Dhekli* and *Charas* systems to animal - drawn *Rahat* system of mid-20th Century and then to engine-operated tubewell systems of the modern time, there seems a fast increase in the irrigated areas. In India, only 17.55 percent of total NSA (20.85 million hectare) was irrigated by various sources in 1950-51, which rose to 22.17 per cent (31.10 million hectare) till 1970-71 and further to 31.16 percent (43.05 million hectare) till 1987-88. At present , nearly one-third part of the total NSA is irrigated by various sources. The irrigation factor in the agricultural development has a great importance because more than two-third part of the country fall under semi-arid and arid agro- climatic conditions, although the soils of these parts are fertile and suitable for agriculture. Thus, the soils of the entire upper and middle parts of Indo-Gangetic plains including the Thar of Rajasthan are more thirsty than hungry. It is pertinent to note that these areas of fertile soils have significant share of irrigated land, as more than 50.0 percent land of total NSA of these areas of high land productivity have intensive irrigation facilities (Fig.-3.8). Further, size of operational land holdings is also important factor to intensify the modern technology. The marginal farmers who have small and very small size of land holdings (below 2.0 percent) are not in position to establish their own agricultural infra-structure . Land productivity may, therefore, be recorded low in Bihar, Kerala and Tamilnadu where more than 80.0 percent of the total number of operational holding are marginal and small (below 2.0 hectare) in size (Table- 3.4). The effects of other elements of modern agricultural technology on land productivity will be described in detail under the separate heads after interpreting the regional pattern of agricultural growth in relation to land productivity levels for understanding the agricultural growth - productivity relation over space.

(D) Agricultural Growth by Land Productivity: Spatial Pattern and its causes

The spatial pattern of agricultural growth - productivity relationships are infact the result of the intensification of output - augmenting practices (specially the increasing use of modern technology and irrigation). The application of these input factors increases level of land productivity and rate of agricultural output (Binswanger and Ryan 1977, Binswanger 1978). It is consequently hypothesized that the areas of high productivity should follow fast agricultural growth rate with strong growth - productivity relations. But, if output augmenting technology is applied in the areas of low levels of land productivity where magnitude and intensity of agricultural growth potential are enough to use, the optimally balanced regional pattern of agricultural growth - productivity relations can be achieved. Detailed description of agricultural growth potential would although be made separately in the next Chapter, yet the existing patterns of these attributes must be put forward here.

Table- 3.4: State-wise Percentage Share of Number and Area of Operational Land holding Sizes (1985 - 86).

(Figures in percent)

	States		Marginal (1ha>)	Small (1-2ha)	Semi-medium (2-4ha)	Medium (4-10ha)	Large (10ha<)
1.	A.P.	N	54.20	20.82	15.23	7.98	1.77
		A	14.50	17.33	23.95	27.30	16.19
2.	Assam	N	60.00	22.57	13.40	3.80	0.25
		A	19.00	24.07	27.65	15.22	14.08
3.	Bihar	N	76.65	11.33	8.12	3.45	0.44
		A	30.31	17.15	23.79	21.04	7.70
4.	Gujrat	N	25.47	23.43	24.79	21.56	4.46
		A	4.18	10.85	22.43	41.45	21.09
5.	Haryana	N	37.27	19.67	20.86	17.74	4.45
		A	6.16	10.31	21.27	37.94	24.29
6.	H.P.	N	61.49	20.58	12.22	4.79	0.80
		A	20.51	22.75	26.02	21.22	9.69
7.	J&K	N	73.84	15.78	8.27	1.94	0.08
		A	32.68	24.78	25.66	12.49	4.39
8.	Karnatka	N	36.43	26.28	21.04	13.13	3.11
		A	7.29	15.89	24.23	32.67	19.90
9.	Kerala	N	90.58	6.40	2.36	0.56	0.09
		A	45.84	21.62	15.39	7.41	9.73
10.	M.P.	N	35.95	21.21	20.95	17.03	4.90
		A	5.48	10.62	20.08	71.71	28.22
11.	Maha.	N	30.71	25.97	24.16	16.26	2.91
		A	5.77	1.57	25.85	36.82	16.87
12.	Orissa	N	52.09	25.38	16.26	5.69	0.58
		A	17.47	24.20	29.78	22.18	6.35
13.	Punjab	N	23.53	19.12	26.75	23.90	6.80
		A	3.38	7.58	20.47	38.72	29.85
14.	Rajasthan	N	28.63	19.40	20.64	20.79	10.56
		A	3.11	6.44	13.55	29.88	47.01
15.	T.N.	N	71.34	16.35	8.42	3.38	0.51
		A	25.88	—	22.80	19.34	9.23
16.	U.P.	N	72.59	15.61	8.33	3.17	0.29
		A	28.29	22.73	76.05	19.13	4.81
17.	W.B.	N	70.85	19.17	8.42	1.53	0.02
		A	32.27	31.06	87.82	8.61	3.54

Abbreviations: N = Total Number and A = Total area of the land holdings for various sizes.

Source: *Agricultural Census*, 1985 - 86.

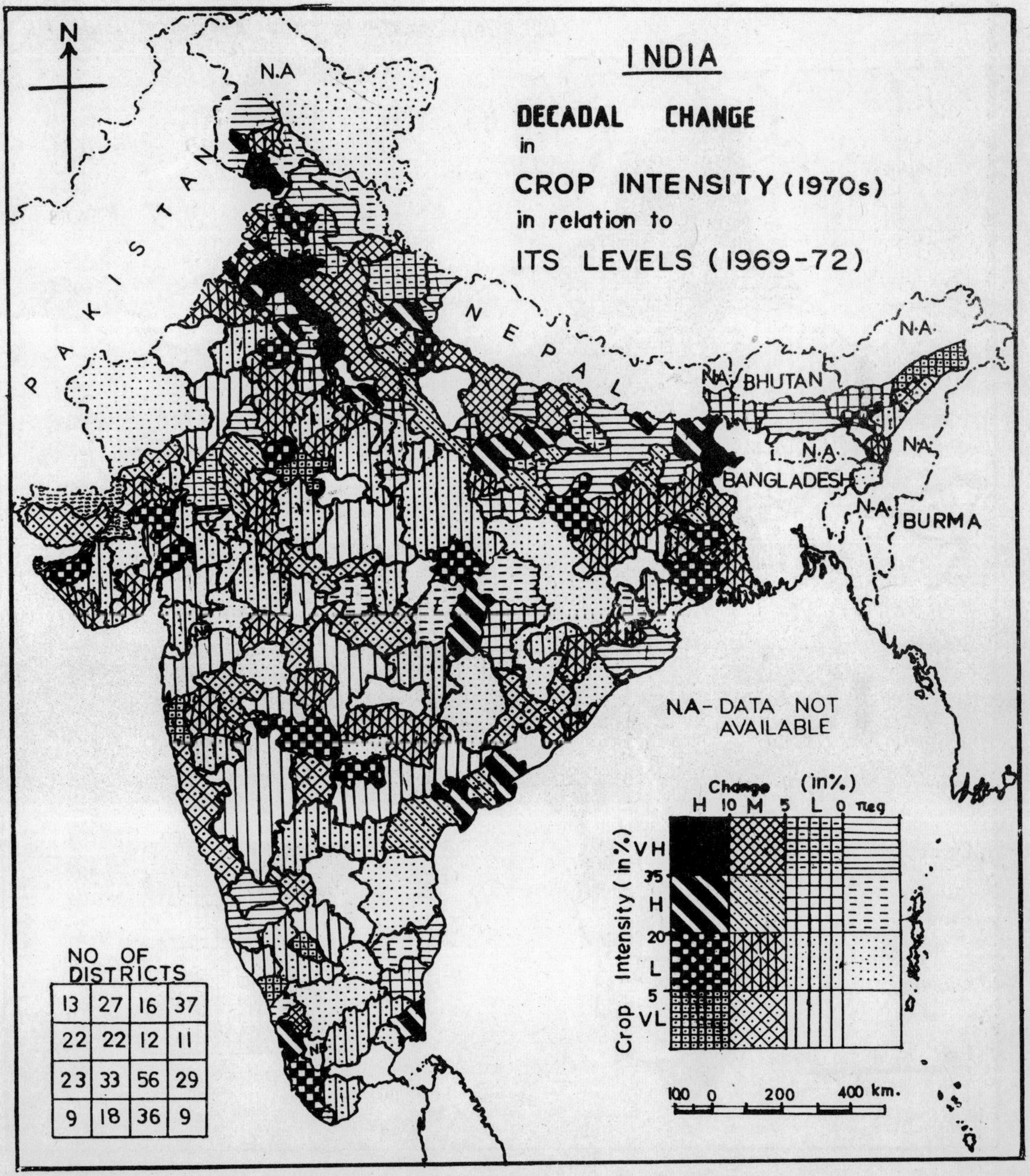
INDIA
DECADAL CHANGE
in
CROP INTENSITY (1970s)
in relation to
ITS LEVELS (1969-72)
N
PAKISTAN
NEPAL
BHUTAN
BANGLADESH
BURMA
N.A
NA - DATA NOT AVAILABLE
Change (in%)
H 10 M 5 L 0 neg
Crop Intensity (in%)
VH
35
H
20
L
5
VL
NO OF DISTRICTS
13 27 16 37
22 22 12 11
23 33 56 29
9 18 36 9
100 0 200 400 km.

Fig.- 3.6

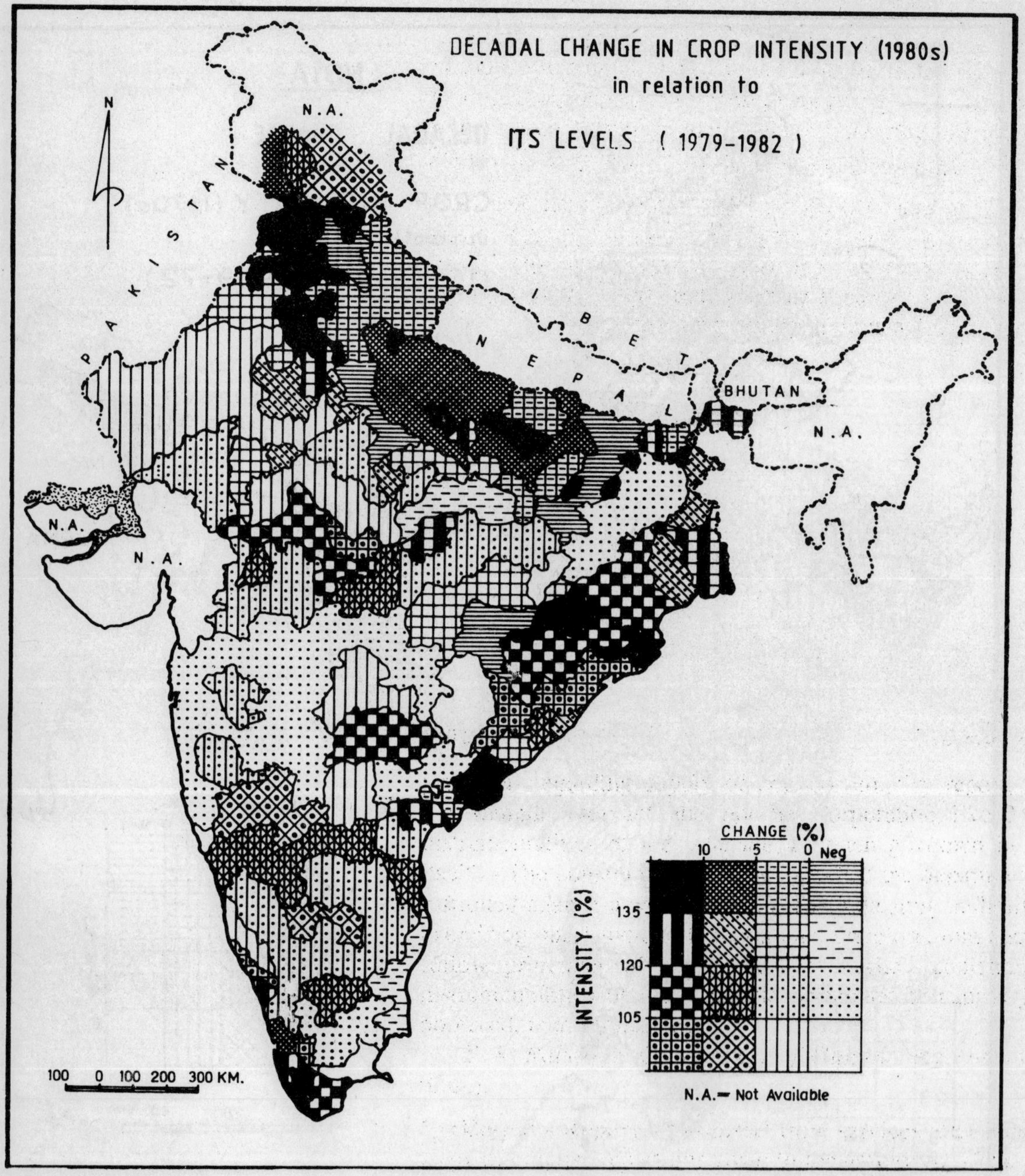
DECADAL CHANGE IN CROP INTENSITY (1980s)
in relation to
ITS LEVELS (1979-1982)
N
PAKISTAN
TIBET
NEPAL
BHUTAN
N.A.
N.A.
N.A.
N.A.
CHANGE (%)
10
5
0
Neg
INTENSITY (%)
135
120
105
N.A.— Not Available
100 0 100 200 300 KM.

Fig.- 3.7

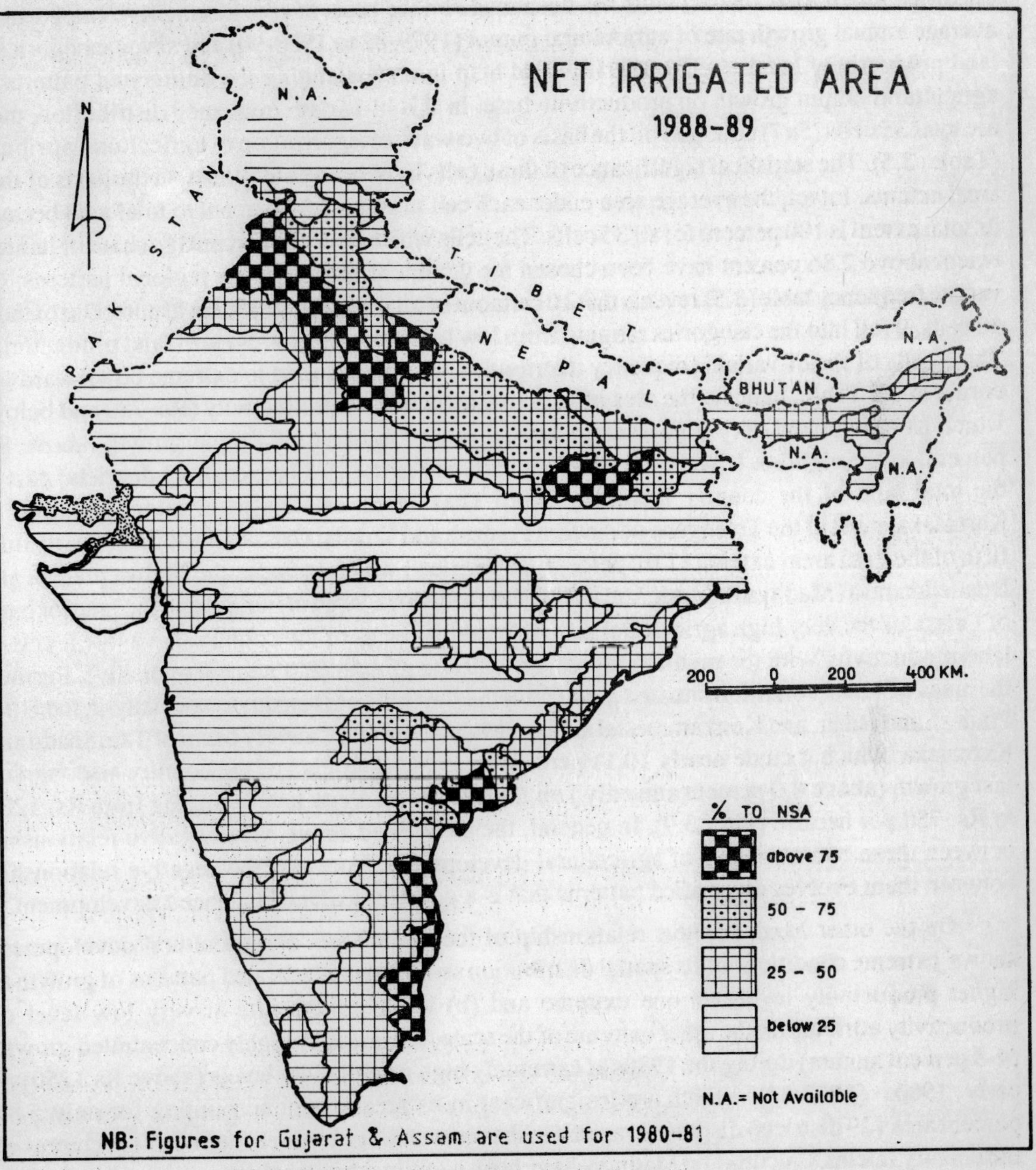
NET IRRIGATED AREA
1988-89
N
N.A.
PAKISTAN
TIBET
NEPAL
BHUTAN
N.A.
N.A.
N.A.
200 0 200 400 KM.
% TO NSA
above 75
50 - 75
25 - 50
below 25
N.A.= Not Available
NB: Figures for Gujarat & Assam are used for 1980-81

Fig. 3.8

To study the growth - productivity relationship in its spatial perspective, a cross-classification of total district units has been made on the basis of considering five categories of average annual growth rate of agricultural output (1979-82 to 1988-90) and seven categories of land productivity levels (1979-82). It would help in understanding the obliterated patterns of agricultural output growth on productivity base. In this bi-variate frequency distribution, there are total 35 cells (5x7) emerged on the basis of two ways categorization of agricultural attributes (Table- 3.5). The statistical significance of these cells have been determined on the basis of their areal extents. Infact, the average area under each cell must be 2.86 percent to total area because its total extent is 100 percent for all 35 cells. The cells which have the percentage share of its areal extent above 2.86 percent have been chosen for the interpretation of the regional patterns. Bi-variate frequency table (3.5) reveals that 10 cells out of total 35 are significant to note. Out of these 10 cells, 9 fall into the categories ranging from low to extremely low levels of land productivity. The 3 cells of the bi-variate frequency distribution which are suited to extreme down ward left corner in the Table, indicate the area of very low level of land productivity (Rs. 750 and below) which have high and very high average annual rate of agricultural output growth (above 8.0 percent) in the eighties. It accounts for more than one-fifth (21.37 percent; 48 districts) part of the total land of the country including entire Thar desert of Rajasthan, interior plateau of Karnataka, most of the Telengana of Andhra Pradesh and Coastal Orissa. In addition, nearly one-fifth of the total areal extent (17.01 percent; 46 districts) which includes the Malwa plateau and Bundelkhand of Madhya Pradesh, Vidarbha of Maharashtra, Arawali ranges and the interior parts of Orissa of the very high agricultural growth potential areas of the country, have low levels of land productivity with the medium rate of agricultural growth (8-4 percent annually). Further, the areas of *terai* condition situated along with the foot hills of Himalayas specially in the Uttar Pradesh and Bihar, and Konkan coastal areas of Maharastra and Cauvery basin of Tamilnadu and Karnataka which include nearly 10.11 percent areas (43 districts) of the country also marked fast growth (above 8.0 percent annually) on the low productivity levels ranging from Rs. 1250 to Rs. 750 per hectare (Fig.- 3.9). In general, the areas cited above have negative relationship between these two attributes of agricultural development. Note that the negative relationship between them evolves diversified patterns that is a good indicator of balanced development.

On the other hand, positive relationship of these attributes of agricultural development shows extreme conditions of its spatial distribution scale :(a) concentrated patterns of growth at higher productivity levels on one extreme and (b) weak growth rate at very low level of productivity attribute on the other extreme of the scale. The areas of highly concentrated growth (4-8 percent annum) during the 1980s at extremely high productivity levels (above Rs 1250) of early 1980s (1979-82), which are insignificant in its areal extent accounting for only 5.84 percent area (29 districts) dispersed mainly in the surroundings of three metropolitan centres of the country (Delhi, Calcutta and Madras), have been evolving through the forces of urbanization, increasing food demand of ever increasing population pressure, agricultural commercialisation and productivity augmenting practices through diffusion of agricultural innovations and better availability of transport facilities from these main centres to their peripheral areas. Thus, the validity of growth centres approach of agricultural development is found significant in these concentrated agricultural patterns (Hagen 1975, pp.198- 202). At the opposite end of the positive growth-productivity relationships, the areas of low and even negative growth (below 4 percent) with very low productivity (below Rs 750) are incorporated. It includes one- seventh part of the total land (14.58 percent; 41 districts) mainly dispersed in the central Deccan plateau of the arid conditions (Rayalseema division of Andhra Pradesh, interior Karnataka plateau and the central longitudinal part ofMadhya Pradesh).They are still backward in connection with agricultural growth- productivity patterns (Fig.- 3.9).

It has generally been observed that a significant change has taken place in the spatial pattern of growth- productivity relationship from its concentrated patterns of the seventies to diversified ones evolving during the eighties. The validity of the facts can empirically be tested by comprising the results produced by Bhalla and Tyagi (1989, pp.133-153) specially for 1960s and 1970s. On the basis of Tables 4.15 to 4.21 prepared by Bhalla and Tyagi in understanding the structural features of development of Indian agriculture and Table-3.5 of the present text, the following salient features of evolving spatial patterns of agricultural development may be marked.

Table- 3.5: Bi-variate Frequency of the Percentage Share of Area and Number of Districts of Productivity Level(1979-82) and Output Growth (1979-82 to 1988-90).

Productivity Classes (Rs/ha)	Average Annual Growth Rate (in percent)					Total
	12-< (VH)	12-8 (H)	8-4 (M)	4-0 (L)	0-> (neg)	
1750- <	1.98	1.26	3.26	2.58	1.66	10.74
(EH)	(10)	(9)	(16)	(13)	(13)	(61)
1750- 1500	1.30	0.08	1.52	1.08	0.94	4.92
(VH)	(5)	(1)	(5)	(4)	(6)	(21)
1500- 1250	0.62	1.51	1.70	0.82	1.87	6.52
(H)	(5)	(8)	(9)	(4)	(11)	(37)
1250- 1000	2.45	2.47	2.63	1.01	2.55	11.11
(M)	(11)	(14)	(12)	(4)	(9)	(50)
1000- 750	2.76	2.43	3.51	2.53	2.80	14.02
(L)	(9)	(9)	(12)	(10)	(10)	(50)
750- 500	5.89	5.98	9.02	7.06	3.12	31.08
(VL)	(13)	(17)	(24)	(22)	(9)	(85)
500- >	9.50	1.23	4.46	4.40	2.01	21.60
(EL)	(18)	(2)	(10)	(10)	(6)	(46)
Total	**24.50**	**14.96**	**26.09**	**19.48**	**14.96**	**99.99**
	(71)	**(60)**	**(88)**	**(67)**	**(64)**	**(350)**

N.B. Figures in parentheses denote number of districts in each category.

Abbreviations : EH= Extremely High, VH= Very High, H= High, M= Medium, L= Low, VL= Very Low, EL=Extremely Low, and neg= negative growth rate.

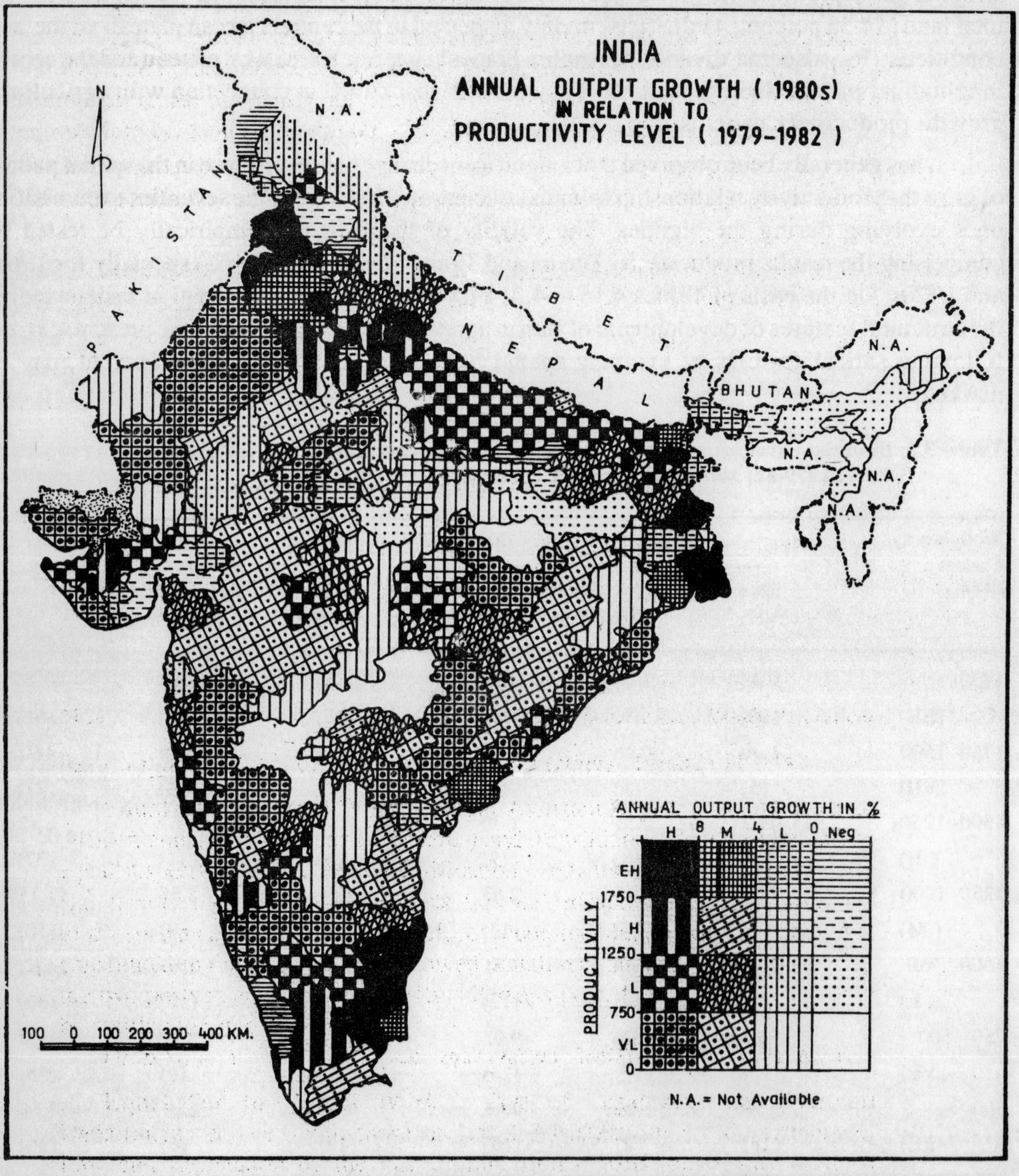
INDIA
ANNUAL OUTPUT GROWTH (1980s)
IN RELATION TO
PRODUCTIVITY LEVEL (1979-1982)
N
N.A.
PAKISTAN
TIBET
NEPAL
BHUTAN
N.A.
N.A.
N.A.
N.A.
100 0 100 200 300 400 KM.
ANNUAL OUTPUT GROWTH IN %
H 8 M 4 L 0 Neg
PRODUCTIVITY
EH
1750
H
1250
L
750
VL
0
N.A. = Not Available

Fig.. -3.9

(1) Of course, higher degree of positive relationship between agricultural development attributes indicates concentration and their inverse relationship denotes diversification its regional patterns. The degree of correlation between agricultural growth and land productivity has been recorded to be significantly high (r =.671) in the sixties, lower (r = .325) in the seventies and very low and insignificant (r = .109) during the eighties. Decreasing degree of relationship over time leads to a conclusion that the concentrated regional pattern of agricultural development has been weakening and transforming into diversified ones. It is a healthy symptom of balanced development. The distribution map which shows the regional patterns established on the basis of agricultural attributes (Fig.-3.9) examines the validity of the same facts.

(2) The concentrated regional patterns of growth productivity attributes have been highly 'area-specific' particularly during the sixties and seventies (Mohapatra 1982, pp.220-43), when two areas of the great plains of India : (i) the peripheral areas of Delhi metropolitan (Punjab-Haryana- Western Uttar Pradesh), and (ii) surrounding areas of Calcutta centre (lower parts of West Bengal), have emerged as the core-regions of strong agricultural growth-productivity relations.

(3) The reasons behind the fast emergence of these areas of concentrated patterns are obvious. They have been 'crop-specific', i.e., wheat dominated cropping pattern. During the first phase of green revolution (the 1960s and 1970s), there has been marked substantial increase in wheat - yield which rose nearly 60.0 percent from 8.87 quintal per hectare to 14.0 quintal per hectare and, in wheat-area, it increased by 59.27 percent from 12.84 to 20.45 million hectare during the successive period of ten years (1965-66 to 1975-76). Very high rate of wheat-yield and its areal expansion might have been recorded particularly in the core-areas of concentrated patterns (Punjab- Haryana- Western Uttar Pradesh). It happened on account of three main reasons: use of HYVs of wheat seeds (e.g., Mexican and newly developed Indian varieties like Sonalika 1553, Sona 1593, Hira, K-68), subsidised low costs of chemical fertilizers and cheaper electricity rates for irrigation, and rise in the procurement price of wheat particularly in the states of Punjab and Haryana; it increased by 38.16 percent from Rs. 76 per quintal to Rs. 105 per quintal (as recommended by the Agriculture Price Commission).

(4) The evolving features of Indian agriculture have been generalised by comparing the results produced by agricultural intensification tables (Table- 3.6 & 3.7). These tables explain the facts that, in the first phase of agricultural development (1969-72 to 1979-82), the productivity levels in India as a whole have been raised by 2.12 percent per annum (from Rs. 936 to Rs. 1135 per hectare) by increasing average annual rate of 13.0 percent in fertilizer consumption, 4.1 percent in the number of tractors and 4.3 percent in irrigation pump sets per areal unit of cultivated land. Infact, the production processes have not been operated economically when rate of input intensification has been recorded higher than the rate of productivity increase. But, in the second phase of agricultural development after green revolution (1979-82 to 1988-90), the average annual rate of increase of these inputs have been recorded comparatively lower as 3.4 percent for the use of chemical fertilizer intensity, 3.7 percent for number of tractors and 1.7 percent for irrigation pump sets per areal unit. However, these rates of input increase have still been recorded higher than the rate of productivity increase (i.e., 3.35 percent per annum) during the same period.

It may be concluded here that land productivity has been marked increasing with its increasing rate in the two decades of agricultural development, while inputs are being intensified with their diminishing rates (Tables -3.6 & 3.7). It means that the agricultural production increase is not only the function of intensification of modern technological inputs but also due to its proper utilization over space. Therefore, there seems a gradual change in the regional patterns of land productivity. During the first phase of development (the 1970s), productivity patterns have been observed concentrated with its fast increase (.20 percent annually) in the areas falling under the categories of high and very high productivity levels and, on the other hand, rapid decrease in productivity levels (about 3.0 percent per annum) especially in the areas of low and extremely low productivity classes. Note that these patterns have marginally diversified during the second phase of development (in the 1980s) by shifting the rate of productivity increase from high and very high productivity areas to the medium productivity level areas (Table- 3.2). There are three main reasons behind the areal shift of agricultural intensification observed in the land productivity patterns:

(a) The law of diminishing marginal return to input intensification is operative in the all developing agricultural economies (Miller 1966, Kata 1990, pp.5-18). As a result, in the areas of high productivity, the farming practices become less profitable and, consequently, the application of modern technology should shift from the areas of high productivity to low and then to extremely low productivity areas. The empirical evidences given in Table- 3.2 also confirm the same facts. For instance, the marginal annual increase in the use of chemical fertilizers (2.0 to 4.0 percent) and irrigation pumpsets (1.0 to 3.0 percent) and fast decrease in the annual rate of number of tractors per areal unit in the areas of high and very high productivity on one hand and, the higher rate of increase of these input intensities in the areas of low and very low productivity classes, on the other hand, have been observed during the second phase of agricultural development in India (1979-82 to 1988-90) (Table -3.7).

(b) The second reason of diversified productivity pattern is related to the initiatives taken by Planning Commission, New Delhi to pursue the agricultural growth especially in the backward areas where agricultural growth potentials are sufficient to use. During the period of last 10 years, Planning Commission has laid emphasis on regional aspects of agricultural development through formulating and implementing the concept of agro-climatic regions for 'area specific' strategy of balanced development (Planning Commission 1987,1989).

(c) The poly-cyclic landscape of agricultural development which has been pursuaded by the diffusion processes of agricultural innovations accelerated through and 'spread' of these innovations occurred from main central places and growth centres of the areas (Hagrestrand 1973/74, Carlstein 1977) are also expanding areal boundaries of high productivity patterns with occurring the changes in the growth and productivity relationships. The centre -dependent agricultural development patterns which are based on the Perroux (1955) hypothesis and Myrdal's (1957) thesis of 'spread' and 'backwash effects', expand in the concentric zones from the growth points. Therefore, greater efficiency of agriculture in the hinterlands of these centres is a striking feature of agricultural development forms (Fig.- 3.3). But changes in growth-productivity relationship patterns might be breaking up the norms and patterns of labour -

productivity with creating many and varied problems of labour - employment and labour wage differentials, which should be analysed separately in the following manner.

Table - 3.6 : Intensification of Agricultural Technology in Various Land Productivity Categories.

Productivity Classes (Rs./ha)	Fertilizer Consumption (kg/ha)			No. of tractors (per ,000 ha.)			Pumpsets (per , 000 ha.)		
	70	80	90	70	80	90	70	80	90
1750- <	68.80	116.37	143.39	6.93	6.14	6.11	68.32	96.69	111.32
1750-1500	47.26	89.17	103.28	4.41	3.24	3.12	65.37	75.29	93.31
1500-1250	32.82	55.36	73.23	2.09	2.30	2.35	49.97	53.70	68.59
1250-1000	20.85	43.30	61.39	1.53	1.58	1.63	27.85	31.56	39.63
1000- 750	17.07	26.26	32.51	1.06	1.28	1.48	14.21	29.52	32.52
750- 500	10.96	19.41	18.30	0.78	0.84	1.03	18.98	22.65	29.31
500- >	8.04	7.67	6.73	0.40	0.83	0.99	15.84	15.90	16.20
Total	**19.18**	**44.13**	**56.12**	**1.44**	**2.03**	**2.63**	**25.56**	**36.59**	**41.59**

Abbreviations: 70 = 1969-72, 80 - 1979 82, 90 = 1988-90.

Source : Statistics for the early 1970s and 1980s are compiled from Bhalla & Tyagi (1989), Appendix 4 B & C.

Table - 3.7: Average Annual Change in Agricultural Technological Inputsin Various Land Productivity Categories.

Productivity Classes (Rs./ha)	Annual Average Change (in percent) in: Fertilizer Consumption (kg/ha)			No. of tractors (per ,000 ha.)			Pumpsets (per , 000 ha.)		
	70	80	90	70	80	90	70	80	90
1750- <	6.91	2.90	6.00	-1.14	-0.06	-0.65	4.15	1.89	3.49
1750-1500	8.86	2.03	6.58	-2.65	-0.46	-1.62	1.52	2.99	2.37
1500-1250	6.87	4.05	6.84	1.00	0.27	0.69	0.75	3.47	2.07
1250-1000	10.76	5.21	10.80	0.33	0.39	0.36	1.33	3.20	2.35
1000- 750	5.38	3.03	5.02	2.07	1.95	2.20	10.77	1.27	7.18
750- 500	7.71	-0.71	3.72	0.77	2.83	1.78	1.93	3.67	3.02
500- >	0.46	-1.53	-0.90	10.75	2.41	8.19	0.03	0.02	0.13
Total	13.01	3.43	10.70	4.10	3.69	4.59	4.31	1.72	3.48

Abbreviations: 70 = 1969-72, 80 = 1979-82, 90 = 1988-90.

Source : Statistics for the early 1970s and 1980s are compiled from Bhalla & Tyagi (1989), Appendix 4 B & C.

(E) Agricultural Labour Productivity

Since income, daily wages and standard of living of the agricultural population are determined by the output per agricultural worker, it is worthwhile to interpret the inter - regional pattern of agricultural labour productivity (Bhalla and Tyagi 1989, pp.38-43). Labour absorption capacity of agricultural sector may also be assessed to study the changing patterns of agricultural labour productivity. In a country like India where the conditions of unlimited supply of labour prevail in the agricultural production processes, it is obvious to study the agricultural workforce in relation to agricultural output. It has already been discussed that labour productivity is the product of two major attributes of agricultural production system: land productivity and land-labour ratio (eqn. 1.5). Increase in output per worker will, therefore, depend not only on factors influencing the land productivity but also on the increase in the size of farm labour. The rate and direction of change in the size of agricultural workforce and land holdings are obviously the important determinants of the changes occurring in agricultural labour productivity (Johnston 1980, p.227). Infact, various socially determined factors like relative prices of agricultural production and input costs are also important for determining labour productivity (Johnston and Kilby 1975, p.391) (Fig.- 3.10).

So far as increase in agricultural labour productivity is concerned, it is obvious from the data that, inspite of 2.98 percent annual average increase in land productivity in the 1980s (from Rs.1135 per hectare in1979-82 to Rs.1439 in 1988-90 as described in the earlier section of this chapter) which is the main attribute of labour productivity, the annual average rate of increase in agricultural output per worker has been recorded very low, i.e., 0.174 percent only during the same period (see foot note of Table- 3.9). The labour productivity was marked Rs.1090 per worker in 1981 and Rs.1109 in 1991. It means the second attribute of labour productivity (i.e., land- labour ratio) directly or indirectly stabilizes its increase.

On account of very fast increase in total agricultural work force recorded at 2.52 percent per annum from 14.81 million in 1981 to 18.52 million persons in 1991 (Table - 3.8) and negligible increase in the cultivated land (NSA plus fallow land) recorded to be .055 percent per annum from 165.14 million hectare in 1981-2 to 165.78 million hectare in 1987-8, the land - labour ratio, a major attribute of labour productivity, diminishes and hence, the labour productivity rises marginally. State-wise figures of the increase in agricultural labour force (Table- 3.8) show that Rajasthan, West Bengal and Bihar are noticeable for very fast increase of agricultural work force with 3.35, 2.82, and 2.60 percents per annum respectively. The fast increase in these states may be attributed to fast growth of total main workers and its increasing proportionate shares in agricultural activities (Table- 3.8).

Direct effects of land- labour ratio on areal patterns of labour productivity are clearly observed. These facts may also be examined by comparing distribution maps of land productivity (output per hectare) and labour productivity (output per worker). Areal classification of total districts into six semi - interval productivity classes for 1981 and 1991 (Table- 3.9), which demarcates the homogeneous inter - regional patterns of labour productivity, reveals itsstructural features. In general, labour productivity patterns are more or less similar to the patterns of land productivity (compare Figs.-3.11 A and B). The entire peninsular India

Table- 3.8: Total Agricultural Work Force, its growth and Agricultural Labourer - Cultivators Ratio.

(Workers in ,000 persons, Growth 1981-91)

	States		Total Main Workers		Total Agricultural Work Force*		% Share of Ag.Work Force		Agricultural Labourers per 1000 of Cultivators
			Total	Decadal growth%	Total	Decadal growth %	Total (%)	Decadal Variation	
1.	A.P.	1981	22,629		15,733		69.53		
		1991	28,393	25.3	19,454	23.6	68.52	-1.01	1469
2.	Ass	1981	NA		NA		NA		
		1991	7,068	-	4,533	-	64.13	-	252
3.	Bih	1981	20,753		16,409		79.07		
		1991	25,653	23.6	20,680	26.0	80.61	1.54	857
4.	Guj	1981	10,984		6,603		60.12		
		1991	14,109	28.4	7,964	20.6	56.45	-3.67	686
5.	Har	1981	3,664		2,227		60.78		
		1991	4,588	25.2	2,703	21.4	58.91	-1.87	496
6.	H.P.	1981	1,471		1,042		70.80		
		1991	1,729	17.5	1,188	14.0	68.71	-2.09	54
7.	J&K.	1981	1,769		1,097		-		
		1991	NA	-	NA	-	-	-	-
8.	Kar	1981	13,651		8,877		65.03		
		1991	17,244	26.3	10,881	22.6	63.10	-1.93	837
9.	Ker	1981	6,791		2,805		41.30		
		1991	8,197	20.7	3,117	11.1	38.03	-3.27	2074
10.	M.P.	1981	20,041		15,272		76.20		
		1991	24,959	24.5	18,811	23.2	75.37	-0.83	453
11.	Maha	1981	24,302		15,007		61.75		
		1991	30,887	27.1	18,445	22.9	59.72	-2.03	820
12.	Ori	1981	8,635		6,450		74.70		
		1991	10,306	19.3	7,530	16.7	73.06	-1.64	652
13.	Pun	1981	4,928		2,859		58.03		
		1991	6,036	22.5	3,389	18.5	56.15	-1.88	710
14.	Raj	1981	10,442		7,196		68.91		
		1991	13,861	32.7	9,608	33.5	69.32	0.41	171
15.	T.N.	1981	19,026		11,597		60.95		
		1991	22,972	20.7	13,575	17.1	59.09	-1.86	1369
16.	U.P.	1981	32,397		24,135		74.50		
		1991	41,342	27.6	29,798	23.5	72.07	-2.43	364
17.	W.B.	1981	15,424		8,482		54.99		
		1991	20,530	33.1	10,872	28.2	52.96	-2.03	863
	All	**1981**	**222,516**		**148,023**		**66.52**		
	India+	**1991**	**285,423**	**28.3**	**185,238**	**25.2**	**64.90**	**-1.62**	**675**

N.B.: * It includes cultivators and agricultural labourers. + It excludes J.& K. for 1991 and Assam for 1981 where censuses were not been held. NA = Data Not Available.

Source: Census of India, 1981, series 1, *General Economic Tables,* part IIIA(i), and Census of India, 1991, series 1, *Provisional Population Table,* paper -3 of 1991.

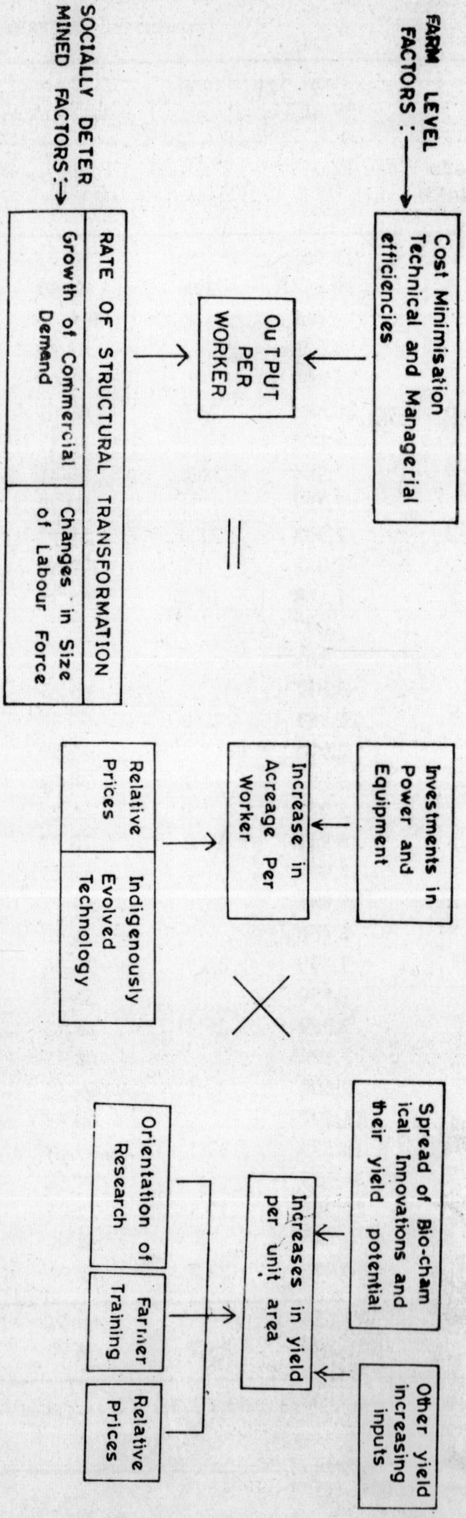

Fig.- 3.10 : Principal Factors Influencing Changes in Agricultural Productivity (After Jonston & Kilby 1975, p.391)

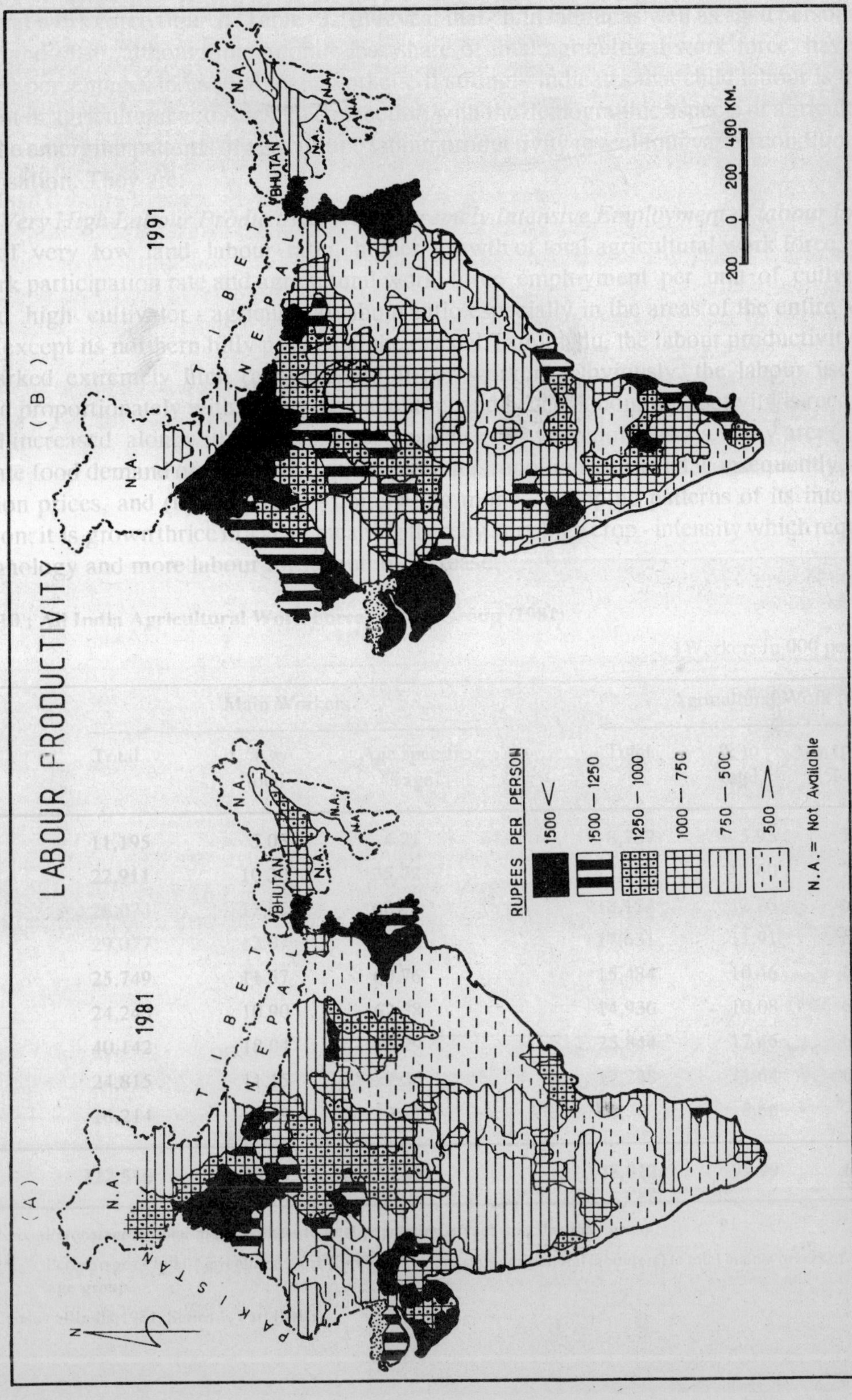
LABOUR PRODUCTIVITY
(A)
1981
(B)
1991
TIBET
NEPAL
BHUTAN
PAKISTAN
N.A.
RUPEES PER PERSON
1500 <
1500 — 1250
1250 — 1000
1000 — 75C
750 — 50C
500 >
N.A. = Not Available
200 0 200 400 KM.
N

Fig.- 3.11 A & B

including Thar desert of Rajasthan, large parts of eastern Bihar and entire Brahmaputra valley of Assam have been identified as the areas of very low and extremely low levels of labour productivity (below Rs.1000 per worker) in the early 1980s (Fig.- 3.11 A). There has been, of course, a gradual areal shift in the areas of low levels of agricultural labour productivity patterns during 1981 to 1991. Low productivity areas which accounted for two - thirds of the country's land has been reduced by nearly 7.0 percent in the 1980s (Table -3.9). It has been on account of increase in the labour productivity especially in the low productivity areas of entire Thar desert of the Rajasthan (from Ganganagar district to Bikaner of the boarder district) and the longitudinal coastal plains of Tamilnadu which incorporate the districts of North and South Arcot, Thanjavur and Ramanathpuram. The labour productivity in these areas might have increased because of intensification of green revolution technology rather than improvement of land - labour ratio which has been declining over time on account of increasing burden of agricultural labour force. Thus, the conditions of unlimited supply of labour as proposed by Lewis (1954) is applicable in the operation of agricultural production processes in India. Of course, the age - specific

Table-3.9: Percentage Share of Area in the various Categories of Labour Productivity in Agriculture (1981 and 1991).

(Area in sq.km)

	Productivity Categories	1981		1991		Decadal Variation	
		Area	%	Area	%	Area	%
1.	Extremely High (Rs.1500 <)	418,181 (47)	14.39	606,681 (68)	20.87	188,500	6.48
2.	Very High (1500 -1250)	169,780 (17)	5.84	329,540 (29)	11.34	159,760	5.50
3.	High (1250-1000)	401,418 (45)	13.81	277,232 (37)	9.54	-1241,186	-4.27
4.	Low (1000-750)	372,839 (45)	12.83	480,070 (58)	16.52	107,231	3.69
5.	Very Low (750-500)	810,782 (99)	27.90	724,263 (91)	24.92	- 86,519	-2.98
6.	Extremely Low (500- >)	732,993 (98)	25.22	488,207 (66)	16.80	-244,786	-8.42
	Total	2905,993 (351)	99.99	2905,993 (351)	99.99	—	—

N.B.: (i) The decadal increase in the national average of labour productivity which has been recorded 1.74 percent from Rs.1090 (1981) to Rs.1109 (1991), is calculated by taking into account total Agricultural work force of the country.

(ii) The figures in parentheses show the number of the districts in each category.

agricultural work force figures (Table -3.10) reveal that child labour as well as aged persons (0-19 years and 60+), although incorporate less share of total agricultural work force, have the noticeable percentages to its total main workers. It strongly indicates that child labour is fairly prominent in agricultural activities. In connection with the demographic aspects of agricultural labour, the emerging patterns of agricultural labour productivity reveal four varied conditions of its stabilisation. They are:

(a) Very High Labour Productivity with Extremely Intensive Employment of labour force: Inspite of very low land- labour ratio, higher growth of total agricultural work force, very high work participation rate and agricultural work force employment per unit of cultivated land and high cultivator - agricultural labour ratio especially in the areas of the entire West Bengal (except its northern hilly parts) and the coastal Tamilnadu, the labour productivity has been marked extremely high (above Rs.1500 per worker). Obviously, the labour use has increased proportionately with an increase in output and hence, labour productivity is recorded high and increased alongwith output increase because of two major reasons. They are: (a) the immediate food demand of the urban population of metropolitan cities and, consequently, high production prices, and (b) the paddy - dominating mono - cropping patterns of its intensive cultivation; it is grown thrice in a year, meaning thereby very high crop - intensity which requires less technology and more labour for its output increase.

Table -3.10 : All India Agricultural Work Force by Age Group (1981).

(Workers in 000 persons)

Age Group	Main Workers			Agricultural Work force		
	Total	% to total	Age specific %age*	Total	% to total	Age specific %age**
0 - 14	11,195	5.03	4.21	8,787	5.93	78.49
15 - 19	22,911	10.30	35.72	17,157	11.60	74.88
20 - 24	28,074	12.65	48.96	18,154	12.26	64.66
25 - 29	29,077	13.07	57.32	17,631	11.91	60.63
30 - 34	25,749	11.57	60.76	15,484	10.46	60.13
35 - 39	24,243	10.90	62.38	14,930	10.08	61.58
40 - 49	40,142	18.04	63.29	25,844	17.46	64.38
50 - 59	24,815	11.15	59.34	17,238	11.64	69.47
60 - +	16,214	7.29	3.71	12,740	8.66	78.57
Total	**222,516**	**99.99**	**33.40**	**148,022**	**99.99**	**66.52**

N.B.: * Percentage of total main workers to total population ofeach specific age - group.

** Percentage of total Agricultural work force (cultivators plus agricultural labourers) to total main workers of pecific age-group.

Source : Census of India,1981, Series 1, Part IIIA(i).

(b) Very high Labour Productivity with Intensive Use of Green Revolution technology: The areas of the Punjab, Haryana and Western Uttar Pradesh (which incorporate the fertile tracts of the Upper Ganga valley, especially Ganga- Jamuna *doab* and Rohilkhand of Uttar Pradesh and Sutlej - Ghaghar basins of Punjab and Haryana) where percentage share of agricultural work force is lesser than that of the national average because of significant occupational shift from agriculture sector to non - agricultural sectors, lower value of cultivation - agricultural labourer (agriculture labour per cultivator), less concentration of size of land holdings, better labour - wage conditions, higher output growth with diversified cropping - patterns, the commercialisation in agricultural practices through intensive irrigation and bio- chemical technology are the peculiar conditions of labour productivity increase. Land - labour ratio is very high in these areas. The fertile desert of Rajasthan and the Kutch - Kathiawar areas of Gujarat of high labour productivity where the same conditions of agricultural labour force prevail, may also be included in the same category.

(c) Low and Very Low Labour Productivity with Stagnant Labour conditions: The entire northern Bihar (middle Ganga valley of the fertile soils), coastal Orissa and Andhra Pradesh (Koromandal areas), the Kerala state of coconut and cardamom cultivation (Malabar coastal areas) and the middle and western parts of the Assam state (middle Brahmaputra valley of fertile land) where, inspite of very high land productivity during early 1980s as agricultural output is recorded above Rs.1500 per hectare of NSA (Fig.-3.2), the labour productivity has been assessed very low and somewhere extremely low as below Rs.750 per agricultural worker (Fig.-3.11). It means that the second component of agricultural labour productivity, i.e., land - labour ratio (see eqn. 1.5) is very weak in these areas. The low value of this component may be due to prevailing conditions of very high density and fast growth of population. Therefore, there is the demographic pressure on cultivated land. High percentage share of total work force engaged in agricultural activities (more than 75 percent in 1991) with its increasing proportions (specially in Bihar as 1.54 percent during the 1990s), very high labour intensity (above 200 persons per 100 hectare of NSA) with high agricultural labour - cultivator ratio (above 1300 labour per 100 cultivators in 1991), and insignificant shift in the occupational structure from agriculture to non agricultural activities have been recorded in these areas of low labour productivity except Kerala state where low productivity is recorded because of non - inclusion of commercial crops of the state in calculating agricultural output (Table- 3.8 and Fig.- 3.11).

(d) Very Low Labour Productivity with Diversified Labour conditions: In entire central parts of the Deccan plateau, the conditions of very low and even in some areas extremely low labour productivity (below Rs.750 per worker) prevail. These areas incorporate nearly one - third part of the country including the areas of: (i) the Vidarbha and Marathwada regions of interior Maharastra, the most backward areas because of wide spread deforestation, heavy soil erosion and low level of agricultural productivity (Monte 1992); (ii) the interior parts of Karnataka where rugged topographic and arid climatic conditions stabilize the level of agricultural productivity, diversify the cropping patterns, and compel the labour to migrate toward cities; (iii) Telengana of the interior Andhra Pradesh (former state of Hyderabad) where backwardness and low level of labour productivity prevail due to concentration of all industries and infra - structure only in and around the twin cities of Hyderabad and Secunderabad (NCAER 1962, Ramanathan

1959); (iv) the Malwa plateau including central parts of Madhya Pradesh where crop intensity as well as agricultural productivity is recorded low because of diversified labour structure; and (v) most parts of the Chotanagpur plateau (North - Eastern foreland of the Deccan) which incorporates the areas of south Bihar, interior Orissa and eastern Madhya Pradesh - the tribal dominated and backward areas with very low level of agricultural productivity (Fig.-3.11 A & B). The diversified agricultural and demographic conditions of these areas influence the patterns of labour productivity and destabilise them. Inspite of low and very low intensity of agricultural work force (below 150 persons per 100 hectare of NSA, for detail see Fig.- 3.12), a reciprocal attribute of land- labour ratio, has a negative influence on labour productivity, and hence, labour productivity has been recorded very low in these areas. It may be because of two major reasons: (i) the low and very low levels of land productivity (below Rs. 1000 per hectare, see Fig.- 3.3) because of diversified cropping patterns in these semi- arid climatic conditions and

Table-3.11:Number of Districts by the categories of Proportion of Agricultural Workers (Cultivators & Agricultural Labourers) of Male Main Workers in Rural Areas (1991).

	States	Total No. of Districts	% of Agricultural Work force in Categories			
			<-70	70-80	80-90	>-90
1.	Andhra Pradesh	22*	-	20	2	-
2.	Assam	23	11	6	6	-
3.	Bihar	42	1	1	29	11
4.	Gujrat	19	7	10	2	-
5.	Haryana	16	5	8	3	-
6.	Himachal Pradesh	12	8	3	1	-
7.	Jammu & Kashmir	-	-	-	-	-
8.	Karnataka	20	5	2	13	-
9.	Kerala	14	14	-	-	-
10.	Madhya Pradesh	45	-	5	36	4
11.	Maharashtra	29*	8	8	13	-
12.	Orissa	13	-	6	7	-
13.	Punjab	12	4	4	4	-
14.	Rajasthan	27	2	11	14	-
15.	Tamilnadu	20*	10	6	4	-
16.	Uttar Pradesh	63	8	16	24	15
17.	West Bengal	16*	6	8	2	-
	All India**	**446**	**122**	**125**	**169**	**30**

N.B.: * The districts which are wholly urban have not been included. They are Hydrabad (A.P.), Greater Bombay (Maharastra), Madras (Tamilnadu), and Calcutta (W.B.).

** It excludes the 14 districts of Jammu & Kashmir state.

Source: Census of India, 1991, *Provisional Population Table*, Series 1, Paper-3 of 1991 (statement 5-9), p.43.

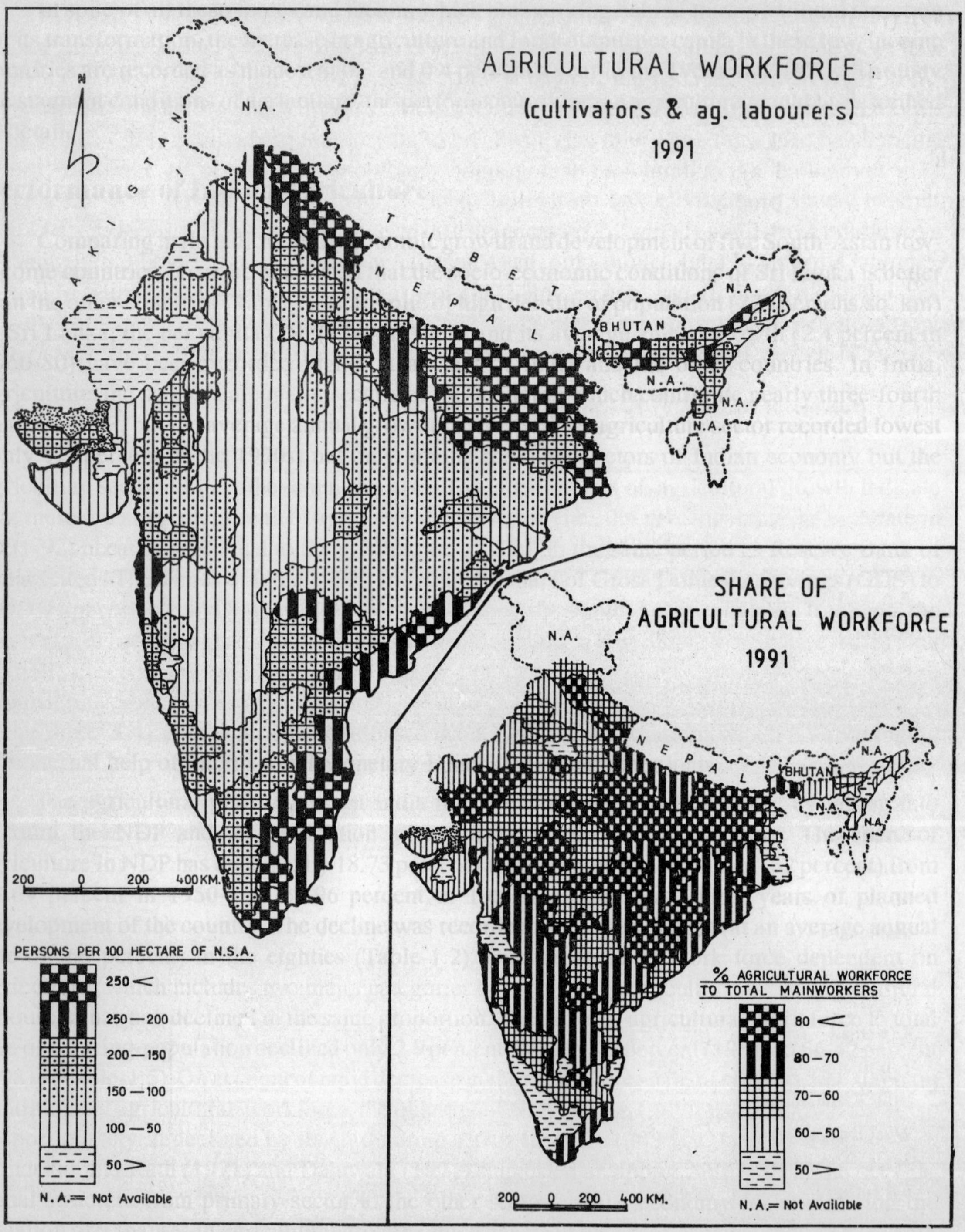
AGRICULTURAL WORKFORCE
(cultivators & ag. labourers)
1991
N
N.A.
PAKISTAN
TIBET
NEPAL
BHUTAN
N.A.
200 0 200 400 KM.
PERSONS PER 100 HECTARE OF N.S.A.
250 <
250—200
200—150
150—100
100—50
50 >
N.A.= Not Available
SHARE OF
AGRICULTURAL WORKFORCE
1991
% AGRICULTURAL WORKFORCE
TO TOTAL MAINWORKERS
80 <
80—70
70—60
60—50
50 >
200 0 200 400 KM.

Fig.-3.12

weak diffusion processes of agricultural innovations from the city centres to the surrounding rural areas, and (ii) stagnant conditions of agricultural labour force and static occupational shift as more than 80.0 percent share of total main workers are engaged in agricultural activities (Fig.-3.12 Inset). To support this fact, the districts are classified according to percentage share of agricultural work force of male main workers of rural areas (Table -3.11). It reveals that most of the districts of Bihar (40 out of 42), Madhya Pradesh (40 out of 45), 13 districts of interior Maharashtra, 7 of interior Orissa and 13 of interior Karnataka (Table -3.11) carry more than 80.0 percent agricultural work force of male rural workers. On account of abundant supply of labour force in agricultural activities, the labour wages in rural areas are very low and marginal productivity to labour input is stagnant at its low level. As a result, rural to urban migration can be observed everywhere in these areas of low labour productivity.

In the end, it can be said that the degree of the determinants of labour as well as land productivity indices and of agricultural growth index and their interactive nature can be studied with the help functional analysis for the distributive phenomena of development. It would help to understand the focal strategic points for proper persuasion of agricultural extension services.

Functional Analysis

The discussion in the preceding sections of this Chapter has been confined to the relevant characteristics and salient features of the patterns of land and labour productivity occurring in the regional agricultural production processes in India. The main factors and reasons behind the inter - regional variations of agricultural productivity are also important to interpret. But the validity testing of these production factors is a useful task to identify their priorities in order to search the principal determinants of the forms and patterns of agricultural production. Three major agricultural production components: land productivity, labour productivity and agricultural growth, have been considered for the purpose. The variables which are explaining spatial variations of these agricultural components are generated on the basis of some relevant hypotheses and interrelationships. The present discussion is persuaded towards three major directions of the functional analysis of agricultural production phenomena as (a) the generation of agricultural variables, (b) the generalisation of inter - related production attributes which would be interpreted with the help of 'correlation coefficient method' for finding the common characteristics of the phenomenal attributes (Pal 1968, Rao 1968, Singh 1988, p.86-96), and (c) the variables' effects and the explanation of spatial variances of agricultural components which would be described by step- wise multiple regression analysis of these explanatory variables.

(A) Generation of Variables and Hypotheses

Over all, twenty six variables depicting various characteristics of each and every areal unit (district) of the country were generated from the raw data provided by many and varied published and unpublished sources. Infact, the agricultural production processes form the complex nature of production attributes and are influenced by various geographical factors and forces. Therefore, the explanatory variables represents the group of agro- ecological attributes, infra-structural variables, socio - economic factors and demographic characteristics of the areal units. The rationale for selecting or generating these variables for the production components are discussed in the following manner.

So far as the explanatory variables for the spatial variations of land productivity component is concerned, the total thirteen variables are taken into account. Out of them, four variables: mean annual rainfall, potential- evapotranspiration, moisture index and soil fertility index, which are agro - ecological variables, were considered to show the effects of physical elements on agricultural productivity. These variables are interrelated themselves and control the optimal limits of agricultural production intensification (McCarty and Lendburg 1967). It is obvious from various studies that, in a tropical country like India, soil moisture and soil fertility are the crucial factors affecting directly agricultural production and land productivity (Sen 1975, Singh and Sharma 1985, pp. 5 - 200). Therefore, the positive relationship of land productivity is expected with these variables of agro - ecological characteristics. Seven variables are chosen to represent the agricultural characteristics related to intensification of agricultural production techniques. Four explanatory variables out of seven, namely, irrigation index (percentage share of Net Irrigated Area to NSA), irrigation intensity (Gross Irrigated Area per 100 unit of NIA), mechanization (tractors, agricultural machine tools, and other sowing and harvesting machine in value added term per areal unit) and the use of chemical fertilizers (the total quantity of N P_2O_5 and K_2O in Kgs per areal unit of NSA), are related to non- land capital inputs of agricultural productivity. In the induced agricultural innovations hypothesis of Binswanger and Rayan (1977, p.217) in which they asserted that, in semi- arid and semi- humid climatic conditions where soil moisture is available in limited quantity for growth, the irrigation makes a long run significant contribution to the expansion of agricultural production and crop - yield increase. The conditions of limited soil moisture availability is prevailing in more than three- fourth part of the country excluding Brahmaputra Valley of Assam, the lower parts of the Ganga Valley which includes most of the areas in West Bengal and the coastal plains of Eastern as well as Western Ghats. Therefore, irrigation and its intensity are the significant explanatory variables for land productivity increase. In addition, increased use of chemical fertilizer and machine tools (especially tractors which is multi - purpose tool for farmers for the irrigation, sowing, harvesting the crops and even for transportation of surplus production) are positively related to expansion of irrigated areas because of modern technological package of yield- augmenting techniques (Bhalla and Tyagi 1989, pp. 58-72). The validity of the same facts is stated by Johnston and Kilby (1975, chs. 6 & 8) in their hypothesis of yield - increasing innovations in which they stated that growth of farm productivity and income are overwhelmingly dependent on mechanical and biological-chemical innovations together with complementary investments on irrigation and drainage (Fig. 3.10). In countries such as Japan and Taiwan, engine - powered equipment became a major source of increase in productivity in the early stages of development and it contributed to realization of the yield potentials of High Yielding Varieties of seeds and expanded use of chemical fertilizers. In this context, it can be said that tractor has become a powerful tool for realization of the agricultural growth potentials through which two major processes of agricultural landuse, expansion and intensification, are accelerated for agricultural production growth and land productivity increase. Thus, these explanatory variables of modern agricultural technology might positively be related to land productivity index.

On account of labour intensive characteristic of Indian agricultural systems, agricultural labour and draught animal force per unit of cultivated land which are considered as labour inputs, are also important explanatory variables for interpreting spatial variations of land productivity. Infact, animals and agricultural workers have been engaging simultaneously in the operation of agricultural systems from the ancient times when Indian culture was totally based on agricultural activities and its transformation from *'cow- culture'* to *'plaugh- culture'* was made on the basis of intensive use of oxen together with man to increase agricultural production. As a result, density distribution of work- animals and agricultural labour force are positively related to each other. It is stated by Dayal (1984, p. 113) that there is no significant contribution of the density of agricultural workers and work animals to the spatial variance of land productivity in India where they contribute insignificantly only 3.0 and 1.0 percent of spatial variances respectively (see Table-4 of the Dayal's text). Therefore, density of work- animals is not considered here as an explanatory variable. Only density of agricultural worker is taken into account for further study.

Of course, farming intensity is the result of intensification of these factors of agricultural production. Intensity of cultivation clearly has a significant effect on the net income and agricultural output. It is also a reflection of intensity of labour use and farm size. Therefore, it has been considered as an explanatory variable by several writers (Bardhan 1973, Dayal 1984). The comparison of the distribution maps of land productivity and crop intensity (Figs.- 3.3 & 3.7) depicts that farming intensity is positively related to land productivity.

Further, two explanatory variables of land productivity are incorporated to reflect the economic characteristics of agricultural operations. They are : the average size of operational land holdings and agricultural labour wages. Infact, size of operational land holdings indirectly influences to the land productivity of an area. The degree of commercialisation in agriculture, which is to be positively associated with land productivity, has positive relationship with the size of land holdings especially in Indian conditions. As noticed earlier that the unit of land, if it is large in size, would produçe larger output because of greater application of modern technology and higher level of inputs per unit area with diversifying the cropping patterns of agricultural system. For example, the larger operational landholding size of Punjab and Haryana is one of the reasons of green revolution. On the other hand, low levels of land productivity are recorded in Bihar because of high population pressure, weak shifting tendencies in occupational structure from agricultural to non - agricultural activities and smaller size of land holdings in which the farm - technology is difficult to implement. Hence, a positive relationship is expected between land productivity and size of operational land holdings.

The economic theories of wage and employment suggest that there is a positive relationship between agricultural wages and land productivity (Hayami and Ruttan 1970). The reasons behind this relationship is obvious that, in the high - productivity areas, the former will get more profit through putting out the agricultural labour. But application of appropriate technology requires skill labour whose wages will be higher than the wages of unskilled labour force. The migration of labour from one part of the country to the others may also be seen because of wage - differentials and a real differentiations in the levels of land productivity. Obviously, these aspects of wage - differentials are more related to labour productivity which should be described in the next section. But it is important to note here that agricultural wages are highly correlated to urban population (r = .89) and hence deleted from the list of explanatory variables in the present context.

So far as generation of variables and its related hypotheses for explaining the spatial variations of agricultural labour productivity are concerned, the explanatory variables are chosen on the basis of considering the major components of labour productivity. Of course, the level of agricultural labour productivity is by definition determined by the output level and the number of agricultural workers employed to produce that output. Further, it is the product of two major components, namely, land productivity and land-labour ratio (eqn. 1.5). Because of limited scope for increasing land under cultivation which has already been discussed in the previous sections of the present Chapter, the agricultural output increase is wholly dependent on crop-yield augmenting technology and hence, the variables explaining the spatial variations of land productivity have much significance to explain the variability of labour productivity; it has already been discussed that land productivity is much stronger component of labour productivity and the patterns of land and labour productivity are more or less similar to each other (compare Figs. 3.3 and 3.11B). As a result, all thirteen variables discussed above are taken into account for the explanation of spatial variations of labour productivity. In addition, the seven variables which are closely related to the second component of agricultural labour productivity (land-labour ratio) have also been included in the present context. The two variables: agricultural workers per unit of cultivated land (i.e., labour input which has already been incorporated) and cultivated land per agricultural worker (which reflects land-labour ratio) are reciprocal to each other. However, cultivated land per agricultural worker (A/L in eqn. 1.5) is directly related to labour productivity. Hence it is expected that cultivated land per agricultural worker is positively related to labour productivity. On the contrary, the variable agricultural worker per unit of cultivated land (L/A by definition, eqn. 1.5) is supposed to be inversely related to labour productivity as well as to the variables related to yield-augmenting inputs (modern agricultural technology) (Thakur 1987). The validity of this fact has been proved by establishing the componental relationship of labour productivity in two ways: declining marginal productivity of labour and diminishing rate of labour absorption capacity in agricultural production processes. Lewis(1954) asserts in his hypothesis of labour productivity with unlimited supplies of labour that, because of increasing pressure of labour and its easy availability for production at very low (even at subsistence) level wage rate, the marginal productivity of labour must decline to stagnate the production processes where marginal productivity is marked negligible or even zero prevailing the conditions of disguised unemployment. Inspite of favorable agro-ecological conditions in the central and northern parts of Bihar and Eastern Uttar Pradesh (fertile alluvial soils, enough soil moisture availability, good soil-retention capacity), the labour productivity has been recorded declining during the 1980s (as discussed earlier) because of high population pressure, cheap supply of skilled as well as unskilled agricultural labour and very low level of marginal productivity of agricultural labour. The Fie-Ranis model of low- productivity of agricultural worker for Japan also refers the same facts (Fie and Ranis 1961, 1964).

The fact of inverse relationship of labour productivity with agricultural work force per unit of cultivated land can also be put forward by describing the rate of labour absorption capacity in agricultural sector over time. Considering agricultural labour per unit of cultivated land (L/A) as dependent variable and outputper unit of cultivated land (i.e.,land productivity, O/A) as independent variable and calculating elasticity coefficient of labour absorption with respect to agricultural output with the help of linear equation in the distribution for different period of times (see foot note of Table- 3.12), the declining trend of labour absorption elasticity in the Indian agricultural practices has been observed. Its declining rates were slower in the 1960s (.65 percent), fast in the 1970s (7.54 percent) and very fast in the 1980s (10.47 percent) (Table-3.12). Fast declining rate of labour absorption elasticity indicates substitution of agricultural technology for labour. Thus, agricultural output growth is mainly because of technology rather than increasing labour. However, the agricultural work force per unit of cultivated land and land productivity are likely to have positive relationship as stated earlier. On account of agricultural labour per unit of cultivated land as a divisor of land productivity for labour productivity, it must predict a negative relationship with labour productivity. While declining labour absorption capacity of agriculture practices reflects the substitution of modern technology for labour input and paralyses labour productivity system where marginal product to labour is negligible. Consequently, poverty and unemployment, larger wage differentials, rural-to-urban migration, rapid urbanization, ever increasing population as well as labour pressure on agricultural practices, and so on can be seen and have been significant explanatory variables for areal patterns of labour productivity.

Table-3.12: Elasticity of Labour Absorption in Agriculture Sector in India.

Period	Rate of Marginal Labour to Output (b)	Labour per thousand unit of Output (L/O)	Elasticity Coefficient (Ec)	Decadal rate of rate of elasticity decline (%)
1959-62	.7098*	1.19	.5965	-
1969-72	.5927*	1.00	.5927	0.64
1979-82	.5069*	0.92	.5510	7.54
1988-90	.4440	0.90	.4933	10.47

N.B: * Figures are taken from Bhalla &Tyagi (1989,Table-2.17 on p.43).

Formula: 1. (L/A)= a + b(O/A), where (L/A) is agricultural worker per hectare of cultivated land (as dependent variable), (O/A) is output per hectare of cultivated land, a is constant and b indicates the rate of marginal labour to output because, $b = \Delta(L/A) / \Delta(O/A)$.

2. Coefficient of elasticity (Ec) is as $Ec = b/(L/O)$.

The variable agricultural wage rate and its relationships with productivity has already been discussed. But, it is important to note here that the economic theories of wages suggest a direct relationship of wage rates with labour migration, employment conditions, and per capita income (Hicks 1932, Bardhan 1973). Theoretical explanation for the relationship of these attributes of socio-economic characteristics is provided by Harris and Todaro (1970). They argued in their 'rural-to-urban migration hypothesis' that migration of rural labour to urban areas is dependent on wage-differentials. The migration of the rural labour will continue at a rate that will not permit urban unemployment to disappear until the differential between the rural-to-urban incomes shrinks to a certain minimum. Rate of increase in employment in urban areas stimulates rural labour to migrate towards towns or cities. Thus, urbanization is directly related to migration factor. It influences the labour productivity in a positive manner. The other related explanatory variables which are associated with the socio-economic and demographic characteristics are also generated in the following manner.

The five variables which influence the inter-regional patterns of agricultural work force to create areal variations in labour productivity are considered here. They are: per capital agricultural income (agricultural output per person), population pressure (density of population), work force share of agricultural sector (percentage share of agricultural worker to total workers), impact of urbanization and industrialization on agriculture (share of urban population to total population), and rural literacy (percentage share of literates in rural areas) (Table- 3.13). Indeed, the level of labour productivity reflects the standard of living of agricultural workers as well as the whole population especially in India (Bhalla and Alagh 1983) and hence a positive relationship is to be expected between labour productivity and per capita agricultural income.

Despite the applicability of the law of diminishing marginal returns of agricultural production to labour, which generally predicts the negative relationship of population density with agricultural productivity (Leff 1969), the recent Boserup hypothesis of agricultural growth under population pressure stresses the positive effects of population pressure on agricultural development (Boserup 1965, 1981). It seems true in Indian conditions where the areas of high population density, namely, middle and southern parts of West Bengal, Coastal Andhra and Tamilnadu, have been the areas of high level of land productivity (Fig.-3.3). But, contrary to that, they have very low level of labour productivity except a few patches of its high levels particularly nearer to the urban centres where urbanization and migration may be the other causes of high labour productivity (Fig.-3.11). As a result, a negative relationship between labour productivity and population pressure and the positive relationships of labour productivity with urbanization and rural literacy are expected.

Lastly, the spatial variation in the third components of agriculture, i.e., agricultural output growth, is explained by choosing nine variables of their magnitudinal changes. Economic theories of production growth suggest the positive relationship among production growth, productivity, income and employment. On account of chief weaknesses of the Keynesian analysis and the Harrod-Domar model of production growth (as these are classical growth models) in which the new elements of growing economies had not been incorporated, the new growth models of Samuelson, Solow, Meade and others have been developed for the explanation of today's competitive market economy and composition of capital in the determination of production and productivity (Brahmananda 1979). There are broadly two approaches to identify the determining factors of production growth, though various attributes and components of growth have been described in the previous Chapter of the present book. First, the Verdoorn law confirms the positive relationship of the output growth with the increase of labour productivity stating a direct linear form of this relationship (Verdoorn 1949). The same fact of Verdoorn law has been tested by Casetti (1981) for the growth of agricultural output and found its validity at a significant level of 1.0 percent. Thus, growth of agricultural output must be positively related to the increase in labour productivity. It is obvious from various.statistical studies conducted for the growth of U.S. economy (Solow 1956, Kennedy and Thirlwall 1972, Hagen 1975,pp.255-58), that increase in output per worker (marginal productivity of labour) is due either to increase in the quantity of inputs or to increase in output per unit of total inputs (average productivity).

Table- 3.13: Variables and their Definitions.

	Name of Variables	Year	Definitions
(A)	**For Land and Labour Productivity**		
1.	Normal Annual Rainfall (P)	1901-1950	Annual mean in mm.
2.	Evapo-Transpiration (PE)	1901-1950	Mean Annual in mm.
3.	Moisture Availability Index	1901-1950	(P-PE)/PE
4.	Soil Fertility Index physical factors of land	1956	Basedonvarious
5.	Per Capita output	1988-90	in Rs per person
6.	Crop Intensity	1988-90	(GCA/NSA)100, (IN %)
7.	Net Sown Area per Agricultural worker	1988-90	A/L in hectare
8.	Share of Agricultural work force to total workers	1991	in percent
9.	Density of Agricultural workers	1991	Ag. worker per na.of NSA.
10.	Irrigation	1988-90	% share of NIA to NSA
11.	Irrigation Intensity	1988-90	(GIA/NIA) in %
12.	Mechanisation	1988-90	Ag. implement in Rs/ha. of NSA
13.	Use of Fertilizer	1988-90	Consumption in Kg. per ha.
14.	Operational size of land-holdings	1988-90	NSA per cultivator.
15.	Population density	1991	Persons per sq. Km.
16.	Urbanisation	1991	% share of urban population.
17.	RuralLiterates	1991	% share of rural literates
(B)	**For Growth of Agricultural Output**		
18.	Changes in land productivity	1979-82to 88-90	in % per annum
19.	Changes in labour productivity	1981-91	in %
20.	Changes in crop-intensity	1979-82 to 88-89	Decadal change in %
21.	Change in irrigation	1979-82 to 88-90	Decadal change in %
22.	Annual irrigation frequency	1988-90	Irrigation Intensity(see No.11)
23.	Increase in Agricultural work force	1981-91	in %
24.	Change in density of Agricultural Woks	1981-91	in %
25.	Population growth	1981-91	Decadal (in %)
26.	Population density	1991	Persons per sq. km.

N.B: Land and labour productivities and output growth are also considered as variables for generalising the facts. Land productivity is defined as agricultural output in Rs. per ha. of NSA for 1988-90, labour productivity as output per agricultural worker for 1991 and growth rate of agricultural output as average annual growth in percent during 1979-82 to 1988-90.

Infact, the changes in labour productivity is due to changes in its components: total output and agricultural workforce; they may be considered as per unit of cultivated area (and hence it is termed land productivity) and agricultural worker per unit of cultivated land because of divisor factor of cultivated area for both the components of labour productivity. Further, the agricultural labour productivity has been increasing with a decreasing rate in India during the last four decades (Table- 3.14).

Table- 3.14: Changes in Agricultural Labour Productivity in India.

Period	Agricultural Output Total (in million Rs)	Decadal change Abs	Decadal change %	Agricultural Work Force Total (in million)	Decadal Change Abs	Decadal Change %	Labour Productivity Output per Worker (in Rs)	Decadal Change Abs	Decadal Change %
1959-62	109891	-	-	131.1	-	-	838	-	-
1969-72	131100	21209	19.30	125.8	-5.3	-4.04	1042	204	24.34
1979-82	161324	30224	23.05	148.0	22.2	17.65	1090	48	4.61
1988-90	200440	39116	24.25	180.7*	32.7	22.09	1109	19	1.74

NB: 1. Agricultural work force includes cultivator and agriculturallabourers.

2. Totals of agricultural work force are Census figures.

* Figure is provisional for 1991. It excludes the figures of J.& K. and Assam States.

Abbreviations: Abs= Absolute values.

The simple reason behind the convex trend of labour productivity is the record of fast increase in the rate of agricultural workforce as 26.13 percent in the last four decades from - 4.04 percent during 1961-71 to 22.09 percent during 1981-91. It has been recorded faster than the increasing rate of agricultural output as only 5.0 percent from 19.30 percent during 1961-71 to 24.25 percent during 1981-91 (Table-3.14). Increase in agricultural output (i.e., numerator of labour productivity fraction) increases the trend of labour productivity but fast increase of agricultural worker (denominator of labour productivity) diminishes its rate. Further, this fact may also be confirmed by comparing growth rate of agricultural output and increasing rate of agricultural workforce. The growth rate of agricultural output exceeds the rate of agricultural workforce with a big margin in the 1960s and with a small margin in the 1980s. It reflects high growth of labour productivity in 1960s and its slow growth in 1980s (Table-3.14). The same fact has also been highlighted by Alagh, Bhalla and Bhadurai (1978) and Ishikawa (1981) by developing 'rectangular hyperbola hypothesis' of land productivity and land-man ratio relationship (c.f. Bhalla and Tyagi 1989, pp.38-43). Thus, obviously the variables related to increase of land productivity, namely, change in crop intensity, increase in irrigation facilities and other modern technological inputs are expected to be positively related to agricultural output growth. The positive relationship between production growth and changes in factor productivity has also established for industrial production by Solow(1957) which was later on applied by

Mc Closkey (1968) for the British pig iron industry. However, production growth of agriculture is also influenced by the physical conditions of the area. The nature and degree of intensity of technological inputs and its applicability are controlled by physical conditions. Thus, the different packages of inputs are required for different sets of agro-ecological conditions. Dayal(1984) concludes in his analysis of Indian agricultural production structure that irrigation is the most significant factor of agricultural growth because the intensification of other modern inputs like uses of chemical fertilizers, HYVs seeds and pesticides and weedecides, is entirely based on irrigation facilities, its areal expansion and frequency. Therefore, two explanatory variables related to irrigation facilities: Net Irrigated Area and irrigation intensity, are considered leaving aside the variables associated with the bio-chemical increase. Further, the variables related to increase in total agricultural workforce, namely, increases in population pressure (i.e., population growth), agricultural work force and its density would be predicted negative relationship with agricultural output growth(Casetti 1981). Thus, the eight variables as described above are included for the explanation of spatial variance of agricultural output growth in the present analysis (Table- 3.13).

(B) Dropping of Variables

Out of total twenty- nine variables (26 independent and 3 dependent) of agricultural growth and development (Table- 3.13), twenty- six are the common ones. The symatric matrix of simple correlation coefficients for all possible combinations of variables were computed for observing the interrelatedness of the complex phenomena and also for dropping the variables which fail to explain variability of the dependent variables of agricultural system. A careful examination of the correlation coefficients of all possible pairs of these variables would show the problem of multicolinearity within the independent variables, which was reduced by dropping out some independent variables from the functional analysis. For instance, Net Sown Area per agricultural worker is perfectly and inversely related to agricultural worker per hectare of NSA (r = -.992) because of reciprocal to each other. Rainfall and potential evapotranspiration are highly 'correlated themselves (r = .839). Therefore, potential evapo- transpiration variable was dropped out at the initial stage of matrix formation. Now, correlation matrix of 25x25 dimensions (Appendix- III) is prepared to drop out further some independent variables. Correlation matrix reveals that per capita income is highly related to labour productivity itself (r = .620); crop intensity is significantly related to irrigation (r = .491), to its intensity (r = .447), and population density (r = .379) and then to use of fertilizer (r = .373); irrigation intensity is highly related to crop intensity (r = .447), irrigated area (r = .361) and to the use of fertilizer (r = .422); the percentage share of agricultural work force is significantly, though negatively, related to the share of urban population (r = -.615), to rural literates (r = -.501) and than to population density (r = -.308); and rainfall is highly positively related with moisture availability (r = .737). Therefore, these seven independent variables which are having multi-colinearity problems are dropped out from the factorial analysis of land and labour productivity. Similarly, the independent variables, irrigation intensity, increase in agricultural work force, and population density are also dropped out from the factorial analysis of agricultural growth. Now, the relative importance and significance of spatial variance of explanatory variables for land and labour productivities and output growth components of the agricultural system have been revealed by using 'step-wise multiple regression model'

(C) Regression Analysis

Dropping out the above variables from the list of proposed explanatory variables, ten variables for explaining the spatial variance of land and labour productivity (Table-3.15) and six variables for the growth of agricultural output (Table- 3.16), have been included for the application of multiple regression model. Obviously, the regression model using land and labour productivity indices as dependent variables is explaining nearly 42.25 percent of the total variance, that is although not much significant, however, is able to explain some salient features of productivity indices.

Table- 3.15: Simple Correlation Coefficients(r) and Multiple Regression Coefficients(b) of ten Explanatory Variables, Regressed Against Land and Labour Productivity (1988-90).

	Explanatory Variables	Land Productivity			Labour Productivity		
		r	b	%CoV	r	b	%CoV
1.	Moisture Availability	.099	306.19 *	3.306	-.243	-12.72	2.476
2.	Soil Fertility	.298	23.48 **	7.611	.202	14.56 **	5.169
3.	Density of Agri. Workers	.252	79.58	.013	-.286	-188.55 *	15.178
4.	Irrigation	.441	3.19 *	13.278	.456	12.80 **	10.176
5.	Mechanisation	.286	.18	.098	.292	.19	.037
6.	Use of Fertilizer	.544	10.92 **	9.504	.512	7.22 **	4.124
7.	Landholding size	-.185	-3.48	.265	.353	470.80 **	10.293
8.	Population Density	.420	1.09 **	4.253	.092	.13	.005
9.	Urbanisation	.051	3.14	.307	.180	3.44	.315
10.	Rural Literacy	.045	14.35 **	3.613	-.017	-8.59	.634
	Constant(a)	-	-367.75	-	-	-575.64 **	-
	Degree of determinant(R^2)	-	-	42.246	-	-	48.407

N.B: 1. Step-wise regression model is used for calculation of percentage contribution to variance(CoV). 2. For definition of explanatory variables, see Table- 3.13. 3. Total number of observations(N) are equal to 348. 4.** Significant at .01 level, and * significantat .05 level.

(i) Land Productivity: Irrigation and use of fertilizer still hold their importance as together they account for nearly 23 percent of the areal variation in land productivity (Table- 3.15). The emergence of irrigation as the most important variable in explaining land productivity is especially noticeable, as it denotes the importance of irrigation in fast acceleration of agricultural production processes through intensification of non-traditional inputs. Thus, irrigation has become a pivotal factor of the whole package of modern agricultural technology. A slight increase in irrigated area of 41.47 percent from 31.10 million hectare to 44.08 million hectare during post-green revolution period (1970-1 to 1989-90) has stimulated fast application of chemical fertilizers as an increase of 509.60 percent from 13.13 kg/ha to 66.91 kg/ha. during the same period of time. Very high and significant correlation between irrigation and use of fertilizer (r = .627) indicates that the fertilizer application is increasing in the irritated areas though its use is also spreading into rain-fed agriculture in several states. For example, the annual rate of increase in the use of fertilizer during post green revolution period, especially from 1983-84 to

1989-90, has been recorded marginally higher in the rain-fed states of the country, namely, West Bengal (25.33 percent), Assam (22.20 percent), Tamilnadu (19.0 percent). Thus, fairly wide-spread use of fertilizer and significantly high its coefficient of correlation with land productivity (r = .544) produce the evidences of the diffusion of modern innovations in Indian agriculture. There are several studies which reveal the importance and effect of irrigation and use of fertilizer on agricultural productivity. The optimal limits of agricultural production which are controlled by physical factors can only be relaxed through increasing irrigation facilities. Irrigation has a direct effect on productivity by helping to avoid crop failure, by sustaining the ideal cropping pattern, by increasing crop-yield and so on (Dayal 1984).

After the effects of irrigation and fertilizer use have been accounted for, soil-fertility appears to have a significant positive influence on land productivity. It accounts for near about 7.61 percent of the areal variance of land productivity (Table- 3.15). There appears to be a good accord in the spatial pattern among land productivity, soil fertility and moisture availability. Moisture availability explains only 3.31 percent of spatial variance of land productivity. Thus, the hypothesis of Singh and Sharma (1985, pp.5-200) which is related to strong relationship between land productivity and soil fertility is valid in Indian conditions but, in regression model, it is third on priority basis.

Further, the independent variable, population density which is highly related to land productivity, explains nearly 4.25 percent spatial variance of land productivity in the early 1990s. It implies that, in the areas of high population density, the land productivity is also high. It confirms the validity of Boserup's hypothesis that intensification of agriculture will lead to high land productivity (output per hectare) but only when population increase is accompanied by an increase in technology (Boserup 1965, p.56). It means that land productivity increases with irrigation and use of fertilizers and then it is influenced by population pressure because of more demand for food for the local people.

(ii) Labour Productivity: In the multiple regression model, three explanatory variables,viz., irrigation, average size of landholding and density of agricultural workers, explain nearly 36.0 percent out of total 48.4 percent spatial variance of labour productivity. It has already been described that irrigation and use of fertilizer are the most significant variables for explanatory variable of land productivity, while land productivity is directly proportional to the labour productivity (eqn. 1.5). Therefore, irrigation and fertilizer use which account for nearly 14.3 percent of spatial variance of labour productivity (Table- 3.15) appear to be an important variable. Similar conclusions have also been drawn from the study on agricultural labour productivity done by Vaid and Datye (1991). Density of agricultural workers on cultivated land and size of land holdings are the most important variables influencing labour productivity (Table- 3.15). It means that, in the areas of smaller size of operational landholding where peasants and cultivators are engaged in agricultural practices, the agricultural production processes are labour intensive (because they have their own family labour). Consequently, size of land holdings is related negative to the density of agricultural workers on cultivated land (r = -.666). But on account of negative relationship between density of agricultural workers (explanatory variable) and labour productivity (r = -.286) which is also valid theoretically as labour input is, according to equation (1.4c) inversely proportional to labour productivity, the size of landholding must

logically be positively related to labour productivity which is as r = .353. As a result, density of agricultural workers appears to be first in priority to explain spatial variance of labour productivity. The same fact is also highlighted by Thakur (1987) to test the validity of labour input influence on the spatial patterns of labour productivity emerging in the areas of Western Uttar Pradesh. Further, the spatial patterns of labour productivity are highly and directly related to the spatial patterns of land productivity (r = .567) and per capita agricultural income (i.e., output) (r =.620). It implies that, in the areas of high land productivity of the country, higher will be the agricultural income which will increase the level of labour productivity. The validity of the facts has also been examined by Bora(1991) considering the most favorable agro-ecological conditions of the upper Brahamputra valley. Of course, the negative relationship of the density of agricultural workers on cultivated land and its importance in explaining the spatial variance of labour productivity provide additional strong support for Boserup's thesis as examined in the earlier part of this present discussion.

Besides, explanatory variables related to agro- ecological conditions, namely, moisture which is generally insignificant in understanding the explained variance of land productivity, are significant and contribute together nearly 7.5 percent of spatial variance of labour productivity (Table- 3.15). It is obvious that these variables are closely related to land productivity and hence, they have their importance for labour productivity in an indirect way. Overally, it is pertinent to note that the spatial variance of labour productivity is contributed by many additional variables including the explanatory variables of land productivity. It is because land productivity is one of the important components of labour productivity.

(iii) Agricultural Output Growth: Increasing rates of productivity, land as well as labour, are the most important explanatory variables which contribute 53.6 percent of total spatial variance of agricultural output growth (Table- 3.16). The other variables of agricultural growth are very weak and might be having indirect influence on it. Obviously, increasing land productivity will increase proportionately the total agricultural output and hence, there must be/ has been the strong positive relationship between changes in land productivity and agricultural growth (r = .591). The labour productivity which is influenced by many and varied factors of agriculture, appears to be the most important and significant variable of spatial variance of agricultural growth. In fact, higher rate of increase in labour productivity leads to higher increase in land productivity (so they have positive relationship, r = .386) and consequently, agricultural growth proceeds fast. The positive relationship between the rate of increase in labour productivity and rate of growth of agricultural output has been an empirical evidence which provides support to the Verdoorn's (1949) law of production growth (c.f. Casetti 1981). Another explanatory variable of agricultural growth which is highly significant (at 5.0 percent level) and negatively related (r = -.181), is population growth. It accounts for only 1.6 percent contribution to the spatial variance of agricultural growth. It has been claimed that high rates of population growth are related to the levels of lower savings, and at the same time tend to channel a larger portion of available savings to 'demographic' investments as opposed to the investment of the savings to economic progress (Coale and Hoover 1958). Therefore, rate of population growth and agricultural progress is negatively related . Thus, population growth appears to be weak variable which has negative impact on the spatial patterns of agricultural growth.

Table-3.16: Simple Correlation Coefficients and Multiple Regression Coefficients of Six Explanatory Variables Regressed Against Growth of Agricultural Output (1988-90).

	Explanatory variables	Correlation coefficient (r)	Partial Regression coefficient(b)	% Contribution to Variance
1.	Changes in Land Productivity	.591	0.3740 **	25.653
2.	Changes in Labour Productivity	.658	.0497 **	28.012
3.	Changes in Crop Intensity	-.129	-1.5249	1.002
4.	Changes in Density of Agricultural Workers	-.043	-0.0013	.124
5.	Changes in Irrigated Area	.075	.0166	.561
6.	Population Growth	-.181	-0.0862 *	1.589
	Constant (a)	-	**4.9853 ****	-
	Degree of Determinant (R^2)	-	-	**56.941**

N.B.:
1. Step-wise Regression model is used for calculation of variance of each variable separately.
2. See Table-3.13 for definition of explanatory variables.
3. Total number of observations (N) equal to 348 (Districts)
4. ** Coefficient significant at .01 level, * significant at .05 level.

Concluding Remarks

The regional variations of land and labour productivity and agricultural growth have been examined in the previous section of the present Chapter. There is a good deal of spatial accord among variables factors influencing the regional patterns of the attributes of agricultural growth and development. Some general remarks which would highlight the salient features of the regional patterns of agricultural attributes, must be presented here in the following manner.

(1) There is a poly-cyclic evolution of land productivity patterns which has been emerging because of the use of modern agricultural technology in its diversified manner. Intensification of modern agricultural technology diversifies productivity patterns because its diffusion processes are artilculated by various imposed ways of productivity enhancement. Therefore, there seems to be a weak relationship in the spatial accord of the levels of land productivity and agricultural growth (r = .109). It is becoming weaker over time when productivity patterns are highly influenced by the modern agricultural technology. In the present phase of agricultural development, irrigation and use of fertilizer appear to be the most important determinants of high productivity levels. This conclusion is also confirmed by the regression results (Table-3.15). Infact, in the core areas of green revolution, irrigation has been the only determinant which rapidly boosted up the level of agricultural productivity.

(2) The regional patterns of labour productivity are much diversified than the pattern of land productivity because of inclusion and interference of some additional factors related to the regional variations of agricultural work force. Size of landholding and density of agricultural labour appear to be the most important explanatory variables for the spatial variance in labour productivity. Of course, the conditions of intensive labour use particularly in the smaller size of land holdings result diminishing returns to labour input and consequently, labour productivity level remains stagnant. For example, very low levels of labour productivity may be observed in the areas of Middle Ganga Plains (the Eastern Uttar Pradesh and Bihar plains) where labour intensive peasant farming is being practiced.

(3) Agricultural growth patterns are highly influenced by increasing rates of land as well as labour productivity. Thus, agricultural growth is still affected by technological changes. But the decentralized pattern of growth may be the better expression of its regional diversity which can be seen in its emerging patterns for the 1980s. However, it is difficult to sound whether these patterns are optimal in its specific agro-ecological conditions or not. If not, what ought to be ? The answer for this question can only be given by applying the 'production function approach' by which the attributes of agricultural growth potential can be studied to keep them in their proper form and place in the suggested agricultural production function. Thus, production function must be based on some norms and laws of agricultural growth in order to follow its potential attributes.

-----o0o-----

Chapter - 4

Agricultural Growth Potential and Production Function

The dictionary meaning of the word 'potential' is a self explained concept in the present context. In the Webster's Seventh New Collegiate Dictionary, the word has been defined as (adjective) 'existing in possibility : capable of development in actuality' and again as (noun) 'something that can develop or become actual'. The hidden capacity of production and the possibilities of its utilisation for the improvement of agriculture and its sustainable growth are, thus, the literal meanings of defined terms of agricultural growth potential. In present context, we are particular about the assessment of magnitude and intensity of agricultural production potential in its quantitative term, so that the causes of its inter-regional variations and its logical relationship with the other agricultural attributes can be studied. These aspects of agricultural characteristics should help to prepare the 'area-specific strategy' and proper expansion of agricultural services. Keeping in view theses aspects of agricultural growth potential, the present Chapter is devoted: (a) to assess agricultural production potential and its regional variations in India and changes therein over time, and (b) to develop an agricultural production function in which agricultural production potential would be acting as one of the major attributes by which varied and many parameters of agricultural growth and development can be prepared and interpreted.

Assessment of Agricultural Production Potential

Generally, magnitude of agricultural production potential is closely related to availability of natural resources, especially water and soils of the area/region, and their utilization processes operating through modern technology. Before discussing the guiding processes and their resulted typography of production potential, it is necessary to understand the background material and related terms which are useful in the present context. The classical theories of agricultural production explain agricultural growth in relation its natural conditions which delimit the boundary of crop production and control its optimal limits (McCarty and Lindburg 1967). According to the classical theories, land capability which is determined by physical properties of land and its natural processes, is the most important determinant of agricultural production potential. It is attributed by agro-ecological concept of land which was developed for land evaluation by many landscape synthesizers and landuse planners (Stamp 1950, 1958, 1961; Oschwald 1966; Riquier 1971, 1972; Vink 1955, 1975, pp. 353-66). It is useful for understanding natural resource potential of land for agricultural land suitability.

On the other hand, the classical models of agricultural production are basically based on marginal productivity theory, in which production elasticity has been recognised as a major criterion for suggesting production growth and its system's optimality (Hagen 1975, pp. 406-24; Jorgenson 1961, 1967; Kahn 1951; Johansen 1961). Production elasticity criterion provides micro-economic causes of production growth. It is widely recognised that the law of diminishing marginal return is operative in agricultural practices every where especially in the developing economies. The theory of marginal productivity and elasticity criterion are based on this law whose importance was recognised by Recardo and others of the classical period of England (Schumpeter 1963). The other two older marginalists, Von Thuenen (Germany) and Longfield, were also important to alter the theory of marginal productivity of distribution (Schumpeter 1963). The causes of diminishing marginal return with respect to application of production factors especially in agricultural practices are closely related to agricultural production efficiency (i.e., determined by production potential) rather than production elasticity which is simply based on the variation of distribution. Without assessing the maximum expected level of agricultural production either in its aggregated terms or crop-wise separately, the agricultural production efficiency cannot be measured, while maximum expectations of agricultural production are only possible through the assessment of land capability/suitability for which agro-ecological aspects are essential to study.

So far as land evaluation for agricultural activities is concerned, there are two major physical attributes of land, the soil fertility and the moisture availability, which have direct impact upon plant growth and crop-yield, are the fundamental determinants of agricultural production potential (Vink 1975, pp. 15-16). Further, it is noticeable that the application of modern technology in agricultural practices is greatly dependent on the availability of agricultural production potential, otherwise agricultural practices will not be profitable after exhausting them. Therefore, inclusion of production potential attribute is equally important in understanding agricultural production function.

The agro-ecological approaches for assessing agricultural production potential and for the supporting capacity of land have been put forward by many environmentalists (Dougrameji 1970, Vink 1975) which was later modified by FAO experts by measuring climatic-potential of land for agriculture on the basis of climatic conditions especially of moisture availability and showing negative effects of soil conditions with production-potential. FAO (1982) model considers the soil as a major constraint of yield-potential because various physical factors of land like slope, drainage, soil-erosion, etc., have the inverse effects on soil fertility (Fig.-4.1). Grosjean and Messerli (1988) supported this idea of physical barriers on soil fertility and exemplified that high erodability, bad rootability, low soil water storage capacity, low oxygen availability in the root zone, low cation exchange capacity, soil toxicity (i.e., high concentration of minerals) and salt/soda contents in the soils and so on decrease the degree of soil fertility. Thus, the magnitude of production-potential is controlled by agro-ecological conditions and

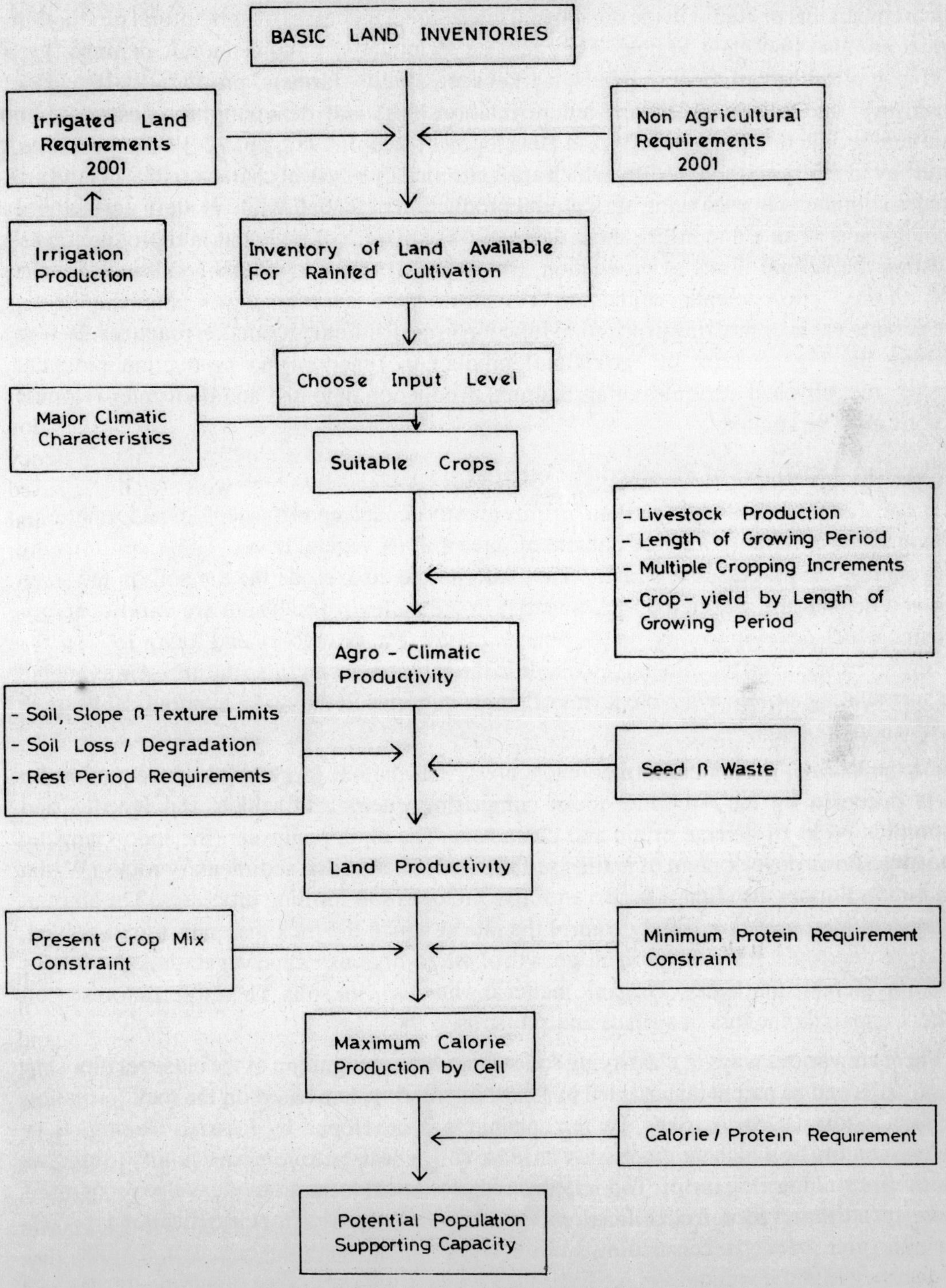

Source: FAO 1982, p.63

Fig.- 4.1 : Potential Population Supporting Capacities.

physical constraints of land. On the other hand, micro-areal processes of agricultural production potential are also important to note. They impose technological and economic ceilings (i.e., related to applicability of modern inputs, market accessibility, farmers' profitability-like price mechanism) and social (like land-tenure relationships) and demographic constraints on agricultural production potentials (World Development Report 1982, pp. 72-3). On the whole, moisture availability and soil fertility which are controlled by physical characteristics of land are the major stimulants in enhancing agricultural production potential, while modern agricultural technology acts as an aid to utilize them. It is good converter of potential into production by exhausting the natural limits of production. But note that socio-economic conditions are the checks on production potential utilization. Therefore, there is a triangular relationship of the above parameters in optimizing production function in agricultural production practices. Before describing the logical form of agricultural production function and production potential processes, the physical attributes of agricultural production potential and their inter-regional variations must be studied.

(A) Physical Attributes of Production Potential

i) Soil Fertility : Soil types and soil fertility greatly depend upon the geological formations, the topographic conditions and the climate of area and its vegetal cover. These soil forming factors operate the processes to add organic matter to the dust, erode the top soil on the steep slopes and deposit the weathered rock material in the valley sides. There are various micro-organisms which develop feeding on the organic matter (Raychaudhury and Rajan 1971, p. 7). These organisms convert the minerals available in the parent rocks and also the nitrogen available in the surrounding air into available forms of plants nutrients. It may take hundreds of years to build up an inch of soil.

On the basis of geological formations, it is obvious that the larger parts of the peninsular India is occupied by the Archaean rocks comprising gneiss and schists and igneous and metamorphic rocks of diverse origin and characters. The extra-peninsula (the Indo-Gangetic Plains) area shows development of marine sediments of all ages and sedimentary rocks (Wadia *et. al.,* 1935). Further the climate is also an active factor in soil forming processes. The amount and distribution of moisture largely control the rate at which the rock materials are dissolved, leached and deposited. It also helps in the growth of micro-organisms and vegetation. Dry leaves of the plants increase the degree of organic matter and humus in the soils. Therefore, deforestation has direct impact in the loss of surface and sub-soils in the areas.

There are various ways of classifying soil system. The recognition of the close relationship between soils and its parent material led to a classification system based on the rock formation processes (Wadia 1975). A triangular relationship was developed by Russian Geologists in eighteenth century by which the emphasis was led to soil genesis and more particularly to climate as a dominant soil forming factor. Topography and geological formations were also recognised as important attributes for soil classification. The integrated approach for classification is proper which may give better understanding to soil types for agricultural potential. Shome and Raychaudhury (1960) prepared soil fertility index for each district of the country on the basis of the soil forming processes and the genesis of the soils (cf. Jakhada and Shivamaggi, 1969). It is a practicable soil classification and reflects soil-fertility, a direct indicator of production potential and land management which is useful in the present context. Thus, soil fertility index prepared by Raychaudhury is useful for understanding the causes of production potential variations.

So far as major soil groups of India are concerned, Troup (1921) recognised ten different geological-forest regions and, later on Wadia, *et.al.* (1935) have prepared a detailed soil map of India on the basis of geological formations. On the other hand, some geologists and climatologists also described soil groups on the basis of climatic conditions to recognise a direct relationship among temperature, rainfall and the soil formation (Basu 1937, Kendrew 1944, Viswanath and Ukil 1944). On the basis of integrated effects of climate, vegetation and topography on soil formation, Raychaudhury and Mathur (1954) divided India into 16 major and 108 minor basic regions. But Raychaudhury and Rajan (1971) studied the soils of India to put them into four major and four other soil groups (total eight). They belong to the alluvial soil of Indo-Gangetic Plains and the coastal areas, the black soil of the Deccan trap, the red soils of the central part of peninsula, and the lateritic soils of moist and humid parts of the country. The other soil groups include soils under forests, desert soils, saline and alkaline soils and Marshy soils (of *Tarai* and *Bhawar* areas). But the soil map of India which was prepared by Viswanath and Ukil in 1944 was modified by the All India Soil and Landuse Survey Organisation in 1956 to conduct extensive soil surveys in different parts of the country. The detailed soil map shows 24 major soil types (cf. Raychaudhury and Rajan 1971). But the soil map which is used by Krishnan and Singh (1968) for the study of agricultural growth consists of ten major soil types excluding mountain and *Tarai* soils (Fig.- 4.2). They prepared 'soil-climatic zones' of India for assessing the agricultural potential and also tried to develop this map on the basis of considering district unit, so that it may be used for the administrative purpose of proper agricultural management and policy implementation.

ii) The Moisture Availability : The moisture factor, which is the most important determinant of production potential, has been described by many climatologists (Koppen 1900, Thornthwaite 1931, 1948, Papadakis 1966) by determining the effects of evapo- transpiration on plant growth. The pioneer and preliminary attempt made by Koppen (1900) was the first recognition of the physical processes accelerated by temperature and precipitation of the climatic conditions. The main attributes which he includes in his climatic system are : temperature of the the coldest and warmest months and occurrence of a dry period. He classified world into five major climatic zones accordingly (Table-4.1). The physical processes of evapotranspiration subject to its biological changes recognised as the major determinant of the moisture available or the degree of humidity/aridity which have been studied by establishing temperature-moisture relationship in order to prepare precipitation-effectiveness and temperature-efficiency indices by Thornthwaite in 1931 and, later on, he rationalized this relationship considering potential evapotranspiration as a fundamental determinant of moisture availability (Thornthwaite 1948). The direct relationship of mean temperature and average precipitation with crop-growth, which gives a better indication of crop-ecological extremes, has also been described by preparing specific kind of climatograms by Papadakis (1965).

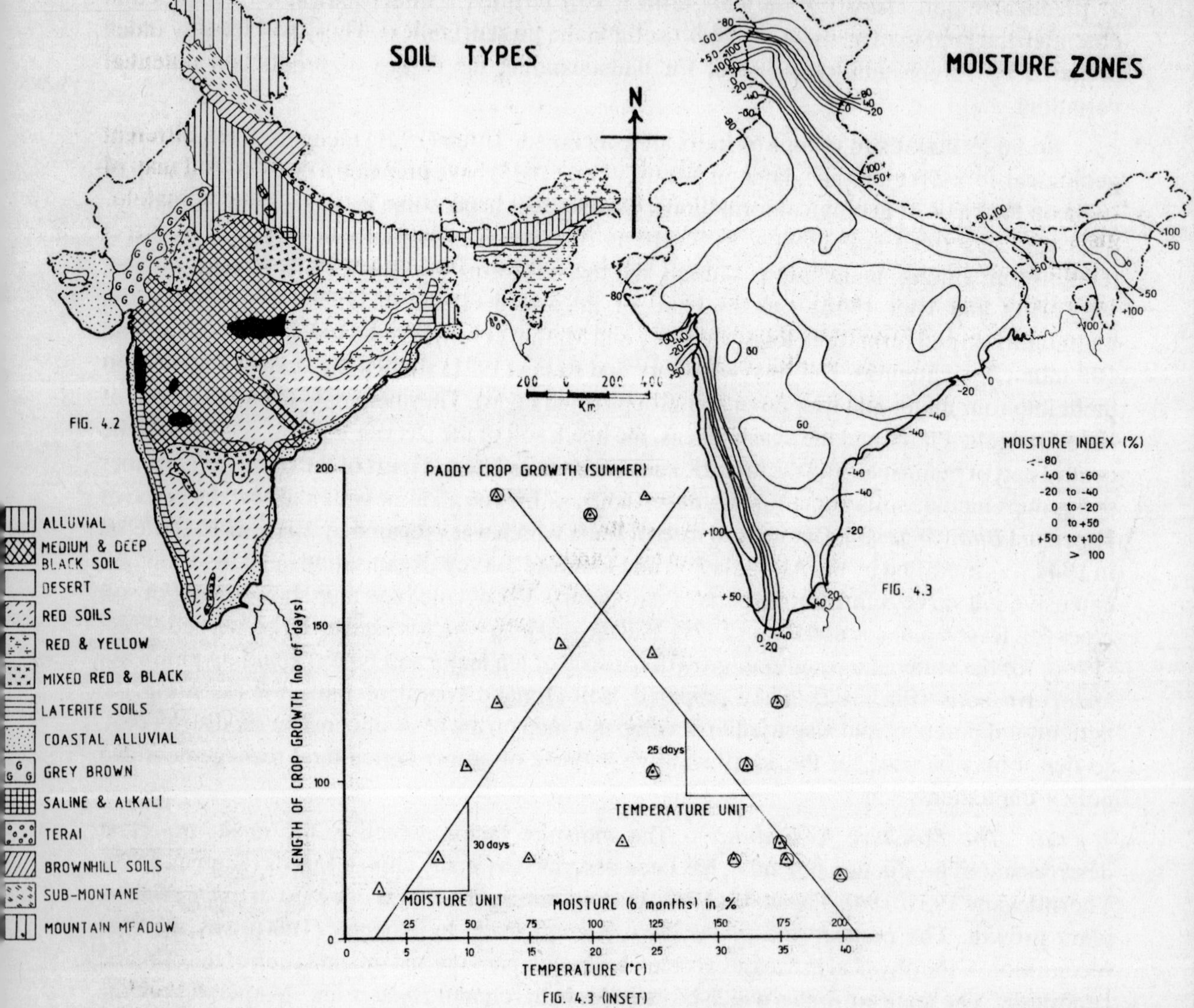

Fig.- 4.2 & 4.3 and in set

Table - 4.1: Climatic types of the World according to Koppen (After Koppen and Geiger 1928).

A) ***Tropical Rainy Climates*** (average monthly temperature above 18°C)

1. Humid and Warm :

- Af : always humid (atleast 60 mm precipitation in the driest month).
- Am : monsoon climate with moderately dry season.

2. Periodically Dry :

- Aw : Savan climates with dry winter.
- As : Savana climate with dry summer (rare).

B) ***Dry Climates*** (determined by the relation between annual precipitaion and annual temperature)

- BS : steppe climates
- BSh : hot B climate
- BSk : cool B climate
- BSk′ : cold B climate
- BSn : B climate with frequent fog.
- BW : desert climates

C) ***Warm Temperate Rainy Climates*** (temperature of the coldest month between 18°C and 3°C)

- Cw : warm climate with a dry winter.
- Cs : warm climate with a dry summer.
- Cf : humid temperate climate.

D) ***Sub-Arctic Climate with Cold Winter*** (temperature ranges between -3°C in the coldest month and 10°C in the warmest month)

- Df : continuously humid.
- Dw : climates with a cold dry winter.

E) ***Polar Climates*** (warmest month temperature between 10°C and 0°C)

- ET : Tundra climates.
- EH : High altitude climates.
- EF : Climates of permanent frost.

Table - 4.2a : Scale for Defining Climatic Zones in India (by Krishnan and Singh 1968, cf. Krishnan 1980).

	Moisture Belts		Temperature Belts		
	Name	Index Value (%)		Name	Mean Annual Temperature (in °C)
1.	Extremely Dry	-80 & Below	A	Very Hot	28 & More
2.	Semi-Dry	-60 to -80	B	Hot	25 to 28
3.	Dry	-40 to -60	C	Mild	20 to 25
4.	Slightly Dry	-20 to -40	D	Cold	10 to 20
5.	Slightly Moist	0 to -20	E	Very Cold	10 or less
6.	Moist	0 to 50			
7.	Wet	50 to 100			
8.	Extremely Wet	100 & above			

N.B. : 1. Moisture Index (in Per cent), MI, is calculated as: MI = [100(P-PE)/PE], where P = monthly precipitation, and PE = mean monthly potential-evapotranspiration which is computed by Thornthwaite method.

2. For regional variations, see Fig.-4.3.

So far as regional variations in the moisture conditions in India is concerned, Krishnan and Singh (1968), two agricultural scientists of ICAR, New Delhi, calculated moisture index following Thornthwaite's formula of humidity/aridity calculations (Thornthwaite 1948) and demarcated moisture belts by dividing India into eight moisture belts and five temperature zones (Table-4.2a). Moisture belts of India which are closely related to the distribution of rainfall indicate a clear four-fold division of climatic conditions as wet, moist, dry and extremely dry (arid) from the eastern to the western parts of the country (Fig.- 4.3). The seasonal variations in moisture availability is because of areal as well as seasonal variations in rainfall. Telangana and Rayalseema of interior Andhra Pradesh, interior Karnataka and Rajasthan areas are the driest parts of the country (Table-4.2b). Further, available storage of moisture in the soils is dependent on the available moisture contents in the air, the total surface area of the soil constituents, moisture contents and the size distribution of pores in the soil (Gupta 1973). The crop-growing period, which directly influences the crop-yield potential, is directly proportionate to the moisture availability and inversely proportional to the temperature. Plotting the data on the duration of growth of the summer paddy crop of various sample places taken from the homogeneous alluvial soils of India as dependent variable and average moisture index and mean temperature of the same places (for six months of summer paddy cultivation from June to November) as independent variables, it is found that per unit increase of one percent in moisture availability in the environment increases the length of crop-growth at a constant rate of six days. While increasing temperature declines the length of crop-growth at a constant rate of five days per degree Celsius of temperature (Fig.- 4.3 inset). As a result, in the dry and hot climatic conditions, the crop growth duration is recorded shorter than the humid climatic conditions. The ideal conditions for plant growth in the alluvial soils of North Indian Plains vary the range of moisture availability from 75 to 125 per cent and temperature range from 20^{0C} to 35^{0C}. These conditions can be observed in the longitudinal *tarai* belts of foot hills of the Himalayas (Northern Uttar Pradesh and Bihar areas) and in the lower parts of Ganga plains (Southern and Central West Bengal) where agricultural production potential can be predicted higher in its magnitude and intensity.

Moisture availability in the soils which reflects soil-water relationship is of considerable importance in agriculture. Soil moisture characteristics are mostly studied by considering its three major aspects, namely, the soil-moisture tension (effect of the force of gravity on the variations occurring in the amount of water in the soils), secondly, the soil water retention capacity and rate of its movement (i.e., related to the size distribution of the pores which is determined by the textural and structural arrangement of the soil particles), and thirdly, infiltration and the rate of capillary rise which refers to the rate of water intake (i.e., directly influenced by the moisture contents available in the surface conditions of the soils). In general, permeability of soil is the main determinant of soil moisture availability which is estimated by the study of hydraulic conductivity in relation to the availability of clay contents in the soils. There are various methods for permeability determinations (Seth and Yadav 1958, Gupta 1966). According to Harris (1931) equation, permeability is inversely related to the intensity of clay contents in the exponential form.

Table- 4.2b: Normal Monthly Rainfall of Climatic Sub-Regions of India (1901-1950).

(figures in mm)

	Sub-Divisions	J	F	M	A	M	Ju	Jul	Au	S	O	N	D
1.	Assam Meghalaya	16	33	68	184	313	534	513	334	282	117	25	16
2.	Sub Himalayan WB	17	30	61	166	283	511	538	442	380	157	10	9
3.	Gangetic W.Bengal	10	23	24	45	88	234	275	266	241	135	12	16
4.	Orissa	13	22	22	31	48	33	496	320	233	141	33	11
5.	Bihar Plateau	16	28	21	27	80	191	299	292	218	85	10	6
6.	Bihar Plains	13	16	12	17	44	153	288	280	211	67	5	3
7.	E. U. P.	15	20	10	7	15	98	271	266	197	54	7	5
8.	Plains of W.U.P.	19	22	12	8	14	77	236	238	170	38	5	12
9.	Hills of W.U.P.	49	75	NA	121	42	159	365	421	199	61	8	19
10.	Haryana & Delhi	17	22	17	9	13	49	151	152	103	21	3	10
11.	Punjab	25	31	23	14	14	40	160	146	95	26	5	14
12.	H. P.	66	86	89	48	65	93	343	331	170	52	16	42
13.	J. & K.	64	162	127	134	6	62	258	321	137	37	31	76
14.	W. Rajasthan	4	6	7	3	11	33	84	102	66	6	2	4
15.	E. Rajasthan	6	6	5	4	11	53	202	199	105	18	4	6
16.	W. M. P.	11	10	9	4	10	108	287	254	191	33	13	9
17.	E. M. P.	17	24	20	18	16	156	639	327	192	55	7	10
18.	Gujarat Region	2	1	3	2	4	119	362	229	174	21	4	3
19.	Saurastra & Kutch	1	2	4	1	4	76	213	112	79	15	4	4
20.	Konkan & Goa	1	0	0	10	35	632	1011	599	376	95	23	9
21.	C. Maharashtra	3	2	3	17	30	145	264	164	153	71	24	10
22.	Marathwada	5	5	11	18	20	139	177	165	168	47	18	16
23.	Vidarbha	11	10	17	15	14	148	286	230	208	50	12	17
24.	Coastal A. P.	7	9	9	18	46	108	151	146	159	200	92	11
25.	Telangana	5	8	10	27	29	129	206	189	184	78	17	6
26.	Rayalseema	4	6	5	24	42	59	76	94	127	122	73	26
27.	T.N. & Pondicherry	34	14	19	54	22	52	67	92	94	211	183	83
28.	Coast Karnataka	1	0	1	28	166	832	1078	597	288	191	60	14
29.	N.Interior Karnataka	3	4	7	36	44	94	133	110	140	97	24	7
30.	S.Interior Karnataka	4	7	8	52	93	149	270	170	130	157	52	13
31.	Kerala	16	26	46	153	271	673	697	389	227	306	149	41

Source : Reports on Rainfall from Indian Metrological Department, Pune.

The soil-moisture tension (pressure difference across the air-water interface) varies in various soil zones because of its composition of various types of clay-minerals. In India, soils clay-minerals vary from *kaolinitic* (fine white clay availability) in the red and laterite soil groups, *illitic* in the alluvial and desert soils, to *montmorillonitic* in black soil group (Gupta 1973). The amount of organic matter varies from less than 0.4 per cent in desert and alluvial soils to more than 4.0 per cent in the mountainous and forest soils. Because of these variations in clay-minerals, clay contents and organic matter, the texture and structure of soils vary significantly which directly affect the coefficient of hydraulic conductivity and soil-moisture tension. It is obvious from various studies conducted on different soil types of India (Rao and Ramacharlu 1959, Ali *et.al* 1966, Sekhon and Arora 1967) that moisture content decreases with increase in soil moisture tension while its rate of decrease is dependenton the soil types (cf. Gupta 1973, Tables 1 to 3). One important observation regarding hydraulic conductivity coefficient in surface and sub-surface soils, which has been reported by Soni and Chakravarti (1959), shows that its coefficient decreases with increase in depth, especially in the Siwan areas of North Bihar where alluvial soils are dominant. Further, there is a positive relationship between hydraulic conductivity coefficient and percentage of soil moisture.

The amount of water stored in soil profiles in watersheds and lakes, lost as run-off is dependent upon infiltration capacity of the soil which depends upon the slope, surface roughness, vegetal cover and soil management. Patnaik and Virahi (1962) reported that the infiltration rates in the *'Doon'* valley are greatly influenced by surface cover. It decreases with the increase in infiltration time. In the Siwalik foot hill areas of the *'Doon'* valley, infiltration rate varies from 2.70 cm/hr. to 7.30 cm/hr. in the cultivated plain areas, from 7.10 cm/hr. to 9.60 cm/hr. in the cultivated areas of Himalayan uplands where surface has some small stones. It ranges from 3.65 to 8.95 cm/hr. in the forest areas (Table- 4.3).

In the end, it can be said that these micro-organisms of soil greatly affect the soil moisture availability, control the plant growth, and fulfill the water requirements of the plants. In fact, water deficiency in the soils for plant growth is removed by utilising surface and sub-surface water through various irrigation means. It is the question of the application of modern technology for agricultural growth which should be elaborated separately.

(B) Irrigation and Modern Technology as Major Attributes of Potential Generation

Irrigation intensity and use of HYVs seeds are also important influents of agricultural production potential generation. Irrigation requirements are based on total available water (achieved by rainfall and soil moisture availability for plant growth), average field capacity, bulk specific gravity and effective depth of plant-rooting. There are three important determining factors of suitable irrigation schedules. They are related to soils, plants and climate. Relatively frequent irrigations are required where the conditions of plants, soils and weather are as : slow-growing root plants with more fresh weight yields of reproductive organs; shallow soil of poor structure and slow infiltration; high fertility and very high temperature soils; high evaporation rate and less rainfall especially during growing seasons (Prashar and Hagan 1970). The general rule tells that HYVs crops need optimum ecological conditions and greater use of chemical fertilizers which determine the water consumption of a field (Yaron, *et.al.* 1973). Some on-farm

Table - 4.3 : Infiltration rates in the Doon Valley investigated (cf. Patnaik and Virahi 1962).

	Sites	Infiltration rate cm/hr.	
		Ist Hr.	2nd Hr.
(A)	***Cultivated Area***		
1.	Dholkot - under cover crop, surface siol having no pebbles/stones	4.00	2.75
2.	Sahaspur - Ploughed fallow with a few pebbles	3.55	1.92
3.	Lakhenwala - Harvested rice field	2.70	1.90
4.	Tapkeshwar - Ploughed field with stones	4.50	2.25
5.	Babagarh - Fodder harvested, no pubbles	7.30	4.55
6.	Bhurpur - Ploughed field, no stones	3.75	0.85
(B)	***Cultivated Himalayan Upland with Some Stones on Surface***		
7.	Sinola - Ploughed land	7.90	4.20
8.	Kinderwal - Ploughed land	7.50	4.40
9.	Bakhtawarper - Ploughed land	7.10	6.65
10.	Donga - Ploughed land	9.50	5.10
11.	Ruderpur - Ploughed land	9.60	5.10
12.	Khalagaon - Rice harvested	2.05	0.75
(C)	***Forest Areas***		
13.	Bidhuali-Sal forest with good leaf	8.95	5.90
14.	Horawala-Sal forest with little leaf	3.65	2.00
15.	Anari R.F. - Sal forest	4.55	2.45
16.	Chandpur R.F. - Sal forest	4.85	2.55
17.	Dholkot R.F. - Sal forest	7.35	6.00
(D)	***Forest Siwalik Slopes***		
18.	Kargapani Fireline - Sal forest	5.35	2.30
19.	Kargapani R.F. - Sal forest	2.80	1.15
20.	Sabhawala Fireline - Sal forest	3.70	2.70
21.	Sabhawala Forest Chawki- Miscellaneous Forests withcompact surface	4.15	2.00

Source : Patnaik and Virahi (1962).

experiments report that, in the good quality land of north Bihar where enough moisture in the soil is available, two doses of nitrogen fertilizer of 42 kg per hectare each which are given after 30 days of planting are required for optimal increase of 42.3 per cent in maize crop-yield (Sinha, *et.al.* 1979). Obviously, two doses of 42 kg per hectare are worthwhile for *terai* maize crop (Table- 4.4).

Therefore, HYV crops, use of chemical fertilizers and irrigation requirements which are the elements of 'green revolution technology', greatly affect maximum expected crop yield levels and hence, they accelerate the agricultural production potential generation processes in indirect ways. The assessment of the maximum expected yield of each principal crop for various environmental conditions is done by a team of expert committee under the Demonstration Scheme of agriculture extension services. It was successfully done on on-farm experiment basis.

Table - 4.4 : Yield of Maize at Different Nitrogen Doses of 42 kg/ha each after 30 Days of Planting (1976-77).

	Nitrogen Doses	Yield qu/ha	Rate of Yield Increase	
			Absolute	in %
1.	Without any dose	5.6	-	-
2.	Environment plus first dose	5.9	0.3	5.35
3.	Environment plus second dose	8.4	2.5	42.37
4.	Environment plus third dose	9.3	0.9	10.71

Source : Sinha, *et.al.* (1979).

Further, if agriculture is considered as 'industry like-activity', the production potential of crops and the implementation of modern technology in relation to the agro-ecological conditions are important aspects of preparing regional investment strategies of a region/country. The triangular relationship among production (existing yield conditions), production potential (optimum agro-ecological conditions) and production factors (modern technology and labour as inputs) is essential to study for achieving optimum levels of agricultural production practices. Therefore, the objective function of agricultural production must be based on the acceleration of trilateral processes of production activities as : to maximise the use of production potential, to optimise the production factors (input intensification) and to maximise the farmers' profitability subject to their production-price and input costs. The validity of these optimised production conditions would empirically be tested after rational discussion on production function and its normative quantitative form for generating important variables which would describe the inter-regional variations in agricultural production potential.

Components of Agricultural Production Potential and Their Established Relationships

Production function approach, which is infact based on 'marginal productivity theory of production', gives insights of the interconnected components of production system because it describes its six main aspects : (i) factor share (factor ratios for production), (ii) factor contribution (the marginal productivity of a factor in production processes), (iii) factor elasticity estimates (proportionate change in production with respect to proportionate change in production factors), (iv) the estimates of factor efficiency (ratio of marginal revenue to marginal cost of the system), (v) substitutability/complementarity pattern of the factors employing in production system, and (vi) the estimates of return to scales as constant/increasing/ decreasing. On the basis of these aspects, resource allocations and planning strategies of production growth can be/ have been prepared even for agricultural production activities. It is noted here that, in this economist's approach of production growth, the efficiency criterion of production factor is solely based on production-price and input-costs of the system. But they are the influencing factors rather than determinants of the system. Agricultural production efficiency is directly related to the agricultural production potentials. Soil fertility and moisture holding capacity of soils which depend on chemical composition and physical properties of soils, as described earlier, are the physical determinants and the packages of agricultural modern technology (irrigation, fertilizer doses and HYV seed rates) are the man-made determinants of the maximum expected yield of various crops (or the maximum expected agricultural production level). In various environmental conditions with suitable doses of irrigation, fertilizer and HYV seeds, the maximum expected yield levels of various crops are altered which have been assessed by ICAR under its field-experiment based Demonstration Projects and transfer of Technology Projects (Prasad *et.al.* 1987). Since the district-wise data of maximum expected yield of principal crops of the country are available, it would be helpful for preparing maximum expected production index and showing the regional variations in agricultural production potentials. It would be discussed separately in the next section of this Chapter, but here the major components of agricultural production system in order to preparation of its regional planning strategy must be elaborated precisely.

There are two types of measurements of agricultural production components. First is related to the absolute measurement by which the relationships of only production attributes are established. The second is associated with the contextual measurements of production attributes under which the production and production factors relationships are estimated. The agricultural production components have been interpreted here in connection with these two measurements.

Since total capacity of land to produce agricultural production is known to assess the Maximum Expected Production (i.e., yield) level, A, and the used capacity of land is referred to as the Existing Production Level, Y, in the agricultural production system, the latent capacity of land for agricultural production (that may be called usable production, but it is named here the *total Magnitude* of *Production Potential,* P) must be the difference between A and Y, as:

$$P = (A - Y), \text{ with condition } A > Y \qquad \ldots \quad \ldots \quad \ldots \qquad (4.1)$$

Many economists and agronomists have recognised it as 'yield-gap' of the various crops (Kumar 1986, Varadarajan 1986). It can be assessed in its physical term or in term of money value. Further, *Intensity of Production Potential,* Ip, refers to the ratio of maximum expected production to existing production because,

$$Ip = \{Y + (A - Y)\}/Y = 1.00 + (A - Y)/Y = A/Y, \qquad \ldots \quad \ldots \qquad (4.2)$$

with condition $Ip > 1$, because $A > Y$.

Another important component of the agricultural system is *Production Efficiency* (i.e., yield-efficiency), PE, which refers to the share of existing production to maximum expected production in the system as :

$$PE = Y/A. \qquad \ldots \quad \ldots \quad \ldots \qquad (4.3)$$

Note that PE is the reciprocal form of production potential intensity, Ip, as one compares Equations 4.2 and 4.3.

Now, these absolute measurements of agricultural production system can be interpreted in their contextual forms to establish their relationships with input factors, X, of the system with some assumptions and normative conditions.

1. Assumptions

The triangular relationship among three major production components : the magnitude of production potential, existing production and input factors (P, Y and X), can not be stated without specifying the variable forms of P and Y with respect to input factors as P(x) and Y(x). A few but important real conditions and assumptions are imposed to study the componental relationships. They are as follows :

(a) Because A > Y (by definition), then the magnitude of production potential must be greater than zero, P > 0.

(b) If Y is the function of X, and P is dependent upon Y (eqn. 3.1) then P must also be function of X.

(c) It is widely recognised that agricultural production function follows law of diminishing return because of utilization of production potential. Marginal productivity must diminish in the system.

(d) Assumed that non-applicability of any type of inputs which means non- interfearence of human activities on the piece of agricultural land (X = 0) does not produce any production (Y = 0). However, land has maximum magnitude of production potential at this stage which is equal to A. It means X and Y are non-negative variables and hence, origin (0,0) of the graph is the starting point of production function curve. The upper limit of this curve must always be below the maximum expected production level, A.

(e) Production prices, p, and the input costs, k, are the marketable factors of farmer's profitability and land-rent maximization. They are considered as constants in present context.

2. Normative Conditions

There are *two* conditions which explain the extreme ends of the scale of production variables with respect to the variations occurring in the factors of production. They are :

(a) In the case of non-applicability of input in agriculture production system, the existing production must be equal to zero (Assumption - d) and the magnitude of production potential must be the highest as equals to maximum expected production level as:

P = A, subject to X & Y approaches to zero. ... ... (4.4)

(b) In the other extreme condition of production variation as the input applicability at infinite level of the system (as X tends to infinite), the production level will be maximum (Y = maxi) and the magnitude of production potential must be minimum (P = mini). It means production increases with absorbing the magnitude and intensity of production potential in the system (for more clarity, see Figs.- 4.4 a, b & c). Now, let us speculate the range of variation occurring in the magnitude of production potential for its per unit of input applicability. According to the above conditions, it must vary from A/X (eqn. 4.4) as maximum to {(A-Y)/X} as minimum because A >Y (assumption - a). Infact, the total magnitude of production potential must be proportional to the difference occurring between the magnitude of production potential per unit of input on these two extreme conditions of its variations expressed as

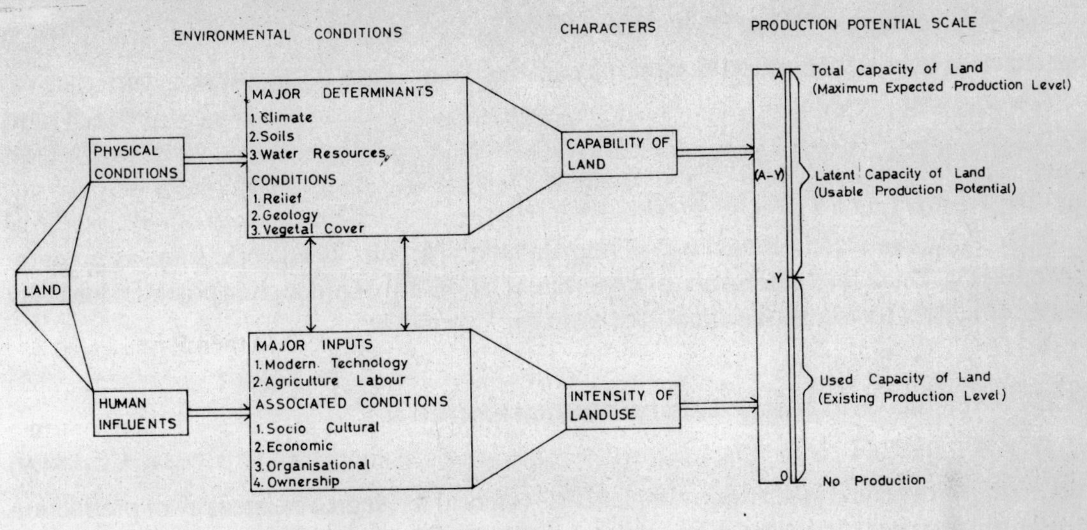

Fig.- 4.4a : Componental Interactions and Production Structures.

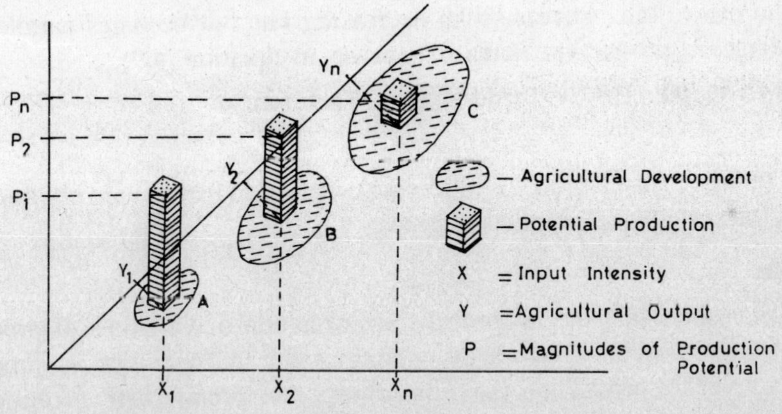

Fig.- 4.4b : Three-Fold Relatons of Agricultural Systems.

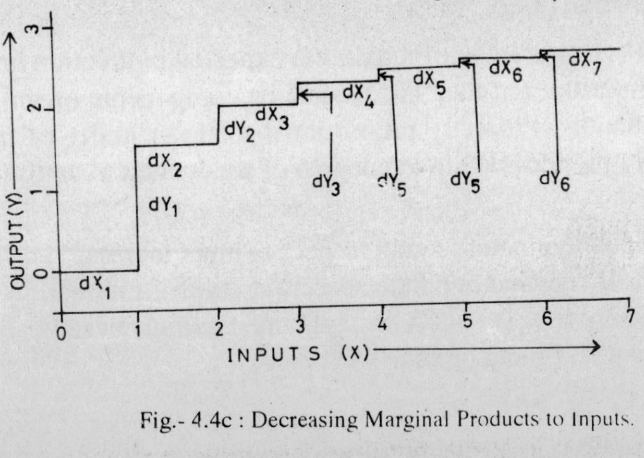

Fig.- 4.4c : Decreasing Marginal Products to Inputs.

(A - Y) is proportional to [A/X - {(A - Y)/X}]. ... ... (4.5)

Constant B is imposed on the RHS term for equating them. Then it specifies,

$$(A - Y) = B\,(Y/X), \quad \ldots \quad \ldots \quad \ldots \quad (4.6)$$

in which $\{(A - Y)/Y\} = B/X$,

and $\{1 + (A - Y)/Y\} = (1 + B/X)$. ... ... (4.7)

The same facts can also be stated by solving Equation (4.1) in its algebric form as given in Appendix- IV. There is an emergence of important relationship of production potential intensity with input factors for which the simplified form for Y^{-1} must be,

$$Y^{-1} = A^{-1} + (B/A).\, X^{-1}, \quad \ldots \quad \ldots \quad \ldots \quad (4.8)$$

which yields a real form of agricultural production function as

$$Y = A\,(1 + B/X)^{-1}, \quad \ldots \quad \ldots \quad \ldots \quad (4.9)$$

in which the term placed in denominator (1 + B/X) refers to the degree of intensity of production potential in its contextual form as Ip(x) (see eqn. 4.7). Further, the major characteristics of production increase is related to the general nature of the present agricultural production function. It follows asymptotic nature (i.e., increase with decreasing rate but becomes parallel to the horizon at the later stages of production increase) because, in equation (4.9),

if X tends to infinite, then B/X will tend to zero. Therefore,

$$Y = A. \quad \ldots \quad \ldots \quad \ldots \quad (4.10)$$

On the basis of the above discussion, the following generalized features are inferred for the detail elaboration of the agricultural production system.

3. Generalizations

(i) Equation 4.8 ensures that the reciprocal transformation of variables of production function, X^{-1} and Y^{-1}, leads to the co-linearity conditions for the operation of production processes, and hence, present production function follows 'reciprocity law' of agricultural production increase rather than logarithmic form predicted by Dauglas and Cobb (1928) and the exponential yield function of Spillman (1922, 1933).

(ii) Agricultural production is the quotient of maximum expected production level to the degree of production potential intensity (as they are the major components of the system). Consequently, agricultural production is directly proportional to the quantity of maximum expected production and inversely proportional to the degree of production potential intensity (equation 4.9).

(iii) Rate of agricultural production increase with respect to input increase (i.e., marginal product to input, dY/dX) is implicitly depend upon the absorption rate of production potential intensity (i.e., $dIp/dX = -BX^{-2}$, where $Ip = (1 + B/X)$ as explained earlier) because first order differentiation of the present production function (eqn. 4.9) is as:

$$dY/dX = [\,- BA\,(1.0 + B/X)^{-2}.\, X^{-2}]. \quad \ldots \quad \ldots \quad \ldots \quad (4.11)$$

Thus, marginal product to input is indirectly depend upon the denominator of the above equation. Marginal product decreases with increasing input intensity.

(iv) Since Agricultural Productivity Capacity (APC) is difficult to measure, the economists usually measure it in the form of production elasticity of demand. APC is closely related to these two components of agriculture system as described above. APC is obtained here by applying marginal productivity theory and its coefficient is found to get the ratio of production change with the change occurring in production-potential intensity (i.e., marginal product to production-potential intensity, dY/dIp). In the present function, APC (dY/dIp) is :

$$dY/dIp = -A(Ip)^{-2}. \quad \ldots \quad \ldots \quad \ldots \quad (4.12)$$

Since production elasticity of production-potential intensity is constant at unity in the present production function, the APC must be equal to production per unit of production-potential intensity, because,

$$dY/dIp = Y/Ip, \text{ subject to } Ip > 1.0 \text{ then } APC < Y.$$

Substituting equation 4.2 in the above equation, one finds,

$$APC = (Y/A).Y = (PE)\ Y. \quad \ldots \quad \ldots \quad \ldots \quad (4.13)$$

Note that the values of APC may also be calculated over time by obtaining rate of production growth with the proportional changes in yield-potential intensity within the specific points of time.

The present discussion leads to an important conclusion that the absorption rate of production potential intensity and marginal product to input are the major determinants of agricultural production increase. They follow concavity (diminishing with decreasing rate non-negatively) in the distribution. The inter-regional variations in these determinants of agricultural production can be revealed by calculating their values with the help of above equations since district-wise empirical data of A, Y and X are available. Before describing the empirical results of its regional variations, one can move towards logical discussion regarding the causes and effects of these determinants on the agricultural production system.

The numerator of the present production function, A, is directly related to the ***yield - stimulating factors*** because increasing magnitude of A increases the level of crop-production. But it is interesting to note that it acts as constant and does not have any effect on the marginal product to factor input (eqn. 4.11) in agricultural production system. However, its magnitude varies according to variations occurring in the agro-ecological land conditions. These conditions are changeable temporally and hence, it also changes over time. For instance, in the areas of suitable agro-ecological conditions for plant growth where soils are fertile with daily mean temperature ranging from 10^{0C} to 30^{0C} with sufficient moisture availability (i.e., the mean monthly rainfall greater than half of the potential - evapotranspiration, $p > 0.5$ PE), the rates of plant seed germination and plant growth will be higher because of greater magnitude of production-potential availability and fast acceleration of potential generation processes in these high land-capacity areas. Since plants are good converter of soil nutrients into agricultural production, higher the soil fertility, higher will be the marginal product of seed and hence, positive relationship between soil fertility and seed rate exists (Kata 1990, pp. 95-96). As a result, the magnitude of A must be higher in these areas. Further, biological researches are the stimulating factors of crop-yield increase and hence, they also increase the level of A.

On the other hand, degree of production-potential intensity Ip(x), that is the denominator term of the production function, is inversely related to input intensity. It means increasing labour and/or technological inputs must diminish the degree of production potential intensity because,

$$dIp/dX = -BX^{-2}, \quad d^2Ip/dX^2 > 0. \qquad \ldots \qquad .. \qquad \ldots \qquad (4.14)$$

Indeed, increasing farm technology or labour absorbs production potential intensity at BX^{-2} rate for the increase of crop-yield. The absorption rate of potential intensity is checked by some factors, which may be called, ***yield restricting factors***. Undoubtedly, diminishing rate of production-potential absorption (as stated by eqn. 4.12) diminishes rate of crop production and therefore, production increases with decreasing rate. As a result, agricultural production function always follows the law of diminishing marginal return. These processes of agricultural production potential generation as well as utilization influence to alter the agricultural landuse patterns of an area in which the magnitude of production potential are absorbed over time for intensification of landuse patterns (Table- 4.5, Fig.- 4.5).

Table- 4.5: Stages of Transformation, Levels of Modernization and Production Potential Absorption in Agricultural System.

Agricultural Characteristics	Stages of Transformation		
	Initial Stage (t_{n+0})	Growing Stage (t_{n+1})	Saturation Stage (t_{n+2})
Agricultural Systems and types	Traditional System and Subsistence type of Agriculture	Transitional System with Intensive Subsistence Grain farming in Agriculture	Modernized System with the capital intensive commercialised farming
Landuse Patterns	Generalization of crops	Intensification and Diversification of Crops	Specialization of Crops
Levels of Modernization	Rudimentary Technology: work done by hand or with the help of animal power	Sub-Technical Level: some mechanization & moderate use of chemicals for land operations	Technical Level: Regular use of mecha- of mechanical aids & agricultural chemicals
Productivity Levels Leves and Rates of Yield Potential	Very Low Very high levels with extremely high rate potential absorption	High Moderate availability with high rate of potential absorption	Very High Low level of yield potential with very low rates of its absorption

N.B.: For detail, see Fig.- 4.5.

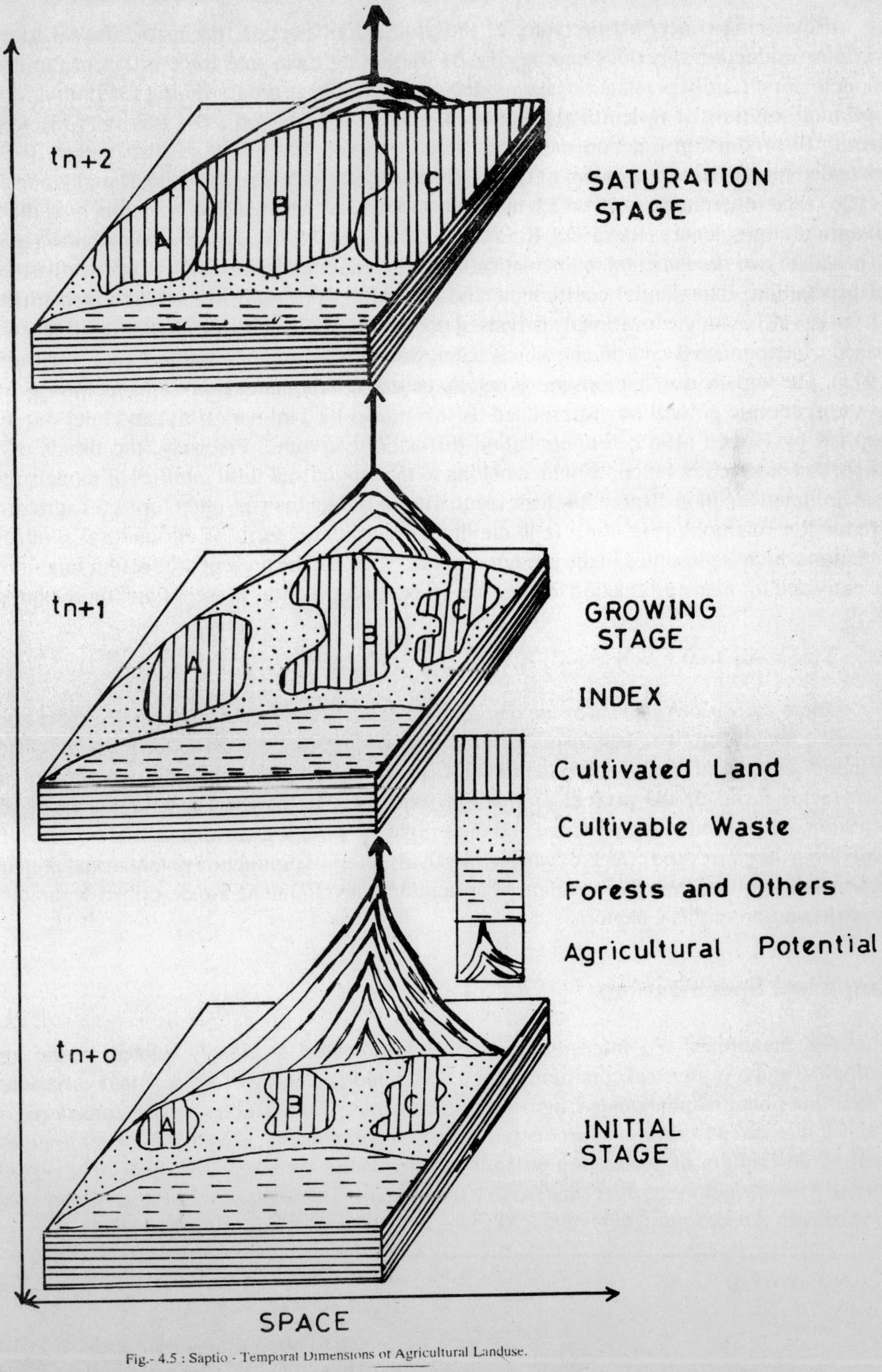

Fig.- 4.5 : Saptio - Temporal Dimensions of Agricultural Landuse.

Reviewing concerned literature of the production function, the mathematical forms of various production functions can be studied by putting them into three different families of models. First family is related to the models based on linear programming for finding out the optimum solutions of agricultural production (Khusro 1968, Singh 1974, Rakita 1975). Second family of production function models is based on quadratic nature of distribution. It is the extended form of linear equations of its non-linear nature (Ram Sharan 1965). Dauglas and Cobb (1928) used logarithmic form which is later on applied by many Indian researchers in the field of agricultural sciences (Rao 1968, Kata 1990). The third family of production function models is based on two fundamental mathematical theories: exponential as well as logistic distribution of production. Exponential coefficients and constants were used in the elaborated forms by Hudsom (1972) for the locational analysis of geographical diffusion, while Spillman function is based on exponential coefficient which regresses in its asymptotic manner (cf. Abler, *et. al.* 1971). The logistic distributions are generally based on exponential and semi-reciprocal forms as the economic growth was formulated by this model by Tintiner (1961) and later on, it was applied by Brown (1965) for innovation diffusion over time. Precisely, the trends of five important production functions which belong to the second and third families of models reveal that Spillman function displays the least inequality and better than the other forms for agricultural production functions (Fig.-4.6). It is similar to reciprocity form of agricultural production function which is presented in the present context. Note that the present production function can be extended for many production factors. Many-factor form of the present function is expressed as :

$$Y(x) = A\,[\,1.00 + B_1X_1^{-1} + B_2X_2^{-1} + B_3X_3^{-1} + \ldots + B_nX_n^{-1}\,]^{-1}. \quad \ldots \quad \ldots \quad (4.15)$$

There are various aspects of the marginal productivity theory which can be studied in the present context. But two major aspects of the theory which are related to the marginal product to inputs and rate of production potential absorption capacity, are taken into account to apply 'two-factor form' of the present production function. The imperial specifications of these determinants of production potential and their regional variations, which should be helpful for explaining the causes and effects of various physical factors of production potential and preparing regional investment strategy for balanced agricultural development, are described separately in the next section of this Chapter.

Empirical Specifications

The magnitude and intensity of production-potential is closely related to the agro-ecological and bio-physical conditions. For a better understanding of the regional variations of production potential phenomena, agro-ecological zones of the country can be considered as a base for regional description of production potential components. It would be better to give the detailed description of production potential by analysing the yield gaps and yield potential intensity for various crops over time, so that the temporal fluctuations of these components can be specified. Accordingly, the concerned material is arranged into two broad heads.

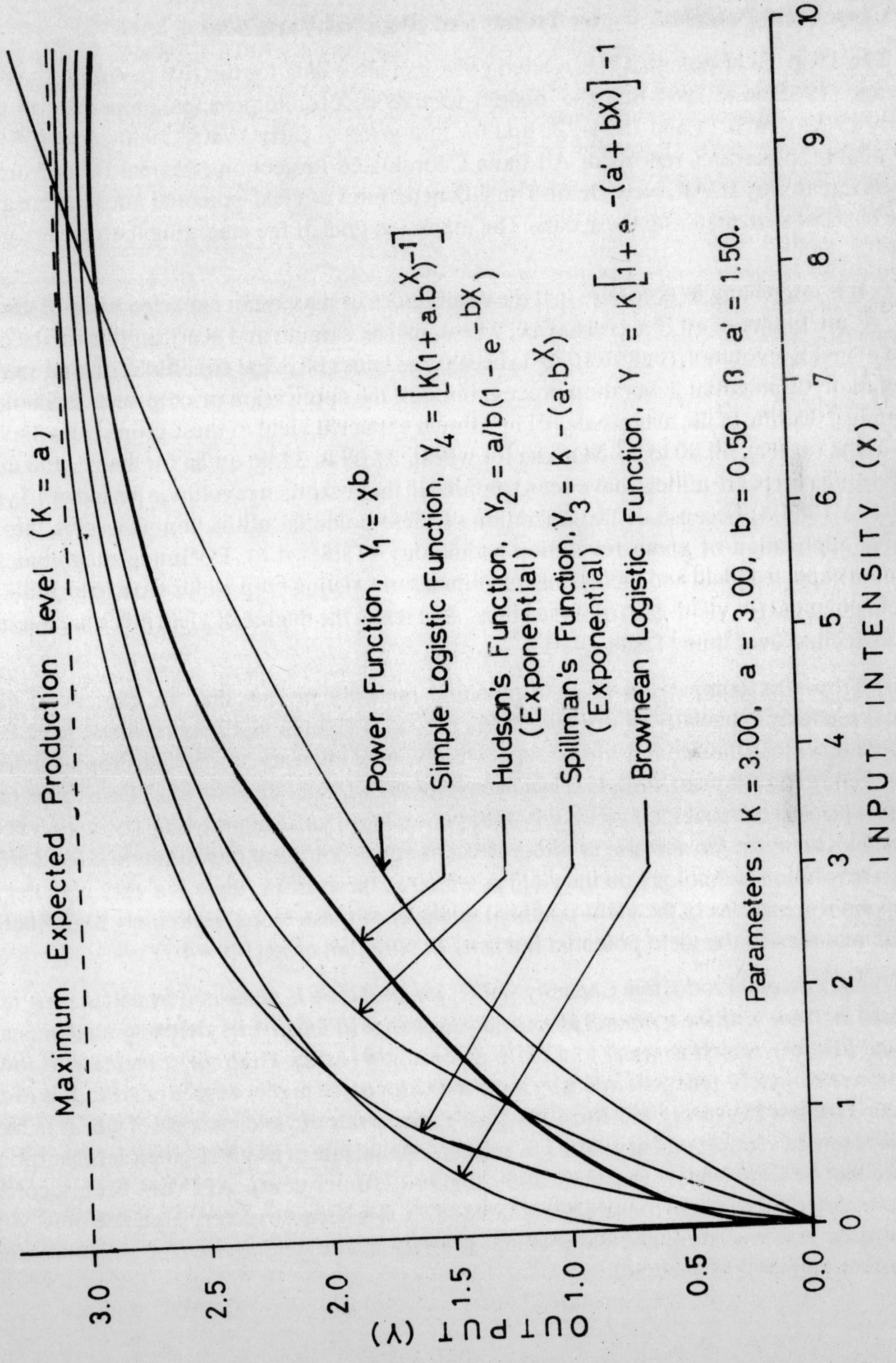

Fig.- 4.6 : Various Production Functions with its Known Parameters.

(A) Crop Yield Potential — Its Trends and Regional Variations

The crop yield potential (i.e., called yield-gap also) data for the five major crops for the 20 years (1965-66 to 1984-85) and district-wise its data for all principal crops for two years of early 1970s (1970-71 and 1971-72) and for four years of early 1980s (1980-81 to 1984-85) are available in various reports of All India Coordinated Project on National Demonstration Projects initiated by ICAR, New Delhi. The salient features of yield-potential intensity are given on the basis of systematizing these data. The major insights of the emerging features are given below.

i) It is interesting to note here that the magnitudes of maximum expected yield of various crops, A_i, are higher of all five crops (rice, wheat, maize, sargum and pearl-millets) in the early period of green revolution (before 1970-1) because of better physical conditions of land and fast acceleration of potential generation process through the application of crop-seed technology. The gradual decline in the magnitudes of maximum expected yield of these crops from 37.93 to 32.24 qu/ha for rice, 40.80 to 35.54 qu/ha for wheat, 37.89 to 34.96 qu/ha for maize, and 28.76 to 23.88 qu/ha for pearl-millets, have been recorded in the post green revolution period of 15 years (1970-1 to 1984-5) because of fast operation of yield potential utilization processes through intensive application of green revolution technology (Table- 4.6). Declining magnitudes of maximum expected yield and increasing magnitudes of existing crop yields have been reducing the yield potential (or yield-gap) of these crops. As a result the degree of yield potential intensity tends to decline over time (Table - 4.6).

ii) Crop-wise comparison of yield-potential intensity reveals that the degrees of yield potential intensity especially of dry land crops (maize, sorghum and pearl-millets) have been recorded higher than the rice and wheat crops. The potential intensity of sorghum crop is recorded highest (5.63) and for pearl-millets it has been very high (4.12) in 1984-85. These crops have better prospects to increase their yields through application of yield-augmenting (irrigation-seed-fertilizer) technology. On account of direct effect of agro-ecological conditions and least effect of green revolution technology on the yield potential of these crops, there is a very high degree of temporal fluctuations in the yield-potential intensity of these crops. Extremely high fluctuations are recorded in the yield potential intensity of sorghum crop (Fig.- 4.7).

iii) Agricultural Productive Capacity (APC) for each crop is measured by calculating ratio of its yield increase with the temporal proportionate change (dY/dt) of its yield potential intensity over time (dIp/dt), which is equal to dY/dIp as equation (4.12). High yield increase at lower absorption rate of yield-potential intensity is the indicator of the higher degree of APC. It is found that, during the last 15 years (1965-6 to 1984-5), the annual rate of yield increase of wheat in India has been recorded at 6.32 percent with a 3.02 per cent annual rate of its yield-potential absorption. It means the APC of wheat is significantly higher (210 per cent). APC has been recorded extremely high (282 percent) for sarghum (Table- 4.7). It is because of very high rate of its yield increase at the very low rate of its yield potential absorption. The APC of rice crop is also recorded significantly higher (215 percent).

Table- 4.6: All India Maximum Expected Yield (A), Existing Yield (Y) and Yield Potential Intensity (Ip) of the Principal Crops (1965-66 to1984-85).

Years	Rice			Wheat			Maize			Sorghum			Pearl-Millet		
	A	Y	Ip	A	Y	Ip	A	Y	Ip	A	Y	Ip	A	Y	Ip
1965-66	27.96	8.62	3.24	39.61	8.27	4.79	39.76	10.05	3.95	3.76	4.29	7.40	27.06	3.24	8.62
1966-67	31.96	8.63	3.70	36.82	8.87	4.15	43.76	9.64	4.54	27.15	5.11	5.31	30.43	3.65	8.34
1967-68	35.56	10.32	3.44	41.78	11.03	3.79	42.36	11.33	3.77	35.53	5.45	6.52	33.55	4.05	8.28
1968-69	39.64	10.76	3.68	40.90*	11.69	3.50	43.88	9.97	4.40	46.69	5.23	8.93	33.01	3.15	10.08
1969-70	37.93	10.73	3.53	40.70	12.09	3.36	42.40	9.68	4.38	35.90	5.22	6.88	32.40	4.26	7.60
1970-71	37.90	11.23	3.37	40.80	13.07	3.12	37.89	12.79	2.96	35.96	4.66	7.72	28.76	6.22	4.62
1971-72	36.78	11.41	3.22	45.01	13.80	3.26	39.17	9.00	4.35	42.61	4.60	9.26	26.81	4.52	5.93
1972-73	34.78	10.70	3.25	33.02	12.71	2.60	38.59	10.94	3.53	30.74	4.49	6.84	29.62	3.33	8.89
1973-74	35.13	11.51	3.05	37.03	11.72	3.16	34.88	9.65	3.61	32.17	5.44	5.91	26.20	5.00	5.24
1974-75	32.12	10.45	3.07	34.46	13.38	2.57	36.51	9.48	3.85	38.73	6.43	6.03	23.87	2.90	8.23
1975-76	34.31	12.35	2.78	39.14	14.10	2.77	32.38	12.03	2.69	35.54	5.91	6.01	21.42	4.96	4.32
1976-77	34.33	10.88	3.15	32.80	13.87	2.36	30.88	10.60	2.91	40.40	6.67	6.05	25.90	5.44	4.76
1977-78	34.51	13.08	2.64	36.65	14.80	2.47	34.30	10.51	3.26	42.95	7.39	5.81	26.22	4.26	6.15
1978-79	34.64	13.20	2.62	35.07	15.68	2.24	36.54	10.76	3.39	35.24	7.08	4.98	24.88	4.89	5.08
1979-80	31.96	10.74	2.97	36.85	14.36	2.57	33.23	9.79	3.39	40.79	6.99	5.83	23.64	3.78	6.25
1980-81	30.42	13.36	2.28	33.54	16.30	2.06	32.67	11.50	2.84	33.18	6.60	5.03	31.65	4.58	6.91
1981-82	32.30	13.08	2.47	37.15	16.91	2.19	32.57	11.62	2.80	34.03	7.27	4.68	25.23	4.70	5.37
1982-83	32.06	12.30	2.61	40.10	18.36	2.18	31.58	11.02	2.86	36.14	6.63	5.45	26.08	4.72	5.52
1983-84	32.18	14.58	2.21	31.82	18.51	1.72	30.86	13.46	2.29	34.71	7.34	4.73	24.34	6.46	3.76
1984-85	32.24	14.25	2.26	35.54	18.73	1.90	34.96	14.41	2.43	40.36	7.17	5.63	23.88	5.79	4.12

N.B. : Ip = (A/Y) which refers to Yield Potential Intensity. * = estimated yield.

Source : Prasad,C., *et.al.*,(1987): *First Line Transfer of Technology Projects*, Publication & Information Division, ICAR, New Delhi, Table- 2a, p. 12.

Table - 4.6

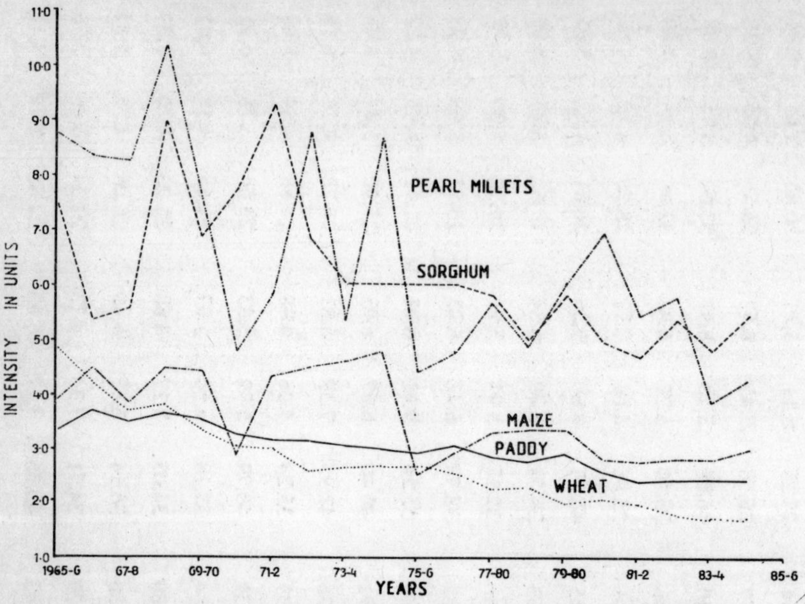

Fig.- 4.7 : Yield Potential Intensity of Various Crops in India

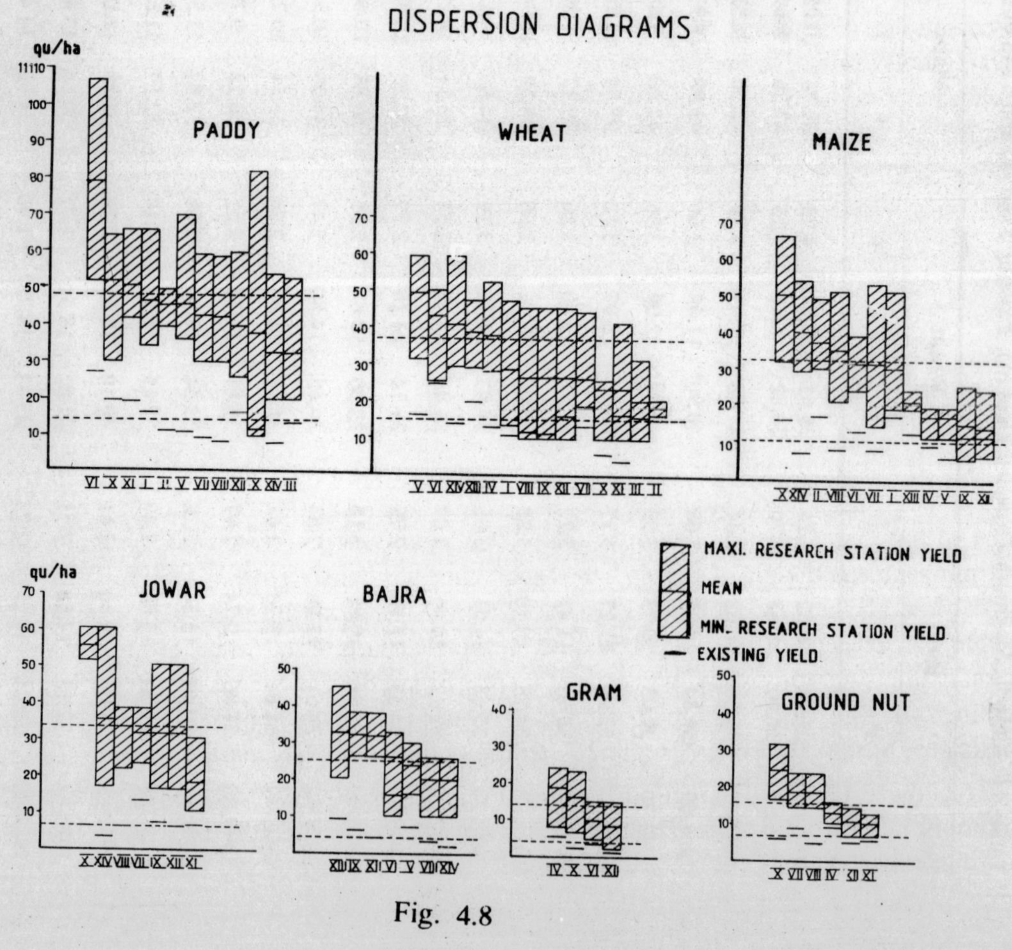

Fig. 4.8

Table- 4.7: Agricultural Production Capacity (APC) of Various Crops.

	Crops	Annual Rate of		
		Yield increase (%)	Yield potential absorption (%)	APC (%)
1.	Rice	3.26	1.51	215.89
2.	Wheat	6.32	3.02	209.27
3.	Maize	2.17	1.92	113.02
4.	Sorghum	3.36	1.19	282.35
5.	Pearl-Millets	4.22	2.61	161.68

N.B.: Annual rates are calculated on constant change of concerned phenomena. For the same, 1965-66 is considered as base year and 1984-85 as current year.

iv) Of course, the regional variations marked in the magnitudes of yield potential of various crops occur because of regional variations in bio-physical factors of land and technological constraints. The dispersed nature of maximum expected yield and existing yield magnitudes (that are the major components of crop yield potential) is interpreted in order to show the effects of physiographic conditions by arranging yield potential data of various crops according to physiographic zones of the country. Considering physiographic attributes with administrative boundaries, Indian Statistical Institute, New Delhi tried to delineate physiographic regional complexes for practical purpose (Bhat 1968) which was, later on, used by Planning Commission (1987) for interpreting agro-ecological conditions. The dispersion diagrams showing inter- and intra-regional variations of growth components depict that :

(a) The magnitudes of crop yield have very low degree of regional variability of different crops in various physiographic conditions of the country. For example, paddy yield varies from 26.6 qu/ha recorded in the Punjab plains to 8.5 qu/ha in the central plateau, wheat yield from 25.5 qu/ha of Punjab plains to 5.7 qu/ha of southern plateau, maize crop yield from 18.5 qu/ha recorded in southern plateau to 8.7 qu/ha of dry zone of Rajasthan. Very low degree of regional variations are recorded in groundnut crop-yield, that is from 11.4 qu/ha to 5.0 qu/ha (Table-4.8).

(b) The degree of regional variability occurring in the magnitudes of maximum expected yield of the crops is observed very high in case of rice and very low for groundnut. The variability range of this component is determined by taking data of maximum and minimum levels of maximum expected yield of various crops available at on-farm research station level. It is found that paddy and wheat are the crops which have the maximum variations in its maximum expected yield levels. The areas of Punjab plains and the western parts of the forelands of Deccan Plateau are markable for paddy yield-expectation levels (Fig.-4.8). The intensive application of HYV seed in paddy cultivation in Punjab plains and change in physiographic conditions in the central upland are the main reasons of regional variability of paddy yield expectations.

(c) Jowar, bajra and groundnut, the dry land crops, have very low range of variations in the maximum expected as well as existing yield magnitudes in India. It is because of their natural growth resistance.

Table- 4.8: Maximum Expected Yield (A) and Existing Crop Yield (Y) of Major Crops in Various Agro-Ecological Zones (1984-85).

(yield in qu/ha)

Agro-Ecological Zones	Paddy		Wheat		Maize		Jowar		Bajra		Gram		G. Nut		Moong		Arhar		Potato		S. Cane		Jute		Cotton	
	A	Y	A	Y	A	Y	A	Y	A	Y	A	Y	A	Y	A	Y	A	Y	A	Y	A	Y	A	Y	A	Y
I	47.1	16.1	28.6	11.5	31.0	18.1	-	-	-	-	-	-	-	-	-	-	-	-	-	-	-	-	-	-	-	-
II	46.5	11.1	18.7	11.5	38.0	18.2	-	-	-	-	-	-	-	-	-	-	-	-	-	-	-	-	30.0	14.6	-	-
III	32.6	14.4	20.8	16.7			-	-	-	-	-	-	-	-	-	-	-	-	-	-	-	-	52.0	13.1	-	-
IV	44.6	10.2	37.5	13.1	17.1	11.6	-	-	-	-	19.5	7.0	13.0	11.4	-	-	-	-	-	-	-	-	-	-	-	-
V	46.1	10.5	49.7	16.4	17.1	7.1	-	-	23.0	7.3	-	-	-	-	7.4	1.7	20.4	11.7	249.8	88.2	-	-	-	-	-	-
VI	78.8	26.6	43.7	25.5	32.5	14.1	-	-	25.4	23.5	10.0	6.2	-	-	-	-	-	-	-	-	-	-	-	-	-	-
VII	43.3	9.3	26.5	13.6	31.3	9.1	31.4	21.5	-	-	-	-	18.3	9.5	-	-	-	-	-	-	-	-	-	-	-	-
VIII	42.2	8.5	26.6	12.0	36.3	8.9	33.3	5.6	19.5	4.3	-	-	18.3	5.0	-	-	-	-	-	-	-	-	-	-	-	-
IX	38.5	12.0	26.8	11.6	16.3	13.1	31.1	7.3	31.7	5.2	-		-	-	-	-	-	-	-	-	-	-	-	-	18.0	0.7
X	52.3	19.2	23.8	5.7	51.0	18.5	55.1	5.2	-	-	16.2	2.5	25.0	6.3	7.9	2.0	-	-	-	-	-	-	-	-	24.3	1.9
XI	50.6	19.1	23.6	4.6	-	-	16.5	7.5	26.7	7.6	-	-	10.9	7.1	-	-	-	-	-	-	142.5	85.8	-	-	-	-
XII	40.0	16.0	26.6	15.6	15.0	13.1	31.1	5.6	31.7	4.4	8.3	3.5	11.5	8.1	-	-	-	-	-	-	-	-	-	-	-	-
XIII	-	11.6	39.0	20.0	21.6	13.1	-	6.4	32.3	8.8	-	-	-	-	-	-	-	-	285.4	179.0	-	-	-	-	-	-
XIV	33.0	8.8	41.6	14.6	40.8	8.7	35.3	3.4	19.5	2.3	-	-	-	-	-	-	-	-	-	-	-	-	-	-	-	-
All India	48.3	13.4	37.1	15.8	32.6	11.5	34.0	6.9	25.2	4.3	14.1	8.0	16.7	8.1	6.9	3.0	-	-	240.7	130.0	-	-	-	-	-	-

N.B. : For the name of Agro-Ecological Zones, see Table- 4.10.

Table 4.8

Table- 4.9: Yield Potential Magnitude (P) and its Intensity (I) in Various Agro-Ecological Zones (1984-85).

Agro-Ecological Zones	Paddy		Wheat		Maize		Jowar		Bajra		Gram		G. Nut		Moong		Arhar		Potato		S. Cane		Jute		Cotton	
	P	I	P	I	P	I	P	I	P	I	P	I	P	I	P	I	P	I	P	I	P	I	P	I	P	I
I	31.0	2.92	17.1	2.89	12.9	1.71	-	-	-	-	-	-	-	-	-	-	-	-	-	-	-	-	-	-	-	-
II	35.4	4.19	7.1	1.63	19.8	2.09	-	-	-	-	-	-	-	-	-	-	-	-	-	-	-	-	15.4	2.05	-	-
III	18.2	2.26	4.1	1.24	-	-	-	-	-	-	-	-	-	-	-	-	-	-	-	-	-	-	38.9	3.97	-	-
IV	34.4	4.37	24.4	2.86	5.5	1.47	-	-	-	-	12.5	2.78	1.6	1.14	-	-	-	-	-	-	-	-	-	-	-	-
V	35.6	4.39	33.3	3.03	10.0	2.41	-	-	15.7	3.15	-	-	-	-	5.7	4.35	8.7	1.74	161.6	2.83	-	-	-	-	-	-
VI	52.2	2.96	18.2	1.71	18.4	2.30	-	-	1.9	1.08	3.8	1.61	-	-	-	-	-	-	-	-	-	-	-	-	-	-
VII	34.0	4.65	12.9	1.95	22.2	3.44	9.9	1.46	-	-	-	-	8.8	1.93	-	-	-	-	-	-	-	-	-	-	-	-
VIII	33.7	4.96	14.6	2.22	27.4	4.08	27.7	5.95	15.2	4.53	-	-	13.3	3.66	-	-	-	-	-	-	-	-	-	-	-	-
IX	26.5	3.21	15.2	2.31	3.2	1.24	23.8	4.26	26.5	6.10	-	-	-	-	-	-	-	-	-	-	-	-	-	-	17.3	25.71
X	33.1	2.72	18.1	4.17	32.5	2.76	49.9	10.60	-	-	13.7	6.48	18.7	3.97	5.9	3.95	-	-	-	-	-	-	-	-	22.4	12.79
XI	31.5	2.65	19.0	5.13	-	-	9.0	2.20	19.1	3.51	-	-	3.8	1.53	-	-	-	-	-	-	56.7	1.66	-	-	-	-
XII	24.0	2.50	11.0	1.70	1.9	1.14	25.5	5.55	27.3	7.20	4.8	2.37	3.4	1.42	-	-	-	-	-	-	-	-	-	-	-	-
XIII	-	-	19.0	1.95	8.5	1.65	-	-	23.5	3.67	-	-	-	-	-	-	-	-	106.4	1.59	-	-	-	-	-	-
XIV	24.2	3.75	27.0	2.85	32.1	4.69	31.9	10.38	17.2	8.48	-	-	-	-	-	-	-	-	-	-	-	-	-	-	-	-
All India	34.9	3.60	21.3	2.35	21.1	2.83	27.1	4.93	20.9	5.86	6.1	1.76	8.6	2.06	3.9	2.30	-	-	110.7	1.85	-	-	-	-	-	-

N.B. : (1) Yield-Potential Magnitude is difference and its Intensity is the ratio between A and Y, (2) For the name of Agro-Ecological Zones, see Table- 4.10.

table 4.9

v) In India, the yield-potential intensity of jowar and bajra are recorded extremely high, 4.93 and 5.86 respectively. The suitable areas of their proper utilization are the Thar and central parts of the Deccan plateau of arid conditions (Table-4.9). Intensity and magnitudes of paddy crop potential are recorded higher in the North-Eastern Regions (specially in Brahmaputra valley) and the Middle Ganga plains of Bihar and West Bengal where paddy yield can be increased at minimum input costs. The magnitude of wheat yield-potential is recorded highest (33.3 qu/ha) in the Upper Ganga plains particularly in the Western Uttar Pradesh (Table-4.9).

vi) To optimise the agricultural production conditions, the alteration in the cropping pattern and crop priorities must be determined on the basis of intensity and magnitudes of crop yield potentials, while the changing patterns of present day are being attributed to agricultural price - cost mechanism which diversifies crop-combination in India as described earlier in Chapter-2. The optimal crop-combination regions which are demarcated by Husain (1979, p. 125) by considering areal importance of the crops, must be proposed on crop-yield potentiality basis because it is the reflection of the best suitable agro-ecological conditions for crop-growth and yield- increase. For example, if a crop has greater magnitude and higher intensity of its yield-potential in the homogeneous set of agro-ecological conditions, it should be put on first in relation to crop preference in the crop-combination of the area. Thus, the optimal crop combination pattern must follow crop-yield potentiality criterion rather than land-occupancy one. This criterion of optimal crop combination may also be helpful for fixing up the priorities of input structure, infra-structural agricultural variables and the normative requirements of the agriculture sector specially for the agro-ecological zones. Following same criterion of the optimal cropping patterns for different sets of physiographic conditions of the country, it can be realised that paddy should be the first ranking crop in the areas of Western Himalayas, the North eastern parts (specially Brahmaputra valley) and the eastern parts of Chhota Nagpur plateau while entire central part of Deccan plateau (agro-ecological zones VIII, IX and X) has dry land farming for which jowar and bajra are the suitable crops in their diversified optimal cropping patterns (Table 4.10).

Table- 4.10: Optimal Crop Combinations Based on Yield Potentials.

S. No.	Agro-Ecological Zones	Crop Combination	No.of Crops
I	Western Himalayas	P-W	2
II	N.E. Mts & Valleys*	P-Ju-W	3
III	Lower Ganges Plains	Ju-P	2
IV	Middle Ganges Plains	G-W-M-P	4
V	Upper Ganges Plains	Mo-P-G-Po-W-S	6
VI	Punjab Plains	G-T-P	3
VII	Central Plateau	P-M-B-W	4
VIII	Central Highlands	B-Gn-P-W-J-M	6
IX	North Deccan	B-J-W-C	4
X	South Deccan	J-W-Mo-Gn-G	5
XI	East Coasts	W-M	2
XII	Western Coasts	B-G-M-W	4
XIII	The Gujarat	J-Po-B-P	4
XIV	The Thar	M-W-B	3

N.B.: * It includes Brahmaputra valley (Assam State) only. The ranks of various crops is fixed according to the degree of their yield potential intensities upto a level of significant crops.

Abbreviations: P= Paddy, W= Wheat, J= Jowar, B= Bajra, M= Maize, G= Gram, T= Tur (Arhar), Mo=Moong (Pulse), Gn= Ground-Nut, Po= Potato, S= Sugar Cane, C= Cotton, Ju= Jute.

Same crops are also significant in the optimal cropping patterns in the Western Coastal Areas and the Gujarat plains of humid climate (Agro-ecological zones XII and XIII) because of availability of their HYV's for wheat cultivation. HYV maize crop should get first priority in Rajasthan while wheat has second rank in proposed cropping pattern in this area (Table-4.10). The yield of these crops can be increased by increasing irrigation facilities. It should always be kept in mind that because of changes in potential generation forces, the magnitude and intensity of crop-potentials are changeable according to time as described earlier. Therefore, the optimal crop combinations and the priorities of the crops are also changeable.

(B) Agricultural Production Potential — The Regional Patterns

In the preceding section of this chapter, the individual crop-wise trends and regional variations of crop-yield potential have been described. But the aggregate picture of these crop-yield potential would produce a synthetic view of production-potential. District-wise aggregated production-potential index is prepared by using the same formula of agricultural output aggregation in terms of money value (see eqn. 1.4a). It is assumed that land-occupancy and production prices are the weight and conversion factors in this equation. The yield of various crops is the main component of agricultural output. Replacing crop-yield by maximum expected yield of the crop for each district (which is available in the various reports of the All India Co-Ordinated Projects on National Demonstration Projects of ICAR, New Delhi at site sample of on-farm research level, see Prasad, *et al.* 1987), and putting the same values of land-occupancy of crop as weight, and production prices as conversion factor in equation (1.4a), the aggregated output of maximum expected yield per hectare of cultivated land (i.e., called maximum expected production, A) is calculated for each district. Land productivity which is aggregated output per hectare of cultivated land as described earlier in Chapter-3, is called here existing production, Y, for the measurement of magnitude of agricultural production potential, P, as stated in equation 4.1. P increases since A is increased by accelerating potential generation processes and it decreases when Y is increased in agricultural systems.

Visualizing distributional patterns of the magnitudes of production potential (Fig.-4.9) and comparing them with the patterns of land productivity (agricultural output per hectare of cultivated land) as shown by Fig.-3.3, it is interesting to note that the areas of high land productivity as the entire great plains of North India including the Coastal plain areas, have high and very high magnitudes of production potentials (above Rs. 3000 per hectare). It might be on account of extremely high levels of maximum expected production. With high soil fertility in these alluvial soils and climatic suitability for crop grain weight, length of crop growing period, crop plant density (which are the determinants of production potential generation), the value of maximum expected production, A, is recorded very high in these areas. It varies within high level range from Rs. 12553 to Rs. 4053 per hectare in the Great Plains of Northern India (Table-4.11). The Brahmaputra valley is marked favourably for future growth of agriculture where magnitude and intensity of production potential are recorded extremely high.

On the other hand, areas in arid climatic conditions, namely, the Thar desert and the central parts of the Deccan plateau, have low and very low magnitudes of agricultural production potential (below Rs. 1500 per hectare) in the early 1970s and is expected to continue in the same range in future because of very low level of maximum expected production (Table-4.11). The main causes of low magnitude of production potential are :

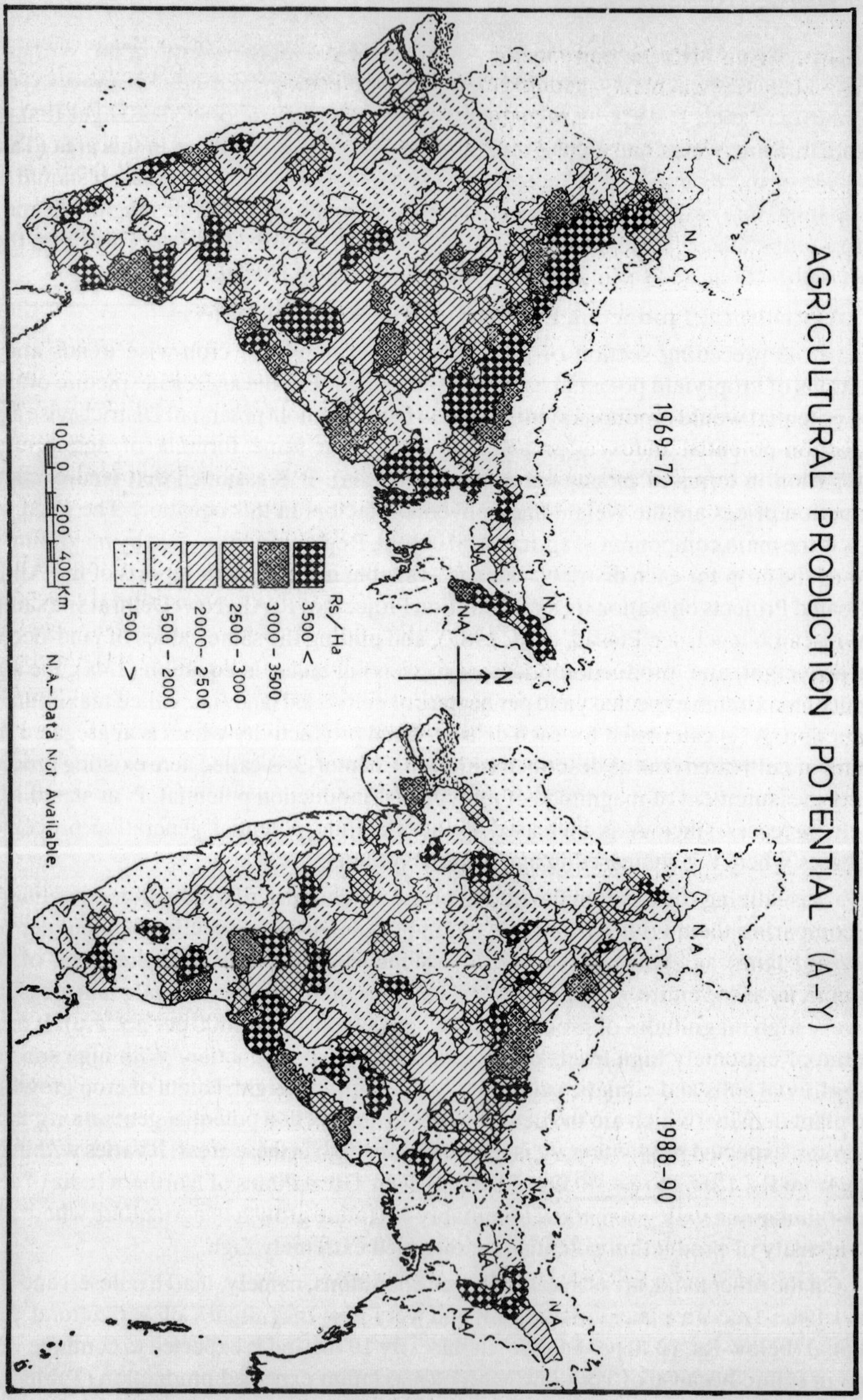
AGRICULTURAL PRODUCTION POTENTIAL (A-Y)
1969-72
1988-90
Rs/Ha
3500 <
3000 – 3500
2500 – 3000
2000 – 2500
1500 – 2000
1500 >
100 0 200 400 Km
N
N.A
N.A.–Data Not Available.

Fig. - 4.9

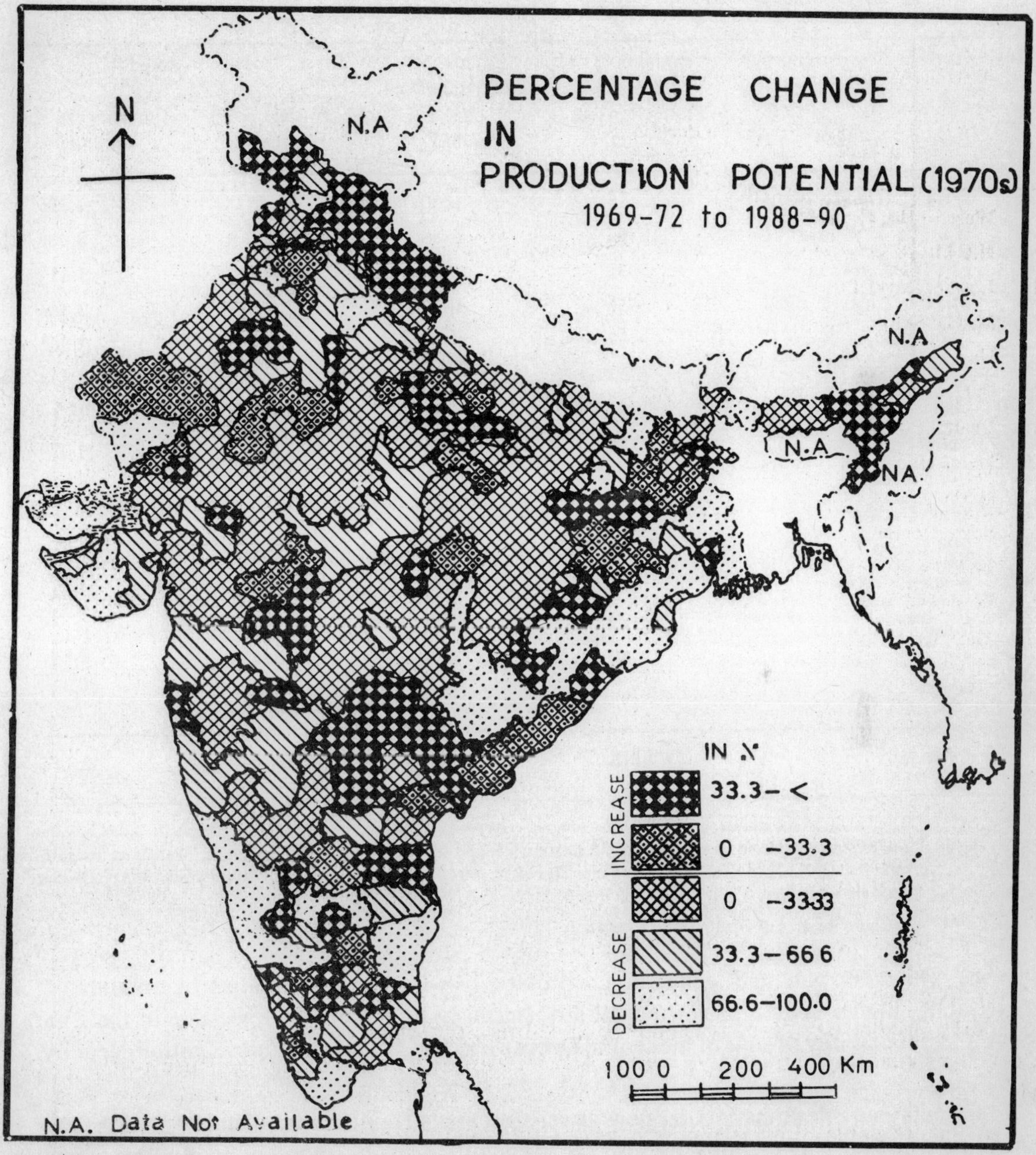
PERCENTAGE CHANGE
IN
PRODUCTION POTENTIAL (1970s)
1969-72 to 1988-90
N
N.A
N.A
N.A
NA
IN %
INCREASE
33.3– <
0 –33.3
DECREASE
0 –33.33
33.3–66.6
66.6–100.0
100 0 200 400 Km
N.A. Data Not Available

Fig. - 4.10

Table-4.11: Magnitude and Intensities of Agricultural Production Potential in Various Physiographic Zones (1988-90).

	Agro-Ecological Zones	Maximum Expected Production (A) (Rs./ha)	Existing Production (Y) (Rs./ha)	Production Potential	
				Magnitude (A-Y) (Rs./ha)	Intensity (A/Y) (in unit)
I	Western Himalayas	3113	1350	1763	2.306
II	N.E.Mts & Valleys**	12553	1568	10985	8.006
III	Lower Ganges Plains	5032	2770	2262	1.817
IV	Middle Ganges Plains	3556	1026	2530	3.466
V	Upper Ganges Plains	3957	1431	2526	2.765
VI	Punjab Plains	4053	2140	1912	1.894
VII	Central Plateau	2903	756	2146	3.840
VIII	Central Himalayas	2798	686	2113	4.079
IX	North Deccan	2517	609	1907	4.133
X	South Deccan	4222	751	3471	5.612
XI	East Coasts	3485	1494	1991	2.331
XII	Western Coasts	1451	616	835	2.355
XIII	The Gujarat	2420	1132	1288	2.138
XIV	The Thar	1160	266	894	4.361
XV	Islands	-	-	-	-
	All India	**3215**	**1184**	**1681**	**2.717**

N.B. : * The values of maximum expected production, A, are based on 1984-85 crop-data. It is composite index in value added term calculated by aggregating the maximum expected production of principal crops. There is an insignificant fluctuation in the level of A over time. Therefore, 1984-85 data is used for 1988-90 for which crop production data are available.

** Includes the area of Brahmaputra valley only.

a) The weak potential generation processes owing to soil constraints like undulating topography, higher degree of soil erodability (made by wind-erosion specially in the Thar areas), less rootability of soils of the central Deccan trap and its less moisture retention capacity, and

b) unfavourable climatic conditions as very low annual rainfall (less than 800 mm) in these areas, less moisture availability and higher variations in daily, monthly as well as annual temperature ranges which directly affect germination of seedlings and growth of plants. Water availability is the biggest constraint of production potentials in these areas of low level of maximum expected production. Calculating coefficients of simple correlations and multiple regression for four explanatory variables related to natural conditions of land suitability for agricultural production potential generation processes (rainfall, soil fertility, moisture index and irrigation) which explain spatial variation in maximum expected production level, it is found that these variables are explaining more than 95.0 per cent variability in the arid areas of the country, whereas only 4.8 per cent spatial variation of maximum expected production is explained in the areas of semi-humid conditions (Punjab, Haryana, Western Madhya Pradesh, Central Maharashtra, Karnataka states) without the significance of any variable. In the humid conditions of Brahmaputra valley and lower Ganga plains including coastal areas of the South India, the moisture and irrigation are the main factors for accelerating production potential processes, though the spatial variation of maximum expected production level is explained only of 40.4 percent by these four variables (Table- 4.12).

Table- 4.12: Simple Correlation Coefficients and Multiple Regression Coefficient for four Explanatory Variables Regressed against Maximum Expected Production in Various Climatic Zones (1988-90)

		Rainfall (mm) (X_1)	Soil Fertility Index (X_2)	Moisture Index (%) (X_3)	Irrigation (NIA in %) (X_4)	Constant (a)	Degree of Determinant (R^2)
I	**Arid Zone (N=17)**						
	1. r	0.3151	0.0010	0.7742	0.2132		
	2. b	-0.0054	0.4960*	1.8371*	-0.0064	139.2220*	0.9591
II	**Semi Arid Zone (N=37)**						
	1. r	0.0066	0.1110	0.1468	0.1768		
	2. b	-0.0023	0.1096	0.3295	0.1337	35.7581*	0.0480
III	**Humid Zone (N=39)**						
	1. r	0.1713	-0.2651	0.5096	0.3310		
	2. b	0.0090	-1.4713	0.7917**	0.7666*	86.7265	0.4040
IV	**All India (N=93)**						
	1. r	0.2375	0.0393	0.4312	0.2809		
	2. b	0.0008	-0.1387	0.4664*	0.2981	45.734	0.2195

Abbreviations : r = Correlation Coefficients, b = Multiple Regression Coefficients, and N = Number of Observations (i.e., sample districts) chosen for present study.

N.B. : ** Significant at 0.01 level, * Significant at 0.05 level.

These empirical observations stand testimony to the facts that moisture availability which is insignificantly related in negative manner to irrigate area (r = - 0.142), is the main determinant of the maximum expected production. The magnitude and intensity of production potential can only be engendered through providing canal irrigation in the arid areas in the country because of inaccessible and limited source of underground water availabilities. The dry land farming and suitable crop-combinations as given in table may help to increase the production and productivity in these areas of low production potential. It is interesting to note that a significant increase of about 33.3 percent in these areas of low magnitude of production potential is recorded during the last 20 years (Fig.- 4.10). It is primarily due to fast acceleration of potential generation processes through extension of irrigation facilities.

(C) Production Potential Intensity versus Agricultural Efficiency

Measuring production potential intensity is helpful in understanding the inherent characteristics of agricultural growth and strategy to prepare for its proper utilization. Equations 4.2 and 4.3 express logically the reciprocal relationship between production potential intensity and agricultural efficiency. Obviously, the value of production potential intensity will always be greater than unity because it is the ratio of maximum expected yield with existing crop yields (eqn. 4.2 & Assumption- a) and hence, the value of agricultural efficiency must be lesser than unity because they have perfectly inverse relationship between them. It may be noted here that agricultural efficiency is the coefficient of agricultural production per hectare of land for Agricultural Productive Capacity and hence, APC is the product of agricultural efficiency and land productivity (eqn. 4.13). On the other hand, production potential intensity, which is usually called realization factor of agricultural growth by many agricultural scientists (Kumar 1986, Varadarajan 1986) determines the rate of agricultural production increase in the system. Since agricultural efficiency is perfectly and inversely related to production potential intensity in the agricultural system, the regional patterns of one of them, especially of agricultural efficiency, are essential to describe the observations of its impact on other components of the system in relation to its areal perspective.

Classifying all areal units into five equi-interval agricultural efficiency classes, namely, very high (above 60 per cent), high (45-60), medium (30-45), low (15-30) and very low (0-15 per cent), the maps of efficiency patterns are prepared for early 1970s and late 1980s (Fig.-4.11). They show that the areas of the lower Ganga plains, Punjab plain and the east and western coastal parts of Andhra Pradesh, Tamil Nadu, Kerala and Maharashtra have high and very high degree of agricultural efficiency (above 45 per cent). Nearly 15 per cent area has recorded an increase under these categories in the last 20 years (Table-4.13). Low and very low efficiency (below 30 per cent) areas which are situated mainly in the arid conditions of Rajasthan, Madhya Pradesh, Maharashtra and Karnataka have reduced in its areal extent during the same period of time (Fig.-4.11). Nearly 30 per cent reduction of low efficiency areas of the arid zone of the country has been possible because of increase in land productivity through the use of modern irrigation-seed-fertilizer technology, while the maximum expected production level, A, remained almost constant during the successive period of time. In the fertile plains of the country, agricultural efficiency has been rising by intensifying production processes through provision of better infrastructural facilities (market accessibility and transport efficiency) with balanced price and costs economic scheme, changing crop-combinations from food-fodder based to cash-crop dominated and spreading the effects of new agricultural researches and its applications. Note that, in the areas of high agricultural efficiency, the degree of production potential intensity is very low on account of higher absorption rate through yield-augumenting techniques. The rate of production increase in relation to production potential absorption can be studied in detail under separate head.

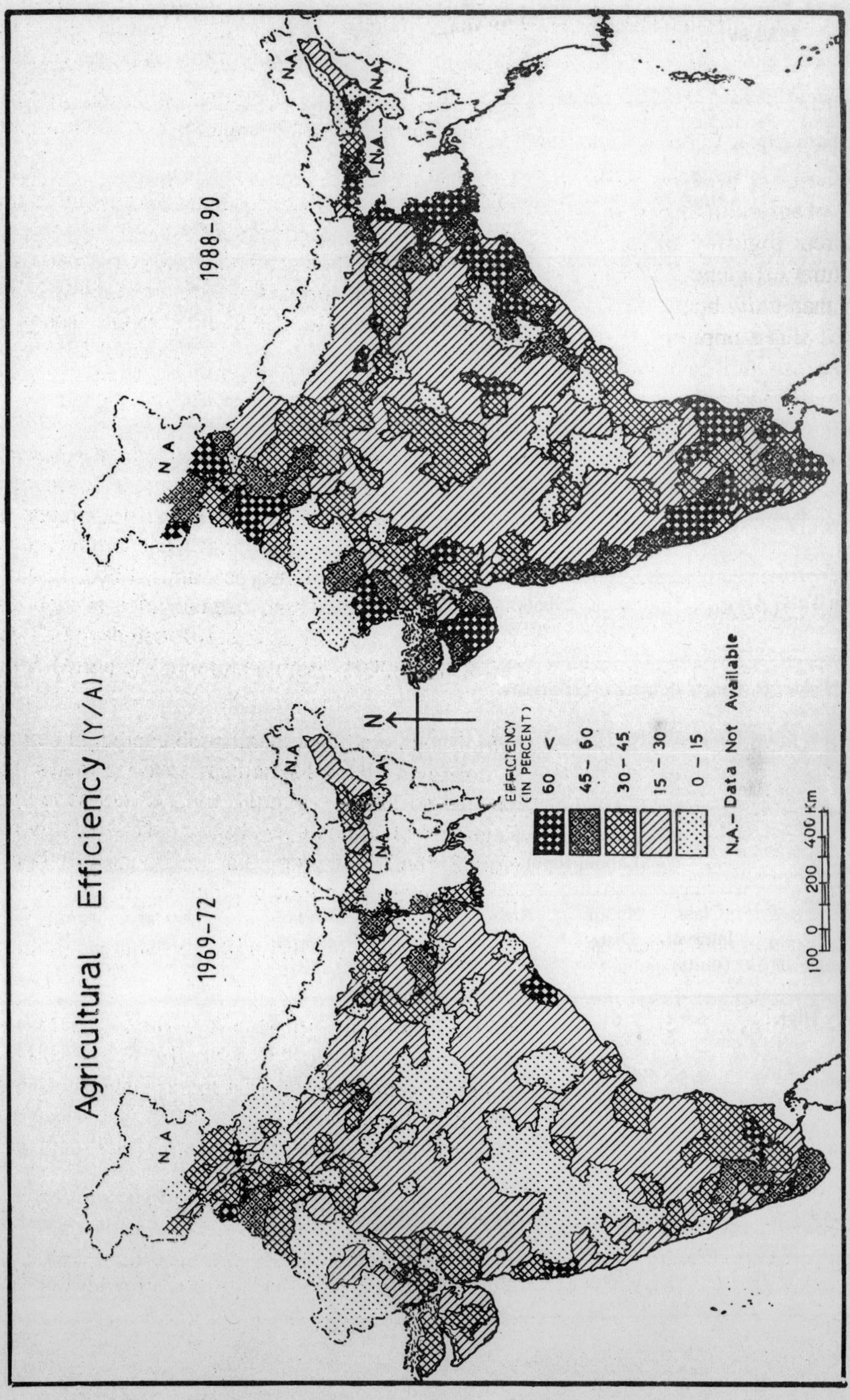

Agricultural Efficiency (Y/A)
1969-72
1988-90
N.A
N
EFFICIENCY (IN PERCENT)
60 <
45 - 60
30 - 45
15 - 30
0 - 15
N.A.- Data Not Available
100 0 200 400 Km

Fig. - 4.11

Table- 4.13: Changing Agricultural Efficiency/Production Potential Intensity Patterns in India (1969-72 to 1988-90).

(Area in Sq. km.)

Agricultural Efficiency Classes (in %)	Production Potential Intensity (in Unit)	Area and Its Percentage Share				
		1969-72		1988-90		
		Area	%	Area	%	Changes (in %)
60 &<	1.666-below	82028 (10)	2.82	340024 (43)	11.70	8.88
45-60	1.666-2.222	250085 (30)	8.61	430548 (52)	14.82	6.21
30-45	2.222-3.333	397539 (48)	13.68	863697 (104)	29.72	15.04
15-30	3.333-6.666	1075377 (130)	37.00	1035254 (24)	35.62	-01.38
0- 15	6.666-above	1100971 (132)	37.89	236477 (27)	8.14	-29.75
All India Total Area		**2906000** (350)	**99.99**	**2906000** (350)	**99.99**	

N.B. : Number of districts are given in parentheses.

Table- 4.14: %age Share of Area Under Various Categories of Marginal Product to Input Intensities (88-90).

(Area in Sq. km.)

Catigories	Marginal Product w.r.t. Labour Input				Marginal Product w.r.t. Capital Input			
	Class Interval (units)	No. of Dist.	Area	%	Class of Interval (units)	No. of Dist.	Area	%
Extremely High	5&<	61	511474	17.60	a) 36 & <	40	333294	11.47
					b) 36-25	29	241913	8.32
Very High	4-5	17	141148	4.86	25-16	27	224287	7.72
High	3-4	18	149451	5.14	16-9	60	498071	17.14
High Medium	2-3	43	350023	12.04	9-4	122	1011840	34.81
Medium	1-2	85	705744	24.28	4-1	66	546908	18.82
Low & Low	0-1	126	1048160	36.07	1-0	6	49607	1.71
Total		**350**	**2906000**	**99.99**		**350**	**2906000**	**99.99**

(D) The Marginal Products and Production Potential Absorption

Higher the magnitude of marginal product in response to input intensification, greater is the availabilities of production potential in the areas. It implies a higher absorption rate of production potential intensity. Regional variations in the magnitude of marginal product are studied with respect to two factor inputs : agricultural labour and non-land capital (technological) inputs. Converting agricultural workforce (cultivators plus agricultural labourers) per hectare of land and technological inputs (which includes irrigation, machine fertilizer and seed costs) into its money term because they are needed for comparison; it is done because homogeneous production and production factors scale, and then putting these values of input variables separately in equation 4.11, the magnitudes of marginal product to labour and to technological inputs are calculated for each district of the country. They are grouped into six categories of marginal product to input intensities to distinguish their regional patterns. Being very high degree of variability of the marginal product to non-land capital input (coefficient of variation is 417.88 percent) then the areal variability of the marginal product to labour input (240.48 percent), the distribution map of marginal product to technology is prepared by scaling class-intervals in its square form (X^2) while the distribution of latter one is shown on simple scale of equal interval. Table-4.14 reveals that, in more than one-third part of the country (36.07 percent), the magnitude of marginal product in response to labour increase is low and very low (below - 1.0 percent). It means per unit increase in agricultural workforce is not capable of increasing one unit of agricultural production in these areas. They are mostly the parts of entire Deccan plateau including most of middle Ganga plains. The state of Kerala and the interior Orissa have extremely low magnitude of marginal productivity of labour (Fig.-4.12, A). On the other hand, the areas in Western Himalayas, Brahmaputra valley and the upper parts of the Ganga valley (agro-ecological zone I, II and V) have very high and extremely high magnitude of marginal productivity of labour input (Table-4.14). These areas are perhaps able to absorb more labour force in agricultural activities at its markable productivity level and hence the wage rates of agricultural labour are comparatively higher in these areas. Thus, the absorption rate of production potential intensity is recorded higher therein.

Further, the magnitude of marginal product with respect to non-land capital is very high throughout the country except a few small pockets situated in the Karnataka coastal areas and in the central Tamilnadu where agricultural technological enchancement is not profitable. The Brahmaputra valley and the lower Ganga plains have the extremely high values of marginal product (150.0 and 135.3 units respectively) at the per unit increase of technological input (Table- 4.15, Fig.-4.12, B). Modern agricultural technology should accelerate fast production processes with least absorption of production potential in these areas. The Thar desert is also noticeable in this connection (Fig.-4.12, B).

Further, it is interesting to note that, though production elasticity is lesser than unity everywhere in the country because of 'diminishing production return' in agricultural practices, yet the significant high elasticity coefficients (above 0.750) are marked in the Brahmaputra valley (0.8751), the south Deccan (0.8458), the Thar of Rajasthan (0.7707), the north Deccan (0.7576) and in the central high lands (0.7552) (Table- 4.15), where production potential intensity is recorded very high (Table - 4.11). It implies that production elasticity is positively and highly related to production potential intensity. Very high coefficients of production elasticity of these areas of extremely dry as well as of very high humid conditions of the country imply that agricultural production can be raised significantly in response to the changing levels of production factors. These areas, therefore, have been taking advantage of high production return conditions.

Table- 4.15: Production Elasticity, Marginal Products and Absorption Rate of Production Potential Intensity in Various Agro-Ecological Zones (1988-90).

	Agro Ecological Zones	Production Elasticity*	Marginal Products with respect to		Absorption Rate of Production Potential Intensity with respect to	
			Labour Input	Non-Land Capital	Labour Input	Non-Land Capital
I	W. Himalayas	0.5663	8.8483	29.9806	0.01511	0.05121
II	NE Mts & Valleys**	0.8751	3.8851	150.0171	0.02004	0.79111
III	L. Ganges Plains	0.4495	1.4559	135.3386	0.00095	0.00750
IV	M. Ganges Plains	0.7115	0.7487	5.7707	0.00253	0.01949
V	U. Ganges Plains	0.6383	4.0434	5.8105	0.00781	0.01123
VI	Punjab Plains	0.4717	1.8745	3.2261	0.00166	0.00285
VII	Central Plateau	0.7392	1.3557	22.8096	0.00688	0.11585
VIII	Central Highlands	0.7557	2.0739	12.3644	0.01233	0.07347
IX	North Deccan	0.7576	0.9677	7.6135	0.00718	0.05167
X	South Deccan	0.8458	0.9435	5.1937	0.00781	0.03888
XI	East Coasts	0.5713	1.0283	6.4612	0.00129	0.01001
XII	Western Coasts	0.5755	0.3053	3.9086	0.00117	0.01494
XIII	The Gujarat	0.5322	1.8311	7.0297	0.00345	0.01324
XIV	The Thar	0.7707	0.7354	13.8936	0.12876	0.22949
XV	Islands	-	-	-	-	-
	All India	**0.6914**	**3.6830**	**22.5160**	**0.02510**	**0.29285**

N.B. : * Production Elasticity figures are calculated simultaneously in response to labour and non-land capital inputs.

** It includes the area of Brahmaputra valley (Assam State) only.

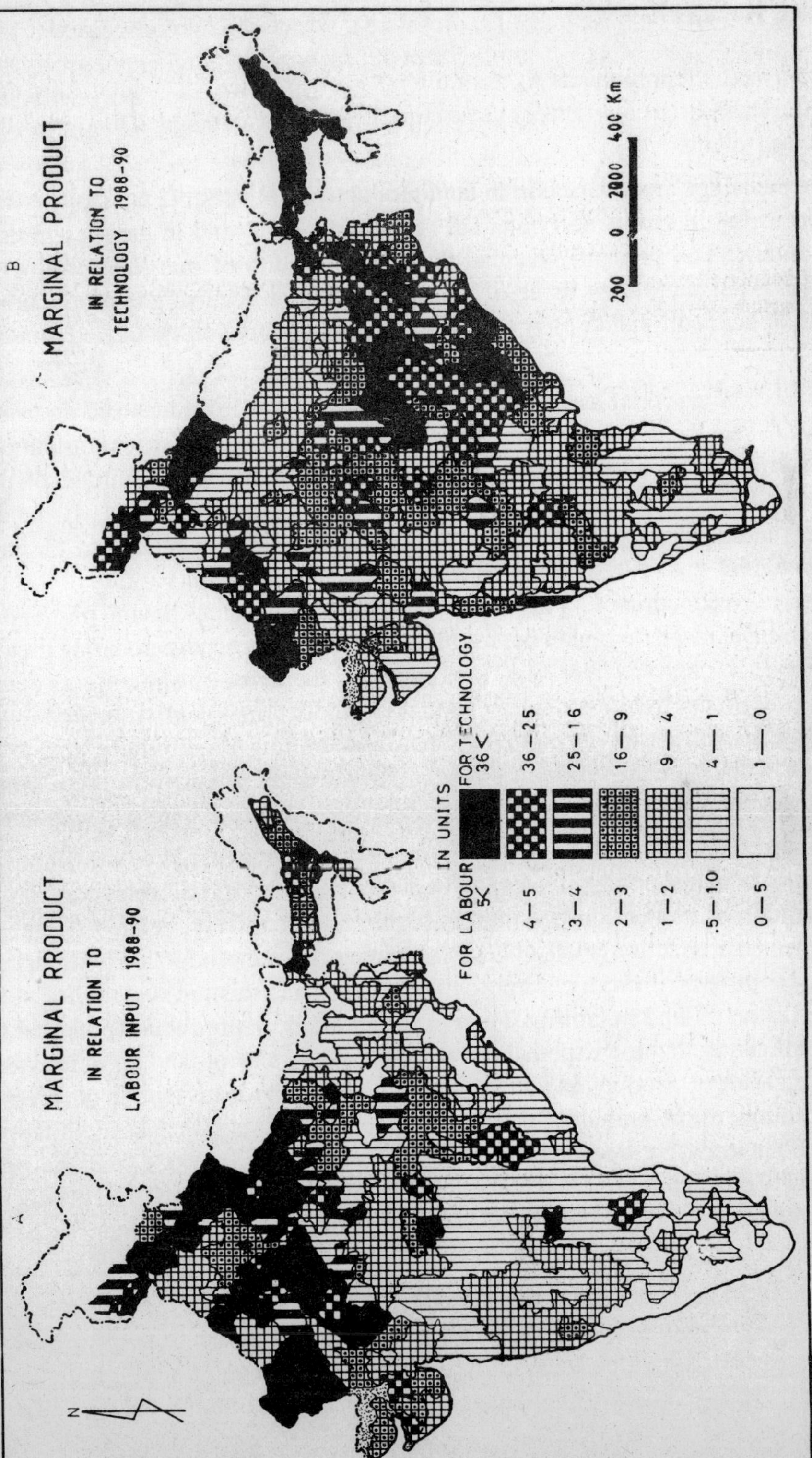
A
MARGINAL RRODUCT
IN RELATION TO
LABOUR INPUT 1988-90
N
B
MARGINAL PRODUCT
IN RELATION TO
TECHNOLOGY 1988-90
200 0 200 400 Km
IN UNITS
FOR LABOUR 5<
FOR TECHNOLOGY 36<
4—5 36—25
3—4 25—16
2—3 16—9
1—2 9—4
.5—1.0 4—1
0—5 1—0

Fig. - 4.12

Concluding Remarks

The interrelated components of agricultural growth potential, which form its complex nature, and the areal differentiations of these complexities, are concluded to generalize the facts in the following manner.

1) The explained areal variation in land productivity (Cv. 80.92 per cent) is due to areal variations occurring in production potential (106.80 per cent) and in the maximum expected production level (73.58 percent) whereas the areal variation of marginal product to labour intensity (240.48 per cent) is the result of the areal variations occurring in production potential intensity (58.30 per cent) and density of agricultural work force on cultivated area (53.68 per cent).

2) Correlation matrix of interrelated production potential attributes and their influencing variables reveals that the regional patterns of land productivity (agricultural output per hectare of cultivated land) are positively and significantly related to the magnitude of production potential (r = 0.1632), the level of maximum expected production (r = 0.6414) and also to the patterns of agricultural efficiency (Fig. - 4.11), and are negatively related to the intensity of production potential (r = - 0.4543) (Appendix- III). Theoretically, the validity of this fact is also explainable through equations 4.11 and 4.13. It implies that the areas having higher production potential magnitudes stand for higher degree of land productivity accommodating greater degree of agricultural efficiency and *vice-versa*. As a result, the level of agricultural development (particularly land productivity) is directly related to production potential. Inversely, degree of production potential intensity is higher in the areas of low productivity and low rate of agricultural growth. More absorption of production potential intensity in these areas of low agricultural growth must increase the agricultural growth rate in a self-sustained manner.

3) The correlations of main components of production potential, i.e., maximum expected production and production potential intensity with their explanatory variables confirms the facts that the magnitude of production potential is highly and positively related to the level of maximum expected production (r = 0.8472). Maximum expected production is significantly and directly related to three main production potential factors, viz., moisture availability, soil fertility and irrigation factors of land suitability. Therefore, magnitude of production potential must also be related significantly to these explanatory variables, while size of land holding is negatively related the magnitude of production potential (Table - 4.16). It means that, in the areas of small size of land holdings, the magnitude of production potential is higher because of 'untapped yield-crops' and labour intensive traditional system of agricultural practices. But the production potential intensity is negatively related to these variables of maximum expected production level and hence, maximum expected production level and production potential intensity is insignificantly related to each other (r = 0.039).

4) The application of modern agricultural technology diversifies the agricultural productivity pattern through creating very high variations in the marginal productivity patterns, while the unlimited supply of agricultural labour is available for the operation of production system. As a result, the patterns of marginal product to labour intensity are stable and unified rather than

the pattern of marginal product to non-land capital. It might be because the modern technology applied to the production processes has many constraints in its diffusion processes. However, its impact on production processes is stronger than labour factor. The law of production increase (i.e., reciprocity law) explains that when each of the factors of production (labour and technology) is separately increased in Indian agricultural production processes, while other held constant, the production added by each equal unit of increment of a factor is 3.69 unit in case of labour and 22.52 units in case of technology with a production elasticity of 0.6914 and agricultural efficiency of 48.60 per cent in agricultural system of the country. It implies that technology is a substitute of labour input. But the areal variations of marginal product to labour and to technology explain the complementarity patterns of agricultural production factors rather than their substitution. It is because of smaller size of land holdings (labour intensive) and poor peasants conditions for further investments in the agricultural practices.

Table- 4.16: Simple Correlation Coefficient of Maximum Expected Production (À) and Production Potential Intensity (Ip) with Explanatory Variables (1988-90).

	Explanatory Variables	Correlation Coefficient with A	Correlation Coefficient with Ip
1.	Magnitude of Production Potential	0.8472*	0.3730*
2.	Moisture Availability	0.1093*	0.0372
3.	Soil Fertility	0.2060*	- 0.1234*
4.	Irrigation	0.2181*	- 0.2794*
5.	Density of Agricultural Workers	0.1433*	- 0.0649
6.	Size of Land Holdings	- 0.1947*	0.0582

N. B. : * Significant at 0.05 level.

5) Very high variations of the attributes of agricultural production potential and weak inter relationships of these attributes with the other components of agricultural production, though these relationships are significant upto some extent and form the complex nature of weak interactions, are testimony to the facts that interrelated phenomena of agricultural growth and development which is analysed here must be interpreted to delimit the agricultural regions at meso-and micro areal levels. Region-specific study of interrelated agricultural phenomena may, thus, provide sound base and may give the real picture of weak interacted patterns. The 'regionalisation' is, thus, the ideal approach for finding out the areas of weak agricultural systems for which area-specific feasible solutions of agricultural development may be suggested with sound bases.

-----oOo-----

Chapter - 5

Agricultural Regionalisation: A Strategy For Agricultural Development

The main factors of agricultural development, which have been discussed in the previous Chapters based on 'pattern approach', have led to the conclusion that three sets of agricultural characteristics : the agricultural production (existing conditions of productivity), the production factors (labour and technology as agricultural inputs), and the agricultural potential productivity (i.e., maximum expected yield of various agricultural crops which is the result of various agro-ecological and bio-physical conditions), evolve some specific relationships for explaining the optimisation of agricultural systems. They are different in different physical as well as socio-economic conditions. These relations can be studied with the help of 'system approach' of the subject matter in order to find the regional personality of agricultural phenomena. Regional synthesis of facts and regional interpretation of agricultural phenomena would, no doubt, be useful to be an appropriate tool for agricultural scientists in understanding the inherent regional inequalities of socio-economic development and the dynamics of agricultural production. For the same, a strong regional frame of agricultural characteristics is to be built to understand the regional weaknesses of agricultural systems. A literature survey related to the model-building is required in this connection.

The classical theories of agriculture enable the agricultural scientists to understand the geographical extent in relation to different factors and causes of different agricultural production. Recardean theory of economic rent stresses on the physical suitability of margin of agricultural production. The same idea of economic rent was later on presented diagrammatically and elaborated logically by McCarty and Lindburg (1967) by proposing the limits of physical factors (especially precipitation and temperature) for optimizing the conditions of agricultural production. On the other hand, the agricultural production processes are intensified by spatial organisation of agricultural activities for which location of market is the main factor of the evolution of agricultural pattern in its micro-areal frame as Thuenen's location theory of agricultural production points out (Hall 1966). In isolated state of homogeneous physical and socio-economic conditions of land, the micro-areal processes of agricultural production are location (especially market location) dependent and hence, economic rent diminishes with distance from market and landuse becomes less productive in the peripheral areas of market centre. It changes in relation to market influence, distance and transport costs.

The application of modern agricultural technology which is diffused through the market centres in the agricultural landscape is a major aspect of spatial organization of agriculture (Visser 1980, 1982). Technological inducements, although they relax the limits of physical control of agricultural production, diversify the agricultural landuse patterns as concluded earlier in the previous Chapters, and hence, there seems a widening gap in the intra- as well as inter-regional inequalities. A pioneer work on regional inequalities in India undertook by Mohapatra (1982, pp. 172-218) stresses that intra- regional economic inequalities have increased positively but are slower than the rate of inter- regional inequalities. Prior to this study, the preliminary comprehensive observations and the outcome of the pilot research project on Regional Dimensions of Natural and Socio-Economic Phenomena proceeded under the supervision of Professor Moonis Raza in collaboration with other faculty members of the Centre for the Study of Regional Development (CSRD), Jawaharlal Nehru University, New Delhi, which have been published in various forms and journals especially during the mid 1970s (Raza and Kundu 1975, Raza *et.al.* 1975, Chattopadhyaya and Raza 1975, Raza 1981), and the conclusions derived in the Chapter- 3 of the present research, point out that the regional dimensions of agricultural development of the country have been diversified and regional inequalities in agricultural production structure have widened through the application of modern agricultural technology. The sets of various geographical factors like natural, historical, socio-economic, organizational etc. are also the causes of the differentiated regional structure of agricultural production. This discussion leads us to ***two*** main conclusions on the regional dimensions of Indian agricultural development :

a) Introduction of modern agricultural technology has altered the'process-form' scale of agricultural development of the country from Recardean concept of physical limit of agriculture to the Thuenen's spatially organise dregional structure of agricultural development, and

b) Regional synthesis of spatial characteristics of agriculture must provide feasible solution for the optimisation of agricultural activities.

These conclusions can be extended further by giving the answer of ***two*** research questions related to region-formation processes of agricultural development. They are :

i) What should be the criteria and procedure to delimit the agricultural regions for the purpose of identifying agricultural weak but potentially rich areas of the country?

ii) What are the inherent regional agricultural characteristics at different orders of the optimal agricultural regions for understanding strategic point of agricultural development and planning ?

Thus, the main objective of the present Chapter is to give concrete answers to these questions giving suitable criteria of the selection of attributes/variables from the point of view the sustainable agricultural growth and development. From this perspective, one must support the agro-ecological criterion of agricultural regionalisation.

Choice of the Variables

The first task of regionalisation is to set out the scheme of characteristics of phenomena for understanding the system of regions. Reviewing concerned literature on agricultural regionalisation, it can safely be concluded that there is a variety of criteria for the selection of agricultural attributes for understanding the system of agricultural types. Say for example, the classical scheme of agricultural regionalisation introduced by Baker (1926 to 1932) for interpreting regional dimensions of the United States agriculture was the first mile stone to generate neo-classical models of analysing the multi-structured characteristics of agriculture into its regional frame. Whittlesay's (1936) neo-classical scheme of classification of world agricultural types was perhaps the outcome of Baker's scheme. Whittlesay included five major agricultural attributes into his scheme of classification : crop-livestock association, methods used to grow the crops (farming operations) and crop-specialisation, intensity of agricultural input application, disposal of products for consumption (commerciality), and degree of mobility (nomadic movement). These five dimensions of agricultural characteristics are still marked in the modern taxonomy of the spatial organisation of the world agriculture (Abler, Adams and Gould 1971). The other variables that are closely associated with and similar to more elaborative dimensions of agricultural characteristics, have been incorporated by Kostrowicki (1972) in his new kind of agricultural typology of the world which is shown by 33 model typograms (world types). He selected 20 variables for the types of world agriculture which are grouped into three broad categories of agricultural characteristics (Table- 5.1).

Table- 5.1: Selected Variables Characterising Typology of World Agriculture (Kostrowicki 1972).

Name of the Variables	Name of the Variables
A) *Social and Ownership Characteristics*	C) *Production Characteristics*
1. System of land tenure.	15. Land productivity.
2. Average size of farms.	16. Labour productivity.
B) *Organisational and Technical Characteristics*	17. Level of commercialisation.
3. Input of labour.	18. Degree of commercialisation.
4. Input of animal power.	19. Ratio of animal to total production within gross production.
5. Input of mechanical power.	20. Ratio of animal to total production within commercial production.
6. Organic Maneuring.	
7. Chemical fertilizer.	
8. Extent of irrigation.	
9. System of irrigation.	
10. System of landuse.	
11. System of crop rotation.	
12. Intensity of crop landuse.	
13. Cropping system.	
14. System of live stock breeding.	

On the other hand, some interesting classifications with special reference to agricultural problems were also made by Papadakis (1938, 1966). In his early classification produced in 1938, growth of agricultural crops was characterized by temperature regimes, but his newer system of classification introduces a specific kind of climodiagram by which crop ecological extremes are identified for ecological requirements of agriculture (Papadakis 1966). Note that his classification follows the agro-ecological criteria of agricultural growth but the criteria used in the other classification follow the socio-economic, technological and production characteristics of agriculture. A comprehensive review and comparison of various criteria used for the examination of system of the agricultural regions of the world were produced by Grigg (1969) who pointed out that there seems to be a number of predictable changes going on in agriculture in different parts of the world which will minimize many of the present regional differences. But the principal difference between the systems of world agriculture, although not used as criteria in most systems, is productivity which must be included in the criteria in analysing the system of agricultural regions for accelerating the production processes in future (Grigg 1969, p. 118-120).

In connection with the agricultural regionalisation of India, the agro-ecological attributes, namely, topography, climate and soils, have been considered for macro-agricultural zonation and cropping patterns for meso and micro-agricultural regions (Sen Gupta 1968, Bhat and Learmonth 1968). No doubt, the concept of 'natural regions' has been applied to delineate the agricultural regions especially during the mid of this century because Indian agricultural systems might have been controlled by the ecological constraints (particularly by physical features and climatic conditions) before the green revolution period (Randhawa 1958, ICAR 1964, Planning Commission 1964, c.f. Mamoria 1975). But after green revolution, it appears to be the significant changes in the crop-combinations, productivity patterns and in regional structure of agricultural growth as interpreted in the previous Chapters of the present research. These areal features have been breaking the limits of physical attributes of agricultural systems with a significant transformation of agricultural characteristics from traditional less-productive system to modern systems of more productive ones with rapid growth. Consequently, the criteria of analysing the present day system of Indian agriculture, although they are still under the influence of agro-ecological conditions, must follow integrated approach of region-formation processes and variable selection. The chosen variables must represent agricultural productivity and growth, so that the regional characteristics of agricultural production processes can be assessed for further resource allocation. Keeping this view in mind, the total twenty variables have been chosen for the agricultural regionalisation in India. The selected characterized variables which are reproduced in Table- 5.2, have been grouped broadly into the following four categories.

a) Agro-ecological Characteristics

Out of the total twenty variables, two belong to the group of agro-ecological conditions. Moisture in the surface air which is directly controlled by the *two* fundamental biological and physical processes of environment, evapotranspiration and rainfall, is a most important variable of plant growth and agricultural productivity. Instead of rainfall, moisture availability index is taken into consideration. Soil fertility is also an equally important variable for productivity enhancement of agriculture system. Infact, soil fertility is the outcome of various physical and climatic factors, like geological formations, slope, drainage density, temperature and rainfall and so on and agricultural productivity is positively related to soil fertility. Therefore, the agricultural types of India is controlled by physiographic features especially before green revolution and hence, most of the agricultural regionalisation of that time have been completely 'natural region-based' (Sen Gupta 1968). Inspite of relaxation of natural limits of agricultural production processes through the application of modern agricultural technology, the soil fertility still holds strong crop-ecological and environmentally-oriented bases of agricultural development (Bhat 1988).

Table- 5.2: Selected Attributes for Agricultural Regionalisation, Their Definitions and Coefficient of Variations.

Name of the Attribute		Definitions	Mean	C.V.(in %)
(a)	*Agro Ecological Characteristics*			
1.	Moisture index	[(P-PE)/PE]	- 0.151	-
2.	Soil fertility index	(unit)	61.908	15.26
(b)	*Production Characteristics*			
3.	Per capita agricultural output 1991	(Rs./person)	280.601	130.04
4.	Average annual growth rate of Agricultural output 1979-82 to 1988-90	(%)	8.439	149.23
5.	Land productivity (Y) 1988-90	(Rs./ha)	1576.620	80.92
6.	Labour productivity 1991	(Rs./person)	1189.411	98.37
7.	Crop intensity 1988-90	(%)	134.219	19.60
(c)	*Growth Potential Characteristics*			
8.	Potential productivity index (A) 1988-90	(Rs./ha)	3228.081	73.58
9.	Magnitude of production potential (A-Y) 1988-90	(Rs./ha)	1681.635	106.80
10.	Production potential intensity (A/Y) 1988-90	(Ratio)	2.578	58.30
11.	Marginal product to labour input	(unit)	3.688	240.48
12.	Marginal product to technological input	(unit)	22.515	417.88
13.	Absorption rate of potential intensity w.r.t. labour	(unit)	0.025	356.00
14.	Absorption rate of potential intensity w.r.t. technology	(unit)	0.292	506.51
(d)	*Organisational and Technological Characteristics*			
15.	Input of labour	(Rs./ha)	512.782	85.15
16.	Input of non-land capital 1988-90	(Rs./ha)	96.819	104.76
17.	Extent of irrigation 1990-91	(in %)	35.584	75.76
18.	Mechanisation 1988-90	(Rs./ha)	55.310	145.98
19.	Use of chemical fertilizer 1988-90	(Rs./ha)	43.991	104.27
20.	Size of operational land holding 1991	(NSA/Cultivator)	1.466	61.05

N.B.: C.V.= Coefficient of Variation.

b) Production Characteristics

This group incorporates five variables. Out of them, three are directly related to existing production structure of agriculture. They are: land productivity (agricultural output per unit of cultivated land), labour productivity (agricultural output per person of agricultural work force) and crop intensity. Agricultural growth which is an important variable of development, and per capita agricultural output which reflects the availability of production indicating food deficiency/ surplus patterns in relation to food requirements of the population, have been included in this category of variable choices. Infact, degree of crop commercialization which has been considered as important attribute of agricultural typology, is not included in the present classification because of its non-existence in the regional dimensions of Indian agriculture. Say for example, in modern Indian agricultural practices, the most of the farmers of various land holding sizes have been altering their cropping patterns and are intensifying crop-production through system's price-mechanism. Since agricultural practices have become price- oriented rather than demand-based, each and every crop whether it is staple food-grain or locally consumed production like wheat and paddy cultivated even in the marginal size of land holdings in the densely populated areas of West Bengal and Bihar, is grown as commercial crop for maximizing net return to land.

c) Agricultural Growth Potential Characteristics

Agriculture is an integral part of environment. But in this materialistic world, fast accelerating technological processes of development forever increase human needs which are operating in inhuman manner and are unfit within the limits of environmental conditions. Consequently, imbalances in utilisation of environmental resources are apparent. Looking at the degradation of environmental resources, the United Nations Conference on Environment and Development (Known as Earth Summit) held at Rio-de-Janeire, Brazil, during 3-14 June 1992, raised the issues of sustainable development and resolved them by proclaiming that environmental protection is the integral part of development. Therefore, the components of agriculture related to environmental protection and sustainable development of agriculture must be the part of our regional-investment-strategy. The attributes of agricultural growth potential which are characterized by assessing the maximum expected yield levels, are solely based on the available agricultural resources under the specific set of environmental conditions. The attributes which are incorporated in this group must reflect the inherent structural characteristics of agricultural development possibilities and agricultural efficiency, the dimensions and ways for agricultural expansion, and intensification programmes, and the available intensity of untapped agricultural resources.

Seven principal attributes/variables have been included in this group. Out of them, three variables are associated with the magnitude, intensity and degree of agricultural growth potential. They are : potential productivity (maximum expected production per unit of land, A), magnitude of production potential (the difference between actual land productivity and potential productivity indexes, A-Y), and production potential intensity (ratio of potential productivity and actual productivity, A/Y). Remember that the reciprocal form of production potential intensity yields the coefficient of agricultural efficiency (see eqn. 4.3). Thus, instead of agricultural efficiency, production potential intensity index is chosen as an appropriate and main variable of this group. The rest of the four variables of this group are related to the rate of change in production as well as in the production potential intensity with respect to input factor, namely, labour and non-land capital (technological) inputs (Table- 5.2).

d) Organisational and Technological Characteristics

There are several attributes related to the intensification of agricultural production of an area. But in the present scheme of classification, six important variables have been chosen. They are : input of labour, input of mechanical power, extent of irrigation, number of machine tools per areal unit, use of fertilizer, as the main input for agricultural intensification. In the end, one variable, namely, size of landholdings, which reflects the ownership characteristic of land and is indirectly related to the agricultural intensification, has also been included in this category of the present scheme.

The Procedure for Identifying the System of Regions

Identification of the system of regions for agriculture must provide the solution of two major problems of the regional interpretation of the concerned agricultural phenomena. First, it would provide a tool or scale for measuring the regional differentiations of agricultural phenomena and, secondly, the characteristics of agricultural systems and sub-systems evolving within the regional frame. But question arises as how to delimit the boundaries of the region of given set of agricultural characteristics? This question is directly related to the approaches and methods of identification of system of regions and appropriate and applicable procedure for regionalisation or the grouping of the areal units for deriving the regional boundaries of agricultural characteristics.

Broadly, the synthesis of regional dimensions of areal characteristics, in which observations are defined as areal units (i.e., districts in present case) and properties of any observation as elements, can be made by classifying or grouping the areal units into areal classes/regions (Bunge 1962). Thus, identification of a system of regions is to group the objects into classes on the basis of properties or relationships they have in common (Grigg 1965, 1967). Methodologically, the logic of the system of regions leads to understand the grouping of objects that can be derived either on the basis of similarity between objects (association by similarity) or on the basis of relationship between connected and different objects (association by contiguity) which leads to the two distinct methods of grouping : *Classification* and *Division* (Simpson 1961, Grigg 1965, Singh 1974). Of course, classification of the objects is a logical division because co-incidence or inter - relationships of the properties of objects which follow some laws/rules of the regional systems determine the association by contiguity by which the universe is divided into parts. There are three main approaches of the regionalisation or classification.

a) The Analytical Approach -through which the regional characteristics of the properties of geographic phenomena are interpreted by dividing logically the universe into its constituent parts. Say for example, Koppen's climatic classification, the Harbertson's system of natural regions, Whittlesay's agricultural regions of the earth are based on the analytical approach of regionalisation because they follow some rules of inter-related properties for demarcating the regional boundaries.

So far as regionalisation of India is concerned, the procedures for the formation of natural geographical regions of India or Indian sub-continent followed by Baker (1928), Stamp (1928), Spate, Learmonth and Farmer (1967, pp. 407-23), Chatterjee (1964), Mishra (1970), Singh (1971, pp. 33-34) are based on classical approach of imposed-regional frame on geographical reality considering the natural boundaries and the criteria of physical factors for region-formation rather than administrative ones. Of course, district is the best suitable micro-areal unit for the purpose of administration, resource management and the plan implementation. Therefore, the administrators, planners and the concerned Central Government Departments have been trying since independence to form the regional frame which must be based on district boundaries at micro-level. For instance, the natural regions formulated by the office of the Registrar General, Census of India, paper No. 2 of 1952; the regions of India demarcated by the 16th round, National Sample Survey, Government of India, 1950-51; the planning regions of India by Regional Survey Unit, Indian Statistical Institute, New Delhi, 1965; Asok Mitra's scheme of socio-economic regions of India published by the Office of the Registrar General, Census of India in its Monograph No. 8 on Economic Regionalisation, all follow the district boundaries for the region-formation. But they all adopted division approach for regionalisation rather than grouping the areal units.

b) The Synthetic Approach of grouping of the objects by which the classification is made and hierarchy of groups of areal classes (objects) is derived on the basis of similarity or contiguity criteria of classification by applying various multivariate techniques especially after the mid of this century when computer had become a helpful tool for iterating and solving the long logical procedures of complicated equations. At this time, different procedures and techniques were developed and adopted to study the logic of the system of regions. For instance, the application of different techniques like (i) the factor analysis to reduce the multi-dimensional characteristics of regional systems used comprehensively by many scientists (Berry 1961, 1964, 1965, Berry and Rao 1968, Verma 1974, Pal 1968, 1975), (ii) the hierarchical group function (Ward 1963, Zebler 1958, 1972), (iii) the cluster analysis on distance function used by Park (1970) and (iv) the discriminating procedure of regionalisation developed logically by applying trigonometric polynomial analysis and tested it with the help of computer by Casetti (1964, 1966) and, later on, explained in a simplified manner by Amedeo in his articles and books (Amedeo 1969, Amedeo and Golledge 1975) are indications of a search of optimal and more logical procedure for regionalisation. It is noticeable here that, in this procedure of region-formation, the tools and techniques used are different for different purpose of region formation. It may be, therefore, called purpose-based approach of regionalisation.

c) Non-Parametric Model for a new approach by which simulation process of classification is rested upon a natural measure of proximities based on the hypervolume of a multidimensional functional set. On these lines of classification, the work of the faculty members especially of the Departments of Geography and Mathematics of the Facultes Universitaires Notre-Dame Dela Paix (F.U.N.D.P.), University of Namur, Belgium, is appreciable. They open new horizon for functional partition of space by applying uniform density function of transformation of functional dimensions rather than normal density function of its classical type. Rasson and others (1988, 1989) contribution is recognizable in this connection. They point out that the discriminant rules are associated with the Poisson Process Hypothesis by which the volume of a multidimensional set can easily and correctly be measured. This model was later on applied by other faculty member of F.U.N.D.P. for solving space-partition problems (Orban-Ferague, Rasson and Granville 1991, 1992). Infact, the Rasson's algorithm of space partitioning is based on the paradigm of 'convex hulls' to calculate the similarity matrix for classification.

The procedures of region-formation are infact different while approaches and methods of the conceivement of the systems of regions vary. For instance, analytical approach of regionalisation imposes the regional frame to search the reality of phenomena while synthetic and non-parametric approaches assimilate the spatial contiguity and phenomenal proximity by following convex hull procedure of unclassified areal units. In the assimilation process of regionalisation, the regional forms which emerge out on the basis of internal assemblages of phenomenal properties and their determining underlying regional patterns, can be distinguished to calculate the deviations of the properties of two areal units (that is called the taxonomic distance between two objects) in the discriminant space. Its utility in the formation of regions is well defined by Casetti (1964, pp. 30).

> "... when the centroids of the classes are chosen as representative points, the classification generated by the Discriminant Iterations from an initial classification has a smaller within class variability that the initial classification. In turn, smaller variability corresponds to a smaller average distance among the points in the same classes".

The contiguity criterion of regionalisation has also been described by Amedeo (1969, p. 27) in the following manner.

> "... the desirable outcome (of discriminating procedure) is to obtain that set of regions such that members (unclassified areal units) of the same region in the set are as similar as possible and members of different regions in the set are as dissimilar as possible. It is intuitively clear that the more homogeneous each region in the set is made, the more total distance (deviation) is lowered, and each region in the set becomes more recognizable".

Discriminating procedure of region-formation follows three major steps : (a) generation of discriminant space from multi-dimensional originary problem-space which is associated with the transformation of variables, (b) system arrangement of areal units which are shown by the points of distribution in the discriminant space, and (c) evaluation of relative quality of classification/ regionalisation. The first step is necessary because, at initial stage, the areal dimensions of various properties on which classification is based, are at various scales and hence, transformation of these properties is essential to put them on a homogeneous scale. These multidimensional properties may be transformed by applying normal density function for the purpose, for generating the discriminant space. Mean and variance free 'Z' score transformation of the original variables/properties is the initial stage of discriminating procedure. However, linear or non-linear (polynomial) transformations may also be adopted for generating discriminant spaces. The second step is closely related to the measurement of functional distance between two areal units and its ordering (Singh 1988, pp. 8-9). These distances which reflect the degree of spatial contiguity at each level of regionalisation (Sokal and Sneath 1963, King 1969) have been measured by numerous logicians and taxonomists either by tracing out the common features of areal properties drawn with the help of factor analysis (Professor B.J.L. Berry has been the pioneer applicator of this technique for regionalisation), or by calculating proportionate loss of the detail informations of areal properties at each level of assimilation. Since discriminant procedure of regionalisation starts in assimilating areal units into the classes, the degree of loss of informations at the stage of beginning becomes zero per cent (the case of complete detailed informations), but informations are lost and loss increases gradually until the discriminating procedure becomes complete at its highest order (the case of complete generalisation). It is the stage of 'uniform-universalisation' in regionalisation (Amedeo and Golledge 1975, pp. 160-170). Further, it is worthwhile to note here that the factor analytic approach (that is fundamentally correlation method-based) is not more appropriate for calculating the functional distance among areal units especially for agricultural regionalisation of India where green revolution effects have diversified the regional dimensions of agricultural phenomena and hence, the correlations among the agricultural characteristics are weak and even insignificant as already described in the previous Chapters, though this method has been applied by many agricultural scientists. Thus, Euclidean distance function, which is based on the Pythagorean Theorem and has been used in its various forms for different purposes of measuring the nearness of points in the discriminant space (Casetti 1964, pp.6-10), is used to systematize the spatial variance of set of multidimensional agricultural properties (for details, see Appendix- V).

The last but the most important step of the region-forming process is to form optimal groups of areal units (i.e., OTUs) in order to minimise the degree of spatial contiguity and its measurement for knowing the relative quality of classification/ regionalisation. This step is , of course, associated with a repetitive process of minimizing the functional distance from the main distance matrix. Further, the significance of regionalisation's quality can be tested by calculating the difference between classification and its limit. The classification nearer to its limit is better with respect to given variables and hence, the smaller values of ratio of inbuilt class variability to total class variability correspond to higher homogeneity of the regions and *vice-versa.* Before, discussing the stability and significance of agricultural regionalisation in present context, one must be interested to understand the main steps of discriminant algorithm, although its computer programme for larger dimensions of raw data is available with the author*. The main steps in the process for finding the optimal solution of spatial contiguity at each level of assimilation of OTUs/observations are given below :

Step-1: Set the values of given attributes/variables, m, for n observations/OTUs which will form n.m dimensional input data matrix where i and j are specific observations and k specific variable with the condition i & j = 1,2,3,...,n and k=1,2,3,...,m.

Step-2: Transform m dimensional attributes into discriminant spaces through normal density function (Zscores) and create standardized data matrix (Z-matrix of the same

* The programme on discriminant analysis for optimal solution of spatial contiguity is developed by the computer centre, Bijni Complex, North-Eastern Hill University, Shillong, and is available in the Department of Geography, North-Eastern Hill University, Shillong (India).

n.m dimensions).

Step-3: Compute Dij with the help of formula given in Appendix for all possible ij pairs of n observations and prepare distance matrix (D-matrix) of n . m dimensions.

Step-4: Find minimum value of Dij in D-matrix, combine ith and jth observations of Dij minimum in Z-matrix by calculating means of their kth variables separately,and reduce dimension n.m of **Step-2** to (n-1).m.

Step-5: If n.m > 1.m go to **Step- 3**, if n.m = 1.m go to **Step- 6**,

Step-6: Write the value of Dij and its coordinates at each level of reduction.

Step-7: Stop.

Spatial Contiguity Constraints and Optimal Regional Partitioning

We can now begin the discussion on the results of forming the optimal agricultural planning regions of India which have been derived from the assimilation of OTUs (districts) for which twenty agricultural attributes have been taken into account (for name of agricultural variables, see Table- 5.2). The spatial variances of various groups of OTUs are carefully adjusted to consider the spatial contiguity to delimit the optimal agricultural regions. We have a finite set of 348 OTUs of 20 dimensional features of agricultural characteristics that we want to classify. It is bare fact that at macro-regional level, physiography is the major partitioning base of agricultural characteristics and hence, assuming that the macro-agricultural regions are analogous to physiographic regions of the country, total OTUs have been classified by following the physiographic regional scheme of macro-level. These regions are called Macro-Agricultural Regions. They are arranged according to their levels of assimilation and degree of their similarities of agricultural characteristics.

Having run the computer programme for optimal solution of the ordering of spatial variance as logically discussed earlier, it is found that there are atleast three basic concerns regarding the partitioning of contiguous boundary areas and the formation of optimal agricultural planning regions which have to be dealt with while analysing the result of assimilation processes for various Macro-Agricultural Regions, namely, (A) The Coastal region, (B) The Deccan Plateau, (C) The Western Himalayas, (D) The Great Plains, and (E) The Rajasthan Plains. The salient features of assimilation of OTUs and formation of agricultural regions are being elaborated here keeping in mind these basic concerns of the level of assimilation, degree of spatial variance within the emerging group of similar OTUs and stability of areal classes when emerging groups are put together to remove spatial contiguity constraints. The region formation of Indian agriculture has the following inherent characteristics and salient features of its spatial variations.

a) In the assimilation process of the five macro-agricultural regional units, the coastal region is assimilated with the Deccan Plateau at the lowest assimilated level of 3.20. It accounts for 40.78 per cent of the spatial variance of the region-formation system. It means they are most different in physiographic as well as agricultural conditions, though they have been assimilated at first level of assimilation process by forming a complete picture of peninsular India. Similarly, the regions of the Western Himalayas and the Great Plains are the most dissimilar with regards to their physiographic conditions but seem to be least dissimilar in agricultural characteristics recording only 4.62 per cent of total spatial variance. On the contrary, at the last step of assimilation, the Great Plains and the Rajasthan Region, although geographically most homogeneous, are significantly dissimilar in their agricultural characteristics (Table- 5.3).

Table-5.3: Assimilation Process and Groupings of the Macro- Agricultural Regional Units.

Groups	Assimilation of macro-units	Within group D values	% of variance	
			cumulative	Absolute
Prior to grouping	-	0	0	0
After I grouping	A/B	3.204	40.78	40.78
II grouping	AB/C	6.144	78.20	37.42
III grouping	ABC/D	6.551	82.82	4.62
Final grouping	ABCD	7.857	100.00	17.18

N.B. : 1. Final grouping is the stage of complete generality where total informations of the spatial system are lost. For assimilation of the agricultural regional units, see inset of Fig.- 5.3.

2. For names of macro-regions, see abbreviation in the foot note of Table- 5.4.

b) The range of assimilation levels within the macro-agricultural regional units is recorded very high in the Great Plains Region, from 0.857 to 17.570 (that includes 95.12 per cent of total spatial variance) with starting assimilation processes from very low level, although it is physiographically most homogeneous part of the country. It means that there is recognizable diversities in the agricultural characteristics and hence, the formation of agricultural regions especially at micro-level might have been influenced by the factors of green revolution and the application of modern agricultural technology. Contrary to the fact, the process of assimilation starts from a higher level (i.e., 3.266) and ends at 7.05 in the Rajasthan Region. There seems to be a high degree of spatial variation with the loss of 46.33 per cent informations of agricultural phenomena at first level of assimilation (Table- 5.4). It may be on account of direct control of physiographic factors on the spatial dimensions of agricultural phenomena.

c) The micro-processes characteristics of assimilation of OTUs for various micro-agricultural regional units, which have been depicted by the graphs and dendrograms (Figs 5.1 & 5.2), reflect a wide range effects of physiographic as well as agricultural production characteristics on the assimilation process of agricultural regionalisation. Larger the difference of assimilated groups of OTUs from its pre-group conditions wider the spatial gaps of agricultural characteristics and less degree of stability of a agricultural region formation. Say for example, the degree of functional differences appears to be very high in the Peninsular Plateau Region

Table- 5.4: Assimilation Levels and Loss of Agricultural Information in the Regionalisation of Various Macro-regions in India.

	Items	Macro Regions					
		A	B	C	D	E	All India
1.	Number of districts	52	143	23	117	11	5 regions
2.	Lowest level of assimilation	1.322	.841	2.237	.857	3.266	3.204
3.	Upper level of assimilation	9.092	14.269	6.587	17.570	7.050	7.857
4.	Absolute difference	7.770	13.428	4.350	16.713	3.784	4.653
5.	% loss of informations at lowest level of assimilation	14.54	5.89	33.96	4.88	46.33	40.780
6.	% loss of informations from Ist to last level*	85.46	94.11	66.04	95.12	53.67	59.220

N.B.: 1. **For the percentage loss of informations in the assimilation process of regionalisation at its each stage, see Fig.-5.2 (dendrograms).**

2. **Assimilation levels for all India are based on five macro- regions.**

3. **Loss of informations in percent are calculated from the total variation, i.e., upper level of assimilation of OTUs.**

Abbreviations :

A = The coastal regions, B = the Deccan plateau C = the western Himalayas, D = the Great plains E = the Rajasthan plains.

* **It is difference between rows 2nd & 3rd and shows percentage of total spatial variance taking into account in the assimilation process.**

specially at its lower level of assimilation, and hence, it show a wide range of fluctuations at the latter stages of assimilation. Thus, the region building is not much stable and, consequently, the region formation in this region have four tier system of areal hierarchy with some indifferent regions at meso and micro regional levels in the region-formation processes. There are many tevidences to confirm the facts about the degree of stability of region-formation. For instance, four out of total nine agricultural planning regions of the Peninsular Plateau at meso-level (namely, Aravali Hills, North Deccan, Andhra Interior and the Tamilnadu Uplands) have the degree of spatial variance of more than 100 per cent. Even some micro-level regions, namely, the Narmada Valley, the Maharashtra Hills, and the Balaghat (a unique micro-level region) have very high degrees of their spatial variances (Table- 5.5). On the other hand, very high degree of spatial variance within the micro-agricultural region of the Great plains with its smooth fluctuations at its each level of grouping/clustering can also be seen (Fig.- 5.3). Among them some agricultural

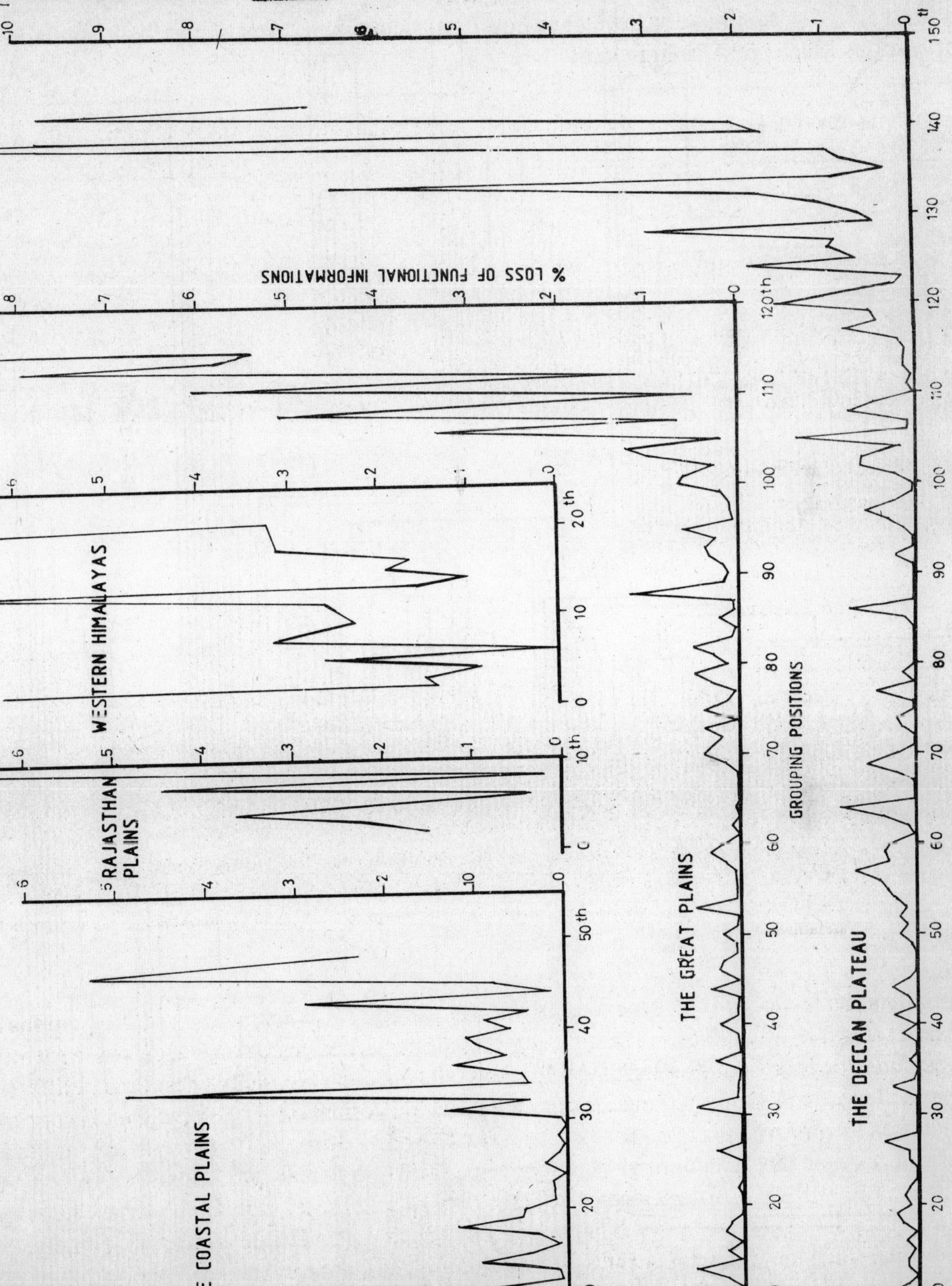

Fig. -5.1 : Assimilation Tendencies of OTUs at its Grouping Levels.

DENDROGRAMS

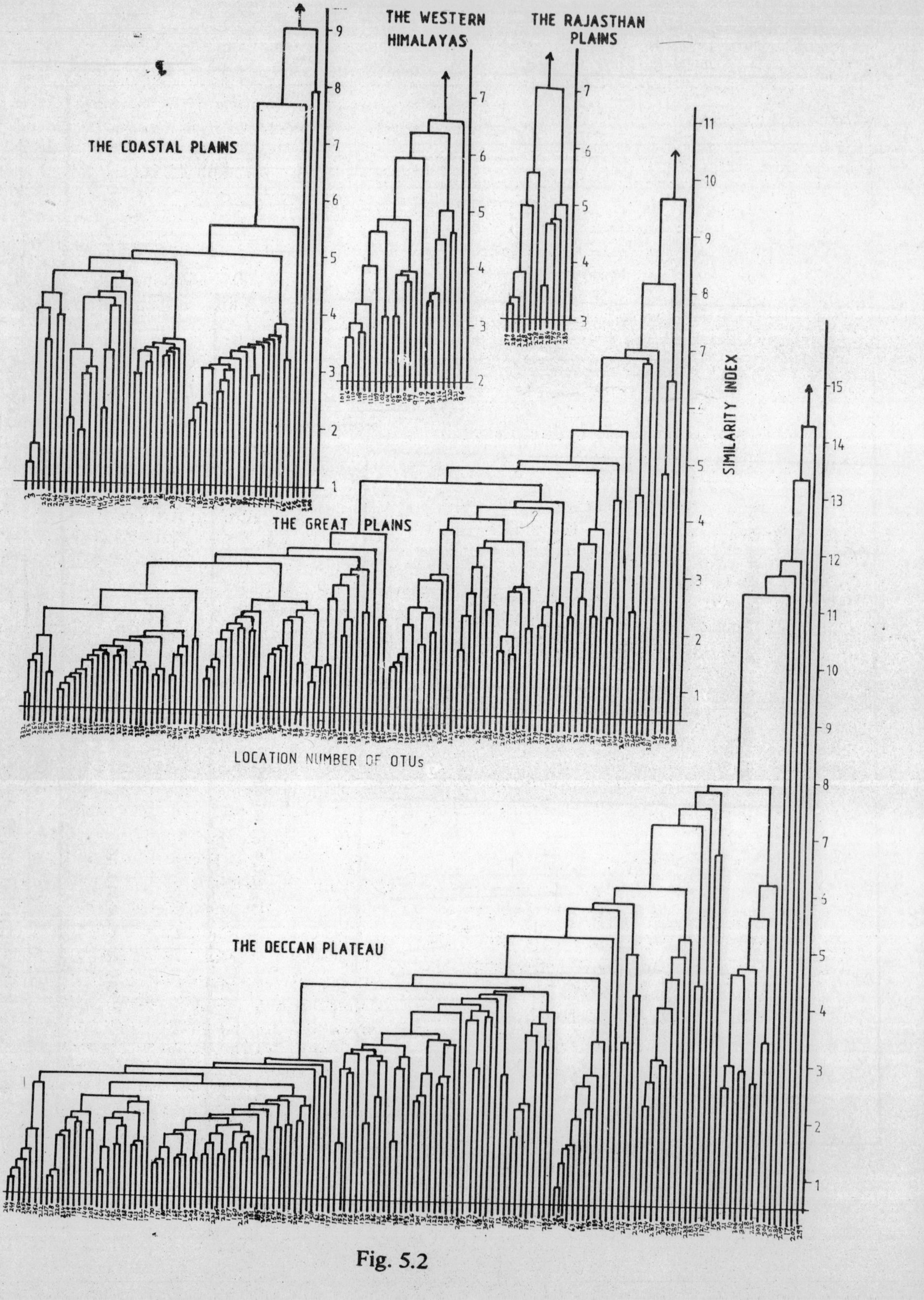

Fig. 5.2

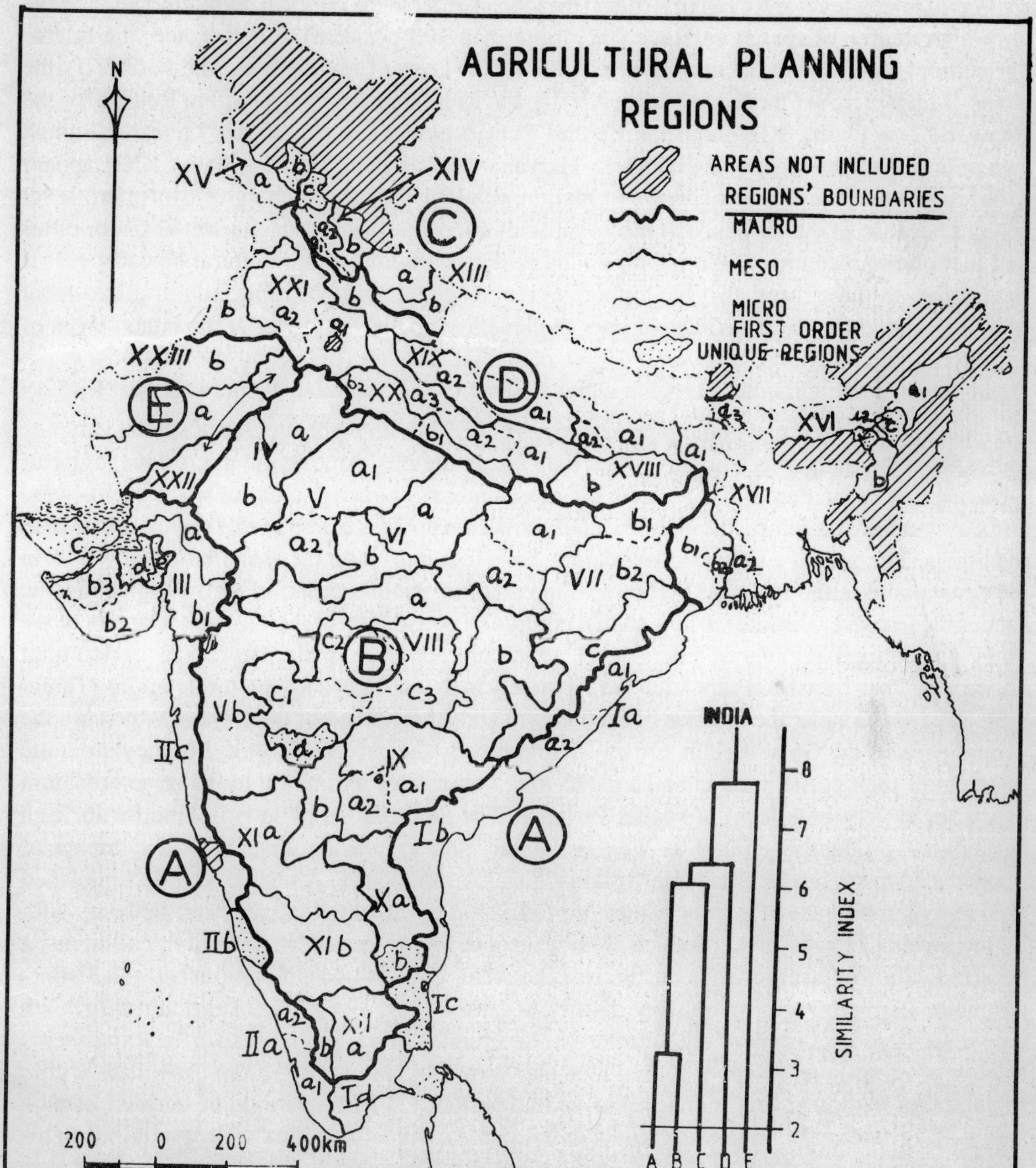
AGRICULTURAL PLANNING REGIONS
N
AREAS NOT INCLUDED
REGIONS' BOUNDARIES
MACRO
MESO
MICRO
FIRST ORDER
UNIQUE REGIONS
A
B
C
D
E
XV
XIV
XIII
XXI
XXIII
XXII
XIX
XX
XVIII
XVII
XVI
IV
V
VI
VII
VIII
III
IX
Vb
IIc
XIa
XIb
Xa
IIb
XII
IIa
Ia
Ib
Ic
Id
200 0 200 400km
INDIA
SIMILARITY INDEX
8
7
6
5
4
3
2
A B C D E
Macro-Regions
NB : For name of the Regions, see Table — 5.5

Fig. 5.3

regions of micro-level and even first order (the lowest order in the regional hierarchy) levels have very high degree of spatial variance (i.e., more than 100 per cent). For instance, the micro-agricultural regions of the Central Bengal (a unit of the Lower Ganga-Plains, number XVII), the Trans-Ganga plain (of the Bihar plains, XVIII), the Rohilkhand-Upper Ghaghra Region (of the *Bhawar-Terai* Plains, XIX), and the Central Punjab plains and the Border Lands of Punjab (which are the micro-regions of the Punjab- Haryana- Western Uttar Pradesh plains, XXI), appear to be less stable in the process of region formation, although they are much significant micro-level regions because of the influence of micro-agricultural processes and the impact of major cities and metropolitan centres of the region on the spatial variations of agricultural landscape. It is interesting to note here that the higher degree of spatial variance especially at micro-level region-formation as described above rises the levels of spatial variances at the latter stages of assimilation and increases an overall degree of spatial variance (or loss of informations) in the Great plains macro-agricultural region which has been recorded nearly 95 per cent (Table- 5.4).

d) The emergence of homogeneous groups of OTUs with higher degree of spatial variance indicates non-contiguous zonation rather than stable regions. Among the micro-level agricultural regions of the Peninsular Plateau, the non-contiguity over agricultural space seems wide and obvious and, therefore, the stability of assimilation process is less in this region rather than the others. The spatial contiguity constraints have less impact on the assimilation of OTUs in the Great plains, although it has higher spatial variation, yet this variation is also appeared to be sequential in space. Despite various spatial contiguity constraints in region-formation, there are many agricultural regions of micro-level which are 'unique' in its nature and agricultural characters. They have been kept bounded separately in the scheme of agricultural regions (Table-5.5). Say for example, the districts of Sundargarh and Ahmedabad of the Gujarat which are the central parts of the Gujarat plain, are physiographically the part of one unit. But they are quite different in their agricultural characteristics and, hence, they assimilate in the regionalisation processes at very high level of spatial variance. The Ahmedabad plain is unique for its high agricultural productivity (land as well as labour) and growth because of direct impact of Ahmedabad town, but the Sundargarh plain which is contiguous to Ahmedabad is distinguished unique region because of greater values of production potential magnitudes and intensity with higher levels of its marginal products with respect to labour as well as technological inputs, a good indication of fast growth in the future. Like-wise, Osmanabad is distinguished as a distinct unique small micro-region of only one district, because of very low values of agricultural growth potentials. A good example of unique micro-agricultural region is also marked in the Rayalseema Region of meso-level (number X) inwhich shevaroy and Javadi Hills (Xb) assimilate within Rayalseema Region at very high level of spatial variance (14.26). It might be because of high levels of agricultural production, productivity and growth as raw data table highlights. This region is spatially contiguous to the Madras plain, a micro-agricultural region (Ic) of the East Coastal plains. It has very low degree of spatial variance (13.46 per cent) with a very high level of assimilation (9.02). However, the region shevaloy and Javadi Hills have been assimilated to group with the meso-agricultural region of Rayalseema (X) rather than the Madras plains of the East Coastal region (Ic).

Table- 5.5: Nomenclature and Hierarchy of Agricultural Planning Regions with the Degree of Their Spatial Variances

	Name of the Regions	No. of OTUs	Assimilation Levels		Within Region Variation	
			Mini	Maxi	Absolute	%
	(1)	(2)	(3)	(4)	(5)	(6)
A.	<u>**The Coastal Regions**</u>					
I.	***East Coast Plains***					
a.	Coromandal East	7	1.32	4.37	3.05	231.06
	1. Utkal plain	4	3.48	4.37	0.89	25.57
	2. Andhra east plain	3	1.32	1.64	0.32	24.24
b.	Andra Plains (Central Coast)	7	3.25	4.01	0.76	23.38
c.	Madras Plain (Unique)	2	7.95	9.02	1.02	13.46
d.	S. Tamilnadu Plain	3	3.10	3.31	0.21	6.77
II.	***Western Coastal Plains***					
a.	Malabar Coasts	11	2.13	4.12	1.99	93.43
	1. South Kerala	7	2.27	4.12	1.85	81.50
	2. North Kerala	4	2.13	3.31	1.18	55.40
b.	Karnataka Coastal Plain (Unique)	1	0.00	4.55	4.55	-
c.	Konkan Coastal Plain	5	2.16	2.99	0.83	38.42
III.	***The Gujarat Plains***					
a.	Panchmahal-Sabarkantha	3	3.27	4.43	1.16	35.47
b.	Central Plains	11	2.63	3.21	0.58	22.05
	1. Mehsana-Baroda Plain	6	3.03	3.21	0.18	5.94
	2. Coastal Kathiabar	3	2.63	2.81	0.18	6.84
	3. Interior Kathiabar	2	0.00	3.27	3.27	-
c.	Kutch Peninsula (Unique)	1	0.00	4.43	4.43	-
d.	Sundernagar Plain (Unique)	1	0.00	7.65	7.65	-
e.	Ahmedabad Plain	1	0.00	5.55	5.55	-
B.	<u>**The Peninsular Plateau**</u>					
IV.	***Aravali Hills***					
a.	Eastern Rajasthan	6	2.32	4.20	1.88	81.03
b.	Aravali Ranges	7	3.15	5.22	2.07	65.71
V.	***The Central Plateau***					
a.	N.W. Madhya Pradesh	21	1.25	2.28	1.03	82.40
	1. Chambal Basin	13	1.42	2.28	0.86	60.56
	2. Malwa Upland	8	1.25	1.68	0.43	34.40
b.	Maharashtra Shayadri	9	1.24	1.70	0.46	37.10

Contd...

	(1)	(2)	(3)	(4)	(5)	(6)
VI.	***The Bundelkhand-Malwa Plateau***					
a.	Bundelkhand	8	1.05	1.91	0.86	81.90
b.	East Malwa Plateau	5	1.32	2.00	0.68	51.51
VII.	***The Eastern Plateau***					
a.	Benghelkhand	7	3.40	5.51	2.11	62.06
	1. The Sonpar Hills	4	3.40	4.81	0.41	12.06
	2. The Maikal-Ramgar Hills	3	4.12	5.51	1.39	33.74
b.	Chotanagpur Plateau	10	0.97	2.85	1.88	193.81
	1. Hazaribagh Plateau	4	0.97	1.35	0.38	39.17
	2. Ranchi Plateau	6	1.12	2.85	1.73	154.46
c.	Orissa Hills	6	0.84	1.71	0.87	103.57
VIII.	***The North Deccan***					
a.	The Narmada Valley	8	1.25	2.93	1.68	134.40
b.	Bastar Hills (including Mahanadi Basin)	4	2.30	3.29	0.99	43.04
c.	Wardha Plateau	12	0.88	2.30	1.42	161.36
	1. South Central Plateau	4	0.88	1.96	1.08	122.73
	2. Ajanta Hills (N. Central)	4	1.58	2.30	0.72	45.56
	3. Wardha Valley	4	1.52	1.93	0.41	26.97
d.	Balaghat Range(Unique, Osmanabad)	1	0.00	2.52	2.52	-
IX.	***The Andhra Interior (Telangana)***					
a.	N. Telangana Upland	8	2.41	6.71	4.31	178.84
	1. N. Andhra Upland	6	2.61	4.61	2.00	76.63
	2. Hydrabad Hills	2	2.41	6.72	4.31	178.84
b.	Karnataka East	3	2.91	4.78	1.87	64.26
X.	***The Rayalseema***					
a.	Chitor-Cudapah Upland	3	3.31	3.71	0.40	12.08
b.	Javadi Hills (Unique)	1	0.00	14.26	14.26	-
XI.	***The South Deccan***					
a.	North Karnataka	7	1.92	3.23	1.31	68.23
b.	South Karnataka	11	2.31	3.52	1.21	52.38
XII.	***The Tamilnadu Upland***					
a.	Middle Caveri Basin	4	3.00	5.66	2.66	88.67
b.	Transitional Land of South Sahayadri-Nilgiri Hills	3	3.67	7.15	3.48	94.82

Contd...

	(1)	(2)	(3)	(4)	(5)	(6)
C.	**The Western Himalayas**					
XIII.	***Uttar Pradesh Himalayas***					
a.	Garhwal Himalayas	3	2.94	3.56	0.62	21.08
b.	Kumaon Himalayas	3	4.49	5.09	0.60	13.36
XIV.	***Himachal Himalayas***					
a.	Lesser Himalayas	8	1.00	3.56	2.56	256.00
	1. Siwalik Foothills (Duns)	6	2.24	3.56	1.32	58.93
	2. Main Valleys of Kulu, Mandi & Lahaul	2	1.00	3.16	2.16	216.00
b.	Central Himalayas	2	1.11	3.32	2.23	200.00
c.	Sub-Himalayan Zone (Unique) (Upper ChinabValley of Chamba)	1	0.00	6.58	6.58	-
XV.	**Jammu-Kashmir Valley**					
a.	Punch-Jammu Valley (Siwaliks & Foothills)	5	2.84	4.04	1.20	42.25
b.	Pirpanjal Ranges (Unique)	1	0.00	5.96	5.96	-
D.	**The Great Plains**					
XVI.	***The Assam Plains***					
a.	Brahmaputra Valley	10	2.35	3.84	1.49	63.40
	1. Upper Brahmaputra	3	2.64	3.84	1.20	45.45
	2. Lower Brahmaputra	4	2.35	3.62	1.27	54.04
	3. Tista Plain (N. Bengal Plain)	3	2.35	3.08	0.73	31.06
b.	The Barrak Valley (Kachhar)	2	0.00	4.65	4.65	-
c.	Mikir Hills (Unique) (Karbionlong)	1	0.00	6.63	6.63	-
XVII.	***The Lower Ganga Plain***					
a.	Hoogli River Alluvial Plain	7	2.20	2.61	0.41	18.64
	1. Upper Hoogli Plain	3	2.41	2.61	0.20	8.30
	2. Lower Hoogli Plain	4	2.20	2.41	0.21	9.54
b.	Central Bengal Plain	6	1.89	9.63	7.74	409.52
	1. Rahar Plain	4	1.89	2.25	0.36	19.05
	2. Calcutta Surroundings	2	7.00	9.63	2.63	37.57
XVIII.	***The Bihar Plains***					
a.	Trans Ganga Plains	13	1.13	2.32	1.19	105.31
	1. Muzaffarpur-Saharsa Plain	10	1.14	2.32	1.18	103.51
	2. Ghagra-Gandak Lower Doab	3	1.13	1.36	0.23	20.35
b.	South Bihar Plains	9	1.15	2.23	1.08	93.91

Contd....

	(1)	(2)	(3)	(4)	(5)	(6)
XIX.	***The Bhawar Terai Plains***					
a.	Rohikhand Upper Ghagra Plains	11	1.14	2.36	1.22	107.02
	1. Upper Sarda- Ghagra Doab	5	1.14	1.96	.82	71.93
	2. Ram Ganga Basin (Rohilkhand)	6	1.28	2.36	1.08	84.37
b.	Haryana-Uttar Pradesh Bhawar (Foot Hills)	6	1.96	3.73	1.77	90.31
XX.	***The central Ganga Plains***					
a.	Gomti Central Avadh Plains	15	0.78	1.53	.75	96.15
	1. Central Avadh Plain (E.U.P.)	6	0.93	1.19	.26	27.96
	2. Gomti Plains (C.U.P.)	5	1.19	1.69	.50	42.02
	3. Central Dry Zone	4	.78	1.53	.75	96.15
b.	Lower Ganga-Jamuna *Doab*	9	1.16	1.90	.74	63.80
	1. Kanpur- Allahabad Doab	3	1.16	1.72	.56	48.27
	2. Agra Plain	6	1.33	1.90	.60	45.11
XXI	***The Punjab - Haryana - Western Uttar Pradesh Plains***					
a.	Central Punjab Plains	25	1.16	3.54	2.38	205.17
	1. Delhi Surroundings	10	1.16	1.79	.63	54.31
	2. Punjab - Haryana Banghar	15	1.79	3.54	1.75	97.76
b.	Border Lands of Punjab	2	2.41	6.94	4.53	187.97
E.	**The Rajasthan Plains**					
XXII.	***The Rajasthan Bangar***	5	3.53	5.01	1.48	41.93
XXIII.	***The Marusthali***	6	3.27	5.57	2.30	70.36
a.	Marusthali Central	3	3.27	3.37	.10	3.06
b.	Western Marusthali Border	3	3.37	5.57	.20	59.35

Note : The Andaman and Nicobar, Lakshadweep and Maldive Islands form one separate agricultural planning region and can be placed in the last as meso-region number XXIV in the present scheme of regionalisation. But it is not included in the present scheme because of non-availability of agricultural statistics.

The Agricultural Planning Regions

The calculation and ordering of spatial variance (i.e., based in the functional differentiation of agricultural characteristics) at each level of region-formation (or assimilation of OTUs), which follow the guiding principles of boundary demarcation of agricultural planning regions, classify the total OTUs into ninety five lowest order levels and fifty five micro-level regions of optimal groupings of assimilated OTUs for detail observations and indepth inquiries of agricultural phenomena of its micro-processes regional elements (Table-5.5, Fig.-5.3). For more generalisation of regional agricultural characteristics, these fifty-five micro-level regional units have been grouped into twenty - three meso-level agricultural regions by following the same guiding principles of regionalisation and spatial contiguity constraints.

Looking at the regional boundaries shown on the map and comparing them with the agro-climatic zones demarcated by the Planning Commission (1989) in its recent publication, it can safely be concluded that the macro-regional boundaries of Agricultural Planning Regions (that are five in numbers) and the boundaries of Agro-climatic zones coincide with each other following broad physiographic division of the country. It means physiography especially the relief features and climatic conditions are the controlling factors in the region-formation at macro-regional level. But the boundaries of meso-agricultural regions and agro-climatic zones are coinciding only in the Coastal Regions, in the Rajasthan and the western Himalayan regions where climate is a direct determinant of region-formation of agricultural phenomena. On the other hand, there is a significant boundary deviation and over-lapping of agricultural planning regions and agro-climatic zones especially in the peninsular plateaus and the Great Plain of India of the meso- as well as micro- levels regions (Figs.-5.3 & 5.4). The factors behind this fact are obvious as :

a) Agro-climatic zones demarcated by Planning Commission are basically and initially based on ecological criteria of agricultural attributes rather than its agro-technological, economic and growth potential characteristics. As a result, agro-climatic zones particularly at its meso-regional levels follow the superimposed common boundaries of relief features, geological structure and climatic regions of the country. Therefore, these boundaries are comparable and similar to the Natural regions prepared by Census of India (1952) in its paper no. 2 or to the physiographic regions demarcated by the Regional Survey Unit, Indian Statistical Institute, New Delhi in 1968 (Fig.- 5.4 Inset). For example, the part of the Maharashtra Plateau has different agricultural characteristics from the central part of Malwa Plateau of Madhya Pradesh. But these two agricultural units have been clubbed together in the region-formation scheme initiated by the Planning Commission (1989); this zone is named as, the Western Plateau and Hills (IX). On the other hand, the southern Sahayadri Hills of Maharashtra and the Malwa Plateau which are separate meso-regions demarcated by the Planning Commission, undoubtedly, similar in agricultural characteristics and form a longitudinal agricultural planning region at meso-level of region-formation; according to the present scheme, it is named as 'The Central Plateau (V)'. Another example of the same fact can be cited from the North Deccan Region (VIII), which includes the Wardha Plateau and its surroundings and forms a homogeneous agricultural region of meso-level according to the present region-formation scheme. While the same fact is not shown in the agro-climatic regionalisation scheme which homogeneously forms meso-level agricultural region to club the Wardha and the Malwa Plateau of different agricultural identities.

b) According to agro-climatic zonation scheme of Planning Commission, the boundaries of meso- as well as micro-regions especially in the Great Plains of India follow clearly and solely the rainfall criteria of region-formation rather than the criteria of agricultural production characteristics. Obviously, this part of the country is the most fertile and has the most favourable conditions for agricultural intensification and, consequently, it has been the persuator of green revolution. Indeed, the green revolution effects and the diffusion processes of agricultural

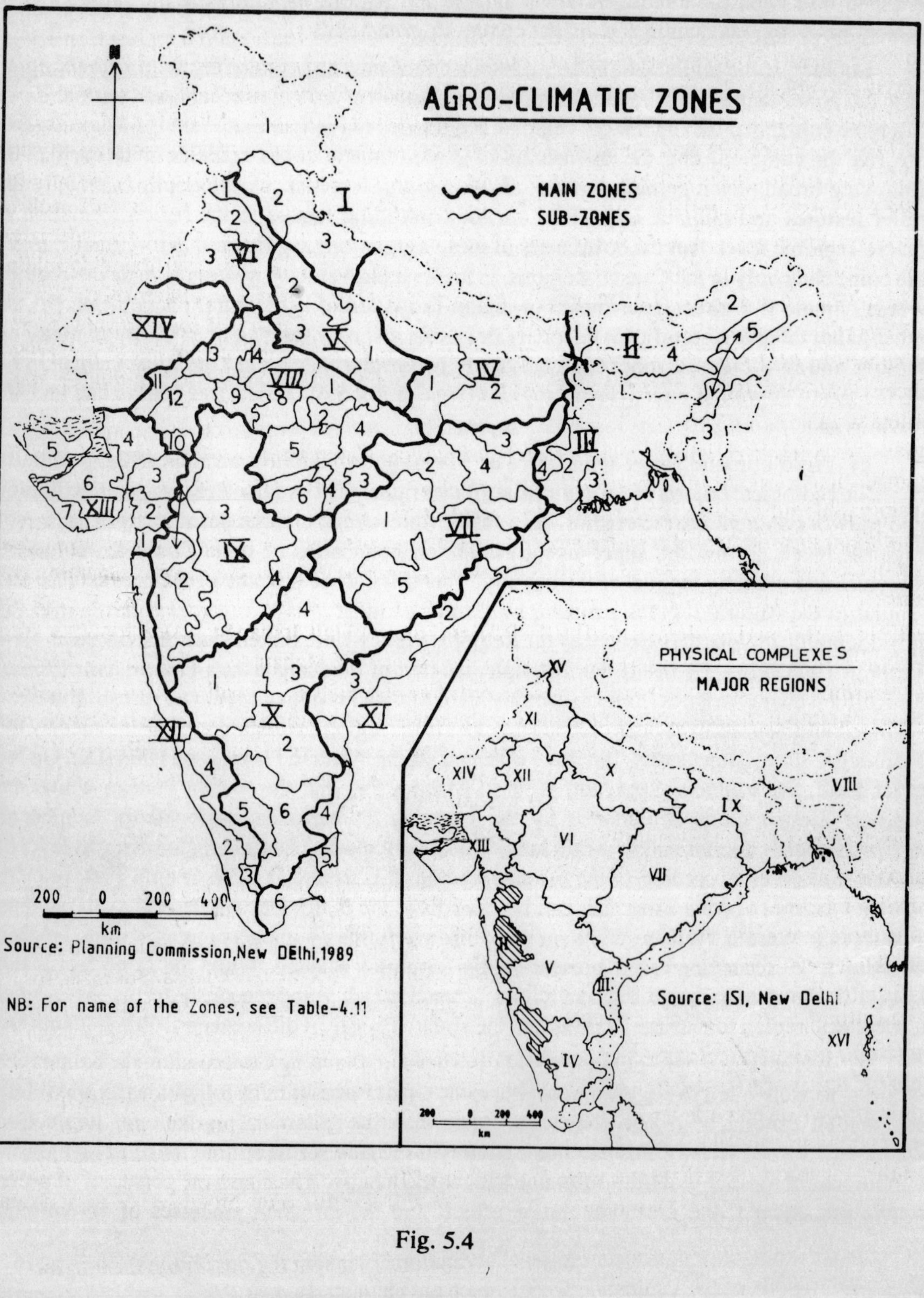
AGRO-CLIMATIC ZONES
MAIN ZONES
SUB-ZONES
Source: Planning Commission, New DElhi, 1989
NB: For name of the Zones, see Table-4.11
PHYSICAL COMPLEXES
MAJOR REGIONS
Source: ISI, New Delhi

Fig. 5.4

innovations have been the most influential factors of region-formation especially at meso- and micro-levels of agricultural regionalisation. The present scheme of agricultural region-formation proves the clear cut and strong evidences of the centre-based growth and formation of planning regions particularly at micro-or first order levels. For instance, the Rahar plain and the Calcutta surrounding regions of the central Bengal Plains (XVIIb1 and XVIIb2), and the Delhi surroundings and the Punjab-Haryana *Banghar* regions of Punjab-Haryana-Western Uttar Pradesh plains (XXIa1 and XXIa2) are emerging as first order regions. It is a reflection of the dominance of agro-technology on the assimilation processes of region-formation.

c) After an introduction of modern technology in the agricultural intensification (especially during post-green revolution period of 1980s), the regional dimensions of Indian agriculture are not solely dependent upon the physical characteristics of the region, though physiographic factors control it at macro-regional level. Green revolution effects lead Indian agriculture towards its diversified areal pattern of agricultural growth and development and hence, regional forms of agricultural characteristics appear to be more complex and non-contiguous particularly at lower-levels of regional hierarchy. The present scheme of agricultural region-formation highlights some relevant facts and inherent correlative characteristics of the regional dimensions of Indian agriculture as some areas/OTUs are most homogeneous in its physiographic attributes but are quite indifferent in its agricultural characteristics. They are emerging as separate agricultural regions of unique characteristics. Say for example, the Madras plain consisting of the district of South Arcot and Thanjavur of the central part of east coastal plains (Ic), the Karnataka plain of the west coastal plains (IIb), and the Kutch Peninsula of the Gujarat plains (IIIc) are agriculturally indifferent at very high assimilation levels (at 9.00, 4.55 and 4.43 levels respectively), though the degree of spatial variance is very low within these regions of unique characteristics. The more elaborations on the regional characteristics of Indian agriculture should put forward separately in the next section of this Chapter.

Agricultural Characteristics in its Regional Frame

The regional characteristics of Indian agriculture can be interpreted in detail in the present context at first-order levels of regional units. But the discussion at this level may deviate us from the main objectives of the present Chapter which we have put forward earlier. A regional analyst who is more interested in the real interpretation of structural agricultural characteristics based upon its interrelationships and spatially co-existing conditions for concrete suggestions made for self-sustained growth and balanced development of agriculture, can pursue his studies on the direction which leads towards the comparative statements and elaborative result of meso-level agricultural planning regions which are the close contiguous and tightly-bound regional units within the macro-regional frame of the country. Thus, the conclusions of the regional interpretation are drawn on meso-level regional units. However, the insights of the present interpretation are elaborated to consider the empirical agricultural informations at first order areal hierarchy. The salient features of agricultural planning regions of India are given below :

A. The Coastal Regions

There are emergence of three meso-level agricultural planning regions within the longitudinal coastal regions of the Peninsular India, which are characterised, as :

AI. *The East Coastal Plain:* which includes 19 districts of the eastern coast of the country and has four micro-level regional units, namely, the Coromandal east, the Andhra plains, the Madras plain of its unique nature and the south Tamilnadu plains. They are agriculturally most homogeneous, though the Madras plain is indifferent from the other regional units at its very high level of assimilation (7.95).

AII. *The West Coastal Plain:* a meso-agricultural planning region of 17 districts which incorporates three stable micro-level regions, viz., the Malabar coasts, the Karnataka coastal plain and the Konkan coastal plain. The degree of spatial variance within the region has been recorded very high (93.43 per cent) in the Malabar coastal region and hence, it has two first-order regional units of the south and the north Kerala.

AIII. *The Gujarat Plains:* which includes five micro-level regional units including these three unique regional units (Table- 5.5). The central plains of Gujarat as one of the most homogeneous agricultural regional unit at micro-level, is most stable and has very low degree of spatial variance (22.05 percent), while the others have much variations in agricultural attributes and hence, they have been declared as unique regions of single districts.

In general, the evapo-transpiration conditions for plant growth are similar in all the regions of coastal plains, inspite of significant spatial variation in annual rainfall. Annual rainfall is recorded 1075 mm in the east coastal plain, 2858 mm in the west coastal plain and 714 mm in the Gujarat plain. Therefore, there is a deficiency of rain water availability particularly in the Gujarat and the east coastal plain regions. The climatic conditions are moist sub-humid in the eastern coastal region to dry sub-humid and semi-arid in the Gujarat plain. The soils are largely coastal alluvium varying from deltaic alluvium to red/gray brown alluvium because of availability of different parental rock materials. But these soils are fertile and favourable for the intensification of agricultural activities. Water deficiency in these soils has been minimised through extensive utilisation of underground as well as surface water sources by increasing irrigation facilities especially in the east coastal region of the country.

On account of favourable agro-ecological conditions, better irrigation facilities (Net Irrigated area has been recorded 53.28 per cent to total NSA in 1988-89) and its fast increase (4.45 per cent) during the 1980s in the eastern coastal region, its agricultural growth potential structure appears to be stronger and suitable for agricultural development. The magnitude and intensity of yield-potentials are, therefore, recorded very high (magnitude Rs. 1906 per ha and intensity 224 per cent), although their absorption rates are very low and, hence, marginal products to labour as well as to technology are recorded very low not only in the eastern coastal region but in the entire coastal region at macro-level also (Table- 5.11). It is interesting to note that, in the eastern coastal region at meso-level, the greater use of chemical fertilizer (58.42 kg/ha), very high use of agricultural labour input (2.17 persons/ha) with greater use of non-land capital input (Rs. 114/ha) have intensified agricultural systems to increase record levels of agricultural output (of about 8.0 per cent), labour productivity (55.65 per cent) and crop-intensity (120.9 per cent) during the last ten years from 1979-82 to 1988-90. Comparatively higher share of work force which is solely dependent on agricultural activities in this region (71.02 per cent in 1991) tends to decrease the operational size of land holdings and NSA per worker (i.e., 0.52 ha/worker) which directly affect the utilisation of agricultural growth potentials. On account of sufficient availability of the magnitude and intensity of crop-yield potential, remarkable increase in labour productivity and land utilisation has been recorded during the 1980s and, therefore, this region of the east coastal plain is called 'Prosperous Agricultural Region'.

On the other hand, on account of sufficient moisture availability in the soils, rice-ragi dominated cropping patterns are marked with very less share of working force employed in agricultural activities (44.55 per cent in 1991) with its moderately low increase (12.37 per cent) during 1980s, though population density is extremely high (691 persons/sq. km. in 1991) comprising of a very high percentage of rural literates (68.11 per cent). It denotes abundant supply of labour in agriculture sector of the west coastal region of the country, the per capita agricultural output, land and labour productivities and their increases in the 1980s have been recorded very low (Tables- 5.6 through 5.11, see Tables in the end of the Chapter). Inspite of these agricultural conditions prevailing in the region for its development, there is sufficient availability but misuse of agricultural growth potentials which can be channelised in future. Therefore, this region can also be called progressive and developing in its nature, although agricultural growth and productivity are recorded very low. It might be because of non-inclusion of horticulture and other crops in our domain of productivity calculation which are dominant in the Malabar and Konkan Coastal Areas. Undoubtedly, the economy of the Malabar coastal areas has been changing fast from food grain rice intensive to coconut horticulture dominated during the past green revolution period.

Thirdly, the Gujarat plain of meso-level region is climatically semi-arid in nature with poor soils of Kutch and Kathiawar hills, although the central plains of Mehsana-Baroda (a micro-regional unit) are most fertile and favourable for agricultural intensification. The moisture deficiency for plant growth (i.e., marked 0.510 moisture index value) is still prevalent in the region which directly influences the cropping patterns and crop-intensity. Therefore, crop-intensity is very low (113.15 percent) with a marginal increase of about 2.0 per cent during 1980s. On account of noticeable share of total work force (57.69 per cent in 1991) engaging in agriculture with its marginal increase of 19.12 percent during 1980s, the labour input per agricultural land unit has been increasing fast at the rate of 36.74 per cent in the last decade and, hence, labour productivity is recorded high (Rs 1446 per person) in 1988-90. Land productivity is marginally lower than the national average. It is because of less and improper applicability of the modern means of agricultural productivity, although production potential intensity is high with significantly high levels of marginal products to labour as well as to technology. It means that the response of the use of technology would be better in future if it is used to increase irrigated areas in this region.

B. The Peninsular Plateaux

The operational taxonomic units (i.e., districts) of entire peninsular plateaux have optimally been grouped into nine meso and twenty- one micro- level regional units considering their contiguity constraints and degree of spatial variances in the assimilation processes of region-formation. The salient features of agricultural development especially at meso-level of agricultural regions are described as follows :

B IV. *The Aravali Hills Region :* It has a separate identity physiographically as well as in agricultural systems. It includes eleven districts of the Aravali Hills and uplands of eastern Rajasthan including two districts of western Madhya Pradesh. Climatically, it is semi-arid and receives only 773 mm average rainfall in a year. On account of high evapo- transpiration (1577 mm annually) and very less rainfall, it is moisture deficient region of the peninsular plateau, but the soils are fertile, red and gray-brown in its texture. Because of favourable agro-ecological conditions especially of soil conditions , the maximum expected yield levels are very high (Rs. 3154 per ha) with high magnitude and intensity of agricultural production potential. The share of Net Irrigated Area is slightly low (34.2 percent) but its decade increase is recorded highest (24.89 percent) during 1980s. The modernisation in agricultural practices is moderate because of high share of work force employed in agricultural activities (71.51 percent in 1991) with its remarkable increase (51.49 percent) during 1981-91. This increase has been recorded far higher, even more than double to the increase of national average (i.e, only 22.37 percent). Very high increase and share of agricultural work force denote the availability of cheap labour for agricultural operations. Inspite of unlimited supply of labour to agricultural system of the region, the marginal product to labour and the absorption rate of production potential with respect to labour have been recording higher (Table-5.11). It means that more labour can be absorbed in the agricultural production processes in future. On the other hand, production potential absorption rate and marginal product with respect to the application of technology have been recorded very low and insignificant. As a result, the growth rate of agricultural output, land and labour productivities are recorded moderately with its very slow rate of increase (Table-5.8).

The level of agricultural productivity can be increased and the process of growth can be accelerated optimally with the proper application of modern technology which would act as complementary to the labour rather than its substitution in the development pattern in the Aravalli Hills Region.

BV. *The Central Plateau :* It is a longitudinal agricultural planning region which incorporates 21 districts of the North Western parts of Madhya Pradesh (the area of Chambal ravines and west Malwa upland, which are first order-regional units of the micro region Va) and nine districts of Maharashtra Shayadri which is a transitional part of Maharashtra Deccan (as Vb). It is a stable micro regional unit of agricultural phenomena.

Though these micro-regional units of this region are quite indifferent physiographically, say for example, North-West Madhya Pradesh has Chambal system of water drainage with mixed red and yellow soils of less fertility where climate is dry sub-humid, while the micro-region of Maharashtra Deccan is a stable micro-regional unit of agricultural phenomena. Though these micro-regional units of this region are quite indifferent physiographically, say for example, North-West Madhya Pradesh has Chambal system of water drainage with mixed red and yellow soils of less fertility where climate is dry sub-humid, while the micro-region of Maharashtra Sahyadri is a water shed divide of about 600 m height and formed by deep black and shallow red soils of lava where prevailing climatic conditions are semi-arid to sub-humid and hence, millets and cotton crops are dominant cropping pattern. Rainfall being less in the entire region of the central plateau (838 mm/annual), there is water deficiency (mean moisture index -.327) for proper plant growth and enhancement of agricultural productivity. As a result, agricultural output growth, productivity levels and their increases have been marked low to very low. For instance, annual growth rate of agricultural output has been recorded 6.69 percent during the 1980s as against 8.44 percent of the national average, low levels of land and labour productivities, Rs. 844/ha and Rs.974/person respectively, with very low increase in their levels as 6.45 and 30.12 percent respectively during 1980s. Farming intensity is very low 118 percent because of low share of Net Irrigated Area to total NSA (22.39 percent), very low irrigation intensity (112 percent), low and very low application of modern machine tools (Rs. 33/ha) and chemical fertilizers (20.27 kg/ha) with low degree of labour as well as of technological inputs, although a noticeable share of total workforce is employed in agriculture sector (73.78 percent in 1991) with its fast increase of 25.37 percent in 1981-91. On the other hand, the stagnant conditions of agricultural growth potential prevailing in the region with the low and very low degree of the magnitude and intensity of production potential, diminish their marginal products of agricultural systems and the absorption rates of potential production with respect to labour and technological inputs that have been recorded very low (Table- 5.11). It may be because of poor agro-ecological, socio-cultural and economic conditions. Thus, this region may be called, 'under-developed agricultural region' of the country.

BVI. *The Bundelkhand - Malwa Region:* The prevailing agro-ecological, and economic conditions of this region are more or less same as of the central plateau region. But the agricultural growth and productivity have been marked extremely low even lowest among all the agricultural planning regions of the peninsular plateaux. On account of very low per capita agricultural output (Rs. 234/person), the lowest annual growth rate of agricultural output especially in the peninsular India (only 1.62 percent in 1980s), lowest level of land productivity (Rs. 595/ha) and extremely low level of labour productivity (Rs. 770/person) with decreasing rate of their changes (land productivity decreases .23 percent and labour productivity 5.21 percent annually during 1980s), the prevailing agricultural situation in the region is the most stagnant and backward (Table- 5.8). The agricultural growth potential attributes are also recorded weak. However, the agricultural production potential intensity is comparatively very high (4.05) with low coefficient of its spatial variation (33.05) (Table- 5.11). Therefore, in near future, these agricultural growth potentials can be utilised to increase their absorption rates by intensifying irrigation and agricultural extension services in the region.

BVII. *The Eastern Plateau :* It includes three micro-agricultural regional units, namely, VIIa: Benghalkhand of Maikal Ramgarh and Sonpar hills (7 districts), VIIb: Chotanagpur Plateau which incorporates the Hazaribagh and Ranchi Plateaux of the eastern foreland of Indian peninsula (10 districts), and VIIc: The Orissa Hills (6 districts of interior Orissa state), which are physiographically different to each other but form a meso-level agricultural planning region with a significant variation in the spatial properties of agricultural attributes. This region has the important mineral belt of India but is a tribal dominated area and, hence, very low literacy rate in the rural areas (29.13 percent) is recorded, although the density of population is low (239 persons per sq. km. in 1991) with moderate decadal growth (24.03 percent). Agro-economic structure is also weak. The region has very low share of Net Irrigated Area (15.58 percent), extremely low application of modern technology as mechanisation index is recorded lowest among all the regions of Indian peninsula (Rs. 6/ha) with very little use of chemical fertilizer (only 9.7 kg/ha). The use of labour input is moderate (Rs. 447/ha or 1.67 agricultural workers /ha in 1991) with a moderate increase of 21.9 percent in the 1980s. The prevailing conditions of weak agro-economic structure of the region, where per capita agricultural output is very low (Rs. 176/ person) with very low annual growth rate of agricultural output (3.57 percent), low levels of land as well as labour productivities with their decadal increase, hamper the agricultural growth potential characteristics of the region. Therefore, the magnitudes of agricultural production potential (yield-gap) has been recorded marginally low (Rs. 1689/ha) with a good deal of its intensity (3.00). Marginal product to labour is very low because of low absorption rate of labour potentiality and traditionalism in agricultural operational systems of the region of agro-ecological diversity. However, marginal product to technology is recorded highest among the other regions of the peninsular India and even higher than the national average (Table- 5.11). Per unit of increasing agricultural technology may increase 37 times level of agricultural production with absorbing only 23.5 percent share of production potential intensity. Thus, technology may be a good complement to labour input to optimally intensify the traditional agricultural systems operated in these areas of the fertile red gravel soils of plateaus and hills of this region.

BVIII. *The North Deccan :* It incorporates 25 districts including 12 districts of south -western parts of Madhya pradesh, 12 districts of the interior Maharashtra and one district of Andhra pradesh. This agricultural region is formed by four micro- level agricultural regional units, namely, VIIIa : The Narmada Valley including Mahadev hills black soils, VIIIb : The Bastar Hills of the Chattisgarh region including the districts of Mahanadi basin (Raigarh Raipur and Durg districts of South Madhya pradesh), VIIIc : The wardha Plateau - an interior part of Maharashtra Plateau which includes south - central plateau, Ajanta hills and Wardha valley of the black cotton soils and VIIId : The Balaghat Ranges (osmanabad districts of Maharashtra) as an unique agricultural micro-level regional unit which is 600 m above the mean sea level. The entire region is moisture deficient (moisture index -.446), although it receives an annual average rainfall of about 1160 mm. Because of high rate of annual potential evapo- transpiration (1513 mm) the climate of this region is semi- arid. Soils are fertile, hard medium to deep black in colour and favourable for cotton crop. Therefore, the region is jowar -cotton - wheat dominated cropping pattern which is best - suited to these agro-ecological conditions. The intensification conditions of agricultural production systems operated in this region are moderate although the future prospects agricultural development are better and favourable for technology extension services. In the moderate demographic and social conditions of the region where less pressure of population on land (174 persons/sq.km in 1991) with moderate rate of its decadal growth (24.15% 1981-91) moderate share of urban population (22.07%) and of rural literates (36.82%), the share of total working force employed in agricultural sector is marginally higher (77.85%) with a moderate rate of its (1981-91) increase of about 19.92%, although the agricultural labour input (i.e agricultural workforce per unit cultivated land) is moderate (1.05 persons/ha) with moderate increase of 25.51% during 1981-91. Inspite of moderate demographic conditions for agricultural growth and development, the annual growth rate of agricultural output has been recorded low (6.18 percent as against 8.44 percent of national average). The land and labour productivities are marked very low (as Rs.783/ha and Rs.713/person in 1988-90) with moderate increase during the 1980s (Table -5.8). The causes of low level of agricultural productivity are perhaps very low farming intensity (112 %) with its decadal decrease of 17 percent and less application of modern tools and techniques with very little use of chemical fertilizers (19.95 kg/ha) though the average size of operational land holdings are larger (1.94 ha of NSA per cultivator) than the national average. No doubt, it is cotton- crop-dominated region for which irrigation and fertilizer is not much required. But it is a commercial crop (raw material of cotton industry) and, thus, agricultural productivity in this region is controlled by the economic laws of demand and supply and the price mechanism of raw cotton. The future growth prospects of this region are better because of enough availability of the magnitude and intensity of agricultural production potentials (Rs.2234/ha and 3.69 respectively) with its marked absorption rate for increasing agricultural output. Therefore, marginal product to technology is recorded as high as 21.47. It means that the increase of one unit of technology in the present agricultural system of this region is capable of increasing 21.5 times of the agricultural output provided the extension agricultural services are utilised properly. On the whole, the region is developing in its nature and it may be suggested a change in the foodgrain dominated agricultural system to horticulture and orchard intensive system which would be more profitable and less risky to the farmers. Fruit cultivation which has been starting in this region is a good sign of changing traditional system agriculture.

BIX. *The Andhra Interior (Telengana):* It is a maso-regional unit of eleven districts which includes eight districts of the North Telengana upland and 3 districts of the Karnataka East with forming separate micro-regional units of agricultural attributes as IXa and IXb. The climate is semi-arid to arid following less amount of annual rainfall (838 mm) with higher rate of potential evapotranspiration (1655 mm/annual) and, consequently, there is noticeable moisture deficiency in the atmosphere (-.518 moisture index). Groundnut, jowar and rice are predominating crops in the cropping patterns of this regions which require less water and comparatively lesser use of fertiliser and modern technology, though the soils are fertile especially in upper Krishna basin which is lateritic, red loamy in the textural contents. In spite of these facts, greater use of machine tools (mechanisation Rs.68/ha), higher use of chemical fertilizers (57.72 kg/ha as against 44.0 kg/ha national average) are recorded. But increasing mechanisation in agricultural practices does not seem helpful to intensify agricultural production. It is surprising to note that, inspite of greater use of labour as well as of technological inputs because cheap labour is available though the share of agricultural workers to total workers is moderate (68.76 percent in 1991) with its moderate increase (18.25 percent in 1981-91), the farming (or crop) intensity is very low (116.86 percent) with its moderate increase (6.82 percent in the 1980s). It might be because of low share of Net Irrigated Area to the total cultivated land (28.7 percent). Therefore, the soils of this region are more thirsty rather than hungry. As a result, in the early 1990s, very low annual growth rate of agricultural output (5.14percent), low levels of land and labour productivities (Rs.988/ha and Rs.670/persons respectively) with a very low level of per capita agricultural output (198/persons) have been recorded, although influence of demographic and social factors are moderate with low density of population (215 persons/sq. km) and moderate urban share of total population (20.80 percent). In addition, the magnitude and intensity of crop production potential (i.e., yield gaps) are recorded very high (Rs.2573/ha and 414 percent respectively). It means that there are possibilities to develop agricultural practices in near future. But there is a variety in the application of modern technology and hence the present system is operative at very high absorption rate of labour potentials with a very low level of marginal product to labour if it is compared to the other regions of the country (Table- 5.11). It means there is a mismanagement of labour resources in the region. On the other hand, marginal products to technology as well as to labour have been recorded low (7.62 and 1.92 respectively) with very low absorption rate of its production potential(.228). It can be concluded that the ratio between the marginal product and the absorption rate of production potential which refers to resource utilization is higher with respect to labour input than to the technological inputs. Therefore, technology is complementary to labour input rather than being a substitution and, it can be said surely that more labour can be employed with simultaneously increasing technology to optimise the agricultural production systems of the region of rugged topography and dry climatic conditions.

BX. *The Rayalseema Region:* It is very small in size (only four districts including one district of Tamilnadu state). It is the driest part of the peninsular India; only 711 mm annual average rainfall with high rate of potential evapotranspiration (1637mm annually) and hence moisture is recorded highly negative as -.551. This region covers most of the southern part of Eastern Ghats where Chittor- Cuddaph uplands including upper basins of the Nandyal and Pennar rivers (300-600 mm in height) of the southern Andhra Pradesh, a micro-regional unit of agricultural characteristics(Xa) and the Shevaroy upland including Javadi Hills of the flat land (300-600 m in height) situated between Cauvery and Palar river basins, especially the North Arcot district of Tamilnadu, which is agriculturally indifferent at very high level OTUs assimilation (14.26), is another micro-regional unit (Xb) of the Rayalseema Regions. The soils of this region are red, sandy and medium black in colour and texture which are enough fertile but thirsty and, hence cropping patterns are diversified dominating groundnut, ragi and jowar crops. The farming intensity in this region is recorded lowest (108.01 percent) with its negligible decadal increase of about 0.54 percent in the 1980s. It may be because of low share of Net Irrigated Area to total cultivated land (27.47 percent) with its very slow decadal increase of only 3.89 percent. The high levels of input intensification, labour as well as technological inputs, through the share of agricultural workers to total workers is moderate (71.82 percent) with its moderate decadal increase of 19.50 percent in the 1980s, have been recorded because of availability of cheap labour (which is unskilled and illiterate) and sufficient use of chemical fertilizers (39.67 kg/ha) and high mechanization (Rs. 93/ha). Unreal mechanization of agricultural practices with unskilled labour of traditional farming and readily available labour at cheaper rate which diminishes the wages and decreases 10.80 percent labour input (in its money term, not in agricultural workers per unit of land) in the last ten years (1981-91). It is direct indication of very low levels of land labour productivities of the region. It is a fact that land productivity is very low (Rs. 914/ha) with its extremely slow increase of 3.99 percent per annum in 1980s and labour productivity is also very low (Rs. 545/person) with its very slow increase of 21.84 percent annually in the same period. As a result, the growth rate of agricultural output is recorded very low (5.6 percent annually) with the lowest level of per capita agricultural output (Rs. 169/person), though the population burden on land is very low (density 175 persons/sq.km.) with its low decadal growth of 19.85 percent. These stagnant and underdeveloped conditions of agriculture of this region can only be altered to accelerate and intensify modern technology, especially water-technology for cheaper source of irrigation, in the agricultural production systems of the region. It is suggested here because of greater availability of the magnitude and intensity of agricultural growth potentials (production potential magnitude 2669/ha and its intensity 4.21) and higher productive capacity of agricultural technology at very low absorption rate of its potential (0.042). The ratio of marginal production to absorption rate of production potential with respect to non-land capital (technology) is higher (116 times) than the labour input (i.e., 77 times). It means that the per unit increase of technology in the existing agricultural system of the region is able to produce 487 percent of agricultural output by absorbing only 4.2 percent of the intensity of production potential, whereas per unit of labour input is capable only to produce 208 percent agricultural potential intensity. Therefore, the marginal returns of agricultural technology are higher and the agricultural practices would be more profitable if they become technology- oriented especially in this region. Thus, the thrust of development strategy must be towards water-resource utilisation and changes in cropping patterns from traditional to more commercial crops with suitable price-mechanism, so that the existing stagnant and under developed conditions of this dry region may optimally be changed with a significant increase in per capita agricultural output, agricultural growth and level of productivity.

BXI. *The South Deccan (Karnataka Interior) :* It incorporates two micro-agricultural regional units, similar in their areal extent and in the number of districts, namely, XIa: The North Karnataka - a micro unit of 7 districts including one district of South Maharashtra and Andhra Pradesh each and XIb : The South Karnataka - which includes 8 districts of the Deccan plateau (Karnataka state including one district of Tamilnadu). Physiographically, the region is the part of most dissected Deccan plateau and has a variety of relief features, geological structure, soil formation processes and its texture that influence directly to the agricultural attributes of the region. But surprisingly, the micro- as well as meso-level regional units do not influence much from the physiographic/agro-climatic conditions of the region, while they are the major determinants of agricultural growth potentials. The demarcation of micro-regional units is east to west for the north and south Karnataka optimal agricultural groupings of OTUs, but physiographically, it has been divided from the central Sahyadri (Western Ghats) of about 600-900 m height to the upper and middle Krishna, Tungbhadra and Cauvery basins (the eastern parts of the region) of about 300-600 m height. It seems that the formation of micro-level agricultural regions of the most homogeneous conditions where the degree of spatial variance within the region is recorded very less (Table- 5.5) is based on the agricultural growth phenomena rather than its physiographic conditions.

Agro-ecologically, the region is not much recognisable. There is a water deficiency of about 480 mm annually because potential evapo-transpiration rate is far higher (1404 mm annually) and, hence, the moisture index is recorded -.266. But the soils are medium black and red loamy in texture and colour and are fertile for crop growth. A diversified crop pattern of jowar-groundnut- rice- cotton is being practised with an introduction of modern technology. Therefore, it has become most developed and prosperous agricultural region of the peninsular plateau. Say for example, the annual growth rate of agricultural output has been marked extremely high (20.09%) as the second highest among the regions of India, with very low degree of its spatial variance within the region (C.v. 60.5%). It is only because of extremely high increase in the land

and labour productivities (23.53% and 22.30% annually) during the 1980's, while their levels moderately low (Rs.1108/ha and Rs.965/person of agricultural worker respectively) with low level of farming intensity (111.20%), less share of Net Irrigated Area (21.52%) and moderate conditions of labour as well as technological inputs (Table- 5.9). Infact, the agricultural growth potentials of this region have been exhausting through intensifying modern technology and no doubt, fast growth of agricultural output is the result of its potential utilisation. Further strategy of balanced development can only be suggested on the basis of growth potential attributes. It is obvious that the marginal productivity to technology is significantly high (32.31) as against national average (22.41) and far higher than the marginal product to labour(i.e, 1.06). Being very high ratio of marginal product to absorption rate of production potential especially with respect to non-land capital (633.5), the modern agricultural technology can be extended upto an optimal extent where it equates its ratio of labour input, which is far lower (212.0) in the existing agricultural production systems operated in the region. Agricultural technology may be applied as substitution for labour if the agricultural systems are able to shift in the occupational structure of the region by generating more employment in non-agricultural sectors and even agro-surplus based- processing activities. The fast emerging agricultural economy of this backward region can only be maintained by intensifying agricultural production processes and changing it accordingly.

BXII. *The Tamilnadu Upland :* It is situated in the extreme southern triangular corner of the peninsular plateau. It is small in size which includes total 7 districts of Tamil Nadu including one district of Kerala, but has a variety of relief features. Thus, it consists of two micro-regional units which are physiographically and agriculturally homogenous. Physiographic features are highly associated with the agricultural developmental patterns of the region. These micro-regional units are XIIa: The Middle Cauvery Basin -which is surrounded by the Sheveroy Hills in the north, South Sahyadri in the South-west, Nilgiri Hills in the West of the heights of 150-300 mtrs, and XIIb: The Transitional Lands of South Sahyadri-Nilgiri Hills which is called the roof of the Tamilnad upland and has the height varying from 300 to 2711 mtrs. Being sub-humid climatic conditions which are favourable for agricultural crop growth, there is less requirements of irrigation facilities in the summers but irrigation is essentially required in the winters for winter-rice cultivation. Soils are fertile, mixed red and valley alluvium. Rice is the dominating crop which is labour intensive. Cotton and groundnut are the chief commercial and industrial crops. Therefore, the annual growth of agricultural output and land productivity have been recorded very high (15.07% growth in 1980s and agricultural output Rs.1652 per hectare of cultivated land in 1988-90), although the share of Net Irrigated Area is very low (21.97%) with its decadal decrease of 2.11%. It is because of moist and humid conditions of the region, which do not have any significant effect on growth and agricultural productivity. The agricultural systems are being operated at high levels of input intensification; labour input is Rs.1025/ha as 2.17 agricultural workers /ha with a moderate increase of 38.62% in 1980s and capital input level is Rs.172/ha because of higher use of fertilisers (79 kg/ha) as against national average (44kg/ha) and high mechanisation (Rs.94/ha). To maintain the rate of agricultural growth in the future in this region, the growth potential conditions are not favourable, although production potential intensity is marked moderate (2.64) with very low absorption rates. Marginal product to labour and technology are also recorded low to very low (Table-5.11). Marginal product-absorption rate of production potential ratio is higher for technology. Therefore appropriate technology can be increased to intensify systems would not be profitable and even would not work in its optimal manner because the share of agricultural workers to total workforce is recorded smaller (47.56 percent) with its low decadal decrease.

C. The Westerm Himalayas

It is physiographically different from the other parts of the country. It follows a variety of relief features like hills, valleys, gorges, canyons and snow covered hill tops and mountain ranges. Therefore, there is a vast inter-regional variation in agro-ecological and agro-economic conditions. Broadly, the OTUs of this macro-region of typical agricultural conditions have three meso-level agricultural regional units which follow state-boundaries and, hence, the nomenclature of these agricultural regions is based on administrative boundaries as:

CXIII. *The Uttar Pradesh Himalayas:* It includes total 6 hill districts of Uttar Pradesh and assimilates into two micro-regional units of the Garhwal Himalayas (XIIIa) and the Kumaon Himalayas (XIIIb). They are slightly different in agricultural characteristics and agro-climatic conditions. It has hill-temperature climatic conditions of very high rainfall (2142 mm annually) with higher rate of potential evapo-transpiration (1286 mm annually), though it is lesser than the receipt of total amount of rainfall and, therefore, there is a sufficient moisture availability for plant growth (0.67 moisture index).

CXIV. *The Himachal Himalayas:* It has three micro-level agricultural units which follows the relief features of the region as : the lesser Himalayas (XIVa) of the Siwalik Foothills and the main valleys of kulu, Mandi and Lahaul districts of the Central Himalayas (XIVb) of 900 to 3000m of height where climate, cropping patterns and operations of agricultural systems are different from the Siwaliks, and, thirdly, the sub Himalayan zone of unique agricultural characteristic (XIVc) which includes the Chamba district of very high altitude with low temperature. The climate of the entire region of Himachal Himalayas is hill-temperate with the moisture availability in the atmosphere through out the year (o.581 moisture index) except a few months during winter. Brown hilly soils are dominant which pursue the cultivation of rice, maize and wheat in the region, especially in the Siwaliks and river valleys.

CXV. *The Jammu and Kashmir Valley:* It has two longitudinal micro-regional units of agricultural characteristics: the Punch-Jammu valley of Siwalik and foothills which has fertile soils of valley alluvium and brown hills for intensive cultivation and the Pirpanjal range of indifferent agricultural regional unit. In the entire region, there is water deficiency of very less amount of rain(-.07 moisture index annually) and the prevailing climatic condition are from humid to semi-arid. Wheat and barley are principal crops of the region which are grown without irrigation.

In general, these meso-level regions of the western Himalayas have very low percentage share of total geographical area under cultivation because of undulating slopes and steep valleys. The flat land is very less and scattered.The population pressure on land is very less in all these three regions as population density is recorded extremely low (91 persons /sq.km in 1991) in the

Uttar Pardesh Himalayas with its low decadal growth (14.50 %). Mostly the population is scattered in the villages and rural literacy rate is higher than the national average. On account of low to very low levels of land and labour productivities with their slow increase; somewhere they have been recorded negative, in its trends (Table- 5.8), the annual growth rate of agricultural output and per capita agricultural output have been marked very low, even negative agricultural growth especially in the Himachal Himalayas where the rural economy is being shifted from foodgrain cultivation to fruit-crop dominated farming. In addition, agricultural growth potentials are moderate in its magnitude and intensity (Table- 5.11), which are being absorbed at a very low rate for the increase of agricultural production (i.e., called marginal products). As a result, agricultural productivities are marked very low in these regions of mountain agro- ecological conditions. However, marginal products to labour as well as to technology are recorded higher. It means a record of agricultural production can be increased optimally through increasing the absorption rate of production potential. Labour intensification would be more appropriate in agricultural production systems of these regions because the ratio between marginal product and absorption rate of production potential with respect to the labour input are higher in all the regions than the technological input, although labour input is employed upto greater extent in the existing conditions of agricultural practices. Orchards, horticulture and tree- gardening are better and more profitable and, hence, the cropping patterns must be changed towards fruit cultivation, so that agricultural growth and productivity may be increased fast to over throw the stagnant and undeveloped agricultural conditions of these areas.

D. The Great Plains

There are the most fertile and rich in underground water resources and are one of the largest and most densely populated alluvial plains of the world, stretching along the foothills of the Himalayas from the upper Brahmaputra in the east to the Punjab plain in the west. Note that the Rajasthan dry plain is also part of the Great Plains. But it is studied to keep aside in a macro-agricultural regional unit because it differs considerably from the Great Plains in the growth and development of agricultural attributes and also in the agro-ecological conditions. In the assimilation process of 118 OTUs of the Great Plains, it forms six meso-agricultural regions and, at a lower level of assimilation, thirteen micro-level and twenty-three first order (lowest) agricultural regional units. The agricultural characteristics and its development possibilities in its regional frame are given below:

DXVI. *The Assam Plains:* These plains consists of (a) the Brahmaputra- Tista valleys (micro-regional unit of the main Assam, XVIa), (b) the Barrak- Surma vallay (another micro- regional unit, XVIb, which incorporates the southern part of the Assam Plains and has *terai* climatic conditions with cherry red loamy soils), and (c) the Mikir Hills (an unique agricultural unit of micro-level, XVIc) which have favourable agro- ecological and biophysical conditions for agricultural practices. However, crop intensity is low (131.63%) with its low decadal increase (3.59% during 1979-82 to 1988-90). It might be because of weak techno-economic structure of agricultural systems. For example, use of machine tools is recorded negligible as Rs.5/ha and use of chemical fertiliser is also marked extremely low as 7.92 kg/ha, although the application of labour input in agricultural practices has been marked very high as Rs.612/ha (in money term) or nearly 2.0 persons /ha with a extremely high increase of 77.03% that is more than double of national average during 1981-1991. Infact, this extremely high increase is recorded not because of the natural growth of rural population but because of immigration especially in rural areas. As a result, labour productivity has been recorded very low (Rs. 902/person) with its harp decline in its annual change (-24.76 percent). Therefore, percapita agricultural output is also recorded very low (Rs.189/person). On the other hand, the conditions of agricultural growth potential are very much favourable for future growth and development of agriculture. Magnitude of production potential has been recorded highest in India (Rs.4022/ha, i.e., two-and-a-half time its national average) with its moderately high intensity (2.52). Marginal productivities and absorption rates of production-potential Intensity are extremely high in this region. It indicates faster agricultural growth at very low increase of labour and technology in agricultural operations. Analysing production potential attributes of the region, it may safely be concluded that labour dominated agricultural systems are more profitable where technology is complementary to them. The causes are obviously the availability of cheap agricultural labour and high magnitude of production potentials.

DXVII. *The Lower Ganga Plain:* It includes entire West Bengal plains of new and deltaic alluviums of the moist sub- humid climatic conditions. High rainfall (1551 mm annually) with the high rate of potential evapo- transpiration (1447mm) and consequently, moisture index is positive (0.236), are the favourable conditions of proper plant growth. Rice and jute are dominating crops; one is foodgrain for local consumption and grown thrice in a year and another is cash and commercial crop which increases level of agricultural productivity. As a result, land productivity is recorded highest (Rs.4568/ha as three times higher than national average) with extremely high annual increase of 12.10 percent (i.e., also one-and-a-half times higher than the national average). Inspite of the highest population density (910 person/sq. km. in 1991) with moderately high growth of 26.01 percent in 1981-91 with moderate urbanisation (19.07 percent) and rural literacy (37.24 percent), labour productivity is recorded very high (Rs.160/ person), but its increase has been slowed (25.31 percent annually) in the 1980s. Consequently, annual average growth of agricultural output has been slightly lower (7.53 percent) than the national average. Farming intensity is high (161.02 percent) with its extremely high decadal increase of 21.43 percent in 1980s, because of high application of chemical fertilisers (60.53 kg/ ha) and labour input (Rs.955/ha, nearly double to the national average though the agricultural workers share is recorded low with its moderate increase). It means that agricultural economy of the region has reached its developed stage of high equilibrium and , therefore, the agricultural growth potential is marked exhausted. Thus, the magnitude and intensity of production potential are low to very low with low levels of marginal products and low absorption rate of production potential . The agricultural areal variations within the regions confirm the facts that the economy of the region is gradually shifting from agriculture to non-agricultural activities and hence the influence of the transport network, urban centres and industrial development in this region can directly or indirectly be seen on the emergence of lower order agricultural regions. For example, the Calcutta surrounding region of the Central Bengal Plain, (XVIIb2) which incorporates only two districts has evolved a separate first-order regional unit in the assimilation process of regionalisation because of the effect of agricultural innovations diffusion from the metropolitan to the surrounding areas. This processes of centre based agricultural development is directly having influence on the levels and increase of land and labour productivities and determines the agricultural regionalisation. Basu's hypothesis of inverse relationships between the average farm size and productivity under the condition of higher urbanisation (Basu 1981) seems significant and valid in the present reference of agricultural development. In fact, this lowest order regional unit of the Calcutta surrounding region (XXVIIb2) which has direct impact of higher degree of urbanisation on the agricultural growth and development signifies that very high agricultural productivities, land as well as labour productivities as Rs.5206\ha and Rs.1742 per agricultural worker respectively, have been attained with very low size of operational land holdings (0.76 ha. of NSA per cultivator in 1991) because of linkage effects of urbanisation on agricultural development (Dasgupta and Basu 1985). It is found that Basu's hypothesis is valid but requires an immediate need of in-depth inquires for searching the causes of inverse relationship between average farm size and productivity.

DXVIII. *The Bihar Plains:* It includes 22 districts of the Bihar Plains of the most homogenous physiographic conditions with moist sub- humid conditions with 231 mm of annual moisture deficiency (1145mm annual rainfall with 1481mm rate of annual potential evapo-transpiration). Water-deficiency is observed especially in the winters (rabi season) which is minimised by tubewell/canal irrigation. Under water resource is easily available and cheaply exploitable for tubewell irrigation in this region. Inspite of higher use of modern technology (i.e, intensification of machine tools, intensive use of chemical fertilizers and irrigation), the levels of land and labour productivities have been recorded very low to extremely low with very slow rate of annual increase; even labour productivity is recorded lowest as only Rs.548/person. In fact, labour productivity is the quotient of total agricultural output (dividend) and agricultural work force (divisor) (see eqn. 1.4c for detail). Since agricultural workforce per unit of cultivated land is extremely high (2.68 persons/ha) with an extremely fast decadal increase of about 126.35 per cent in 1980s, which is more than three-and-half times higher than the national average with a more burden of work force on agricultural activities, it diminishes the level of labour productivity. The agricultural growth potential attributes are very weak and hence the annual rate of agricultural output growth is recorded low (6.13 percent). The reasons of slow growth are obvious. Magnitude and intensity of production potential are moderately low (Table-5.11) with low level of marginal product and low absorption rate of labour as well as of technological production potential. Overall, there is a low level of equilibrium conditions of agricultural development. Occupational shift from agriculture to non-agricultural sectors, fast growth of rural growth centres which would help to process local surplus agro-materials and to employ more rural labour in these agro-industrial activities, and provision of strong infra-structural attributes are only the alternative remedies to fasten the agricultural growth and to increase the land and labour productivities of this region of stagnant and under-developed agricultural economy.

DXIX. *The Bhawar-Terai Plains:* It is a longitudinal region of 17 districts incorporating *Bhawar* belt of about 15 km wide and the *Terai* belt of Uttar Pradesh situated longitudinally in the northern borderlands of Haryana and Uttar Pradesh alongwith the foothills of the Western Himalayan Region. Agro-ecological conditions of this region are very much favourable for agricultural growth and development because sufficient rainfall is available throughout the year

(1109 mm annually), though the rate of potential evapo- transpiration is slightly higher than the receipt of total rainfall, and enough available ground water potentials which can be and are being utilised at cheaper investment rates. The ground water table is in the upper layers of alluvium soils. All these favourable agro- ecological conditions pursue crop- growth. Therefore, land and labour productivities and their increasing annual rate of agricultural output, and per capita agricultural output are marked high to very high with a strong and well- developed infrastructural and agricultural input attributes. The agricultural systems are working at high level of its equilibria conditions with a better socio-economic conditions, though the magnitude and intensity of production-potential are recorded moderately with low level of marginal products with respect to labour as well as technology, but the existing agricultural system of this area is well operative with technological enhancement rather than traditional labour-intensive agriculture, although there is an unlimited supply of labour in the agricultural production processes.

DXX. *The Central Ganga Plains:* It includes the entire eastern parts of Uttar Pradesh plain consisting of two micro-regional units, the Gomati- Avadh plains (XXa) and the Lower Ganga-Jamuna *doab* (XXb) of the fertile alluvial soils with moderate semi- arid to dry sub-humid climatic conditions. Crop intensity is high(148 percent) with its fast decadal increase of about 6.16 percent. The reason of high farming intensity is higher use of machine tools with high application of fertilizers and irrigation. Intensive use of modern technological package increases land productivity as recorded Rs.1963/ha and labour productivity as Rs.1137/person. The increase in labour productivity is recorded moderate (32.16% annually) because of higher degree of agricultural workforce per unit of cultivated land (1.80 persons/ha) which is easily and cheaply available in the rural areas. On account of slow rate of land productivity increase in the region (6.34% annually in the 1980s), the annual growth rate of agricultural output has been recorded low (6.19%). The agricultural growth potential attributes don't seem strong; magnitude and intensity of production potential are recorded moderate with very low absorption rate. But ratio of marginal product to absorption rate with respect to technology is higher (402) than the labour input (308). Therefore, the technological intensification in the agricultural production systems of this area may be profitable and suitable for further growth acceleration.

DXXI. *The Punjab - Haryana - Western Uttar Pradesh Plains:* It is 'wheat bowl' of India which characterises intensive farming with extensive irrigation (more than 80 percent cultivated land is under irrigation), mechanisation (Rs. 134/ha), chemical fertilizer (117.7 kg/ha as highest in India), field operations with bigger sizes (2.14 ha of NSA per cultivator in 1991), and the low degree of labour input (0.89 person/ha) with its moderate increase in 1980s. It is due to fast shift in the occupational structure from agricultural to non-agricultural sectors and, hence, only 59.9 percent of the total work force is engaged in agricultural activities. As a result, land and labour productivities have been marked very high with their moderate increases; note that labour productivity is Rs. 3943 per person in 1991 that is more than three times higher than the national average (Table-5.8). Therefore, per capita output is recorded highest Rs. 920 per person. On account of weak agricultural growth potential attributes, though agro-ecological and agro-economic conditions are favourable, the agricultural growth has been recorded moderate (8.45 percent annually) in the 1980s. Modern agricultural technological inducements in the agricultural systems may be more suitable for this region because of high ratio of marginal product to absorption rate of production potential with respect to technological inputs. The reasons behind high ratio are (a) the direct backwash effects and the effects of diffusion processes of agricultural innovations as growth- centre based strategy of agricultural development and (b) the efficient transport network to regulate surplus agro-based production and to feed the seed fertilizer packages to the rural areas. Consequently, the emerging regional variations which can be seen at first order assimilation of OTUs and its region formation as the regions of the Delhi-surroundings (XXa1) and the Punjab-Haryana *Banghar* (XXIa2), are the realisation and the confirmation of these facts of agricultural characteristics of this region of semi-arid and *banghar* dominated alluvial soils where wheat-rice-sugarcane are the dominating crops in its cropping pattern. Wheat and rice are also cash crops of this region. Therefore, price mechanism, an economic factor of farming intensity and farmers' profitability, has become a dominating reason behind agricultural development of the region. The farmers of this region are now businessmen and traders of agricultural products rather than peasants of traditional thinking.

E. The Rajasthan Plains

It is the driest part of the country. Physiographically and agriculturally, it has two meso-regional units. The Rajasthan *Banghar* which consists of the five central districts of Rajasthan dispersed in a longitudinal strip alongwith the western side of the Aravalli Hills including entire Luni river basin and the Jhunjhunu and Churu districts of Haryana border, and the *Marusthali* which incorporates six districts of the Thar desert. Sand dunes are the main relief features of this region. Agro-ecological, socio-cultural and agro-economic facts of these regions are described in detail in the following lines.

EXXII. *The Rajasthan Banghar :* Climatically, it is semi-arid to dry sub-humid because the total amount of annual rainfall is far lesser than the annual rate of potential evapotranspiration and, therefore, there is a water deficiency of about 611 mm annually (moisture index -0.481). Old alluvial soils of river-born are dominant and hence, this region is called *banghar*. On account of less rainfall and less facilities of irrigation (Net Irrigated Area in only 16.5 percent to total cultivated land in 1988-90), very low applicability of technological inputs (low mechanisation Rs. 33/ha, very low use of chemical fertilizers 14 kg/ha), although there are possibilities to apply intensive modern techniques of farming because of availabilities of larger size of operational landholdings (2.61 ha of NSA per cultivator) and of cheap and better agricultural labour and animal forces. Labour productivity is, therefore, high (Rs. 1488/person) with its fast annual increase of 114.23 percent, i.e., more than double to its national average. But land productivity is recorded very low (Rs. 601/ha) with its moderate increase. The region is characterised as very high annual growth of agricultural output especially in 1980s (16.16 percent, i.e., nearly double to the national average). The causes of high rate of agricultural growth are (i) the exhaustive use of agricultural growth potentials of which absorption rates are recorded very high especially with respect to labour input. While intensification of modern technology is more suitable for faster agricultural growth and land productivity levels because the ratio between marginal product and absorption rate of potential intensity with respect to technological input is recorded high, very high (170.0) compared to labour input (i.e., 64.3), and (ii) very low percentage share of workers engaging in agriculture (53.01 percent) and its slow decadal increase (3.42 percent in 1981-91).

Because of very high intensity of production potential (3.62), the future prospects of this region are better for enhancement of the level of land productivity.

EXXIII. *The Marusthali :* Inspite of extreme arid climatic conditions (a record water deficiency of about 1060 mm annually in the atmosphere) and excessive weathering processes of soil formation (gray brown desert sandy soils) and traditional cropping pattern of bajra-gram-wheat-rapeseeds which caters to the needs of the local people, the labour productivity is recorded higher (Rs. 1779/person) with an extremely fast annual increase of about 492.1 percent (i.e., more than ten times of national average). It is because of very low use of labour inputs (0.58 person/ha) in the agricultural production systems of this region. On the other hand, land productivity that is directly related to the application of modern technology is recorded very low (Rs. 712/ha, i.e., half of the national average). While the annual growth rate of agricultural output has been marked highest in the country (35.16 percent, i.e., four-and-a-half times of the national average) in the 1980s because of extremely high rate of increase of land productivity (27.17 percent, i.e., more than three times of its national average) as well as of labour productivity in the successive period of time. The main causes of fast agricultural growth are high to very high rate of marginal returns in agricultural systems with high absorption rates of agricultural production potentials. However, modern agricultural technology can be intensified in future for optimum use of agricultural resources. Water-use is the primary and appropriate technology to increase the productivity and growth of the region.

Regional Growth Characteristics

The detailed regional characteristics of Indian agriculture which have been discussed in the preceding part of the present Chapter can now easily be interpreted for generalisations of the regional features highlighting the major aspects of agricultural planning. Synthesis of the regional facts of agricultural phenomena particularly for acceleration of decision-making processes is brought out by classifying the agricultural planning regions of meso-regional level into five categories by considering agricultural attributes of existing production system (i.e., the variables of agricultural growth and productivity, crop-intensity and socio-economic variable like urbanization and rural literacy) and the agricultural production growth potential conditions (taking into account the variables of production potential magnitude and intensity, its absorption rates with respect to input factors and labour-capital ratio for absorption of production potential intensity). These categories must explain the conditions and extent of the acceleration of development processes in its regional perspectives. They are :

(i) Underdeveloped Agricultural Conditions with High and Very High Growth Potential - which includes the entire Western Himalayas from Garhwal to Kashmir Himalayan Ranges (XIII, XIV, XV) including two regions of the humid climatic conditions of the Great Plains (Bihar and Assam Plains; XVI and XVIII respectively). These regions have homogeneous agricultural characteristics despite sharply contrasting conditions of physiographic, demographic and economic attributes. They have better prospects for agricultural growth in the future. But the existing conditions of agricultural systems are diversified with stagnant growth.

(ii) Underdeveloped Agricultural Conditions with Low Growth Potential - which incorporate four regions, out of them three are from peninsular India and one from the Coastal Plains (II, V, VI and XI). It covers entire Chambal and Bundelkhand - Malwa Regions of Madhya Pradesh, Sahyadri Hills of the Maharashtra and Karnataka including Malabar- Konkan Coastal Plains of the Western Ghats. Agricultural conditions, despite commercialization in agricultural practices, are weak with its poor growth potential in these regions of rugged and hilly topography of unfavourable climatic conditions. The intensive horticulture and tree - crops farming systems are capable of increasing productivity and to extricate the regions from the present stagnant agricultural growth conditions.

(iii) Developing Agricultural Conditions with High Growth Potential - It includes four agricultural planning regions of two contrast agro- ecological conditions as (a) the Orissa Coastal region and the *Bhawar - Terai* region (I and XIX) of the plain topography of humid climatic conditions, and (b) the regions of Rajasthan plains, which are two in number (XXII and XXIII) where dry *banghar* and *Marusthali* agro- ecological conditions prevail. Agricultural growth and developmental conditions are favourable in these regions because of availability of high magnitude and intensity of agricultural growth potential with its high rate of absorption. It has been possible in these areas to introduce irrigation- fertilizer technology in agricultural practices.

(iv) Developing Conditions with Low Growth Potential - which includes three agricultural regions of various agro-ecological conditions, one each from coastal regions (III), Peninsular India (XII) and from the Great Plains (XX), where agricultural growth potential attributes are weak because of its fast utilisation in the existing agricultural systems. The future prospects of agricultural growth are not good in these areas.

(v) Developed Conditions with Low Growth Potential - where absorption rate of agricultural growth potential is very high and hence, the production potential has been exhausted in the existing agricultural production processes. Consequently, the magnitude and the intensity of growth potential are very low. These conditions prevail in two agricultural planning regions of the Great Plains, namely, the Punjab-Haryana-Western Uttar Pradesh (XVII) and the West Bengal Region (XXI) which are directly influenced by the metropolitan economy of these regions. Delhi and Calcutta are the central places from where the agricultural innovations have been diffusing into their surroundings. Therefore, the agricultural systems operative in these regions are well-developed but their growth potential has been exhausting fast by the technological advancements.

It can be said here that the regional approach which we have applied for inferring the results of self - sustained growth is based on the principle of 'inter-relatedness' of agricultural characteristics. On the other hand, bio-physical and socio-economic conditions of the regional characteristics may be optimised by applying the 'target approach' of resource - allocation for which the regional synthesis of agricultural characteristics must be based on feasibility criterion of production components.

Regional Synthesis and Feasible Solution for Agricultural Production

The agricultural policies questions arise repeatedly about the optimum utilisation of land to meet future food demands of the ever increasing population keeping in view the alterations in the bio-physical and socio-economic conditions (Hopkins, *et.al.* 1982, UN Conference on Environment and Development 1992). The study of agricultural growth potential (which is the attribute closely related to land capability for agricultural production) and its relationship with land productivity is of a great interest for a variety of applications of decision-making planning models. In the present context, the production targets can be achieved and the optimal utilisation of present landuse can be suggested by establishing this relationship in the regional frame of agricultural characteristics.

So far as the assessment of feasibility of production systems is concerned, a region's potential for agricultural production surpasses projected requirements (it means agricultural potential and food target ratio is higher than one) denotes the greater feasibility (i.e., much flexibility) of production system and many options for food production (Smit, *et.al.* 1991). But the degree of feasibility in the specific regional characteristics of agricultural production system is not static over time because of changing conditions of agricultural growth potential phenomena and production needs. However, system's feasibility for various agricultural regions of the country may be assessed to tackle the problems of the preparation of region- specific self-sustained agricultural growth strategies.

Keeping these conditions of the production system in mind, linear programming method which is frequently used to estimate the optimal conditions (or feasible solution) of production process in relation to its production requirements, has been used to consider region-wise statistics of four variables, viz., land and labour productivities, increase in land productivity which is directly and closely related to agricultural growth and agricultural production potential as already described in the earlier section of the present Chapter. The feasible solution of resource allocation is subject to certain constraints of the conventional applications of linear programming (Vajda 1966, Cole and King 1970, Chapman, Smit and Smith 1984). The main constraints which are imposed here in the present case are :

(a) The agricultural productivity (land and labour, X and Z) and its increase (Y), if added, cannot exceed the defined agricultural production potential (i.e., maximum expected yield level, A, in present case and elaborated in detail in the previous Chapter) as

$$X_i + Y_i + Z_i < A_i, \quad i = 1,2,3,...,n \text{ regions.} \quad ... \quad ... \quad (5.1)$$

(b) The production targets can not exceed the production potential in a region because, in the developing stages of the economic conditions where lot of agricultural potential is available to use, the increasing food requirements can easily be fulfilled and the agricultural system is able to produce more food. Therefore, there is much flexibility of the system and many options are available to induce more production.

(c) Non-negativity is also one of the important constraint of the system under which the all variables considered for optimisation are non-negative. Note that, in some agricultural regions, land productivity increase is negative because of deceleration processes of growth. But these figures are used as positive though negligible because of achieving the feasible solution of the production systems as:

$$X_i, Y_i \& Z_i > 0. \quad \ldots \quad \ldots \quad \ldots \quad (5.2)$$

Feasible Solution and the Regional Investment Strategy

Using the statistics of related variables as discussed above and imposing the constraints given by the equations 5.1 and 5.2, the co-ordinate values of three-dimensional space have been created and plotted on the graphs for each of the agricultural regions of the country. The set of these agricultural attributes (vectors), that satisfies the above set of constraints, is a convex set, usually referred to as feasible region by Wu & Coppins (1981) which forms a convex polyhedron consisting of a set of faces. The study of the shape (configuration) and size (volume) of these polyhedrons would indicate the degree of feasibility or the freedom to extend the production limits in the system.

The configuration, an arrangement of faces of the convex polyhedron, must explain the intersecting nature of the linear equations of agricultural attributes. For instance, more number of intersections of the triangles drawn by the equations will give ideal shape of convex polyhedron and *vice-versa.* It means more number of faces of polyhedron with varied types show the contribution of varied types of agricultural regions to the formation of the boundaries of the feasible regions. On the other hand, lesser degree of intersections form a simple triangular faces of the feasible region and show the domination of a few regions' agricultural attributes to form the shape and size of feasible region. Say for example, a well interacted phenomena of agricultural regions of the Great Plains has well-formed shape of the polyhedron of six faces, while the Western Himalayan Region has tetrahedron (four-triangular faces) shape of the feasible region (Fig.- 5.5). It appears that, in the mountain region, the agricultural attributes of the Himachal Himalayas (Region XIV) determine the shape and size of the feasible region. In addition, the distorted shape of polyhedron which is formed by six faces, three triangles and three tetragons, can be seen in the Rajasthan and the Coastal regions of the country. The shape of polyhedron for the peninsular plateau seems flat with six faces of tetragons (Table- 5.12). It is the result of undulating topography and variations in the climatic conditions for diversified regional patterns of agricultural development.

On the other hand, the volume of these solid figures must present the best measurement of flexibility of the system. But question arises how it is to be calculated. An approximate measurement of the volume of polyhedron has been estimated by applying the concept of the centre of gravity (or epicentre) of the solid figure and the best fitted sphere therein (Chapman, Smit and Smith 1984). The distance between epicentre and nearest face of the figure will be the radius of the inscribed sphere and its diameter will provide a direct measure of feasible or predicted figures for future planning. The volume of polyhedrons for various macro regions of the country confirm the facts that the plain areas of the country where agricultural productivity is higher, are still having higher degree of flexibility to increase the agricultural production. The coastal plains (eastern and western coastal regions) and the Great plains of the country have the higher volume of well-formed polyhedron (17.816 and 13.311 cubic units respectively), whereas the peninsular plateau has very low volume of its solid figure (7.798 cubic units) (Table- 5.12).

Table-5.12: Characteristics of Feasible Solution for Various Macro-Regions.

	Regions	Convex Polyhedrons			Coordinates		
		Shape (no. of faces)	Diameter on map* (in cm.)	Volume+ (in cu. units)	X	Y	Z
A.	The Coastal Plains	3-tetragons & 2-triangles	3.24	17.816	1.62	16.20	3.24
B.	The Peninsular Plateau	6-tetragons	2.46	7.798	1.23	12.30	2.46
C.	The Western Himlayas	4-triangles	2.10	4.851	1.05	10.50	2.10
D.	The Great Plains	6-tetragons	2.94	13.311	1.47	14.70	2.94
E.	The Rajasthan Plains	3-tetragons & 3-triangles	2.70	10.310	1.37	13.50	2.70

N.B.: * diameter of the spheres fitted into the Convex polyhedrons for the calculation of their volumes.

\+ Approximate volume of polyhedrons calculated by predicting its shape as sphere. The volume of a sphere, V is calculated by the formula as $V = (4\pi/3)r^3$, where r = radius of the sphere.

The feasible solution would further provide expected optimal changes of agricultural attributes which are necessary to predict the degree of acceleration of decision-making processes. Having calculated the coordinate values of the feasible solution (that are the predicted coefficients of variables/attributes), the predicted figures for agricultural attributes and its expected changes from existing ones have been estimated for each and every agricultural planning region of the country (Table - 5.13). Table reveals that the expected increase in land productivity has been predicted fast in the peninsular plateaus except South Deccan (Karnataka Region, XI). The increase in land productivity has also been recorded extremely high (343.47 per cent) in the West coast plains (region number II) because of high intensity of agricultural growth potentials and favourable agricultural conditions. It is pertinent to note that predicted increase of labour productivity of Indian agricultural systems is recorded lesser than the predicted changes of land productivity. Somewhere labour productivity changes have been marked negative. Since labour productivity is highly dependent on land productivity which is directly influenced by the intensification of agricultural modern technology, the labour productivity can be increased by intensifying technological production factors rather than agricultural labour force. Therefore, technology is the complementary production factor for labour input in existing and predicted forms of agricultural systems. This fact has already been stated in Chapter -3 for existing production processes. Thus, technology is, still and even in future, having positive effects on labour productivity.

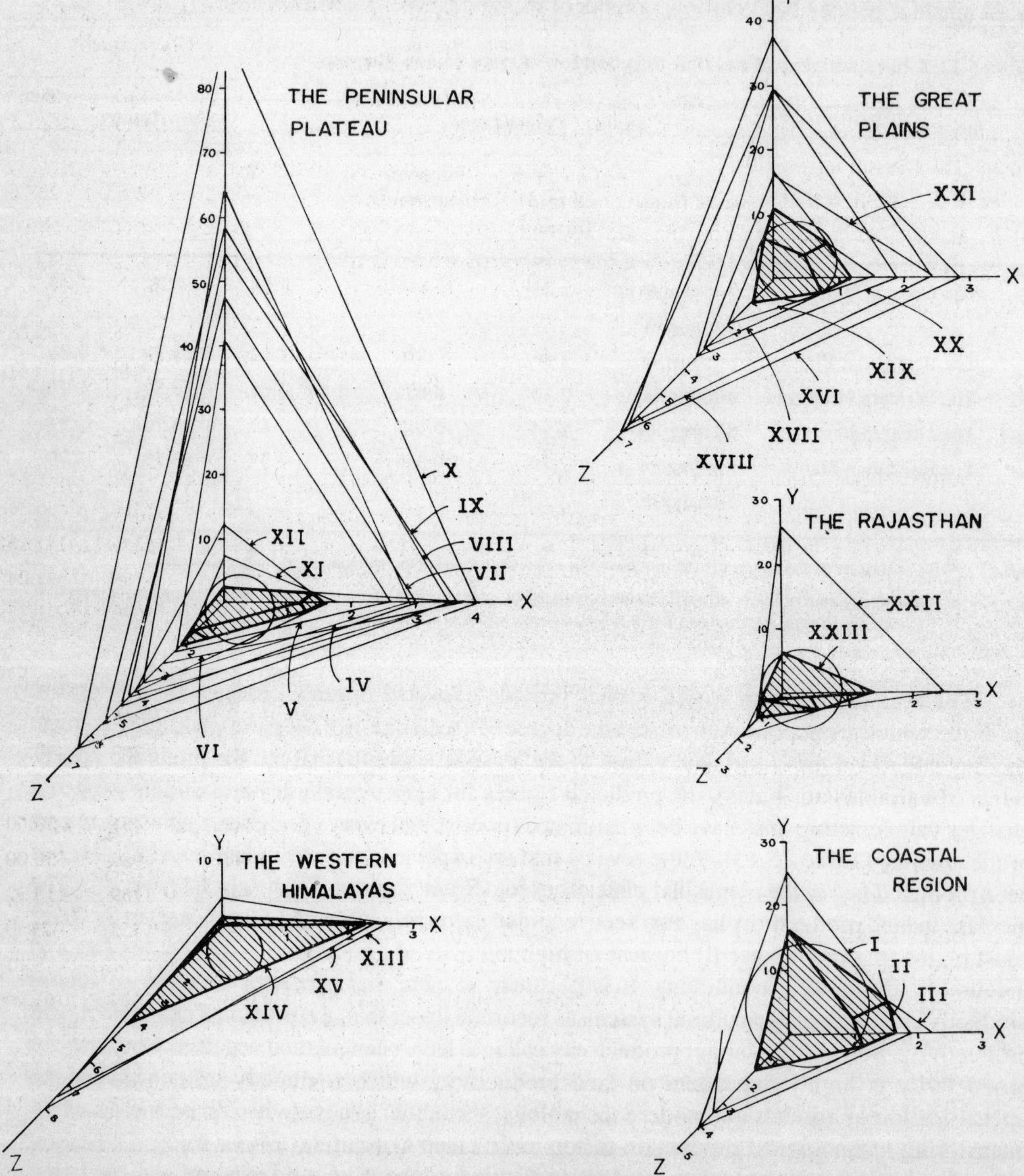

Fig. - 5.5 : Feasible Solution (Convex Polyhedrons).

Table- 5.13: Expected Changes in Agricultural Attributes for Decision Making Processes.

Ag. Planning Regions	Land Productivity (Rs/ha)			Absolute Increase in Land Productivity in 1980s(Rs/ha)			Labour Productivity (Rs/persons)		
	Xe	Xp	Xinc	Ye	Yp	Yinc	Ze	Zp	Zinc
A. The Coastal Regions									
I	1998	2410	20.64	156	241	54.48	958	1205	25.78
II	891	1022	14.70	23	102	343.47	474	511	7.80
III	1304	1643	26.00	157	165	5.09	1446	822	-43.15
B. The Peninsular Plateaus									
IV	1081	2564	137.19	49	256	422.45	816	1185	45.28
V	844	1803	113.62	55	181	229.09	974	833	-14.47
VI	595	1821	206.05	-03	182	—	770	842	9.35
VII	819	2020	146.64	54	204	277.77	522	943	80.65
VIII	783	2453	213.35	57	246	331.58	713	1135	59.19
IX	988	2853	188.81	60	285	375.83	670	1319	96.86
X	914	2913	218.76	136	291	114.34	545	1347	147.15
XI	1108	1644	48.37	261	164	-36.97	965	760	-21.24
XII	1652	2316	40.02	225	232	2.89	623	1070	71.75
C. The Western Himalayas									
XIII	1362	3451	153.38	645	345	-46.51	490	1725	252.04
XIV	1264	2663	110.72	-13	266	—	629	315	-49.92
XV	1404	3156	114.79	-02	315	—	416	208	-50.00
D. The Great Plains									
XVI	2208	4238	91.94	211	423	100.07	902	451	-50.00
XVII	4568	3980	-12.87	553	398	-28.03	1960	980	-50.00
XVIII	1462	2338	59.92	93	233	151.07	548	1169	113.32
XIX	2767	2911	5.22	408	291	-28.67	2035	1455	-28.50
XX	1963	2482	26.44	124	248	100.00	1137	1241	9.15
XXI	2994	2828	-05.53	261	283	8.43	3949	1414	-64.19
E. The Rajasthan Plains									
XXII	601	1116	85.69	57	112	96.49	1488	557	-62.53
XXIII	712	766	7.65	193	77	-60.10	1779	383	-78.44

N.B.: The subscripts of X, Y & Z variables are abbreviated as: e= existing figures for 1988-90,p= predicted figures calculated from feasible solution for future planning, and inc= expected increase in percent.

Concluding Remarks

In the present Chapter, regional processes of agricultural development of India have been studied first by delimiting the regional boundaries at various hierarchic orders of distinguished agricultural characteristics and then by identifying the optimal solution of agricultural regional processes for proper acceleration of decision- making processes for balance development.The classificatory approach of space partitioning for agricultural regionalisation (for which functional distances among OTUs have methodologically been calculated by applying Ward's 'functional distance algorithm') and the linear programming method for optimising the regional features of agricultural attributes have been adopted. There are some important salient features of regional strategy of agricultural development which can be put forward in the following manners.

(i) In the region-formation processes, assimilation of OTUs at micro level has implicitly been influencing by the green revolution technology, especially in the plain areas of the country. In more detail, region-formations at lowest level in respect to its regional hierarchy brought out in the Great plains and the Eastern coastal regions have been emerging under the influence of metropolitan economy. Say for example, the Punjab-Haryana-Western Uttar Pradesh and Calcutta based - Bengal agricultural regions are coinciding the Delhi and Calcutta metropolitan regions' boundaries. Likewise, Madras metropolitan has its own influence of agricultural sub-regions of Eastern coastal regions. Thus, agricultural regionalisation has the impact of agro-ecological conditions at macro level, agricultural production potential attribute at meso, socio-cultural at micro and techno-economic conditions at the lowest levels in the process of region-formation.

(ii) Diversification in the regional patterns of agricultural attributes indicates the lesser degree of region-stability. It might be because of the great variations in bio-physical and socio-economic factors and the concentration of the effect of modern technology only on a few patches of the country. Consequently, space-contiguity constraints are there to delimit agricultural regions.

(iii) The regional patterns of agricultural production potential, marginal products to input factors, and rate of potential absorption for production increase are positively related to each other. The ratio of marginal product to absorption rate of production potential with respect to non-land capital are recorded higher than the ratio to labour-input only in the few regions of the Peninsular India. It means labour factor of agricultural production is still having significant contribution whereas technology is only complementary for labour input rather than its substitution to boost up agricultural productivity levels in the country.

(iv) The feasible solutions are identical for the agricultural regions. In general, it is a fact that the predicted increase in land productivity is appreciated in the regions where agricultural growth is stagnant. Therefore, predicted rate of change of land productivity and agricultural growth rate is negatively related. Thus, the present strategy of growth is based on the decentralised patterns of agricultural development rather than concentration of growth patterns. However, there is a conflicting nature of the process-forms of agricultural landscape. The effects of metropolitan cities concentrate the development patterns, while present strategy suggests diversification of its patterns through proper utilisation of agricultural growth potential in different conditions of the agricultural regions.

A Set of Six Tables from 5.6 to 5.11, showing the Developmental Characteristics of Agricultural Planning Regions

Table- 5.6: Agro-Economic Characteristics of Various Agricultural Planning Regions.

Sl. No.	Annual Rainfall (in mm)		Annual Potential Evapotranspiration		Moisture Index		Soil Fertility Rating Index	
	M	Cv	M	Cv	M	Cv	M	Cv
A. The Coastal Regions								
I	1075	13.81	1499	18.17	-.252	-	66.3	12.57
II	2858	24.85	1762	15.95	.668	56.16	61.9	11.92
III	714	35.24	1521	26.82	-.510	-	50.0	15.76
B. The Peninsular Plateaus								
IV	773	21.92	1577	14.62	-.506	-	61.7	9.33
V	838	18.84	1336	19.53	-.327	-	56.9	12.94
VI	1159	18.53	1574	8.38	-.245	-	49.3	10.72
VII	1354	10.62	1496	12.61	-.075	-	59.1	12.65
VIII	1160	25.65	1513	11.21	-.446	-	61.5	14.54
IX	838	19.16	1665	38.00	-.518	-	67.9	5.48
X	711	11.64	1637	16.53	-.551	-	68.3	17.93
XI	924	49.45	1404	44.58	-.266	-	67.7	14.97
XII	1537	72.17	1430	51.72	.091	719.91	72.0	8.69
C. The Western Himalayas								
XIII	2142	8.32	1286	5.37	.670	13.60	73.8	4.26
XIV	1516	15.45	1050	31.38	.581	78.25	60.3	1.48
XV	762	8.10	961	33.28	-.070	-	60.4	1.10
D. The Great Plains								
XVI	2717	21.84	1387	24.32	.997	39.10	67.6	8.21
XVII	1551	17.30	1447	38.96	.236	89.95	63.9	23.76
XVIII	1145	21.88	1481	27.01	-.058	-	53.8	9.02
XIX	1109	39.45	1190	25.22	-.076	-	68.0	10.49
XX	876	15.64	1252	9.87	-.303	-	62.9	4.88
XXI	599	30.85	1517	29.39	-.567	-	69.1	9.18
E. The Rajasthan Plains								
XXII	738	55.28	1349	13.25	-.481	-	56.5	21.27
XXIII	245	21.49	1305	39.37	-.821	-	58.5	7.90
All India	**1165**	**57.81**	**1449**	**29.28**	**-.151**	**-**	**61.9**	**15.26**

N.B. : For the name of the regions, see Table- 5.5.

Abbreviations : M = Mean, Cv = Coefficient of areal variation within the region (in percent).

Table- 5.7 : Demographic and Social Structure of Various Agricultural Planning Regions (1991).

Sl. No.		Population Density (Persons/ km²)		Decadal Growth of Population (in %) 1981-91		% Share of Urban Population to total population		% Share of Rural Literates to total rural population	
		M	Cv	M	Cv	M	Cv	M	Cv
A.	**The Coastal Regions**								
	I	349	30.34	18.40	23.99	21.09	42.10	40.39	23.10
	II	691	58.36	17.20	65.14	25.88	57.28	68.11	18.69
	III	283	56.89	21.09	36.74	31.89	50.91	45.88	20.51
B.	**The Peninsular Plateaus**								
	IV	237	49.48	29.14	43.68	22.48	52.77	26.82	26.54
	V	202	27.82	26.57	17.03	24.23	47.02	32.04	34.21
	VI	194	53.49	27.05	28.70	30.11	87.86	30.33	17.86
	VII	239	71.25	24.03	24.49	15.20	67.71	29.13	25.07
	VIII	174	35.77	24.15	20.97	22.07	50.07	36.82	29.42
	IX	215	25.66	28.03	36.11	20.80	43.90	26.04	11.05
	X	175	16.59	19.85	12.70	23.22	10.86	34.28	13.50
	XI	273	57.53	19.73	22.03	26.21	30.58	40.05	16.54
	XII	322	33.43	13.28	30.31	24.98	58.31	54.37	20.97
C.	**The Western Himalayas**								
	XIII	91	50.40	14.51	42.55	7.81	28.03	44.15	11.54
	XIV	177	45.55	20.50	20.74	9.03	48.02	50.03	17.62
	XV	175	31.99	16.05	12.18	7.93	16.12	50.00	11.10
D.	**The Great Plains**								
	XVI	365	37.77	47.70	40.29	11.64	67.37	40.22	16.48
	XVII	910	59.25	26.01	14.52	19.07	69.28	37.24	32.71
	XVIII	781	27.50	23.39	10.87	9.72	69.25	28.91	16.31
	XIX	497	29.67	25.89	18.34	20.71	60.39	30.73	41.22
	XX	665	33.28	24.66	15.53	19.93	71.67	31.60	17.08
	XXI	465	47.39	24.43	34.54	26.73	35.29	40.63	19.73
E.	**The Rajasthan Plains**								
	XXII	243	56.65	30.69	37.78	31.92	75.77	28.66	12.78
	XXIII	68	54.84	33.54	18.07	24.25	45.22	19.18	12.14
	All India	**378**	**78.70**	**24.30**	**40.07**	**20.91**	**64.89**	**37.12**	**36.01**

N.B. : For the name of the regions, see Table- 5.5.

Abbreviations : M = Mean, Cv = Coefficient of areal variation with in the region (in percent).

Table- 5.8 A : Productivity and Growth Characteristics of Various Agricultural Planning Regions.

Sl. No.	Per Capita Ag. Output (Rs./persons) 1991		Annual Growth rate of Ag. Output (in %)		Land Productivity (Rs./ha) 1988-90		% Annual increase in Land Productivity,1980s	
	M	Cv	M	Cv	M	Cv	M	Cv
A. The Coastal Regions								
I	257	45.56	8.06	74.29	1998	53.97	7.82	98.09
II	68	78.13	5.98	320.68	891	60.68	.32	999.90
III	257	52.87	5.29	147.94,	1304	55.40	12.03	199.77
B. The Peninsular Plateaus								
IV	212	53.05	6.19	134.85	1081	64.58	1.56	161.93
V	251	21.87	6.69	76.87	844	23.55	6.45	85.17
VI	234	91.69	1.62	181.82	595	26.77	-0.23	-
VII	176	94.15	3.57	204.88	819	51.05	6.57	154.87
VIII	232	33.10	6.18	133.70	783	35.18	7.09	115.91
IX	198	29.48	5.14	75.56	988	48.30	6.11	70.04
X	169	16.03	5.60	42.17	914	34.07	3.99	28.81
XI	241	46.96	29.09	60.51	1108	55.19	23.53	67.28
XII	156	63.07	15.07	132.64	1652	69.21	13.63	227.60
C. The Western Himalayas								
XIII	148	25.92	1.95	114.32	1362	26.19	5.54	93.60
XIV	143	23.04	-0.16	-	1264	26.00	-1.12	-
XV	89	17.25	1.21	169.93	1404	17.95	-0.14	-
D. The Great Plains								
XVI	189	69.29	.47	917.27	2208	109.40	9.56	281.19
XVII	369	43.28	7.53	75.27	4568	36.14	12.10	94.70
XVIII	133	44.24	6.13	67.56	1462	31.38	6.37	100.34
XIX	389	36.46	14.34	51.82	2767	29.79	14.74	56.36
XX	259	59.09	6.19	114.19	1963	27.99	6.34	106.94
XXI	920	109.48	8.45	66.31	2994	42.84	8.72	71.70
E. The Rajasthan Plains								
XXII	386	72.66	16.16	114.83	601	73.67	9.49	212.36
XXIII	371	48.96	35.16	70.36	712	68.18	27.17	63.93
All India	**281**	**130.04**	**8.44**	**149.23**	**1576**	**80.92**	**8.36**	**162.12**

N.B. : For the name of the regions, see Table- 5.5.

Abbreviations : M = Mean, Cv = Coefficient of areal variation with in the region (in percent).

Table- 5.8 B : Productivity and Growth Characteristics of Various Agricultural Planning Regions.

Sl. No.		Labour Productivity (Rs./persons) 1988-90		% Change in Labour Productivity 1980s		crop Intensity (in %) 1989-90		Decadal Change in Crop Intensity (%)	
		M	Cv	M	Cv	M	Cv	M	Cv
A.	**The Coastal Regions**								
	I	958	40.55	55.65	75.53	137.06	15.69	11.14	120.89
	II	474	49.27	20.07	454.27	128.90	13.97	4.17	213.23
	III	1446	51.48	19.34	343.30	113.15	9.28	2.01	103.06
B.	**The Peninsular Plateaus**								
	IV	816	26.60	33.76	385.21	141.00	36.38	2.96	323.13
	V	974	23.51	30.12	141.27	118.10	11.25	4.04	169.74
	VI	770	34.61	-5.21	-	115.21	4.01	3.21	232.30
	VII	522	44.00	8.22	661.01	112.11	10.48	6.59	200.25
	VIII	713	28.75	26.28	202.97	112.70	8.02	-0.17	-
	IX	670	28.11	21.64	166.93	116.86	8.00	6.82	77.88
	X	545	12.71	21.84	89.53	108.01	1.92	0.54	218.32
	XI	965	43.40	223.01	120.87	111.20	5.14	3.17	164.06
	XII	623	46.95	103.81	103.27	113.11	8.58	2.05	433.33
C.	**The Western Himalayas**								
	XIII	490	35.01	-2.33	-	160.15	6.21	-1.28	-
	XIV	629	28.99	-17.15	-	171.17	7.36	3.62	211.81
	XV	416	35.95	-24.02	-	170.00	10.39	5.47	26.20
D.	**The Great Plains**								
	XVI	902	77.64	-24.76	-	131.63	16.83	3.59	253.97
	XVII	1960	44.96	25.31	192.18	161.02	14.83	21.43	105.21
	XVIII	548	35.13	18.52	153.17	145.30	9.57	3.36	277.12
	XIX	2035	43.15	103.31	66.06	154.23	7.64	5.17	100.61
	XX	1137	39.41	32.16	209.66	148.93	6.12	6.16	102.51
	XXI	3949	52.52	46.19	104.65	168.70	8.22	2.71	86.80
E.	**The Rajasthan Plains**								
	XXII	1488	38.10	114.23	105.36	116.56	5.18	6.17	59.78
	XXIII	1779	66.41	492.10	44.58	102.79	1.63	0.36	807.36
	All India	**1189**	**98.37**	**49.00**	**258.26**	**134.00**	**19.60**	**5.33**	**194.01**

N.B. : For the name of the regions, see Table- 5.5.

Abbreviations : M = Mean, Cv = Coefficient of areal variation within the region (in percent).

Table- 5.9A: Agricultural Input Intensity in VariousAgricultural Regions.

Sl. No.	% Share of NIA to Total NSA 1988-89		Decadal Change in NIA (%) 1980s		Irrigation Intensity (in %) 1988-90		Mechanisation (Rs./ha) 1988-90	
	M	Cv	M	Cv	M	Cv	M	Cv
A. The Coastal Regions								
I	53.28	34.02	4.45	189.90	122	13.75	56	111.40
II	16.47	87.67	2.23	209.92	122	14.15	50	116.70
III	22.62	52.96	1.60	49.63	123	8.23	50	67.97
B. The Peninsular Plateaus								
IV	34.20	47.06	24.89	58.08	113	7.57	68	98.69
V	23.29	51.74	6.88	134.30	112	13.24	33	45.96
VI	17.09	54.84	7.30	86.57	108	17.45	20	38.90
VII	15.58	69.00	4.74	94.49	122	17.08	6	82.57
VIII	14.21	77.30	1.75	166.00	145	11.09	20	72.55
IX	28.70	62.03	20.26	189.61	129	11.35	68	91.16
X	27.47	28.13	3.89	27.07	124	4.67	93	68.51
XI	21.52	48.49	3.77	106.65	122	7.70	36	80.87
XII	21.97	82.77	-2.11	-	116	10.42	94	111.12
C. The Western Himalayas								
XIII	10.98	44.85	0.82	242.71	184	5.49	2	128.31
XIV	26.03	76.70	10.82	161.27	158	17.42	3	107.94
XV	21.23	70.24	2.42	77.83	159	19.59	3	113.47
D. The Great Plains								
XVI	30.54	80.10	1.43	69.44	108	5.97	5	70.65
XVII	29.37	70.43	1.72	400.57	116	12.73	43	93.27
XVIII	58.31	39.68	10.70	121.15	118	7.90	138	145.62
XIX	61.54	33.09	9.18	135.40	142	19.84	112	72.22
XX	69.09	16.32	5.80	78.67	134	11.18	71	31.94
XXI	80.70	22.48	10.33	107.72	167	12.40	134	71.44
E. The Rajasthan Plains								
XXII	16.50	13.03	14.06	33.50	112	9.40	33	25.71
XXIII	4.45	59.20	4.45	59.12	135	12.66	4	99.94
All India	35.58	75.76	6.84	180.94	127	19.15	55	145.98

N.B. : For the name of the regions, see Table- 5.5.

Abbreviations : M = Mean, Cv = Coefficient of areal variation within the region (in percent).

Table- 5.9B: Agricultural Input Intensity in Various Agricultural Regions.

Sl. No.		Fertilizer Use (kg/ha) 1988-90		Labour Input (Rs/ha)		Non-Land Capital Input (Rs/ha)	
		M	Cv	M	Cv	M	Cv
A.	**The Coastal Regions**						
	I	58.42	78.32	916	43.50	114	81.77
	II	44.17	53.95	1223	57.23	94	78.58
	III	38.00	59.56	313	62.97	86	61.55
B.	**The Peninsular Plateaus**						
	IV	34.61	115.48	238	174.92	92	117.14
	V	20.27	59.48	367	49.17	52	44.76
	VI	8.75	32.03	345	46.87	28	29.13
	VII	9.70	94.01	447	52.71	16	78.31
	VIII	19.95	185.15	404	42.84	41	97.55
	IX	57.72	106.35	578	46.10	125	63.37
	X	39.67	22.67	567	60.41	133	44.89
	XI	42.85	56.07	398	28.95	77	43.06
	XII	79.00	53.34	1025	4[illegible].59	172	79.59
C.	**The Western Himalayas**						
	XIII	6.83	42.60	12	45.66	14	26.01
	XIV	27.90	31.83	77	54.03	31	35.81
	XV	11.20	64.48	128	83.05	14	49.81
D.	**The Great Plains**						
	XVI	7.92	129.69	612	48.15	14	73.18
	XVII	60.53	71.95	955	29.61	103	75.11
	XVIII	35.04	43.93	1123	26.94	134	23.02
	XIX	82.06	43.87	300	73.40	187	55.87
	XX	72.33	30.19	232	44.28	142	26.23
	XXI	117.70	62.12	462	50.66	265	66.70
E.	**The Rajasthan Plains**						
	XXII	14.00	18.62	163	75.47	40	20.72
	XXIII	10.67	8.84	14	57.29	5	82.43
	All India	**43.99**	**104.27**	**513**	**85.15**	**97**	**104.76**

N.B. : For the name of the regions, see Table- 5.5.

Abbreviations : M = Mean, Cv = Coefficient of areal variation within the region (in percent).

Table-5.10A : Agricultural Labour Structure in Various Agricultural Planning Regions.

Sl. No.		NSA per Ag. Workers (in ha) 1988-90		% Share of Ag. Workers 1991		% Increase in Total Agricultural Workers 1981-91	
		M	Cv	M	Cv	M	Cv
A.	The Coastal Regions						
	I	0.52	36.94	71.02	7.54	10.03	176.94
	II	0.72	49.36	44.55	33.42	12.37	106.65
	III	1.18	36.87	57.69	23.18	19.12	58.23
B.	The Peninsular Plateaus						
	IV	0.90	43.98	71.51	15.90	51.49	116.55
	V	1.19	20.35	73.78	14.31	25.37	61.96
	VI	1.10	78.90	65.30	27.61	16.28	195.59
	VII	0.72	35.43	75.55	16.79	27.98	99.93
	VIII	0.96	19.74	77.85	12.29	19.92	41.62
	IX	0.73	42.69	68.76	21.40	18.25	118.99
	X	0.64	23.97	71.82	1.73	19.50	21.23
	XI	1.16	55.03	63.41	33.17	16.84	144.84
	XII	0.70	73.53	47.58	34.47	-1.93	-
C.	The Western Himalayas						
	XIII	0.42	30:47	79.58	6.76	31.11	140.38
	XIV	0.54	26.20	66.96	16.85	31.22	139.19
	XV	0.36	4.92	79.16	3:62	24.60	31.34
D.	The Great Plains						
	XVI	0.56	30.85	58.33	22.08	34.07	72.83
	XVII	0.48	29.20	63.83	26.47	21.73	98.11
	XVIII	0.41	37.30	80.85	17.93	28.00	85.24
	XIX	0.70	26.41	69.14	23.94	11.01	202.96
	XX	0.59	28.35	73.64	16.75	19.30	91.30
	XXI	1.35	45.62	59.90	17.33	20.06	124.19
E.	The Rajasthan Plains						
	XXII	2.09	29.94	53.01	33.36	3.42	999.90
	XXIII	2.47	50.74	69.57	16.05	43.27	55.57
	All India	**0.86**	**64.74**	**68.17**	**23.34**	**22.37**	**125.78**

N.B. : For the name of the regions, see Table- 5.5.

Abbreviations :M = Mean, Cv = Coefficient of areal variation within the region (in percent).

Table-5.10B : Agricultural Labour Structure in Various Agricultural Planning Regions.

Sl. No.	Agricultural Workforce (Persons/ha) 1991		% Change in Agricultural Workforce 1981-91		Size of Land Holding (NSA/Cultivator) 1991	
	M	Cv	M	Cv	M	Cv
A. The Coastal Regions						
I	2.17	37.25	28.32	129.58	1.26	38.57
II	1.66	36.70	13.16	155.50	1.77	57.50
III	0.97	36.35	36.74	74.20	2.00	46.62
B. The Peninsular Plateaus						
IV	1.37	49.89	36.65	78.52	1.13	36.54
V	0.87	19.54	27.20	110.44	1.75	25.64
VI	0.83	31.22	17.19	96.40	2.20	32.82
VII	1.67	48.78	21.90	156.70	1.09	40.14
VIII	1.05	32.53	25.52	76.51	1.94	39.59
IX	1.63	36.17	10.95	206.54	1.70	48.49
X	1.66	22.91	-10.80		1.67	43.87
XI	1.23	43.78	2.95	811.48	1.82	47.80
XII	2.17	58.48	38.62	216.03	1.67	54.46
C. The Western Himalayas						
XIII	2.52	21.71	34.41	95.89	0.43	31.77
XIV	2.00	25.64	35.27	116.96	0.53	26.79
XV	2.80	4.90	36.71	16.47	0.50	17.71
D. The Great Plains						
XVI	1.97	32.06	77.03	163.77	0.91	55.01
XVII	2.26	27.10	30.95	83.11	1.02	34.18
XVIII	2.68	26.15	126.35	373.57	0.76	24.53
XIX	1.52	26.29	16.57	183.06	1.09	41.40
XX	1.80	23.42	18.73	92.95	0.81	28.06
XXI	0.89	43.31	20.47	127.98	2.14	46.07
E. The Rajasthan Plains						
XXII	0.51	21.30	7.89	305.47	2.61	23.40
XXIII	0.58	64.44	196.89	124.41	3.94	21.43
All India	**1.56**	**53.72**	**35.25**	**377.92**	**1.47**	**61.05**

N.B. : For the name of the regions, see Table- 5.5.

Abbreviations : M = Mean, Cv = Coefficient of areal variation within the region (in percent).

Table-5.11A : Agricultural Growth Potential Structure in Various Agricultural Planning Regions.

Sl. No.	Maximum Expected Yield Level (A) Rs/ha, 1988-90		Yield Gaps(A-Y) (Rs/ha)		Production Potential Intensity(A/Y)	
	M	Cv	M	Cv	M	Cv
A. The Coastal Regions						
I	3905	37.22	1906	52.87	2.24	43.66
II	1655	57.54	829	80.47	2.48	45.87
III	2662	25.60	1357	55.34	2.55	50.54
B. The Peninsular Plateaus						
IV	3154	42.23	2073	68.90	2.92	48.90
V	2218	20.82	1376	36.36	2.75	32.07
VI	2240	27.29	1645	38.25	4.05	33.85
VII	2509	60.87	1689	87.46	3.00	50.91
VIII	3018	45.39	2234	60.57	3.69	43.70
IX	3510	57.89	2573	75.24	4.14	59.18
X	3584	28.35	2669	38.33	4.21	37.51
XI	2022	50.26	914	100.65	2.21	66.10
XII	2848	98.27	1554	144.00	2.64	60.36
C. The Western Himalayas						
XIII	3624	11.94	2262	24.06	2.86	30.72
XIV	2793	18.28	1528	39.62	2.37	33.56
XV	3314	15.72	1910	34.94	2.45	25.99
D. The Great Plains						
XVI	6230	150.96	4022	180:47	2.52	39.02
XVII	5851	30.96	1283	105.29	1.36	35.21
XVIII	3437	18.87	1975	29.30	2.55	30.81
XIX	4280	13.83	1525	50.59	1.62	31.66
XX	3649	19.51	1685	40.32	2.01	39.90
XXI	4158	32.58	1205	56.27	1.47	24.61
E. The Rajasthan Plains						
XXII	1506	33.37	904	40.90	3.62	43.47
XXIII	1035	26.37	439	51.77	1.97	33.55
All India	**3228**	**73.58**	**1672**	**107.44**	**2.58**	**58.30**

N.B. : For the name of the regions, see Table- 5.5.

Abbreviations : M = Mean, Cv = Coefficient of areal variation within the region (in percent).

Table-5.11B : Rate of Potential Absorption and Marginal Productivities of various Inputs in the Agricultural Planning Regions (1988-90).

Sl. No.	Rate of Potential Absorption (in units) w.r.t.				Marginal Productivities (in Unit) w.r.t.			
	Labour		Technology		Labour		Technology	
	M	Cv	M	Cv	M	Cv	M	Cv
A. The Coastal Regions								
I	0.002	120.81	0.055	125.40	0.81	52.04	11.25	95.94
II	0.002	85.54	0.032	125.24	0.43	101.73	5.69	82.76
III	0.006	112.09	0.030	114.33	2.09	49.60	8.94	86.23
B. The Peninsular Plateaus								
IV	0.041	76.26	0.073	109.86	6.37	51.67	10.64	57.96
V	0.012	108.35	0.072	91.09	1.68	83.57	10.30	52.72
VI	0.009	68.49	0.118	73.85	1.36	41.70	16.13	37.66
VII	0.009	105.46	0.235	86.76	1.24	67.17	37.03	52.71
VIII	0.014	111.28	0.156	115.44	1.64	80.47	21.47	92.94
IX	0.040	191.64	0.228	138.76	1.92	107.66	7.62	89.07
X	0.027	120.11	0.042	48.84	2.08	94.95	4.87	40.79
XI	0.005	75.46	0.051	118.22	1.06	102.30	32.31	308.06
XII	0.003	99.52	0.010	81.76	0.48	84.30	2.60	51.80
C. The Western Himalayas								
XIII	0.026	31.24	0.534	61.35	62.22	32.51	126.84	48.18
XIV	0.017	80.74	0.035	77.95	13.20	57.97	29.35	57.35
XV	0.017	49.48	0.089	64.77	9.67	83.28	38.87	18.87
D. The Great Plains								
XVI	0.054	144.21	3.341	157.80	2.99	47.67	156.52	72.20
XVII	0.001	107.65	0.029	191.41	1.15	55.67	17.84	71.64
XVIII	0.002	40.33	0.023	77.61	0.68	42.60	6.21	91.41
XIX	0.012	85.58	0.020	105.29	4.50	57.74	6.62	83.04
XX	0.016	179.50	0.015	48.31	4.73	52.33	6.17	31.32
XXI	0.016	395.15	0.008	125.15	2.55	60.50	5.68	88.03
E. The Rajasthan Plains								
XXII	0.048	108.78	0.043	64.47	3.09	69.50	7.26	40.34
XXIII	0.336	135.20	0.474	98.26	6.38	43.59	31.57	69.84
All India	**0.025**	**356.56**	**0.292**	**505.56**	**3.69**	**240.81**	**22.41**	**240.22**

N.B. : For the name of the regions, see Table- 5.5.

Abbreviations : M = Mean, Cv = Coefficient of areal variation within the region (in percent).

References

001. Abler, R., *et.al.*(1971): *Spatial Organisation- The Geographer's View of the World,* Prentice Hall, Inc., Englewood Cliffs, New Jersey, pp.143 & 340-85.

002. Agricultural Commission (1964): Division of the Country into Homogeneous Crop Regions, *Agricultural Situation in India,* Vol. XIX(No.5), pp.453-71.

003. Ahluwalia, M.S. (1978): Rural Poverty and Agricultural Performance in India, *Journal of Development Studies,* Vol.XIV, pp.298-323.

004. Alagh, Y.K., *et.al.* (1978): Agricultural Growth and Manpower Absorption in India, in Bardhan, *et.al.*(eds): *Labour Absorption in Indian Agriculture,* ARTEP, ILO, Bangkok.

005. Ali, M.H., R.K. Chatterji, & T.D. Biswas (1966): Soil Moisture Tension Relationships of Some Indian Soils, *Journal of Indian Society of Soil Sciences,* Vol.14, pp.51-62.

006. Amedeo, D.(1969): An Optimisation Approach to the Identification of A System of Regions, in M.D.Thomas(ed): *Papers of the Regional Science Association,* Vol. XXIII, pp.25-44.

007. Amedeo, D. & R.G. Golledge (1975): *An Introduction of Scientific Reasoning in Geography,* John Willey & Sons, Inc., New York.

008. Baker, J.N.L. (1928): Notes of the Natural Regions of India, *Geography,* Vol.14, pp.447-55.

009. Baker, O.E. (1926-32): Agricultural Regions of North America, *Economic Geography,* Vol.2, pp.460-93; Vol.3, pp.50-86, 309-39 & 445-65; Vol.4, pp.44-73 & 399-433; Vol.5, pp.36-69; Vol.6, pp.166-92 & 278-309; Vol.7, pp.109-53 & 326-64; Vol.8, pp.326-77.

010. Bandman, M.K. (1978): Structure of Growth Poles of Developing Regions, in Misra, R.P. *et.al.* (eds): *Regional Planning and National Deveplopment,* Vikas Publishing House, New Delhi.

011. Bardhan, P.K. (1973): Size, Productivity and Returns to Scale- An Analysis of Farm Level Data in Indian Agriculture, *Journal of Political Economy,* Vol. 81, pp. 1370-86.

012. Basu, Arait (1981): Location and Utilisation of Land- An Analysis of Agricultural Regionalisation and Its Effects on Farm Size and Productivity, *Indian Journal of Regional Science,* Vol.XIII (No.2), pp.124-39.

013. Basu, J.K. (1937): A Review and Appreciation of Soil Survey Work in India up-to-data with Suggestions for Future, *Proceedings,* 2nd Meeting of Crops and Soils Wing, *Agriculture and Animal Husbandry in India,* pp.226-31.

014. Berry, B.J.L. (1961): A Method for Deriving Multifactor Uniform Regions, *Polish Geographic Review,* Vol.33(No.2),pp.263-82.

015. Berry, B.J.L. (1964): Approaches and Regional Analysis - A Synthesis, *Annals* of A.A.G., Vol.54, pp.2-11.

016. Berry,B.J.L. (1965): Identification of Delimiting Regions, in W.D. Wood & R.S. Thoman (eds): *Areas of Economic Stress in Canada,* Kingston, Ontario.

017. Berry, B.J.L. & V.L.S.P. Rao (1968): Duality in the Regional Structure of Andhra Pradesh, paper presented and discussed in *the Session* of 21st, I.G.C., New Delhi.

018. Bhalla, G.S. (1980): *National and Regional Economic Development in India during 1961-71,*(Memeo, CSRD), J.N.U., New Delhi, pp.11-16.

019. Bhalla, G.S. (1988): Regional Pattern of Agricultural Development in India as An Index of Natural Resource Use, paper presented in *Indo-Soviet Seminar* on Rational Utilisation of Natural Resources and Regional Development, Organised by CSRD, J.N.U., New Delhi (Oct.10-12, 1988).

020. Bhalla, G.S. & Y.K. Alagh (1979): *Performance of Indian Agriculture,* Starling Publishers, New Delhi.

021. Bhalla, G.S. & Y.K. Alagh (1983): Labour Productivity in Indian Agriculture, *Economic and Political Weekly,* Annual Number, pp.825-34.

022. Bhalla, G.S. & D.S. Tyagi (1989): *Patterns in Indian Agricultural Development - A District Level Study*, Institute for Studies in Industrial Development, New Delhi.

023. Bhat, L.S. & A.T.A. Learmonth (1968): Recent Contributions to the Economic Geography of India, *Economic Geography,* Vol.44 (No.3), pp.189-201.

024. Bhat, L.S. (1988): Environment, Resources and Economic Development in India, *Indo-Soviet Seminar* on Rational Utilization of Natural Resources and Regional Development, Organised by CSRD, J.N.U., New Delhi (Oct. 10-12,1988).

025. Bhatia, B.M. (1988): *Indian Agriculture- A Policy Perspective,* Sage Publications Inc., New Delhi.

026. Bhatia, S.S. (1967): A New Measurement of Agricultural Efficiency in Uttar Pardesh, India, *Economic Geography,* Vol.43(No.3), pp.244-60.

027. Binswanger, H.P. & J.G. Ryan (1977): Efficiency and Equity Issues in exante Allocation of Research Resources, *Indian Journal of Agricultural Economics,* Vol.32(No.3).

028. Binswanger, H.P. (1978): Induced Technological Change- Evolution of Thought, in H.P. Binswanger & V.W. Ruttan (eds): *Induced Innovation,* Johns Hopkins University Press, Baltimore.

029. Bora, M. (1991): Agricultural Production Processes in Jorhat District(Assam)- A Geographical Analysis, *M.Phil. Dissertation,* SubmittedtoNorth- Eastern Hill University, Shillong, pp.83-110.

030. Boserup, E. (1965): *The Conditions of Agricultural Growth,* George Allen & Unwin, London.

031. Boserup, E. (1981): *Population and Technology,* Basil Blackwell, Oxford.

032. Boudeville, J. (1966): *Problems of Regional Economic Planning,* University Press, Edinburgh.

033. Brahmananda, P.R. (1979): The New Classical Growth Model, in C.H.H. Rao & P.C. Joshi (eds): *Reflections on Economic Development and Social Change,* Allied Pubs. Pvt. Ltd., New Delhi, pp.91-97.

034. Brown, L. (1965): *Models for Spatial Diffusion Research - A review,* (Department of Geography, N.W. University, Evanston), Technical Report No.3, Contract Nonr 1228(33), p.15.

035. Bunge, W. (1962): *Theoretical Geography,* Series-C(No.1), Lund Studies in Geography, Lund, pp.14-26.

036. Carlstein, T. (1977): Innovation, Time Allocation and Time space Packing, *Lunds Universitets Kulturgeografiska Institution* (Sweeden), paper No.35 (Chapter 17).

037. Casetti, E. (1964): Classificatory and Regional Analysis by Discriminant Iterations, *Technical Report No.12,* Contract NONR 1228(26), North Western University, Evanston, Illinois.

038. Casetti, E. (1966): Analysis of Spatial Association by Trigonometric Polynomials, *Canadan Geographer,* Vol.10.

039. Casetti, E. (1981): Correlates and Determinants of Agricultural Productivity Growth, in Noor Mohammad (ed): *Perspectives in Agricultural Geography*(Vol.IV), Concept Pub. Coy, New Delhi, pp.387-99.

040. Chapman, G.R., B. Smit & W.R. Smith (1984): Flexibility and Criticality in Resource Use Assessment, *Geographical Analysis,* Vol.16(No.1), pp.53-64.

041. Chatterjee, S.P. (1964): Map of Physiographic Divisions of India, *National Atlas Organisation,* I edn, Calcutta.

042. Chattopadhyaya, B. & M. Raza (1975): Regional Development- An Analytical Frame, *Indian Journal of Regional Science,* Vol.VII (No.1).

043. Coale, A.J. & E.M. Hoover (1958): *Population Growth and Economic Development in Low Income Countries,* Princeton University, Princeton.

044. Cole, J.P. & C.A.M. King (1970): *Quantitative Geography,* John Wiley & Sons (III Printing), pp.600-605.

045. Dandekar, V.M. & N. Rath (1971): Poverty in India, *Economic and Political Weekly,* Vol.VI(No.1-2).

046. Dantwala, M.L. (1987): Growth and Equity in Agriculture, *Indian Journal of Agricultural Economics,* Vol.42(No.2), p.149-59.

047. Dasgupta, M. & S. Basu (1985): Urbanisation and Agricultural Yields- A Case Study of West Bengal, *Indian Journal of Regional Science,* Vol.XVII(No.1), pp.25-32.

048. Dayal, E. (1984): Agricultural Productivity in India- A Spatial Analylsis, *Annals* of the A.A.G., Vol.74, pp.98-123.

049. Dayal, E.(1985): Wealth and Poverty in Rural India, *Geo-Journal* Vol.11(No.4), pp.369-82.

050. Dayal, E. (1978): A Measure of Cropping Intensity, *The Professional Geographer,* Vol.XXX(No.3), pp.289-96.

051. Dickenson, R.E. (1969): *The Makers of Modern Geography,* Roultedge & Kegan Paul, London.

052. D'Monte, D. (1992): Pockets of Backwardness, *The Times of India,* Vol.CLV(No.89), p.10.

053. Dogra, B. (1981): How Green was Our Revolution, *The Hindustan Times* (Sunday Magazine), Vol.LVIII(No.300, Nov.1, 1981), p.1.

054. Douglas, P.H. & C.W. Cobb (1928): A Theory of Production, *American Economic Review* (Supplement), Vol.18, c.f., G. Tintner (1952): *Econometrics,* John Willey & Sons, Inc, New York, pp.51-52.

055. Dougrameji, J.S. (1970): Water Requirements of Some Crops in the Baghdad Region, *Technical Report* No.11, Institute for Applied Research on National Resources (UNSF-UNESCO-Ins, Iraq).

056. Dunn, Jr.E.S. (1954): *The Location of Agricultural Production,* University of Florida Press, Gainesvilla.

057. FAO/UNFPA/IIASA (1982): *Potential Population Supporting Capacities of Land in the Developing World,* Technical Report of Project FPA/INT/513, Land Resources for Population of the Future, Rome.

058. Fei, J.C.H. & G. Ranis (1961): A Theory of Economic Development, *American Economic Review,* Vol.51, pp.533-65.

059. Fei, J.C.H. & G. Ranis (1964): *Development of the Labour Surplus Economy,* Richard D. Irwin, Inc., Homewood, Illinous.

060. Ganguli, B.N. (1938): *Trends of Agriculture and Population in the Ganges Valley,* London, pp.93-94.

061. Ghatak, S. & K. Ingersent (1984): *Agriculture and Economic Development,* Select Book Service Syndicate, New Delhi.

062. Grigg, D. (1965): The Logic of Regional Systems, *Annals* of the A.A.G., Vol.55 (No.3), pp.465-491.

063. Grigg, D. (1967): Regions, Models and Clases, in Chorley, R.J. & P. Hagget (eds): *Integrated Models in Geography,* Methuen & Co., London, pp.494-500.

064. Grigg, D. (1969): The Agricultural Regions of the World- Review and Reflections, *Economic Geography,* Vol.45(No.2), pp.95-132.

065. Grosjean, M, & B. Messerli (1988): African Mountains and Highlands- Potential and Constraints, *Mountain Research and Development,* Vol.8 (No.2/3), pp.111-22.

066. Gupta, R.P. (1966): A Permeameter Cell, *Journal of Indian Society of Social Sciences,* Vol.14, pp.37-41.

067. Gupta, R.P. (1973): A Review on Soil-Water Relationship of Indian Soils, *Technical Bulletin (Agri)* No.43, ICAR, New Delhi.

068. Hagerstrand, T. (1973/74): On Socio-Technological Ecology and the Study of Innovations, *Ethnologia Europaea,* Vol.VII(No.1), pp.17-34

069. Hagerstrand, T.(1976): The Diffusion of Innovations, *International Encyclopedia of the Social Sciences,* pp.174-78.

070. Hagen, E.E. (1975): *The Economics of Development,* Richard D. Irwin, Inc., London.

071. Hall, P.(ed) (1966): *Von Thunen's Isolated State:* An Englilsh Edition of *Der Isolierte Staat,* Pergamon Press, London.

072. Haris, A.E. (1931): Effect of Replaceable Sodium on Soil Permeability, *Soil Science.* Vol.32, p.435.

073. Harris, J.R. & M.P.T. Todaro (1970): Migration, Unemployment and Development: A Two-Sector Analysis, *American Economic Review,* Vol.60(Mar), pp.126-42.

074. Hayami, Y. & V.W. Ruttan (1970): Agricultural Productivity Differences among Countries, *American Economic Review,* Vol.60, pp.895-911.

075. Hicks, J.R. (1932): *The Theory of Wages,* McMillan & Co, London.

076. Hopkins, R., R. Paarlberg & M. Wallerstein (1982): *Food in the Global Arena,* Holt, Rinchart & Winston, Toronto.

077. Hudson, J. C. (1972): *Geographical Diffusion Theory,* Studies in Geography (North Western University, Evanstan), No.19, pp.26-27.

078 Hussain, M. (1979): *Agricultural Geography,* Inter-India Publications, New Delhi.

079. ICAR (1964): Division of the Country into Homogeneous Crop Regions, *Agricultural Situation in India,* Vol.XIX(No.5), pp.453-71.

080. Ishikawa (1981): *Essays on Technology, Employment and Institutions in Economic Development,* Kinokuniya Co. Ltd., Tokyo.

081. Jakhade, V.M. & H.B. Shivamaggi (1969): Inter-District Comparison of Agricultural Development and Spread of Banking Facilities in the Rural Areas, *Reserve Bank of India Bulletin,* Vol.XXIII(No.10), Appendix-I, pp.1559-95.

082. Johansen, L. (1961): A Method for Separating the Effects of Capital Accumulation and Shifts Production Functions upon Growth in Labour Productivity, *Economic Journal,* Vol.71(Dec.), pp.775-82.

083. Johnston, B.F. & P. Kilby (1975): Agriculture and Structural Transformation: Economic Strategies in late-developing Countries, New York (see also Johnston 1980).

084. Johnston, B. F. (1980): Socio-economic Aspects of Improved Animal drawn Implements and Mechanisation in Semi- Arid East Africa, in *Proceedings* of International workshop on Socio-economic Constraints to Development of Semi-Arid Tropical Agriculture, ICRISAT, Patancheru(A.P.), pp.221-33.

085. Jorgenson, D.W. (1961): The Development of a Dual Economy, *Economic Journal,* Vol.71(June), pp.309-34.

086. Jorgenson, D.W. (1967): Surplus Agricultural Labour and the Development of a Dual Economy, *Oxford Economics Papers,* n.s.19, pp.288-312.

087. Kahn, A.E. (1951): Investment Criteria in Development, *Quarterly Journal of Economics,* Vol.65 (Feb.), pp.38-61.

088. Kata, V.R.(1990): *Agricultural Production functions: An Appraisal,* Ajanta Pub.(India), Delhi.

089. Kendall, M.G. (1939): The Geographical Distribution of Crop-Productivity in England, *Journal of Royal Statistical Society,* Vol.102(New series), pp.21-62.

090. Kendrew, W.J. (1944): *The Climate of the Continents,* Oxford University Press, Oxford.

091. Kennedy, C. & A.T. Thirlwall (1972): Surveys in Applied Economics: Technical Progress, *EconomicJournal,* Vol.82(March), pp.11-72.

092. Khusro, A.M. (1968): Economic Theory and Indian Agricultural Policies, in A.M. Khusro (ed.): *Readings in Agricultural Development,* I edn., Allied Publishers India, New Delhi, p.3.

093. King, L.J. (1969): *Statistical Analysis in Geography,* Englewood Clifffs, New Jersey, pp.198-204.

094. Kolosovsky, N.N. (1958): Production Territorial Combination (Complex) in Soviet Economic Geography, *Fundamentals of Economic Regionalisation,* Moscow.

095. Koppen, W. (1900): Versuch einer Klassifikation der klimate..., *Geogr. Zeitschr.,* Vol.6, pp.593-611 & 657-79.

096. Kostrowicki, J. (1972): A Preliminary Attempt at A Typology of World Agriculture, *International Geography,* Vol.2 (Abstract of the papers published in the 22nd I.G.C. Montreal, Canada), Paper No.C0908, pp.1097-1100.

097. Krishnan, A. & M. Singh (1968): quoted from, A. Krishnan (1980): *Proceedings of the Climatic Classification - A Consultants Meeting* (14-16 April 1980), ICRISAT centre, Patancheru, Andhra Pradesh, pp.80-84.

098. Krishnan, A. (1980): Agro-climatic Classification- Methods and Their Application to India, *Proceedings of the Climatic Classification - A Consultants Meeting* (14-16 April 1980), ICRISAI centre, Patancheru, Andhra Pradesh, pp.59-88.

099. Kumar, A. (1986): Imbalances in Pulse Productivity, *Agricultural Situation in India,* Vol.XLI(April), pp.23-27.

100. Kuznets, S. (1964): Economic Growth and the Contribution of Agriculture, in Eicher, C.K. & L.W. Witt (eds.): *Agriculture in Economic Development* , McGrow Hill, New York.

101. Leff, N.H. (1969): Dependency Rates and Saving Rates, *American Economic Review*, Vol.59, pp.886-96.

102. Lewis, W.A. (1954): Economic Development with Unlimited Supplies of Labour, *The Manchester School*, Vol.22, pp.139-91.

103. Mahapatra, A.C. (1982): *Regional Inequality in India*, Unpublished Ph.D. Thesis, Submitted to N.E.H.U., Shillong.

104. Mamoria, C.B. (1975): *Geography of India*, I edn, Shivalal Agrawal & Co, Agra, pp.688-700.

105. McCarty, H.H. & J. Lindbarg (1967): *Preface to Economic Geography*, Englewood Cliffs, New Jersey, Prentice Hall.

106. McCloskey, D.N. (1968): Productivity Change in British Pig Iron 1870-1939, *Quarterly Journal of Economics*, Vol.82(No.2), pp.281-96.

107. Miller, J.W. (1966): *The Economics of Agricultural Development*, Vakils, Feffer & Simons, Bombay.

108. Minhas, B.S. & A. Vaidyanathan (1965): Growth of Crop-Output in India, 1951-4 to 1958-61: An Analysis of Component Elements, *Journal of the Indian Society of Agricultural Statistics*, Vol.XVIII(No.2), pp.230-52.

109. Ministry of Agriculture (1991): *Statistics at A Glance*, Department of Agriculture and cooperation, Government of India, New Delhi.

110. Misra, S.D. (1970): *Regions of India*, National Book Trust, New Delhi.

111. Monmonier, M.S. (1972): Contiguity-Biased Class-Interval Selection- A Method for Simplifying Patterns on Statistical Maps, *Geographical Review*, Vol. LXII(No.2), pp.203-28.

112. Myrdal,G. (1957): *Rich Land and Poor*, Harper & Brothers, New York.

113. Nath, V. (1969): The Growth of Indian Agriculture- A Regional Analysis, *The Geographical Review*, Vol.LIX(No.3), pp.348-72.

114. NCAER (1962): *Techno-Economic Survey of Andhra Pradesh*, National Council of Applied Economic Research, New Delhi.

115. Orban-Ferauge, F., J.P. Rasson & V. Granville (1991): About the Measure of the Volume of a Multidimensional Set as Measure of Proximities for a Partition of Space, *Proceedings* of the 7th European Colloquium of Theoretical and Quantitative Geography, Stackholm, Sweden.

116. Orban-Ferauge, F., J.P. Rasson, & V. Granville (1992): A Non-parametric Model for a New Approach of Supervised Remote Sensing Domain, *Abstracts* of the Papers of 27th I.G.C., Washington, pp.481-82.

117. Oschward, W.R. (1966): Quantitative Aspects of Soil Survey Interpretation in Appraisal of Soil Productivity, *Soil Science Society of America and American Society of Agronomy*, Ch.17, p.152.

118. Pal, M.N. (1961): Quantitative Delimitations of Regions, *Bombay Geographical Megazine*, Vol.8/9, pp.69-82.

119. Pal, M.N. (1968): Quantitative Delimitation of Regions, paper presented in *the Session* of 21st Session I.G.C., New Delhi.

120. Pal, M.N. (1975): Regional Disparities in the Level of Development in India, *Indian Journal of Regional Science,* Vol.VII(No.1), pp.35-52.

121. Papadakis, J. (1938): *Ecologic Agricole,* Gembloux, Ducilot.

122. Papadakis, J. (1966): *Climates of the World and their Agricultural Potentialities,* Buenos Aires.

123. Park, J.M. (1970): Fortran IV program for Q-mode Cluster Analysis on Distance Function with Printed Dendogram, *Computer Contribution No.46,* Kansas State Geographical Survey.

124. Patnaik, N. & S.S. Virahi (1962): Field Infiltration Studies in Doon Valley, *Irrigation Power,* Vol.19, p.103-13.

125. Perroux, F. (1955): Note sur la Notion de 'Pole de Croissance', *EconomicApplique,* Vol.8, pp.307-20.

126. Perroux, F. (1964): *La nation de pole de Croissence,. l'economic de xxeme siecle,* II edn, Paris.

127. Planning Commission (1987): *Guidelines for Planning at the Agro-Climatic Regional Level,* Govt. of India, New Delhi.

128. Planning Commission (1988): Guidelines for Integrated Farming, *The Times of India,* June 13, Sect.2.

129. Prasad, C., *et.al.* (1987): *First-Line Transfer of Technology Projects,* Publication & Information Division, ICAR, New Delhi.

130. Rakita, S.A. (1975): Principles for a Quantitative Evaluation of the Impact of National Environment on Econmomic Activity, *Soviet Geography: Review and Translation,* Vol. XVI(No.8), pp.489-502.

131. Ramanandham, V.V. (1959): *The Economy of Andhra Pradesh,* Asia Pub. House, New Delhi.

132. Randhawa, M.S. (1958): *Agriculture and Animal Husbandry in India,* Publication Division, ICAR, New Delhi.

133. Ram Saran (1965): Production Function Approach to Measurement of Productivity in Agriculture, *Journal of the Indian Society of Agricultural & Statistics,* Vol.XVII(No.2), pp.265-78.

134. Rao, K.S. & P.T. Ramacharlu (1959): pF-Water Relationship in Typical Indian Soils, *Soil Science,* Vol.87, pp.174-78.

135. Rao, C.H.H. (1968): Production Functions for Hyderabad Farms, in A.M. Khusro (ed): *Readings in Agricultural Development,* I edn, Allied Publishers India, New Delhi, pp.160-72.

136. Rasson, J.P., *et.al* (1988): A New Approach for a Natural Measure of Proximities also for Non-disjoint Training Sets and for Any Dimension of space, III Meeting of *Euro Working Group on Locational Analvlsis,* Sevilla, Spain.

137. Rasson, J.P., *et.al* (1989): The Supervised Classification Problems: What Happens with a New Basic Hypothesis?, IV Meeting of *Euro Working Group on Locational Analysis,* Chios, Greece.

138. Raychaudhuri, S.P. & L.M. Mathur (1954): *Bulletin National Institute of Science India,* No.3, pp.111-14.

139. Raychaudhury, S.P. & S.V.G. Rajan (1971): *Soils of India* (3rd edn), Technical Bulletin (Agric.) No.25, ICAR, New Delhi.

140. Raza, M. (1981): Regional Disparities in India, in N. Mohammad (ed): *Perspectives in Agricultural Geography,* Vol.IV, Concept Pub. Coy., New Delhi, pp.103-44.

141. Raza, M., A. Kundu & S.Nangia (1975): Urban-Rural Continuum in India, *Indian and Foreign Review*, Vol.12.(No.15).

142. Raza, M. & A. Kundu (1975): Discordance between Industrialisation and Urbanisation in India-Some Aspects, *Proceedings of the Indo-USSR Joint Seminar*, Mosacow.

143. Riquier, J. (1971): The Parametric Method of Land Evaluation (mimograph): *ACL Miscellinous /71/12*, FAO, Rome.

144. Riquier, J. (1972): A Mathematical Model for Calculation of Agricultural Productivitiy in terms of Parameters of soils and Climate, Advance Summery of a paper to be published by Orstom, Paris, FAO, Rome.

145. Shumpeter, J.A. (1963): *History of Economic Analysis*, George Allen & Unwin, London, p.261.

146. Sen, B. (1975): *The Green Revolution in India*, Willy Eastern, New Delhi.

147. Sen Gupta, P. (1968): Agricultural Regionalisation of India, in P. Sen Gupta & G. Sdasyuk: *Economic Regionalisation in India*, Mono. Series Vol.I(No.8), Census of India 1961, pp.101-16.

148. Seth, S.K. & J.S. Yadav (1958): A Simple Field- cum- Laboratory Method of Determining Soil Permeability, *Indian Forester*, Vol.84, pp.397-401.

149. Shafi, M. (1960): Measurement of Agricultural Efficiency in Uttar Pardesh, *Economic Geography*, Vol.36, pp.296-305.

150. Shome, K.B. & S.P. Raychaudhuri (1960): Rating of Soils of India, *Proceedings* of the National Institute of Sciences of India, Vol. 26A, Suppliment- I.

151. Sikhon, G.S. & H.S. Arora (1967): Moisture Retention Characteristics of some Punjab Soils and their Relationship with the Physical and Chemical Propreties, *Journal of Research Ludhiana*, Vol.4, pp.330-37.

152. Singh, Buta (1985): *Convocation Address* (24th Convocation), IARI, New Delhi, pp.3-4.

153. Singh, Jasbir (1971): Agricultural Colonisation of Cultivable Waste land in India, *The Deccan Geographer*, Vol.IX (No.2), pp.135-49.

154. Singh, Jasbir (1974): *The Green Revolution in India- How Green it is*, Vishal Publications, Kurukshetra.

155. Singh, J. & V.K. Sharma (1985): *Determinants of Agricultural Productivity*, Vishal Publications, Kurukshetra.

156. Singh, R.L. (ed)(1971): *India- A Regional Geography*, National Geographical Society of India, Varanasi.

157. Singh, Ram Nagina (1974): The Metaphysics of the Region- Changing Interpretation of Un-changing Theme, *National Geographer*, Vol.IX, pp. 45-55.

158. Singh, S. & V.S. Chauhan (1977): Measurement of Agricultural Productivity- A Case Study of Uttar Pardesh, India, *Geographical Review of India*, Vol.39(No.3), pp.222-31.

159. Singh, S. (1988): *Rural Development and Planning*, Shree Publishing House, New Delhi, (Reprented).

160. Singh, S. (1990): *Integrated Area Development and Planning*, Shree Publishing House, New Delhi.

161. Singhal, K.C. & H.S. Gill (1991): Poverty, Per Capita Income and Per Worker Sectoral Income, *Indian Journal of Regional Science,* Vol.XXIII(No.2), pp.1-10.

162. Sinha, R., *et.al.* (1979): Effect of Source and Time of Nitrogen Application on Chewing Tobacco & Succeeding Maize in North Bihar, *Tobacco Research,* Vol.5(No.1), pp.70-76.

163. Simpson, G.G. (1961): *Principles of Animal Taxonomy,* Columbia University Press, New York.

164. Smit, B., M. Brklacich & T. Phillips (1991): Evaluating Ontario's Potential for Food Production, *Canadian Journal of Regional Science,* Vol.XIV(No.1), pp.1-22.

165. Sokal, R.R. & P.H.A. Sneath (1963): *Principles of Numerical Taxonomy,* San Francisco, pp.169-215.

166. Solow, R.M. (1956): A Contribution to the Theory of Economic Growth, *Quarterly Journal of Economics,* Vol.70(Feb), pp.65-94.

167. Solow, R.M. (1957): Technical Change and the Aggregate Production Function, *R.E. Statistics*, Vol.39.(Aug.), pp.312-20.

168. Soni, B.V. & A.S. Chakravarti (1959): Hydraulic Conductivity in relation to Morphological Characteristics of Soil Profiles of Siwan areas in North Bihar, *Journal of Indian Society of Soil Science,* Vol.7, pp.223-30.

169. Spate, O.H.K., A.T.A. Learmonth & B.H. Farmer (1967): *India, Pakistan and Ceyclon- The Regions,* III edn., Methuen & Co. Ltd., London.

170. Spillman, W.J. (1922): Application of the Law of Diminishing Returns to Some Fertilizer and Seed Data, *Journal of Fertilizer Economics,* Vol.5, pp.36-52.

171. Spillman, W.J. (1933): Exponential Yield Function, c.f., R. Abler, J.S. Adams & P. Gould (1971): *Spatial Organisation,* Prentice-Hall, Inc., Englewood Cliffs, New Jersey, p.143.

172. Stamp, L.D. (1928): The Natural Regions of India, *Geography,* Vol. 14, pp.502-6.

173. Stamp, L.D. (1950): *The Land of Britain- Its Use and Misuse,* 2nd edn., Longmans Green, London.

174. Stamp, L.D. (1958): The Measurement of Land Resources, *The Geographical Review,* Vol.48, pp.1-15.

175. Stamp, L.D. (1960): *Our Developing World,* Faber & faber, London, pp.104-10.

176. Stamp, L.D. (1961): *Applied Geography,* 2nd edn., Pelican, London.

177. Thakur, M.C. (1987): Agricultural Labour Productivity in the Western Uttar Pradesh, *Geographical Review of India,* Vol.49(No.1), pp.33-41.

178. *The Times of India* (1992): Vol. CLV(No.112), May 11, New Delhi, pp.11-12.

179. Thornthwaite, C.W. (1931): The Climates of North America, *The Geographical Review,* Vol.21, pp. 633-55.

180. Thornthwaite, C.W. (1948): An Approach Toward A Rational Classification of Climate, *The Geographical Review,* Vol.XXXVIII (No.1), pp.55-94.

181. Tintner, G. (1961): The Logistic Law of Economic Development, *Arthaniti,* Vol.IV(No.1), pp.75-78.

182. Troll, C. (1950): Die Geographische Landschaft Undihre Erforchung, *Studium Generale,* Vol.3, Heft 4/5.

183. Troup, R.S. (1921): *Silviculture of India,* Vol.I, p.17.

184. UN Conference on Environment & Development (1992): Earth Summit, Rio-de-Janeiro, Brazil, C.f., *The Times of India,* Vol.CLV(No.143) (16 June 1992).

185. Vaid, V. & V.S. Datye (1991): Agricultural Labour Productivity in Maharastra, *Geographical Review of India,* Vol.53(No.3), pp.7-20.

186. Vajda, S. (1966): *An Introduction to Linear Programming and the Theory of Games,* G. Britain, pp.11-13.

187. Varadarajan, S. (1986): Prospects for Pulses in Tamil Nadu, *Agricultural Situation in India,* Vol.XLI(No.8), pp.641-46.

188. Verdoorn (1949): quoted from, Casetti, E. (1981): Correlats and Determinants of Agricultural Productivity Growth, in Noor Mohammad (ed): *Perspectives in Agricultural Geography,* Vol.IV, Concept Publishing Co., New Delhi, pp.387-99.

189. Verma, P.C. (1974): Measurement of Regional Development Levels in Bengladesh, *Indian Journal of Regional Science,* Vol.VI(No.1), pp.1-12.

190. Vink, A.P.A. (1955): Land Classificate, *Landbouwkundij Tijdschrift,* Vol.67, pp.377-89, c.f., H.Th. Riezebos (1988): Land Evaluation and Landuse Planning, Geographical Research in the Netherlands 1978-87, *Netherlands Geographical Studies,* Vol.64 (26th I.G.C., Australia), pp.128-33.

191. Vink, A.P.A. (1975): *Landuse in Advancing Agriculture,* Springer-Verlag, New York.

192. Visser, S. (1980): Technological Change and the Spatial Structure of Agriculture, *Economic Geography,* Vol.56(No.4), pp.311-19.

193. Visser, S. (1982): On Agricultural Location Theory, *Geographical Analysis,* Vol.14(No.2), pp.167-76.

194. Viswanath, B. & A.C. Ukil (1944): Comparative Studies on Indian Soils, *Indian Journal of Agricultural Science,* Vol.14, pp.333-44.

195. Wadia, D.N., M.S. Krishnan & P.N. Mukherjee (1935): Introductory Note on the Geological Forma ion of the Soils of India, *Rec. Geological Survey of India,* Vol.68, pp.363-91.

196. Wadia, D.N. (1975): *Geology of India,* IV edn., Tata McGraw-Hill Publishing Co., New Delhi, pp.287-93.

197. Ward, J.H. (1963): Hierarchical Grouping to Optimise An Objective Function, *Journal of American Statistical Association,* Vol.58, pp.236-44.

198. Whittlesey, D. (1936): Major Agricultural Regions of the Earth, *Annals* of the A.A.G., Vol.XXVI (No.1), pp.199-240.

199. *World Development Report* (1982): Published for the World Bank, Oxford University, London.

200. Wu, N. & P. Copins (1981): *Linear Programming and Extensions,* McGraw Hill, New York.

201. Zipf, G.K. (1949): Human Behaviour and the Principle of Least Effort, Addison Wesley Press Inc., Cambridge(Mass).

202. Zobler, L. (1958): Decision Making in Regional Construction, *Annals* of A.A.G., Vol.48, pp.140-48.

203. Zobler, L. (1972): The Use of Numerical Taxonomy to Evaluate Soil Resources, *International Geography,* Vol.I (Abstract of the papers submitted to 22nd I.G.C.), University of Toronto Press, Paper No.P0322, pp.289-90.

----o0o-----

Appendices

Appendix - I : Agricultural Contribution to Economic Growth.

An expression derived from Kuznets (1964) shows the relationship between agriculture's share of GDP growth (Pa.ra/dP) and change in the share of agriculture sector (Pa.ra), which is positive but non-linear. The established relationship is as :

$$Pa.ra/dP = (1.0 + Pn.rn/Pa.ra)^{-1},$$

where Pa and Pn are the shares of agricultural and non-agricultural sectors to total national product respectively and ra and rn are the growth rates of agricultural and non-agricultural sectors' net product respectively. The simplification of this equation for its reciprocal form shows its linearity as

$$(Pa.ra/dP)^{-1} = 1.0 + Pn.rn\ (Pa.ra)^{-1}.$$

Thus, the relationship stated above follows 'reciprocity law' of agriculture's contribution to the rate of economic growth. It means agriculture's share of GDP growth must increase at diminishing rate when the product of the share and rate of agriculture net product increases.

Appendix- II : Formation of Operational Taxonomic Units (Districts).

District Units based on 1981 (1)	Clubbed Districts 1991 (2)
1. Assam State:	
Golpara	Dhubri, Kokrajhar, Bogaigaon, Golpara.
Kamrup	Barpeta, Nalbari, Kamrup.
Darrang	Sonitpur, Darrang.
Nagaon	Marigaon, Nagaon.
Sibsagar	Golaghat, Jorhat, Sibsagar.
Lakhimpur	Dhemajai, Lakhimpur.
Dibrugarh	Tinsukhia, Dibrugarh.
Cachar	Karimganj, Hailakhandi, Cachar.
2. Bihar state:	
Gaya	Gaya, Jahanabad.
Sehersa	Sehersa, Madipura.
Mungher	Mungher, Khagaria.

Contd...

(1)	(2)
Purnia	Purnia, Areria, Kishanganj.
Dumka	Dumka, Deogarh, Sahibganj, Goda.
Ranchi	Ranchi, Lohardanga, Gumla.
Singhbhum	West and East Singhbhum.
3. Haryana State:	
Ambala	Ambala, Yamunanager.
Jindh	Jindh, Kaithal.
Sonipath	Sonipath, Panipath.
Gurgaon	Gurgaon, Riwari.
4. Karnatka State:	
Banglore	Banglore Urban and Rural Districts.
5. Kerala State:	
Cannanore	Cannanore, Kasaragod.
Quilon	Pathanathitta, Kollan.
6. Maharashtra State:	
Ratnagiri	Ratnagiri, Sindhudurg.
Aurangabad	Aurangabad, Jalna.
Osmanabad	Osmanabad, Latur.
Chandrapur	Chandrapur, Gachiroli.
7. Rajasthan State:	
Bharatpur	Bharatpur, Dholpur.
8. Tamilnadu State:	
North Arcot	N. Arcot, Tiruvannamalai, Sambuvarenja.
Madurai	Madurai, Dindigul-Quade-e-Milleth.
Ramanathpuram	Ramanathpuram, Kamrajen, P.T.Thurimgon.
Tirunelvali	Tirunelvali, Chidambaramar.
9. Uttar Pradesh State:	
Saharanpur	Saharanpur, Haridwar.
Kanpur	Kanpur Nager and Dehat Districts.
Basti	Basti, Sidharthnager.
Gorakhpur	Gorakhpur, Maharajgang.
Azamgarh	Azamgarh, Mao.
Mirzapur	Mirzapur, Son-Bhadra.
Mainpuri	Mainpuri, Firozabad.
10. West Bengal State:	
24-Parganas	North and South 24-Parganas.

Appendix - III : Correlation Matrix (25x25).

	V1	V2	V3	V4	V5	V6	V7	V8	V9	V10	V11	V12	V13	V14	V15	V16	V17	V18	V19	V20	V21	V22	V23	V24	V25
V1	1.000																								
V2	.738*	1.000																							
V3	.082	.102	1.000																						
V4	-.237*	-.213*	.155*	1.000																					
V5	-.168*	-.131*	.148*	.131*	1.000																				
V6	.035	.099	.298*	.299*	.109*	1.000																			
V7	-.156*	-.085	.086	.123*	.591*	.309*	1.000																		
V8	-.286*	-.243*	.202*	.620*	.162*	.567*	.157*	1.000																	
V9	-.195*	-.175*	.084	.150*	.658*	.093	.386*	.234*	1.000																
V10	.076	-.169*	.138*	.229*	-.129*	.492*	-.094	.344*	-.132*	1.000															
V11	.018	.020	-.013	.196*	-.016	.276*	-.016	.242*	-.033	.450*	1.000														
V12	-.269*	-.177*	-.102	-.004	-.002	-.141*	-.031	-.161*	-.094	.021	-.065	1.000													
V13	.079	-.068	-.031	-.083	-.017	-.033	.020	-.123*	-.245*	-.005	-.044	.160*	1.000												
V14	.238*	.332*	-.140*	-.216*	.080	.252*	-.043	-.286*	-.040	.218*	-.045	.062	.014	1.000											
V15	-.008	-.002	-.087	-.015	-.043	.008	.072	-.033	.051	-.003	.001	.047	.131*	.140*	1.000										
V16	-.251*	-.142*	.212*	.267*	.004	.441*	-.039	.456*	-.016	.491*	.174*	.043	-.037	.106*	-.081	1.000									
V17	-.159*	-.089	-.031	.057	.075	-.057	-.011	.081	-.030	.111*	.166*	-.027	.123*	-.038	.010	.161*	1.000								
V18	-.131*	-.059	.298*	.215*	.020	.266*	-.015	.372*	.005	.447*	.063	-.093	.024	.056	-.032	.361*	-.029	1.000							
V19	-.150*	-.144*	.114*	.138*	.064	.286*	.007	.292*	.044	.216*	.064	.094	-.076	.075	-.022	.492*	.072	.163*	1.000						
V20	-.148*	-.136*	.322*	.253*	.032	.544*	.036	.512*	.092	.373*	.145*	-.238*	-.093	.078	-.012	.627*	-.047	.422*	.482*	1.000					
V21	-.199*	-.306*	-.094	.233*	.118*	-.185*	.070	.353*	.232*	.297*	.056	-.231*	-.112*	-.666*	-.007	-.186*	.002	.007	-.043	-.002	1.000				
V22	.199*	.164*	-.078	-.051	-.007	.420*	.032	.092	-.050	.379*	.252*	-.308*	-.062	.377*	.057	.340*	-.088	.068	.237*	.387*	-.209*	1.000			
V23	.030	-.081	-.150*	-.008	-.181*	.044	.038	.019	-.031	-.092	-.050	-.031	.188*	-.053	.091	.002	.078	-.169*	-.092	-.129*	-.036	-.014	1.000		
V24	-.146*	-.213*	.023	.048	.061	.051	.061	.180*	.073	-.168*	.097	-.615*	-.076	-.225*	-.038	.031	-.057	.026	.102	.242*	.311*	.183*	.096	1.000	
V25	.442*	.344*	.141*	-.068	.057	.045	-.114*	-.017	-.104	.077	.022	-.501*	-.176*	.073	-.072	-.081	-.263*	.187*	.064	.193*	.096	.225*	-.325*	.161*	1.000

N.B.: For definition of these variables, See Table- 3.13. * Significant at the confidence level of 5 % with n-2 degree of freedom, where n= 348 (districts).

Name of the Variables : 1= Rainfall, 2= Moisture, 3= Soil fertility, 4= Agricultural output per capita, 5= Annual growth of Agricultural output 1979-82 to 1988-90 (in %), 6= Land productivity, 7= Increase in land productivity, 8= Labour productivity, 9= Change in labour productivity, 10= Crop intensity, 11= Change in crop intensity, 12= Agricultural workforce, 13= Increase in agricultural workforce, 14= Density of agricultural workers, 15= Change in density of agricultural worker, 16= Irrigation, 17= Change in irrigated area, 18= Irrigation intensity, 19= Mechanisation, 20= Use of fertiliser, 21= Size of landholdings, 22= Population density, 23= Population growth, 24= Share of urban population, 25= Rural literates.

Appendix- IV : Solving Proportionality Theorm for Agricultural Production Potential (Algebric Method)

According to Equation (4.1), P= A-Y, which can be written as:

(A-Y)= {A - (A-Y) + (A - 2Y)}.

Dividing above Equation by X, one gets

{(A-Y)/X} - {(A - 2Y)/X} = (A/X) - {(A-Y)/X}.

Taking (A-Y) term common from LHS terms, we get

(A-Y).[Y/{(A-Y)X}] = Y/X.

Simplifying it again for (A-Y) , one gets

(A-Y) = (Y/X).{(A-Y)X/Y},

if the term {(A-Y)X/Y} is taken as equal to B, which is a constant of present production funtion (according to eqn. 4.6 given in the text); it means

{(A-Y)X/Y} = B, then the above Equation can be written as:

{(A-Y)/Y} = (B/X), which is given in text in expression (4.6).

It implies that magnitude of production potential (i.e., yield gap) is proportional to input intensity. Differences in the gap can be due to technological or allocative efficiency. The percentage gap is also proportional to B/X. As X rises, the gap is reduced.

Appendix - V : Creation of Discriminant Functional Space.

If the elements of discriminant space, namely, (i) the observations/areal units are defined as operational taxonomy units (OTUs) and (ii) the agricultural characteristics/properties of areal units as the values of variables (X_k), then in the discriminant process of regionalisation, the degree of spatial contiguity/nearness (i.e., called here taxonomic distance, D_{ij}) between OTUs, i and j of k variables has been calculated by applying the Euclidean distance formula for m-dimensional space as :

$$D_{ij} = [\sum_{k=1}^{m} (X_{ik} - X_{jk})^2]^{1/2}$$

It is a formula for discriminating OTUs on their functional basis, which has been suggested by Ward (1963) for optimising objective function of space partitioning and also by Park (1970) for calculating functional distances. Later on, Monmonier (1972) shown the same procedure by linkage diagram which is called **taxonomic tree** in his own perception.

Discriminant iteration is a process of repetition of events for reducing the number of OTUs by selecting least distance from the distance matrix and averaging them for selecting new OTU from all remaining OTUs. The algorithm continues to pair the next most related OTUs until all have been combine into a single group.

-----oOo-----

Subject Index